Songs in the Key of Fife

Songs in the Key of Fife

*The Intertwining Stories of
The Beta Band, King Creosote,
KT Tunstall, James Yorkston
and the Fence Collective*

VIC GALLOWAY

First published in Great Britain in 2013 by Polygon, an imprint of Birlinn Ltd.

Birlinn Ltd
West Newington House
10 Newington Road
Edinburgh
EH9 1QS

www.polygonbooks.co.uk

ISBN 978 1 84697 235 5
eBook ISBN 978 0 85790 231 3

British Library Cataloguing-in-Publication Data
A catalogue record for this book is available on
request from the British Library.

Typeset in Sabon by Hewer Text UK Ltd, Edinburgh
Printed and bound by

Contents

INTRODUCTION

Songs in the Key of Fife

*Fife for Life . . . Fife, the Universe and Everything . . .
Fife Is What You Make It . . . Fife in the Fast Lane . . .
It's a Wonderful Fife . . . Fife is Fife . . . la la, la la la . . .*

These were working titles for this book, and even for chapters within it, which have mercifully been left as an opening salvo instead. 'Songs in the Key of Fife' is still a little silly, but infinitely better. I couldn't resist it. From a throwaway header on The Aliens' MySpace page, it hopefully delivers a humorous encapsulation of what I'm hoping to achieve as I attempt to sum up the aesthetic and musical ambition of these characters. This loosely connected collection of musicians and artists has conjured up a home-made, homespun, self-sustainable vision that yearns for more and reaches for the sky. The Beta Band and The Aliens went for it, the Fence Collective is quietly getting there, and KT Tunstall has been there, done most of it and come back to earth.

Far from being a definitive guide to all music from Fife, or even the East Neuk, this book talks about and traces the stories of my peer group, musicians I have befriended, crossed paths with and played music alongside. It isn't about me as such, but elements of my own story run through it – a life that started in Fife. Though born abroad, I was raised in the small East Neuk village of Kingsbarns, where my parents moved when I was one year old. My dad was a lecturer in Arabic at St Andrews University, and my mother was a nurse in nearby Craigtoun hospital. I went to school in St Andrews and went through most of my formative experiences in this craggy outpost of eastern Scotland. I made my first friends there and discovered my deep love of music. In fact, as I get older I realise how much of a debt I owe the place, and how much I enjoy going back there. Is it pure nostalgia or Pavlovian conditioning? Do we all inevitably get drawn back to our childhood stamping grounds? Is there anything special about this place at all, or am I just a big sentimental daftie?

The East Neuk is a dreamy enclave where you have trouble getting mobile phone reception, where golfers flock from around the world, where farmers farm, fishermen fish, students learn in isolation and life seems to slow down a bit. The Fife I speak of isn't that of coal-mining, generational poverty or hard-nosed new towns like Glenrothes or Dunfermline. It isn't the story of working-class boys made good. It isn't a history of Ian Stewart (an original member of The Rolling Stones), Nazareth, the Skids, Big Country or Jackie Leven. It doesn't tell the story of linoleum, progressive economics or steelworks, but of an idyllic, pastoral, peaceful place where I grew up without a care in the world.

Although my parents weren't well off, we had no real financial worries, and as a child I was allowed, even encouraged, to let my thoughts run free and wild around the fields, forests, beaches and bays. My parents' marriage fell apart, and I remember harsh winters, school bullies and occasional tales of woe, but my overriding child-hood memories are happy ones of bikes, beach barbecues, playing guitar and drawing comics. I remember laughter, climbing trees, dress-ing up, making crap cine films, shopping for my first 7-inch vinyl singles and a world with infinite possibilities. Without romanticising the past, those memories and instincts have stayed with me and have informed my life ever since.

As I watched many of my contemporaries move into music, art, film, graphic design and so on, I began to think there might be some connec-tion between them, and that that connection might well be the East Neuk of Fife. Was this wishful thinking, some kind of generational fluke? It could happen, I suppose. Maybe the coastal landscape and sea had some influence. Maybe there is some kind of psychogeographical link between creative people and the place they grow up in. Or was there just fuck all to do as a teenager in a largely rural and academic commu-nity in a remote area of 1970s and 1980s Britain? More than likely! Use your imagination or die . . .

I'm not 'going on a journey'. I'm trying to tell the intertwining, inter-locking stories of some truly talented people who all grew up in the same area and have achieved success as musicians, composers, lyricists and writers. Before I was a BBC broadcaster, a journalist, a DJ or an author, I was a musician, and I've played in bands alongside many who feature in this book. I count most of them as friends. It seemed like a good idea to take on the challenge. The stories could fill ten books, but if there's any justice these people will all write books of their own, and probably contradict everything in here. James Yorkston has already written a book of tour diaries, and will have something else published soon. This is not a perfect historical document, neither is it the definitive telling of all these tales. It is what it is, and to my knowledge it's the first time these stories have been told properly. I simply wanted to get it all down.

These are stories that deserve to be told about colourful, interesting and eccentric characters whom more people should know about. There are occasional accounts of big money, showbiz and glamour, but more often of hard work, independence and art. Not everyone lives in a far-fetched world of communal back-slapping, either. With art and inspiration come ego and argument, resentment, rivalry and umbrage. Some I've spoken to feel no sense of unity or collective thinking, and distance themselves from others in this book. My only regret is that Jenny 'HMS Ginafore' Gordon refused to be involved. Her music and story are as important as anyone else's, but she has the right to remain silent. Writing this book has been a mammoth task, like eight biographies in one. I've spent months accumulating interviews with friends and colleagues in order to be as honest, demystifying and straight-talking as possible. I think all the people herein would want that.

The East Neuk might seem an unusual place for a musical revolution, but in among the sleepy fishing villages and rolling fields, a small outsider community of gifted and increasingly well-loved musicians and artists has quietly crept up on the world. *Songs in the Key of Fife* tries to set the record straight and reveal the big picture and the interwoven nature of a flourishing troupe of like-minded souls. Please read on and enjoy . . . just don't tell Stevie Wonder!

I

Eggshell Miles

Kenny Anderson, The Skuobhie Dubh Orchestra and Khartoum Heroes

Without the motivation, drive, camaraderie and vast musical output of Kenny Anderson, it is unlikely that this book would have been written at all. It's not that he persuaded me to do it, or even particularly wants this set of stories told, but that he has been such a catalyst and linchpin in many of our subjects' lives. I've known him for over twenty years, yet he's still something of an enigma to me, with a continual stream of surprises up his sleeve. By far the most prolific songwriter I have ever known, with well over fifty albums in his back catalogue, he has toured and performed relentlessly and has influenced and infiltrated many musical careers from his base in the East Neuk. Kenny is a short, bearded, elfin character usually attired in a baggy jumper and jeans, complete with unkempt hair, dancing eyes and flirtatious smile. He looks more like a fisherman than a celebrity. But over the years he has intrigued, enthused and infuriated many with his charm, talent, obstinacy and contrariness, breaking hearts and settling scores with his most trustworthy of friends and weapons – the song!

Being born into a musical household helps when it comes to making your own music. Kenny recalls: 'The first music I ever heard was probably one of my dad's bands, him playing accordion and rehearsing. I don't remember the radio being a big factor in our house, or albums being played. I don't know if that's because my dad works in music. I'm not sure my dad actually likes other kinds of music. He likes a particular thing and he plays it. He likes Scottish country dance music. He says he likes The Rolling Stones, but I've yet to see him ever listening to or even holding a Rolling Stones record.'

Billy Anderson left school at an early age, playing accordion semi-professionally from the age of fifteen or sixteen. When not working for

Lloyds TSB and as an insurance clerk, he would play with his dance bands as often as possible until he went full-time, when Kenny was about five. He now teaches accordion, plays gigs whenever possible and presents weekly programmes for Radio Tay. In 1975 and 1978 his band embarked on massive US tours, playing every state except Alaska and Hawaii to venues of 2,000–3,000 seats as part of a Scottish revue show with around thirty performers. He was a shrewd operator and made a fair chunk of money from these ventures, investing the finances in independent record shops in St Andrews and Cupar. To fully understand the Anderson brothers and their music, you must not underestimate the importance and influence of their father.

Before going completely professional, Billy would rehearse his band in the evenings in the family's St Nicholas Street flat in St Andrews as the young Kenny listened in. Sometimes, if there was a gig or rehearsal elsewhere, they'd all stumble into the house at 1 a.m., bawdy and raucous with blether, gossip, laughter and nonsense. It was almost inevitable that at least one of the four children would follow their father into music. The actual hit rate would be far higher.

Born on 2 February 1967 at Craigtoun Hospital on the outskirts of St Andrews, Kenny Anderson is a born, bred and raised East Neuker. He has lived all his life in this area and still adores the rolling hills, the coastline, the whitewashed fishing villages, the stone dykes, country roads and paths that link towns, houses and cottages together. His mother Elizabeth is from Crail and his father's from Largoward. Kenny started to play the accordion at seven: being the oldest, and being a boy, he was pretty much expected to learn the instrument his father had mastered. Although he liked certain Scottish country-dance tunes, he wasn't a huge fan of that music at first.

'This was a bit of a bugbear for my dad. He would say: "You should play that and that", but I used to gravitate to the slower, minor-key numbers.' He loved learning the accordion, but says: 'Initially, it felt like an extension of homework. I don't think I'm a typical eldest child, and I was painfully shy. My dad saw this and had to push me into playing and performing. I had a love/hate relationship with the accordion, but like most children I wanted to make my parents happy.'

Billy persuaded Kenny, at a very young age, to play accordion at various functions, whether to pensioners on Christmas Day or taking a solo spot at a Billy Anderson Ceilidh Band hotel show. Unbelievably, knowing what a confident and relaxed performer he is today, Kenny would be sick with nerves and had to be cajoled into those white-knuckle experiences. 'I was not a natural performer and used to shuffle onstage. Bizarrely, I'm kind of glad my dad did that to me, though, because I then started to get work two or three nights a week around St Andrews as a solo accordionist. Quite often I'd be getting paid three times £15 a week at the age of thirteen. Remembering that a paper round paid around £2 a week, I had serious pocket-money for a teenager.'

Never gregarious or outspoken, Kenny was the last pupil to put his hand up in school; he respected his elders and remained within the boundaries his parents set. He was trustworthy and obedient to the wishes of authority figures. He wasn't consciously rebellious or badly behaved in any way. He was also a high-flyer at school. Hardly the stuff of rock 'n' roll . . . but that was to come later.

Kenny's sister, Lynne, was two years younger and a Madonna fan. Although she had the first record player in the family, it was rare for one of her selections to prick up Kenny's ears. 'Aside from my dad's music, the first song that truly connected with me was Charlie Rich's "The Most Beautiful Girl In The World". It still makes me ache when I hear it today. Then as a teenager I remember hearing music in other people's houses, for example Blondie, The Jam and Adam and the Ants, and starting to love them. I enjoyed 2-Tone and became a massive fan of 1980s electronic music and the New Romantic thing. I watched *Top of the Pops* to avoid going to Boys' Brigade on Thursday nights.'

When his younger twin brothers, Een (born Iain) and Gordon, started to listen to and buy music, a connection was made despite five years' age difference. Gordon in particular was into The Beatles, The Rolling Stones and The Smiths, turning his older brother on to music that he'd then search out in local shops Tracks, the Music Shop and John Menzies. In 1982, though, Dexys Midnight Runners' 'Come On Eileen', featuring that most 'folk' of instruments, the accordion, was an epiphany for Kenny. Suddenly the years of practising in his bedroom and performing in front of grannies made sense as he realised: 'Wait a minute, I play that! I don't just have to play jigs and reels.' Over the years that song would continue to gather meaning, getting the cover-version and DJ-set treatment at Fence Collective events more than twenty-five years later.

In his late teens Kenny achieved consistently excellent grades at local schools Kilrymont and Madras College. He hated sports but ended up playing rugby for the 'Madrascals' at scrum-half for a while. He was academic, with no idea of starting a school band. Maths, physics and anything logical and scientific were his strong points. All his musical engagements were as a solo accordionist, mainly for tourists and the elderly. Eventually he played second accordion in his father's dance band on occasion, staying up late and discovering he was a natural night-owl. There was very little under-age drinking, no outlandish behaviour; music was little more than a hobby and a part-time job. He'd contemplated becoming a drummer in the Boys' Brigade pipe band, but still hadn't formed a band or learned a single chord on the guitar. Although his best friends, Stevie Paul and David Wares, were also music-heads, it was solely as fans. Aside from the occasional jam on accordion and drums with Stevie, the thought of writing and performing music of his own hadn't even crossed Kenny's mind. All this was set to change as university loomed on the horizon.

Kenny was perfect material for higher education and had the necessary skills and commitment, choosing Edinburgh University in 1985 for a degree course in physics and electronics despite not having particularly enjoyed classes or having had an in-depth thirst for knowledge at school. Studying and scoring well came naturally and were a means to an end, but university was very different and in one term he realised he had chosen the wrong course. With no desire to spend time in libraries and no real interest in the subject matter, he stuck with it for his parents' sake.

All was not lost, though. An ex-classmate from Madras College, Ralph Hasselgren, who had started at Edinburgh University at the same time, suggested one afternoon, while he and Kenny larked around avoiding class, that they form a band. 'But I only play accordion,' Kenny said. 'You should play the bass, that's easy enough,' was Ralph's response. With the help of their loyal drum machine and a basic reel-to-reel tape recorder, they began mucking about. It should be pointed out that, before this, Kenny had never written a song, a melody, a poem or a lyric. This was a true beginning, and he got the recording bug immediately. 'I have this strong memory of having thoroughly enjoyed the experience, more than anything at university or school. Ralph was reluctant, though. He was into it sometimes and other times not. But I was hooked.'

Kenny then bought a four-track tape-deck, a Roland TR505 drum machine and a sequencer, using his student grant and money from accordion gigs. He started by programming sequenced keyboard and drum parts, overdubbing bass and then adding song ideas on top. 'Some of the songs were absolutely terrible,' he admits, but some weren't. Certain tracks were revisited for future King Creosote releases, including 'Bootprints', 'Marguerite Red' and 'Your Own Spell', their chords, lyrics and melodies all constructed in the middle to late 1980s.

As the music was constructed, Ralph and Kenny searched for a singer. Kenny hadn't discovered his own voice yet, and was petrified of being any kind of spokesperson or frontman. His shyness could be traced back to school, when any public performances would be instigated by his father's boot up his backside. Ralph wasn't keen to sing either, but needs must, and a university refectory gig was planned with the duo, the drum machine and a band name, Uncle Ralph. For musical reference points Kenny had started to listen to Scottish guitar-based bands including Aztec Camera and Lloyd Cole and the Commotions, also buying early U2, Triffids and Smiths albums.

Uncle Ralph briefly expanded with a singer and drummer, played a handful of gigs and considered taking it more seriously. Kenny was spending more and more time doing music and less and less time on coursework, but there was as yet no concept of the band going on after university. But he does say this: 'I went to uni as a wee boy and left pretty much as I am now.' He became politicised in Edinburgh and began to develop strong opinions on all manner of subjects. He still wasn't sure that music was going to figure in his future, but despite a very respectable 2:1 in Electronics and Electrical Engineering he was absolutely sure his future didn't lie there.

In 1989 Uncle Ralph imploded as Ralph acquired a job and Kenny returned to St Andrews. Moving in with his parents again, he started to work full-time at the St Andrews Woollen Mill, a job he'd done part-time during the holidays for years previously. Kenny says this job and this organisation were a key influence on what would become Fence many years later. The truth is that he loved working for the Phillips brothers. Raymond and Bob Phillips had unwittingly started the business in 1962 when funding a holiday to the US by taking a suitcase of tartan scarves with them and selling them within minutes of arriving. This was the beginning of a business that would become an empire of sorts, and an organisation that Kenny massively respected. They were decent people, had respect for their workforce and paid well. Kenny was an all-rounder for the company – driving, working on the shop floor and in the stock department, weeding, vacuuming – anything, really – and would return to work for them many times over the years until they closed their doors in 1999.

Although he was surrounded by friends and settled for a while, nothing much was happening in the East Neuk, and Kenny had only recently turned twenty-two. He yearned for some kind of adventure, musical or not. When a former flatmate, Bruce Bell, taught him three chords on the guitar, accompanied him on the mandolin, and suggested they buy InterRail tickets and take off to the continent for four weeks of fun, he didn't need much persuasion. He dusted down the accordion, four years in its box, and brushed up on a few jigs and reels. Bruce learned a few bluegrass instrumentals, and they had a basic busking set of half an hour to knock out to anyone brave enough to listen.

The trip started with a whimper when they managed to leave days before their InterRail cards were activated, landing in Boulogne with no money, missing rucksacks and train tickets that didn't work. Living out of a bivvy-bag and having to busk for meals and campsite access was a harsh reality, but something that would in many ways change Kenny. Busking would become an important part of his life and shape his psyche as a musician.

When their InterRail passes became valid they made their way to Amsterdam. Any young man or woman with an inquisitive streak and an eye for adventure has to visit this city at least once in their teens or twenties. They made their way straight to the centre of town, grabbed a busking pitch and began to strike up a tune. At that very moment, two shady-looking individuals bounded up to them, armed with a double bass and a banjo. The bassist was some kind of Dutch psychobilly, complete with flat-top hairdo and menacing grimaces, while the banjo player, with his dungarees, striped shirt, ponytail and mischievous Gallic features, could only be a Frenchman.

After listening to a short set, Frenchie and Psycho approached our heroes and offered to back them on a number. 'Bruce and I were really nervous that we'd taken their territorial busking spot and they were coming to get us,' Kenny remembers. 'Thankfully they watched for a while and asked to join in. The second they started to accompany us with the bass and banjo, it was immediate . . . this was the most exciting "folk" music I'd ever heard. We were all shocked at how easily it worked, how good it sounded and how much the crowd loved it.' Within an hour or so they were joined by a classically trained female violinist from the US, dressed in full punk regalia. With even larger crowds amassing, the motley crew now comprised rockabilly Etienne Stekelenburg on bass, bohemian Eric Baeckeroot on banjo, Bruce Bell, in goth/hippie attire, picking a mandolin, Martha Weiss the punk with the fiddle, and Kenny in pork-pie hat and sideburns on accordion. They must have looked like a dishevelled, surrealist gang of gypsies – which, to all intents and purposes, they were.

It was 8 September 1989, and the bare bones of a group were formed. Initially calling themselves La Merde d'Oiseau Quintet (The Birdshit Five) in homage to their being street-musicians, they began to incorporate TV cartoon themes into their live set. Bruce christened them The Scooby Doo Orchestra after the Hanna-Barbera canine detective, and so the legendary, ass-kicking bluegrass combo that is still remembered, revered and respected today first came into existence. The InterRail cards were ditched and the band realised they truly had something, deciding to continue as a semi-serious unit. Within hours of forming they were playing to audiences of around two hundred on the streets of Amsterdam. But this was no flash in the pan. A planned month away turned into two years of busking, and Kenny's future was indelibly marked by the world of street music.

After journeys to Belgium and Germany, the band followed Kenny and Bruce's lead and returned to St Andrews, eventually taking up residence in a cottage near Blairgowrie in Perthshire and bravely busking throughout the winter in Dundee. Within days they were being interviewed and photographed by the local newspaper, the Dundee Courier, and were roped into playing the BBC's *Children in Need* TV charity telethon. The Scooby Doo Orchestra were photographed and interviewed wherever they went in the UK or Europe. They had a magnetism and a fresh-faced charisma that drew people in. They were unpretentious and innocent; they looked like they were having fun.

All was not well at home, however. In his parents' eyes, Kenny had always been the golden boy, but now he had long hair and ripped jeans, played in a busking band and had utterly rejected his school and university successes. Raging arguments ensued and Billy Anderson began to think of Kenny as a tramp, a disappointment and an embarrassment. His mother was also hugely unimpressed, but sneaked him in and out of the family home under his father's nose whenever necessary. Although family relations were unpleasant, Kenny had no intention of changing.

By now the five of them were extremely tight as musicians and going from strength to strength as a group. They could play for hours, drawing on their repertoire of bluegrass, folk and traditional tunes (alongside sillier, improvised moments), all played with sweaty intensity at extreme speed. They were a party band and they knew it, as did their growing audience. Now trading as The Skuobhie Dubh Orchestra, they would record a succession of cassettes with titles such as *Mr Stanbrick Presents . . .*, *Mrs Stanbrick Presents . . .*, *Leaf* and *Stone*. The fake-Gaelic appropriation of the cartoon dog's name looked unusual and helped steer them away from any potential litigation. The cassettes were made up of bluegrass and Irish traditional songs such as 'Wildwood Flower', 'Shady Grove, 'Old Joe Clark', 'Foggy Mountain Breakdown', 'Russian Reel', 'Cripple Creek' and 'Roll In My Sweet Baby's Arms', and were largely instrumental. They were great for selling on the street and picking up more much-needed cash for the Orchestra to live off as a five-piece band.

Unfortunately, things couldn't remain as they were. Martha had a brief relationship with Kenny before switching to Etienne and finally returning to the US. Virtuoso banjo player Eric was darting back and forward to France to keep his successful poster business afloat and keep away from the dreich Scottish east-coast winter.

It's at this point that Een, one of Kenny's younger brothers and twin of Gordon, enters the story. Unlike the academic Kenny and art-school-bound Gordon, Een was a nature lover and had an affinity with wildlife and plants. After school he had entered a land management and groundskeeping course on a neighbouring estate in the Perthshire countryside. Kenny made contact with his then-estranged brother, and Een moved into the cottage. Almost immediately he took a shine to the double bass and eyed it enviously. Although he was five years Kenny's junior and had never played a musical instrument in his life, all who have accompanied him over the twenty-odd years since then acclaim Een ('Pip Dylan') as a total master on a vast array of instruments.

Was this the end of The Skuobhie Dubh Orchestra? Yes and no. By the summer of 1990, despite sporadic gigs, the group had decided to go two separate ways, with Bruce, Etienne and Martha heading in one direction and Kenny travelling to France with Eric to attempt to master bluegrass on the accordion – no mean feat, as accordion is little used in bluegrass, more in Cajun music. Three months later, he'd pretty much done it.

By the end of 1990 the band was no more. Bruce had taken a job as a male nurse, Etienne and Martha had left Scotland, and Kenny and Eric were living in France. On a return visit they hooked up again with Een on Mull and became a trio, buying a half-size double bass from smooth, jazz-flecked Dundee popsters Danny Wilson before retracing their steps to the Dordogne for the winter. Een improved massively on the bass and began to sing harmonies with Kenny, who was now playing the guitar as often as the accordion. Suddenly a singing, harmonising duo had emerged for parties and impromptu gigs when Eric wasn't around to add light-speed banjo licks.

The bohemian, devil-may-care spirit was in full swing, with never a second thought given to the constant flitting between France and Scotland. Possessions were kept to an absolute minimum, with little more than their instruments and a rucksack of tatty clothes to hand. Kenny and Een returned to Fife to look for a place to unleash their growing prowess. Remembering a previous engagement on their travels, they began to attend a weekly open-mic night at the West Port Bar in Dundee. Humble beginnings, but soon they attracted the washboard skills of a young American on a gap year, Joe Collier (one day to be better known in the Fence Collective as MC Quake), who added another rhythmic dimension. Was this the beginning of a new incarnation of the Dubhs?

The next part of the puzzle appeared in the form of Andy Robinson (now renamed Captain Geeko, the Dead Aviator), a Rush and Iron Maiden fan, an excellent drummer and a school acquaintance of Kenny's who had recently left another band, Bedlam. Kenny invited him in, albeit without his prog-rock drum kit and armed with little more than a snare drum and brushes. Finally Eric, the bluegrass maestro, decided to make the journey once again and complete another line-up of the band. After recording a cassette of their live set for sale on the streets of any town that would have them, it was time to hit the road again. To great success and consistently large crowds, they busked throughout France, Spain, Holland, Germany and Belgium until the autumn of 1991.

Although it seems romantic and exotic, the life of a busker can be extremely tiring. In 1991 I too was busking around Europe with school friend Drew Pattison, knocking out dodgy reels, jigs, hornpipes and 1950s rock 'n' roll tunes on guitar and bagpipes – an untutored racket, in all honesty. I wonder what would have happened if we'd crossed paths with the Dubhs? It's certainly true that your musicianship improves, your repertoire increases and your confidence becomes unshakeable when you're busking. However, you do work extremely hard, shivering under the elements and always at the mercy of unforgiving and non-paying crowds. It can feel – God forbid! – like a real job at times.

It was also around this time that the infamous South American pan-pipe bands were emerging, hogging the streets and squares with amplified back-lines and organised merchandise. Anti-busking byelaws were being brought in to ward off the homogeneous teams of cash-hungry Bolivians and Colombians, so it seemed time was up for pure, direct, acoustic street music. With this in mind it was suggested the Dubhs return to Scotland to see out the winter playing proper indoor gigs. After some debate, the decision was made and they were Scotland-bound again.

Despite Joe returning stateside, Kenny worked to secure any gigs he could and establish the band as a real entity. Aberdeen's Blue Lamp bar and venue obliged, and after their first performance there, John Reid of the Granite City Rock agency invited them to play in the Aberdeen area more often. They gladly acquiesced, and a love affair between the Granite City and the band was set in motion. With a new fiddler, Donna Vincent, they gigged hard and often throughout the north-east and the Highlands, building a sizeable fan base, especially in their beloved Aberdeen, where they opened the legendary arts venue The Lemon Tree in 1992, becoming the first band to sell it out.

Their profile was building and there was a tangible buzz around the band. They supported countless Celtic-rock bands such as Wolfstone and the Humph Family, and folkies such as the Old Blind Dogs, around the country, playing their frenetic brand of breakneck banjo-fuelled mountain music, bluegrass, skiffle and early rock 'n' roll. A band logo was scrawled out by Kenny's brother Gordon and emblazoned on T-shirts that sold by the bucketload. Thanks to a tip-off from friends and supporters Old Blind Dogs, Lochshore/Klub Records took an interest in the group after seeing the Dubhs' freewheeling, energetic live shows and hearing the *Van Album* of traditional songs and covers including 'John Hardy', 'Roll In My Sweet Baby's Arms' and 'Mystery Train'.

A cassette, released with their Mystery Machine VW van on the cover, was recorded in ten hours in November 1991 in Land Studios, Kennoway with engineer and producer Dougie MacMillan. It has legendary status among Dubh-lovers to this day. Ask Kenny for a copy or track down an old fan; in many ways it's the definitive Skuobhie Dubh Orchestra album. I remember hearing it for the first time and being blown away by how fast and how expertly executed it was. But that was nothing compared to the live act: they would play three verses and three choruses in under a minute. This was folk music with all the youthful abandon and velocity of punk.

Record company interest in place, the band were asked whether they wanted to be a 'traditional' band doing old songs and covers, or a 'traditional-sounding' band playing originals. Unhesitatingly they went for the second option. Kenny, encouraged by Andy, wanted to write his own material, though with a bluegrass backbeat to fit in with the band's catalogue of covers. Having quietly filled diaries with songs and lyrics since the Uncle Ralph days and during his years of busking, Kenny could now draw on this wealth of material for The Skuobhie Dubh Orchestra's debut album proper, *The 39 Stephs*. He admits he had to go through his songs 'to see which ones could be bluegrassified', but in the spring of 1992 they revisited Land Studios and laid down the bulk of *The 39 Stephs* before the record contract had even been signed, with producer Dougie pushing Kenny onwards with his songwriting and lyrics. With rough mixes ready by the early summer, they then played the Glastonbury Festival, thanks to the Granite City Rock guys. They were on a roll.

Kenny elaborates: 'The Skuobhie Dubh Orchestra taught us how to play and be intuitive as musicians. Een, Andy and I almost developed telepathy as players, but I always felt we were secondary to bands who wrote their own songs. We knew we were a good band and it was a necessity to start doing our own material. I never wanted to be the singer, but someone had to do it! It's fine busking instrumentals and tunes on the street, but when you play forty-five-minute sets in a venue, you need vocals to break things up. By default, I became the singer.'

Een by now had moved from double bass to banjo, filling the gap left by Eric, who was now spending more and more time away from the band in France. By listening to the greatest banjo players of all time – Bella Fleck, Flatt & Scruggs etc – he set himself on becoming the best finger-picking virtuoso in the land. He had never handled an instrument as a child, and he had no official music training, so to prove his worth he had to be faster and more dextrous than anyone else. If Kenny's need was to write unique songs, Een's compulsion was be the greatest technician on bass, then banjo, and eventually every stringed instrument, in the western world!

It was around this point that I, with my childhood pal James Wright (later Yorkston), first saw the Dubhs, playing a sparsely attended gig in Edinburgh toilet venue the Subway. We were utterly blown away. Not only did they play faster than anyone we'd ever seen, but the musicianship was dazzling and the onstage energy electric. Seeing Een Anderson let rip on a five-string banjo was a sight and sound to behold. I soon realised they were from St Andrews too . . . ya wee beauty!

I'd left school in 1990, and in 1991 had formed my first band, Miraclehead, with James. After starting out as a power-trio, with myself on vocals and guitar and James on bass and vocals, we ended specialising in a weird, melodic hybrid of punk, funk, rock and ska and would entertain or annoy audiences with our irreverent stage antics and high-octane pop nuggets, assisted by Cliff Simms on vocals and Stuart Bastiman on drums. We were an eccentric bunch of pierced, dyed, ripped and bleached drop-outs who wanted to play music as fast and as dynamically as possible, and we found solidarity in Kenny and his scruffy gang of acoustic speed-freak gypsies. Although we were a year away from meeting properly again, a mutual appreciation was set in place. Who could have known then that all our futures would be entwined for a very long time to come?

With a growing sense of confidence, the Dubhs started to think more widescreen. Andy expanded his drum kit and Kenny began to introduce songs with more subtlety. 'We were a good band, we had a following, and we could earn money from gigs and from busking. But I was getting sick of shouting throughout the songs. There was no tone control and the lyrics didn't import any real meaning to us. I wanted to be more musical and try to say something that was ours. We were basically singing bastardised versions of songs that were old enough to have been sung on plantations.' They had nailed that sound on *The Van Album* and it was time to move on. Kenny brought in a batch of songs – some bluegrass, some in waltz time, with different tempos. Eric and Andy were keen, but Een, hitting his stride as a bluegrass master, wasn't as impressed. However, that was the way it was: democracy rules. The truth is that Kenny was assuming the role of bandleader, driving force and sole songwriter. 'It wasn't a massive diversion musically,' he says. 'Most of my songs use the old A, D, G, C, E minor and A minor progressions as in folk music.'

They went into Land Studios and recorded ten originals and – at the behest of Klub Records – a few traditional songs. They lifted 'Foggy Mountain Breakdown' from *The Van Album* and recorded new versions of 'Nelly Kane', sung by Een, and an instrumental, 'Wildwood Flower' for which Kenny then wrote lyrics. Bizarrely, Klub then accused Kenny of writing about drugs. They insisted that 'Our Last Needle' and 'Snow Queen' were about substance abuse and Kenny was trying to pull the wool over the eyes of a naive wee folk label. The truth was Kenny couldn't even smoke a joint without flipping out, and wasn't even a big drinker. Drugs would eventually rear their psychedelic heads later in Kenny's life, but then he was totally clean and utterly indifferent.

With artwork from brother Gordon, the first properly released and distributed album by The Skuobhie Dubh Orchestra, *The 39 Stephs*, was born. Not only a play on the John Buchan novel, it was named in tribute to Stephanie, a girl who worked at Land Studios, and to all the other Stephanies who were cropping up in the lives of the Dubhs. The album was warmly welcomed by their growing fan base, who loved the existing bluegrass flavours evident in their frantic live shows but instantly took to the new songs and gentler directions, such as the epic but intimate 'Eggshell Miles'. Here was a song, written about Kenny's new girlfriend, Kirsty Winskill, that captured hearts. 'Dance music is for dancing to, but listening to that fast stuff at home is like listening to a ceilidh band. You need something with more variation and depth,' says Kenny. In the live set the band went from playing almost nothing but covers to almost nothing but originals.

'Eggshell Miles' became the band's most requested song. Lyrically, Kenny covered relationship troubles, falling-outs with brothers and personal woes. 'I'm a two-faced little shit and a coward, so I'll get back at people in the lyrics of my songs. They were mainly from a personal point of view, nothing overtly social or political.' The song 'Precious Days' was a nostalgic look at their busking times, 'Little Wonder' was about turning thirty (although Kenny was only twenty-five), and 'Our Last Needle' was indeed a junkie tale, but not from personal experience. With a real calling card in *The 39 Stephs*, the Dubhs realised it was an experiment that had gone really well. They sold it at gigs and via the label's contacts, but garnered no reviews except for a seven out of ten from *Vox* magazine, with Stuart Bailie remarking: 'While some Caledonian folk acts sound overly dour, the Skuobhies sound like they've got verve in their boots and their radios tuned to busy, noisy channels. Break open a fresh batch of Scooby Snacks and welcome in some shaggy new friends!' Yet they now wanted to be taken seriously, and it was time to attempt something more ambitious.

'For our second album, *Spike's 23 Collection*, at the end of 1992,' Kenny remembers, 'the gloves were off. We really wanted to make something of it. Tempo-wise it was slower, and there were less bluegrass elements on there. It was a little too long, perhaps, with us trying to fit as much as possible on to a CD, but I wanted it to be a real album.' The band were now obsessed with numbers and all the coincidences and conspiratorial connections around the number twenty-three itself. Andy, Een and Kenny noticed them everywhere and anywhere. When they met a couple, Spike and Debbie, on the Teasses country estate in Fife, on which the band had rented a cottage, they found Spike had a collection of them. Spooky but true! Michael 'Spike' Sanderson and Debbie Wheelhouse were to become good friends with Kenny. They became fans of the band's music and influenced the band 'in a magic-mushroom kind of way,' Kenny recalls mischievously.

In their own minds, The Skuobhie Dubh Orchestra and producer Dougie MacMillan had delivered a hefty piece of work that stood up alongside other albums of the time, albeit with an off-kilter Celtic twist. REM, Morrissey, James, Primal Scream, Suede and Counting Crows were all on Kenny's turntable, US grunge was beginning to peter out, and Britpop was about to sink its teeth into the UK music industry. With stand-out tracks such as opener 'The Seminar', 'Swinging On A Gate', 'Fisticuffs' and the breakneck bluegrass of 'Graeme Hallelujah Graeme' as well as more of Kenny's heartfelt laments and 1980s pop-inspired instrumentation, they had tried to make something that stood out from the usual suspects, with longer songs, soundscapes and experimentation. They enlisted John Maclean (soon of The Beta Band) to create the artwork while he attended Edinburgh College of Art. As Kenny's brother Gordon's best friend and a phenomenal artist in collage, this choice made perfect sense. It looked and sounded grander than anything else they'd dreamed of achieving. They had gone to town on making something they thought would, could and should be successful and important.

'We got a two line review in the *Dundee Courier* – that's all we got, press-wise. We were gutted,' Kenny spits. The review goes like this: 'A quick listen shows the Skuobhies in fine form again on this their second album, with good songs and slick production making it well worth checking out.' The album disappeared without a trace. The problem seemed to be that the band's audience weren't old, beardy folk fans, but students and young people who bought their music in indie, dance and rock record shops. The label didn't know what to do with them and continued to sell their CDs in tartan-tat west-coast gift shops to tourists who wanted traditional music as a holiday souvenir. You were more likely to find an SDO album in a Caledonian MacBrayne ferry port than a record shop. There was a huge dichotomy between the way the band were seen by tastemakers and what they were trying to achieve. They weren't a trad band with a comedy name, but an exhilarating live band with an inspired songwriter, trying to push the envelope of what pop, rock, indie and folk could be.

Taking on another fiddler, Jason Brass, a new bassist in Pete Macleod (known today by his Fence pseudonym 'Uncle Beesly') and finally saying goodbye to Eric, they found themselves in a netherworld where folk clubs didn't think they were a true trad band, yet the press and the indie circuit couldn't look beyond their largely acoustic instrumentation and Kenny's Scottish singing voice. They attracted dance fans due to the speed and thumping rhythms of the music, hippies and festival-goers looking for something earthy and real, and those who loved the exquisite musicianship and unusual, contemporary songs. But they didn't attract the hip, cool and trendy tastemakers *du jour*.

Kenny had started out singing on the street and found it natural to pronounce the words in his own accent. He didn't change Scottish words or slang to more conventional rock 'n' roll-speak. Now every indie band in Scotland does exactly this, but in 1992/93 this probably worked against the band. Only The Proclaimers pronounced their lyrics in their own dialect, and outside their fan base and those in the know they were seen as a novelty act. Kenny still thought of himself as a 'singer by default', and The Skuobhie Dubh Orchestra was most definitely a band. If Een wrote a song he sang it, and so on. It just happened that Kenny was the driving force and the most prolific writer in the group – and possibly a control-freak of sorts. He didn't want it to be his backing band, but a unit that worked together. The band members were beginning to think otherwise.

It's here that a young Kate Tunstall enters the fray. 'At the Woollen Mill that summer,' Kenny remembers from 1993, 'I worked with a girl called Siobhan who suggested I go along to the Vic Café to see her pal playing. There was a little oval back-room, and this chirpy little dark-haired lass was surrounded by a load of friends, singing what appeared to be her own songs. Her crowd were very enthusiastic but a lot younger than me, so after chatting to her about maybe having her support the

Dubhs, I sloped off to my own crew. I see from my diary that I'd written down that she was "excellent".'

Here was a bubbly, attractive girl with talent in spades and an unflappable instinct for performance. Confident, for sure, but with a dusty, down-to-earth manner that blew away any air of pretentiousness. 'A few days later,' Kenny continues, 'I met up with Kate at the Vic. She gave me a tape of her songs and I dropped her off at her mum's at closing time. On 2 September Kate joined in with a Skuobhie Dubh Orchestra rehearsal. I tried putting accordion parts on a few of her songs, and she played her first gig with us in that same oval room on Friday, 3 September.' If that turnaround seems quick, it's a testament to Kenny, Kate and the band's abilities as spontaneous musicians.

As the Dubhs were still a fairly sizeable draw, playing as often as possible, Kate became a staple of their live gigs, befriending the boys and making a bond. She regularly joined them onstage for spontaneous backing vocals, bursts of harmonica and added percussion, and occasional versions of her own songs. She was obviously a natural singer and pushed Kenny to perform better too. In the ramshackle world of the Dubhs she was a worthy addition and a little injection of glamour for their audience and her male admirers. One such admirer was Een. With his innocent, country-boy looks and charm, combined with his deadpan Fife humour, here was a ladykiller. But would she feel the same? And could the band handle a romantic entanglement within its ranks?

The wheels, however, were about to fall off the Mystery Machine, spelling disaster for the band's tight core of Kenny, Een and Andy. In early 1994 the Dubhs' new live agents, Active Events, had made their first attempt to get the band gigs in the US, and the overwhelming response from venues, press and radio was that the name of the band was going to be a major problem. Young children and their parents might show up to cuddle and shake hands with the loveable cartoon dog and be confronted by five scruffy Scottish musicians. They were strongly advised to change the band's name by a big US agent who imagined legal threats from Hanna-Barbera. There was a lot of humming and hawing, but at their annual knees-up at the Lemon Tree in Aberdeen that February they announced their decision to do precisely that.

After another series of bad gigs, long drives and speeding tickets, and the realisation that they weren't rising above the UK toilet circuit they'd been playing for years, Andy quit the group. The band weren't progressing career-wise, although their music was. They were gigging around in circles with no sign of the money improving or the audiences growing with them. Andy had seen a chance to return to university, earn money and immerse himself in a serious relationship with his girlfriend, soon to become his wife. Without a decent replacement drummer, the band floundered. Een wanted to pursue more authentic, technical, traditional styles on his own and form a more folk-pop band with Kate, to be called Elia Drew. Kenny was left to call time on a band that could and should have gone the distance. 'It was absolutely gut-wrenching. It was worse than losing a girlfriend, the day Andy left. I remember it clearly, the day he left that note,' Kenny recalls.

Unlike today, alt-folk and nu-folk didn't exist, and the trends of the time, such as Madchester, grunge and Britpop were all electric in sound, aesthetics and rock 'n' roll influence. Creation Records had signed half of Glasgow's indie scene, yet bands from elsewhere of different character, influences and instrumentation didn't stand a chance. Edinburgh got a look-in occasionally but was terminally unfashionable, and places like Dundee, Aberdeen and Fife were almost entirely ignored. Perhaps the band were too late or too early for their time, and would be well-respected elder statesmen in the UK's Americana and folk scenes today had they just carried on regardless. Perhaps their sound harked back to the outmoded 1980s Celtic soul of The Bluebells and Dexys. Possibly the name was a hindrance. We'll never know, but one thing was for certain: they weren't getting to the right ears in the early 1990s and were extremely skilled at avoiding the *zeitgeist* at all times. It was April 1994, and The Skuobhie Dubh Orchestra was no more.

With the bass-playing Pete 'Uncle Beesly' Macleod as his only accomplice, Kenny needed to do something different to rally the troops again. With a change of name imminent, it was time to make a clean break and begin a new group. Initially playing another Lemon Tree gig with reluctant ex-members of the Dubhs as the Barber Hannahs in homage to their potential litigators, Kenny wondered what other cartoon heroes there were out there. In a moment of clarity he stumbled precariously over some daft wordplay and there it was in front of him . . . Khartoum Heroes. It sounded good and, thanks to Gordon, in scrawled logo form it looked good too. In true Kenny Anderson tradition, he had another substantial set of songs that were itching to get recorded too. It wouldn't be a new Dubhs record, but the first under a new name. The despondent group went once more to Land Studios to record the album *Gordonov*, featuring the last recordings of the classic Skuobhie Dubh Orchestra line-up. The songs were as good as ever, if not better, and the band rose to the occasion and created the first Khartoum Heroes LP, with a self-portrait of brother Gordon as the artwork. Now Kenny had a band name and an album – but no band . . .

$$\oint$$

It was at just this time, summer 1994, that my band Miraclehead had lately split-up. James 'Yorkston' Wright and Cliff Simms had unceremoniously walked out, cutting drummer Stu Bastiman and me adrift. Distraught, we desperately wanted to get a new project off the ground. We needed inspiration, and fast. Two months earlier we'd appeared at the Cupar Festival in Fife, playing on the back of a lorry alongside who else but The Skuobhie Dubh Orchestra. We'd all got on famously, getting drunk together and laughing at our bad luck as bands. There was chemistry between us, as people if not as players. When I unwittingly bumped into Kenny Anderson backstage at 1994's T in the Park festival, we let loose our sob-stories and swapped numbers to meet up and cry into our pints if nothing else.

'Honestly,' Kenny recounts, 'I woke up in the night and thought to myself, Vic's a guitar player and he's been left with a drummer. Here I am with a bass-player – that's a potential band. I remember you liked the name Khartoum Heroes, so I phoned you up.' A first, dreadful rehearsal was organised. Here were two bands trying to find a middle ground – Miraclehead was grounded in punk, indie and ska, and we'd never played any kind of folk music, never mind bluegrass. We were moving into classic British songwriting shapes, referencing The Kinks, Madness and XTC, whereas Kenny's songs were more traditional and used at most three chords. Kenny had never really played music with real rock drums and an electric guitar either. However, among the chaos, something clicked. More rehearsals were booked and soon a coherent group emerged.

'I've never experienced anything like it, before or since,' Kenny remembers. 'For a month solid, between collecting Giros [dole money] and having magic-mushroom adventures, we played continually and formed a huge bond as musicians and friends.' It was true: four unlikely lads had summoned some kind of phoenix from the embers of two red-hot bands. For that month or so we lived in Kenny's psychedelic cottage on the Teasses estate near Ceres in Fife, playing Mario Kart, eating gingerbread, tripping on mushrooms and, above all, making music. We had our gear set up twenty-four hours a day and jammed whenever we felt the urge, which was most of the time. With Kenny's seemingly endless book of songs and my angular, melodic contributions we had created our own sound and hours' worth of material. It was a joyful time when music, creativity and merry abandon were the order of the day, and nothing else mattered. Egos were left at the door and all ideas were considered. It was real freedom, and I will remember it as long as I live.

Kenny had confirmed he would honour any outstanding engagements for The Skuobhie Dubh Orchestra under the new name, and Active Events had booked the band on a nationwide UK tour, so our baptism of fire was soon upon us. Expecting acoustic banjo, fiddle and bluegrass, audiences got something altogether different. Here was an electrified quartet playing some recognisable songs of Kenny's, including 'Moonbarking', 'Colossal Angel', 'St Swithin', and 'Spacehopper', from the first Khartoum Heroes album, alongside new, eccentric psych-pop numbers like 'Bathtime Maybe', 'Purple Om', 'Lonely Little Man' and 'Bag Lady'. There were effects on guitars, banjo, fiddle and vocals, and the music was moving into far more contemporary waters. Some Dubh fans went with it and appreciated the seismic sonic shift, others walked away in dismay. We weren't trying to pander to anyone: Khartoum Heroes was what it was, and we brass-necked our way through that tour and a Celtic Connections festival appearance in Glasgow, making friends and enemies along the way.

At an Edinburgh gig in a short-lived venue called Stones, Een Anderson and Jason Brass came to watch what they thought would be a total car-crash. Maybe it was, but they both wanted in. 'Een said to me: "You guys sound like a band and I want to play." I was amazed. I'd actually impressed Een with one of my bands!' says Kenny. The sibling rivalry that had brought the Dubhs to an end was shelved, albeit temporarily. So they re-entered the fold, Een playing banjo (now electrified), mouth-organ, backing vocals and wobbleboard, and Jason back on fiddle. Here was a band that was anything but conventional, traditional or authentically rootsy. It was weird for them, but then it was for all of us. It might have been a strange mismatch of influences but it was also exhilarating.

Khartoum Heroes hit the road continually. We played across Scotland and then the UK. We laid down an odd collection of recordings that was issued on cassette at the time (reissued by Fence later as *Egyptian Skipping*) and sold at gigs. We played festivals, parties, rock gigs, folk clubs, pretty much anywhere people would have us. A friend of ours, Paul Mustarde, became manager, bought a van, and encouraged us to progress as a band. Stu and I learned about folk and bluegrass while opening Kenny's ears to various genres of outlandish indie, rock and electronic music. It was a vibrant, creative and exploratory time.

In the single year we were together as Khartoum Heroes we accomplished some impressive and outlandish achievements. We played in Glasgow's George Square at Hogmanay 1994/95, at the Edinburgh Fringe Festival, and on Ned Sherrin's Radio 4 *Loose Ends* show, and toured across parts of Europe, gigging in France, Belgium and Holland. A highlight for me was performing at and staying in a squatters' club called Bar en Boos in Leiden, Holland. As an anarcho-commune, vegan café, alternative record shop and DIY venue they welcomed this gang of Scottish stragglers to their hearts and home. We briefly became firm friends with the local punks and got trashed on *weissbier* every night. This is what being in a band is all about – travelling wherever, playing to appreciative audiences and cementing real, lasting friendships on the road. Because of that intense and personal time I have an unbreakable bond with those guys, especially Kenny. 'It was like a new girlfriend, that band,' says Kenny. 'We all needed it to be good and to be successful. It was an amazing year.'

After the honeymoon period, band relationships began to blossom and things started to change. If Kenny and I were the motivating force and the songwriting team, Een and Stuart were becoming thick as thieves as players and ladies' men. On our European tour we played electric at night in venues while making extra money busking in acoustic guise during the day. Stu had stepped up as an exceptional drummer and had fully welcomed bluegrass, country, folk and Americana into his life. This pleased Een, and the old ways of the Dubhs began to creep back in. Kenny felt comfortable with this as it reminded him of the good old days of busking, with no real ambition or agenda. Pete was easy-going and enjoyed both the electric and acoustic sides of the band. I yearned for something more, though.

Kenny was beginning to feel internal turmoil building too. Een was forever hounding the band to relocate to France or Spain. As Kenny recalls: 'He'd say "It's Scotland – it's because we're in Scotland that nothing's happening for us. We need to move." But I just couldn't and didn't want to. If I had done, I'd have had nothing in Scotland – no credibility, no history, nothing. Maybe it was to make my dad proud, I don't know. But I needed to establish myself at home, and I just wanted to be in Fife, to be honest.' Ego and vanity played a large part, as did age. 'I felt I was getting too old. Not that I was an old man. It was almost a status thing. Lots of my friends were now incredibly successful in their fields, and here I was playing the same circuit of gigs and going nowhere. I'd told my parents where to stick my degree, but now I felt the pressure of my thirties on my shoulders. In many ways I was on the rebound from The Skuobhie Dubh Orchestra and I was in freefall,' Kenny now says.

On the other hand, I wanted to make modern, electric music and forward-thinking art. I didn't want to be in a busking band, and I didn't want to be playing old Skuobhie Dubh Orchestra songs. Much as I had loved them, I was a man in his twenties on a mission to imprint my own ideas on the world. After a year to the day, in August 1995, I walked away and let Kenny, Een, Stu and Pete mutate into various incarnations of Shoe Market Hour (an anagram of Khartoum Heroes), eventually morphing again into The Skuobhie Dubh Orchestra. It was an incredibly tough decision for me, as they were my close friends and musical companions. We'd undergone a huge amount together and hit the ground running, fuelled by naive hope, youth, enthusiasm and blind faith. We'd done our best, and although I didn't want my friendships to dissolve, I needed to make a different kind of music.

Meanwhile Kenny's mental state was becoming increasingly unstable. 'The demise of Khartoum Heroes was another failure for me,' he says, 'and in retrospect I was letting myself in for another two years of falling apart before I had to confront everything, do something and make sense of it all. I now had three sets of eyes on me – Een, Stu and Pete – all looking for gigs. All I knew was how to be a bandleader and so that's what I did, even though that was the last thing I wanted.' He acted as leader, manager and agent, booking as many shows as possible, eventually playing three or four nights a week in St Andrews alone. He was now the only source of inspiration in the group, and by the end of summer 1995 it was taking its toll. He was starting to have panic attacks, though he didn't know what they were at the time. He was uneasy with everything and everyone. He couldn't be with his family, at work at the Woollen Mill, with his girlfriend or even with the band.

At the start of 1996 Kenny had split with his long-term partner Kirsty, and his cottage on the Teasses estate had been flooded as a result of burst water pipes, destroying almost everything he owned. Emotionally and physically exhausted, he took a well-deserved holiday to the US to visit MC Quake, using up all his savings and staying for a month, thinking this might salvage his mental state and solve his ongoing problems. In retrospect it wasn't perhaps the best of ideas, as the panic attacks increased. Everything there was utter sensory overload and, in his own words, 'totally bamboozling'. He wasn't ready or mentally prepared for somewhere like Las Vegas.

On his return, penniless and emotionally spent, with a banjo tattoo on his arm, he found no one had booked any shows in his absence. He'd handed the gig contacts to Een and Stu, who had done nothing but allegedly break a window and damage the band's PA system. Kenny was at his wits' end. Oddly enough, none of this immediately affected the music, and the group recorded the album *A New Cat*, with Kate Tunstall on backing vocals, a classic release to many fans. The songwriting, playing, production and artwork are all superb. Even under so much pressure, Kenny and the disgruntled gang could still deliver the goods. 'It did feel like a farewell present from them, though,' he says. 'One last album and then goodbye.'

But it was over. Kenny says: 'I was totally wrapped up in my own problems and had become a terrible bandleader. I was on a downward spiral and felt like I was painted black on the inside.' When he discovered that Een, Stu and Pete were all playing in a new, fully rehearsed band behind Kate Tunstall, with whom Een had started a relationship, it was the very last straw. 'It was like rats deserting a sinking ship,' he says. Kenny had been usurped, and he buckled.

2

Dance o'er the Border

Steve Mason, Gordon Anderson, John Maclean, Robin Jones and the Roots of The Beta Band

Steve Mason has always been a bit of a chameleon. For over thirty years he's been into punk, mod, surf, rockabilly, hip-hop, rave, Madchester, electro, reggae, acoustic songwriting and, crucially, a mixture of all of the above. He's a mystery and he likes it that way. When asked if he'd help me with this book he immediately refused, saying he had nothing in common with the other musicians I was writing about. After some gentle persuasion, and a promise that I wasn't doing this to stitch anyone up, he relented and ended up imparting some great stories and intimate details. One thing's for sure, though, he doesn't want to be in anyone's gang but his own.

Not everyone who carves out a career in music comes from a musical family. 'My dad only ever owned one record,' Steve says, 'and that was Bill Haley and His Comets' album *Rock Around The Clock*, which by any stretch of the imagination is a terrible record. My mum had been to art college and enjoyed music, seeing that key Bob Dylan "Judas" gig, among others. But by the time I came along, she'd stopped painting and listening to music to bring up a family.' There was a record player in the Mason household, a copy of The Beatles' *Abbey Road*, a Gilbert O'Sullivan compilation and two Steely Dan albums. Curiously enough, there was also a battered acoustic guitar with missing strings. Steve, intrigued, was the only one ever to give it a go.

Like many boys and girls of a certain age, Steve's first induction into pop fandom was via Adam and the Ants. 'It was a good thing to get into. It was a band, a look and a set of values in a way.' Alongside mutual friend James 'Yorkston' Wright and me, Steve was obsessed, buying all the singles and albums as well as badges, patches, posters and tacky memorabilia. For a couple of years it was nothing less than a lifestyle for the Ant People out there, and no pop or rock star could touch the dandy highwayman. I cast my mind back and realise how subversive Adam Ant was in many ways: a young, muscular, heavily made-up man, dressed as a pirate or Native American, singing songs about sex and bondage over a wall of distorted guitars and tribal drums. Rightfully, he drove the kids wild.

Once the gates had been blown open by the possibilities that pop presented, the next step was to investigate the scary, unruly, vibrant and colourful world of punk. By the early 1980s punk had burned bright and fizzled out in swinging London and hipster New York, but across the provinces of the UK, Europe and the US its force was still being felt. Kids of all backgrounds who felt disenfranchised by the synthetic pop culture and New Romanticism of the day took respite in the aggression, speed and honesty of its music, message and aesthetics. It was vital and fiery and it spoke to thousands of teenagers and pre-teens who needed some tangible excitement in their lives. Some kids loved *Smash Hits* and the likes of Bananarama; others looked further afield.

With punk there was a whole universe to explore, so many strange band names and fashion statements at your disposal. Steve was particularly attracted to bands like the Sex Pistols, X-Ray Spex and The Dead Kennedys. Aged around ten, he'd visit St Andrews record shops Tracks and the Music Shop and order records from their vast catalogues. It must have been strange for the shopkeepers to have a young lad walk through the door asking for 'Oh Bondage Up Yours!' every Saturday afternoon until the damn thing eventually arrived on 7-inch vinyl. At schools across the land kids were punks, mods, skinheads, goths or 2-Tone fans. You chose your gang and aligned yourself with it.

Steve recalls: 'One day I had an epiphany playing that old acoustic guitar. The day I worked out the basic opening line from the Sex Pistols' "Anarchy In The UK", music seemed more real. I can actually do this! It opened up a new world of possibilities and a new kind of magic.' Acquiring a set of drumsticks, he would batter the living daylights out of the cushions and pillows in his room. He'd record the drumsticks on one tape recorder, then play guitar along with the tape and record both on another tape machine. It was basic two-tracking. I had done exactly the same in my bedroom, and then with James above his garage. When you're young, bored and have plenty of time on your hands, it's amazing what you can uncover or invent with no help from others. 'I think the fact I'd thought of it was enough. It was the start of something. The results were always disappointing and the hiss was Biblical, but it was a start,' Steve says.

As his personal youthquake was shaking his life and music was playing a bigger and bigger role, Steve searched out new sounds. While a fan of punk, which was by and large from a few years past, he stepped into the present and became one of St Andrews' first B-Boys. Having befriended a young skinhead John Watson and the Michael Jackson-loving Barry Collins at Kilrymont School, they were soon introduced to the *Street Sounds – Electro 1* album by John's sister, who lived in London. Here was a genuinely pioneering sound for them to get into. 'It's hard to explain nowadays, when so little sounds new or fresh, how it felt to hear something truly groundbreaking like electro. That particular album is now seen as a classic. She then sent us volumes two, three and four and we just loved them. From there were got into Afrika Bambaata and had our minds totally blown,' he says. They saw the film *Beat Street* and the *Style Wars* graffiti documentary, both of which had a huge impact. They then took the look and the sounds to the unsuspecting public in central St Andrews.

Steve's dad worked at a linoleum factory, and the B-Boys would get square metres of the stuff for free to spin on. I remember a summer of Steve and his posse trying to breakdance on the streets of St Andrews in front a huge ghetto-blaster. It was comical but brave. To be dancing as a teenager in Scotland was courageous enough. To do it in the daytime with brightly coloured tracksuits on, playing music that no one had heard before, was faintly ridiculous. I laughed, but I was also impressed. 'It's about the confidence to put something on, put a look together and carry it off. To walk around the streets of a small town like St Andrews and take the ridicule and say: "Well, you don't know what the fuck you're talking about, anyway" was tough. There was quite a bit of violence back then. It took guts to make a statement and dress in a certain way,' says Steve. Things were extremely tribal in these heady times.

Assisted by John Watson and Scott Maclean, Steve tried to form a hip-hop trio at the age of twelve. 'We had a set of bongos and a belt-driven vinyl deck, impossible to scratch on – we assumed scratching was actually impossible, before realising you needed a direct-drive turntable. We couldn't decide who was going to be the MC either.' But this wasn't Steve's first band. He had been part of a beat combo at primary school with James Wright, ambitiously called The Final Transmission, in which he'd rattled upturned oilcans and biscuit tins. They had a manager, Paul Holmes, a cunning businessman at the age of nine, who apparently ripped them off for the 20p it cost to join the band. The split was bitter and acrimonious. If only tapes existed of those seminal outfits . . .

For secondary school, Steve checked into Madras College. The drums were now his chosen instrument, and his mother invested in a lousy bucket of a kit, thinking (and hoping and praying, no doubt) that it was a phase that he would soon grow out of. Instead he immersed himself in the crash-bang-wallop and practised all the time. You could walk down his street and know which house was his by the sound of crashing cymbals and incessant snare pops. He was now a mod, having ditched the B-Boy craze, and was listening to Motown, The Who and surf music. 'I just had an appetite for new music, which was just music I'd never heard before. Every two years or so I'd try something different. I remember going to a breakdance battle in Cupar, and the mods turned up in their parkas playing "Green Onions" by Booker T & the MG's on a ghetto-blaster. I remember thinking: *Those cunts are cool as fuck!* I got into the whole mod thing and that stayed with me for a long time.'

At Madras he met Keith Douglas (now in his own band, The Corps of Discovery) and John Gibbs (now of The Wildebeests and The Masonics). Keith was becoming a tremendous rockabilly guitarist and John enthusiastically rocked along on bass guitar. Their drummer was a hysterically be-quiffed Dick Petrie, whose skills quite frankly weren't up to the job. They'd named themselves the Surfabillies and were soon to play an important gig at the 1,000-capacity Younger Hall, with a host of other local acts on the bill. This show was a rite of passage for much of the town's youth, and the band wanted to impress with a cover of The Surfaris' 'Wipe Out'. Dick couldn't play it, but Steve knew he could. At

John's request there was a trial rehearsal where he nailed the drums on the infamous twang-along. He was instantly in the band and Dick was out.

The gig was a major success and a huge eye-opener for all involved. Local heroes Joe Public, a band in their twenties who were touring the country and being touted in the same breath as acts like Deacon Blue, were headlining. The hall was packed with schoolkids and they screamed for every act, no matter how appalling. The Surfabillies went down well, considering how young and inept they were. This momentous occasion set the wheels in motion. 'It was like being a rock-star. It was mental! People were screaming our names and everything,' Steve laughs.

The Surfabillies soon mutated into The Orang-o-Twangs, playing mainly instrumental rock 'n' roll and R 'n' B. That teenagers in the East Neuk of Fife were playing Link Wray and Duane Eddy songs and perfecting this primal 1950s music is simultaneously fascinating and peculiar. Was this a reaction to the pop *zeitgeist* of the mid-1980s, or just inquisitive young men following a whim? A similar thread seems to run through the music of most of the people in this book, certainly the indigenous Fifers. Perhaps the music our parents listened to was seeping into our own consciousness. Perhaps it was the unabashed simplicity and honesty of this music that connected. It was almost unquestionably a result of living in a creative bubble away from any epicentre of pop culture, without the internet, to experiment and enjoy yourself as you liked.

As their technique improved, the trio of Keith Douglas, John Gibbs and Steve morphed into The Batfinks, named after a cartoon of the time, honing their skills on guitar, double bass and drums. Specialising in 1950s rock 'n' roll and rockabilly cover versions, including obscurities such as 'Rock 'n' Roll Frog', this was in many ways their first serious group. Although still at school, they'd perform all over Fife in pubs and clubs, building up a following and earning money. Even today, over twenty-five years later, music-loving Fifers mention The Batfinks and recall how good they were. However, being hot-headed schoolboys, the band was short-lived; Steve was acrimoniously ejected on account of being too friendly towards John's girlfriend. Laughing now, Steve proclaims his innocence, but John was livid and Steve was out. His next move was a brief sojourn with James Wright and local punk Fraser

MacDonald in the group Verkrampte, mentioned later here, who made an unholy and incompetent racket around St Andrews. Soon, however, Steve's school-band days would come to an end.

Leaving school in 1987, Steve decided to stay in St Andrews and took a job at the delicatessen counter in William Low's supermarket. Hardly ambitious or high-achieving, considering his intelligence, he had no plans for higher education or even taking music to the next level. His parents hadn't encouraged his musical pursuits, wanting him to become a solicitor. Leaving school in fifth year with one Higher and three O-grades, he was hardly qualified for that or much else. 'No one told me about university or college. I just didn't understand. Although there was St Andrews University on my doorstep, I thought: "I can't do that",' he says. 'I knew I wasn't stupid, but I was made to feel stupid because I wasn't academic. My dad had been to university and my mum had been to art college. My parents kind of gave up on me and thought I was a loser.'

He submerged himself in scooter culture, an offshoot of mod life. From 1988 to 1991 he travelled the length and breadth of the UK, attending almost every scooter rally available. It had started with mod rallies, to indulge his musical passions, but developed into a love of scooters themselves. 'Once you've got a fairly reliable scooter, or you learn to fix them, it's an unbelievable sense of freedom, especially in a place like St Andrews. You want to get out, because you know that everything is happening outside here. I'd just open the throttle, point it in the right direction and it would take me anywhere I wanted to go. You'd travel across the country to the rallies and end up talking to people from all walks of life. Your sense of this country becomes a lot smaller.'

The scooter scene wasn't just mods and mechanics, either. At the rallies Steve would meet punks, skinheads, psychobillies, funk and soul boys, casuals and other subcultures, all interested in their two-wheelers and their musical peer groups. It broadened his horizons and his state of mind, making him realise there was more to life than Fife. Every weekend he'd travel to places such as Llandudno, Exmouth or Margate and regale his workmates with stories after the weekend's adventures. They couldn't quite understand or believe what he was up to. For them, it was a big deal to go to Edinburgh. In terms of blowing his own mind, Steve was well on his way. I remember The Beta Band playing the Glasgow Barrowland for the first time, years later, as almost a tribal gathering. In among the indie kids, hippies, hip-hop fans and post-baggy scallies were a large number of mods and scooter boys. These were mates of Steve's who had followed his musical progress and supported his endeavours. He'd always give them a shout-out from the stage.

Out of the blue he had a phone call from an Edinburgh mod band, The Second Generation, asking him to play drums with them. As a result of his scooter obsession, attendance at Northern Soul all-nighters and general mod fascination, the news had travelled that Steve was a very capable player, and they asked if he'd like to play on an album. 'For me it was a huge deal to record an album. I didn't mention it to my mum until I had the album in my hand,' Steve recalls. The album was made at Chamber Studio by Jamie Watson, a stalwart of the Edinburgh punk and post-punk indie scenes, who also ran the Human Condition label. Although called The Second Generation, they were probably about fourth- or fifth-generation mods, and the album is 'dreadful', as Steve now attests. However, it was a first chance to experience a proper recording studio and hear those petrifying three words, 'We are rolling', in his headphones. This album was Steve's first record.

Living with his parents, he began to panic about not having a proper job or profession and, giving in to his father, sold his drum kit, quitting music and The Second Generation in 1989. Showing interest in little other than engines, he was persuaded to enter an apprenticeship as a car mechanic. With his love of scooters, it seemed like an obvious choice to the vaguely clueless teenager. His training began, and regular wages coincided with the arrival of dance music and rave culture via the Manchester indie scene. Suddenly he had disposable income and a new youth explosion to discover.

Introduced to Happy Mondays and The Stone Roses while smoking weed for the first time, it was the Happy Mondays album *Bummed* that first appealed. 'It sounded like nothing I'd ever heard. I then bought *24 Hour Party People*, which is still one of my favourite albums of all time,' Steve says. With The Stone Roses, he was primarily attracted to the look of the band. 'To me, if a band looks interesting then they probably sound quite good too. I loved the fact that they were wearing flares, as they were a complete taboo at the time. I like anything where people are doing the exact opposite of what everyone else is doing.' Here was a band completely wrapped up in the dance culture, playing relatively retro-sounding guitar music among the euphoric, repetitive beats of the time. Steve, being a drummer, admired their funky polyrhythms and was so smitten with the band that he had the iconic lemon slice from the first Roses album tattooed on his arm. A few years later, the Roses' Mani and Reni would be fans of his work with The Beta Band.

Soon he tried his first tab of LSD and was taken to his first rave at the Cronk in Dunfermline, a mecca for Fife's acid-house and techno aficionados. Steve would also frequent Pure in Edinburgh and Glasgow's Sub Club, cementing his love of wild, abandoned clubbing across the land. Increasingly his weekends were taken up with trips to Edinburgh to visit his girlfriend and enjoy this new lifestyle. His friends from school had largely left St Andrews and he began to join a new peer group. He attended fewer scooter rallies and more club nights until his allegiances had dramatically changed, packing in the rallies in 1991 and almost entirely ignoring what was happening in Fife. He was now concentrating on his life and connections in Edinburgh, and it wasn't long before he would meet the people who would completely change his life.

Gordon Anderson and his twin brother Een were born on 18 March 1972, Een being three minutes older. Far from identical in looks or nature, they were 'always fighting', Gordon says. 'We were great friends but we fought a lot. I remember sticking a dart right into his chest. We're great friends now though. We're closer than anyone else in the family. I need to see Een every few days.'

All those who've had the opportunity to get to know Gordon will say that he's a force of nature and a shock to the system. Short and stocky, with boundless energy expressed in quick-fire impressions and a never-ending love of mischief, Gordon never stops pondering, analysing, deconstructing and creating ideas and art. He's cheeky, erratic, arrogant and self-deprecating in equal measure. He's also incredibly warm-hearted, helpful and generous. You won't ever forget spending time with him, if you have the good fortune to do so.

From Kenny's account of the twins, Gordon bossed Een all through early childhood, and as a result can do or say pretty much anything to Een to this day. Although on a far more equal footing now, their bond is stronger, closer and more complicated than most fraternal relationships. They share the same sense of the ridiculous as Kenny, combining down-to-earth humour with off-the-wall surrealism. They're clearly three Andersons to the eye and ear, and extremely talented with it.

Aside from toys, BMX bikes and tearing around the town, one of Gordon's first serious interests was astronomy. He drew his own map of the stars and owned a small telescope. He remembers seeing Halley's comet at St Andrews University Observatory when he was ten. Knowing this today, it's quite telling how the two would develop, musically and otherwise. Being strong-willed and bolshy, Gordon was the boss of Een and friends at school – or so he thought. He was the loudmouth, the instigator and the troublemaker from a young age. He would take the role of gang leader and initiate the adventures and escapades. 'I was a great garden-hopper,' he says, 'and then I became a great roof-hopper. I ended up scaling all the main buildings in town, once making it to the top of the Victoria Hall one night when I was around fourteen. Later on at Edinburgh College of Art, John Maclean and I climbed a university building near Bristo Square. John was petrified and said to me: "That's when I knew you were a nutcase, Gordon!"'

Although immersed in music as children, thanks to their father's career, their older brother's accordion-playing and their sister Lynne's pop collection, neither twin took up an instrument until fairly late on. Asked about his dad's Scottish country dance music, Gordon says: 'It was all around us. We all said we hated it too, although we secretly loved it. We knew all the songs that he and his band would gig.' Gordon's first musical preference, however, was Elvis Presley. He had somehow accumulated a pile of cassette tapes of the King and would listen intently to these and a precious Nina Simone compilation. He was also intrigued and deeply touched by the *E.T.* film soundtrack, something he still loves. Interviewed for this book, he insisted we listen to the very same tape.

One of Gordon's emerging talents was for visual art. He loved drawing, painting and designing pictures and making models with Plasticine, and still does. As a boy he could replicate the cartoon Gaul Asterix's entire village in pen, ink and paint, in minute detail, and soon began to try life drawing at school. Seeing one of his school drawings of a hand and forearm today, it's a testament to how talented he was at a very young age. Een also inherited the creative gene and would convert scrap cardboard into miniature villages and libraries. With humble beginnings, limited finances, lots of time and limitless imagination, life for the Anderson brothers was a question of making their own fun, as it was for everyone else in this book, including me. It was a simple, care-free childhood for all of us, where thoughts could run wild and ideas could come to life.

As the years passed Gordon started to take more interest in music, albeit as a casual listener. He'd sit in Lynne's room as she played single after single on her own private Dansette and read her copies of *Smash Hits*. 'That stuff filters through,' he says. 'She was the most interested in music in the whole family. She had a passion for records.' She was so besotted with the 1980s pop explosion that she started her own Saturday-morning disco in the local Cosmos Centre. Gordon would go, aged eight or nine, to play snooker and chase girls. 'They'd end up just kicking me, though.'

Neither twin was particularly keen on school, and they attended separate classes throughout. This was possibly on purpose, to allow them to develop apart, but Gordon looks back now and thinks it's strange. They didn't see each other that much. Gordon was feisty and fearless, and if necessary would physically take on his adversaries. He was the archetypal wee man who won't back down or be bullied, and it worked for him most of the time. But, as he recounts, things changed. 'My grandfather died just as I was starting secondary school. I went from being leader of the pack in primary to being more withdrawn and private. I avoided confrontation and felt fear for the first time.'

Having sauntered through junior school and into the senior years at Madras College, he never made much of an effort. He was in the top classes, but simply wasn't interested. He now says: 'Do you know what they should have taught? How to fix a car, how to pay your rent, how to make some money, how to fill out forms – things you really need. I just ended up not going in for days and days. No one seemed to notice and no one asked. I'd go in for art and that was it.' He sat various O-grades and Highers, passing some and failing others, unlike Kenny, who was 'always doing homework'.

Moving into fifth and sixth year, Gordon had two massively important encounters. Befriending John Maclean was the first. Although they had been aware of each other in fourth year, their friendship grew, and, as they began taking art classes together, developed into a unique partnership. Dressed in tennis shirts and cutting about with a different crowd, sportier and perhaps a little square, John began hanging out with Gordon more and more. He seemed happy to break away, sharing visual, comedic and musical ideas and taking trips to Edinburgh with Gordon to go record or bike shopping. Inevitably, with Gordon as his accomplice, they got into trouble together too.

They spurred each other on, investigating the culture and music at their fingertips. Gordon's tastes in music widened with albums such as Neil Young's *Zuma* and The Beatles' *Sgt Pepper's Lonely Hearts Club Band* and their *1962–66* and *1966–70* compilations making their way into his collection and consciousness. He loved The Smiths and tried to sound like Morrissey when singing in his attic bedroom. He was introduced to Chuck Berry by John Maclean and Keith Douglas, who also brought his love of 1950s and 1960s rock 'n' roll to the table, and was turned on to some of Kenny's favourites including Simple Minds and Talk Talk. School comrades such as Steve Anderson and David 'Wearie' Waters were into punk, and would blast out their Sex Pistols and Dead Kennedys singles. 'I didn't have to buy records,' Gordon says. 'I got to know a lot of music by accident. Anyway, I had no time for records or collections. I've never been one for collecting someone else's music.'

He did, however, start a lifelong fascination with Prince and went on to buy everything he could by the artist. Both he and John Maclean recall how Gordon would continually chant, sing, scream or whisper the line: 'I'm blinded by the daisies in your yard' from 'Condition Of The Heart' throughout fifth and sixth year. He did it all day, every day for months on end, and naturally it drove John mad. This was, and still is, typical Gordon.

The second important cultural shift came with The Stone Roses. It was more than just music. It was, as Gordon now recalls, the image: 'Here were guys trying to be a bit different, more like The Beatles. We had to go through all that 1980s stuff with guys in make-up, using electronic drumbeats and so on. I liked the occasional tune, but it wasn't my thing at all. This was a little more real.'

$$\oint$$

John Maclean cuts an unlikely figure as a rock star. Tall, skinny, ginger-haired and ever so slightly gangly, it's been remarked on more than one occasion that he resembles Shaggy from *Scooby Doo*. With an acute, dry sense of humour and an attuned, super-creative mind, he laughs in the face of clichéd rock 'n' roll debauchery, preferring to stay in control and one step ahead.

Born in Perth in December 1972, growing up in Gateside and finally settling in Tayport alongside sister Miriam and brother David, John is the son of two artists. His mother, Marian, is a painter who originally specialised in landscapes but more recently has taken a more abstract turn. His father, Will, who concentrates on box construction (a medium involving found objects and collage), is renowned in Scotland and exhibits work internationally, attracting comparisons with Dada artists such as Joseph Cornell. His work draws on Scottish folklore, the Highland clearances and fishing for inspiration, as a result of his having grown up in a Highland fishing community. As well as their Tayport family home, they have a house in the Highlands, a seventh-generation croft that has belonged to the Maclean clan for hundreds of years. Originally an inhospitable hut, there's now a house built on the land that provides the perfect family retreat and a special, almost spiritual home. Not only was this a significant hideaway in childhood years and a place in which his parents could work, it also became a haven for The Beta Band and The Aliens to make videos and generally let the creative juices flow. Have a close look at the video for 'Inner Meet Me' and you'll understand.

Art and creativity are in John Maclean's blood. There were two art studios in the house and the children were encouraged to draw and paint from an early age, and ultimately to go to art school. 'I didn't need much encouragement. I know this was what I wanted to do. I wasn't much good at sums and didn't have any passion for other subjects at school,' John says. As for music in the house, his father strummed a guitar nonchalantly and enjoyed listening to folk and blues, including Bob Dylan, Joan Baez, Pentangle and Steeleye Span. There were some singalong campfire moments, but his parents weren't full-on, flowers-in-their-hair hippies. Their attitude was a little more stoical and Calvinist. There was certainly no 'wacky baccy' in the household either. It was true, honest, forthright folk culture with a 1960s twist.

'I struggled with music,' John says. 'I didn't know what I liked. I didn't like The Smiths and couldn't connect with 1980s music at all until I heard hip-hop. I think I bought *Electro 7* on cassette and just listened to that solidly. I know every song on that to this day.' His horizons widened when he met Keith Douglas in St Andrews around the age of fourteen. Keith introduced him to early rock 'n' roll, and John took to it in a big way, especially Eddie Cochran and Chuck Berry. His first concert was Chuck Berry in Glasgow, a trip he made all on his own at the age of fifteen. How bizarre, but how cool! But music didn't feature heavily in his life. He liked sport and played tennis or football whenever possible.

Enrolling at Kilrymont and then Madras College, like most of our musicians, John scraped by in class and remembers the school as science and maths-led. According to him and others in this book, the art and music departments were lifeless and the teachers lacklustre. He couldn't be bothered with the science subjects and wanted to escape every night to play football, earning a place in the school teams and his local side, Tayport Thistle. It was during school football practice that he first met Gordon Anderson. 'He was this little guy who'd run around the pitch shouting things like "You need brains to play football!" but never actually touched the ball once. I thought "Who is this little shit?",' John recalls. 'But that was him already . . . and he hasn't changed.' Dave Maclean, John's younger brother and drummer/producer in Django Django, says: 'Gordon was a Beatles fanatic like me, so we'd spend a lot of time talking about them. He liked the imaginary alternative covers I used to design for their albums. I took to him straight away, but John thought he was a bad influence on me. One day we went round Tayport sticking huge firecrackers in dogshit to blow it up.'

Although close friends, there was a growing rivalry between them. John and Gordon were in different classes, but Gordon's pictures were shown to John's class as examples of excellence throughout first, second and third year. It wasn't until fourth year that their paths crossed properly and their friendship blossomed. Soon they realised they were kindred spirits and pretty much the only children in the school seriously interested in art. The competition continued as they tried to outdo each other in art. They both replicated Cézanne still-lifes, which the rector of Madras hung in his office. By sixth year they were allowed to drop all their other subjects and concentrate on art, eventually even being given their own room to work in.

Soon John was exposed to a lot more music as Gordon jumped from genre to genre and artist to artist. For a while he was obsessed with Prince, then Mott the Hoople, then The Beach Boys or Neil Young. 'It was all quality stuff even then,' says John, 'although I did have to buy him a Milli Vanilli single once, as he was too embarrassed to go into the shop and ask for it himself.' Before long The Beatles were the band that Gordon would fixate upon during and after school. In 1989 though, the band the two friends would bond on was The Stone Roses. 'They were the first new band I truly liked. I bought all the singles and listened to the album non-stop. I became completely obsessed,' John says. 'I then moved onto De La Soul and then Public Enemy. In fact, I soon realised it was black music that I really liked. The Stone Roses had a lot of those elements and influences in there too.'

Soon Madras was cajoling Gordon to do a technical drawing course at college, and when John suggested Gordon join him at art school, Gordon didn't even know that such a thing existed, but he leaped at the chance. 'At that point, I didn't have a clue and said I wanted to do electrical engineering, simply because Kenny had said the same,' Gordon says. 'I was hopeless at school. John then said: "I'm going to art school – you should too", so I put a portfolio together.' They were both accepted.

So in 1990, aged seventeen and eighteen, the two best friends moved into a flat in Edinburgh to attend the Edinburgh College of Art (ECA). 'I remember feeling very optimistic about it all. I thought it was great fun. But I think Gordon saw some of the more negative aspects of it,' says John. Gordon, however, now states the opposite: 'They were the best years of my life, in a way.'

In 1990 they signed up for the Drawing and Painting BA course. John was very much influenced by the artists of the day and infused all his favourite styles into his own painting. Gordon, by contrast, was far more emotional, more raw and outsider in his outlook. John was more ambitious, whereas Gordon liked painting for painting's sake. They complemented each other, but forged their own paths.

On their first day at ECA they met the baby-faced Robin Jones. John looks back: 'He looked about fourteen years old. Gordon thought he must have been a child prodigy, he looked so young. He had long hair and a Jimi Hendrix T-shirt, and we thought he looked pretty cool. I remember Gordon saying: "We've got to get to know him".' They went up to him and said 'You're with us!', and that was that. Robin was painfully shy, and when two gregarious Fifers approached him he had no choice. 'It was intimidating being at college anyway, and there I was trying to eat my soup in the canteen when along came these two bullies – it was frightening,' Robin adds. His immediate future was set in stone.

Born 26 February 1973, Robin grew up in towns on the outskirts of Edinburgh including Lasswade and then Carlops. With dual nationality as a New Zealander on his mother's side, he had an atypical upbringing in the Scottish countryside. His father had been a Pentland hill ranger, an executive film producer at Nine Mile Burn studios, and even a goat farmer, among other jobs. His mother did secretarial work and brought up the three kids. Robin's sister now works on boats and travels the world, and his brother is a car salesman. Enjoying primary school and hating secondary school in Peebles, he was encouraged to follow science as a career, but when choosing subjects at secondary he fumbled his way into art class and thoroughly enjoyed it. Although urged to forget about his aesthetic ambitions, he became the first person from his school to go to art college. Originally specialising in ceramics, he discovered those in the drawing and painting class were having more fun, so he changed courses. This put him next to the terrible twosome of Gordon and John. He was now very much part of the gang.

Robin was fanatically into Hendrix. He adored Mitch Mitchell's drum fills and was hell-bent on becoming a drummer. With a friend's help he learned some pipe-band snare rolls, but forgot about it when he started college. After a short time, though, his fire was rekindled with regular jam sessions on two drum kits in the ECA's Wee Red Bar with local funk drummer John Hall. He was asked to join the occasional indie band, as drummers were always in short supply. He played in a kitschy indie band called Pop, performing live in local venues such as the Subway. It was fun, but never serious. He'd started playing the drums at sixteen, which is fairly late to start any instrument. As a result he was always learning, trying to overstretch himself. Even in released recordings, his style was loose, raw and full of personality. One of The Beta Band's and The Aliens' finest attributes is Robin's drumming. You can hear that loose-limbed, 1960s feel and a drummer pushing into the outer realms of his own ability. That's when music often sounds most exciting and interesting.

Alongside art school and the constant dedication to their painting, music was playing a more prominent role in their lives. John could play keyboards by ear; he could pick up tunes and imitate jingles, adverts and pop tunes as little more than a party trick. But when he acquired a basic Roland synthesiser, he was determined to make something worthwhile with the tacky noises and pitiful drum sounds. Gordon, on the other hand, was starting to dabble in songwriting. He'd met an Irish singer-songwriter, Brian Mills, who played in a university band called Skinny, White and Happy (later joining The Divine Comedy as a session musician and now in The Kittens), who encouraged Gordon to learn more guitar chords and attempt some songs of his own. Gordon tried, and soon developed a certain amount of confidence. He and John would jam or write together, but it always sounded awful and usually resulted in the instruments being packed away within half an hour. It was nevertheless the start of their musical collaboration and the first time they'd combine acoustic guitar with synthetic beats and electronica, no matter how terrible it sounded.

Now aged seventeen, John was drawn to the breakthrough dance culture. He frequented the Rumba Club in Dundee, where they'd mix Chicago house, Detroit techno and Weatherall's Primal Scream remixes as well as bands such as Talking Heads. He abstained from the hedonistic side, simply enjoying the loud sound-systems, the unbridled dancing and the community euphoria. Soon he was trying to emulate Italo-house on his Roland with staccato piano chords set to drum beats. No one heard these bedroom efforts, but it was a way of keeping his hand in musically and using another creative medium. House and techno soon gave way to the acid jazz craze in second year as he embraced bands like Brand New Heavies and Galliano. Funk, soul and hip-hop ruled, and John would try to play along to his favourite records in his bedroom. 'I didn't know it then, but what I was really into was sampling. I was doing visual collages already, but it probably wasn't until third year that I went "Oh, wait a minute . . ." What I was listening to was similar to what I was making in art classes.' Soon it was all about *Chill Out* by The KLF and Primal Scream's *Screamadelica*. He'd listen to *Chill Out* every night and sometimes smoke a little weed, but he was adamant that he wouldn't be lethargic. 'I made this conscious decision that it had to be creative. It was never escapism,' he says today.

From his Stone Roses period onwards, John had begun to DJ too. He'd play hip-hop, house, funk, ska and techno records, but would also mix in Beatles, Small Faces and Velvet Underground tunes. He set up a monthly night, Club Prague, with his friend Ewan Johns at ECA's Wee Red Bar. Trying to replicate Andy Warhol's Factory, the night was ambitious and eclectic. They'd use projections and visuals with DJs and rooms across two floors. Often they'd give out champagne to people as they arrived and ask bands to play. They even invited Kenny Anderson and the crew as The Skuobhie Dubh Orchestra. It laid the groundwork for future Beta Band events, and John hasn't stopped DJ'ing and collecting records to this day. Yet he still had no aspiration to be in a band. 'People in bands at that time were the miserablists,' he recalls. 'It was bands like Ride with skinny jeans and long hair, and then Nirvana came along. I didn't like any of that. We'd throw parties in our flat and there'd be two rooms – one for dancing and the other for acoustic guitars and songs. I would be in the dance room playing Primal Scream, while Gordon was somewhere in between.'

As their extracurricular lives took control, they delved deeper into what Edinburgh had to offer, always on a quest to further their creativity and adventures. Soon Gordon, John and Robin would connect with someone who'd help shape their futures in Edinburgh and beyond.

Edinburgh is a small city for a capital, but it has an inordinate amount of students. If you participate in its cultural life in any way, you'll almost inevitably meet other like-minded individuals before long. In 1991/92 John Maclean, Gordon Anderson, Robin Jones and new friend Sean McCluskey would frequent the central bars and night-spots, and soon recognised the drummer from Queen's Gardens in St Andrews around the place. Steve Mason remembers: 'I'd bump into them and see them out and about, have a drink and a chat. I began to hang out more and more with them, and it was like stepping into another world. They were art students, with everything that entails – painting, talking about art, going to openings and galleries, reading, writing and talking about poetry. Previously, to me, people who were interested in those things were to be treated with suspicion.'

Though middle-class by background, Steve had taken on working-class values and had never talked about feelings or emotions with friends. Now he'd met a group of people who weren't afraid to talk about esoteric subjects and matters of the heart. He was bombarded with artists, poets and writers, some of whom he loves to this day, such as Yves Klein, Jackson Pollock, Walt Whitman and Jack Kerouac. Discovering visionaries like these and suspecting he might be hanging out with their modern equivalents was incredibly stimulating. This group had their own original ideas and ways of conceptual thinking. 'I'd go to an art show and there would be a load of pallets on the floor with a lamp underneath, and I'd think: "This is bollocks! I'm a car mechanic, get a fucking job!" Then they'd explain things to me.' After a concentrated period of imbibing magic mushrooms, acid and ecstasy while listening to a new kind of music and living under the club strobes, Steve's consciousness was open to new directions. When he met his new gang he felt educated and exhilarated by their knowledge. Although not academic as such, he understood what they were talking about and could comprehend their left-field philosophies. Knowing he had played in various groups and was a nifty drummer, Gordon soon asked if Steve was up for doing some music.

A monumental event that would bring it all together was just round the corner. At the start of third year Gordon took on an exchange trip to Nice art college in Aix-en-Provence, near fellow students Sean McCluskey and Gordon's Japanese girlfriend Tomoko, an artist. Soon their mutual friend Andy Guest decided to hitchhike there to see him with a large amount of hashish and his eye on a good time. After reading *On the Road*, attending art openings and having his mind blown by this new posse of oddball artists, Steve Mason felt he had to be a part of the trip too and quit his car-mechanic apprenticeship just as he was about to become qualified. He needed to be creative again. On arrival in Nice, they took mushrooms and went to the Old Town to watch a funeral. Steve recalls, half-laughing: 'I've never felt sadness like this in all my life. I felt like I was watching my own funeral. We then found a car with the keys in the ignition and . . . acquired it.' Nothing bonds a group of friends like a surreal, drug-induced psycho-adventure in a foreign land, sowing the seeds of further exploits in music and art. From Nice they travelled to Spain, where Steve was overcome by the guilt of not working and returned to Scotland.

These were exhilarating times, but it wasn't all fun and games: at this point Gordon began to take a turn for the worse. His mental state became increasingly fragile as a result of undisciplined drug intake, reckless drinking and an around-the-clock assault of the senses. He was living life to the max and experiencing everything at full tilt. It became apparent that Gordon was extremely sensitive and more susceptible to the effects of drugs than most. For some it was a joyous escape from normality, but with Gordon it activated other worlds. It was his nature to do everything to extremes, so if someone would normally brew a pot of tea containing a hundred mushrooms, he would up the dose into the thousands.

Though Gordon's intake of stimulants subsided as he embarked on a more spiritual inner quest, Andy Guest soon realised there was something seriously wrong with him. Stories go that in France Gordon had tried to live on water alone for a month and slowly became emaciated. 'I was fasting and having a great time in my head,' he says. 'It's a cleansing experience. After fasting for a few days, all the hatred, aggression and envy leave your body and the peace and love flow in.' His descent into mental illness has been documented and discussed by family, friends, colleagues, other musicians and journalists since those times, but no one knows the whole truth. Gordon will talk about it today up to a point, but is keen not to be portrayed solely as 'the mad guy', and rightly so. He is an artist and musician with a huge talent who should be seen as that first and foremost. However, it's impossible to ignore. What seems certain is that a decade of serious mental instability took hold around this time on the French trip.

In Gordon's words: 'Sean and I were crossing a gorge and we saw something in the sky that we couldn't explain. It wasn't a plane or flares or anything, just very weird lights. We thought . . . *aliens!* We recorded the experience on tape and the next day it was all just clicks, bleeps and whirring sounds – like aliens talking! At this point I started writing piles of stuff, including a map of the Great Pyramid. I began meditating on the third eye and I felt like I was working something out . . . working out the way to Jesus! I was trying to find the light. It was the beginning of a five-year journey for me, with me finally reaching Jerusalem.'

I've seen this map, which has thousands of interlinked diagrams including the Star of David, the flower of life, the Great Pyramid, star constellations and the mathematical equation for the speed of light. Although beautiful and fascinating, it makes no sense to me. I've also seen Gordon's journals. He still keeps lots of them, and Kenny has a few as well. Many others have been burnt or destroyed. These are lined A4 art journals packed with doodles, writing, drawings, paintings, found objects and newspaper and magazine clippings. They are incredible pieces of art, but they are also disturbing and utterly incomprehensible, the outpourings from a disordered mind.

A few years later, reminiscing about sharing a cottage in Fife with Gordon, Kate Tunstall says: 'I remember him saying he spent a month taking mushrooms every day. I think the real troubles started with him climbing down the chain of a P & O ferry. It became obvious that he was starting to hear voices, and he started talking about religious stuff.' The P & O ferry story is true. The story goes that, finally on his way back to the UK from France after six months (he was supposed to be there for three), Gordon, who was massively underweight and in bad mental health, supposedly swallowed a sizeable block of strong hash. Once aboard the ferry he was gripped by fear that the ship was sinking and tried to alert the staff, crew and passengers. When they ignored him, he leaped from the ferry's upper deck and swung on the anchor chain. He climbed down to the quay and was met by French border police. After twenty-four hours in their office, where he ranted and raved at the customs officers, he was detained in a mental hospital.

Once they were notified, his horrified mother and father drove through the night from Fife to get Gordon out and bring him home. Initially Gordon's twin, Een, reacted in a very weird way too. He went nocturnal, shadowy and non-communicative. Bizarrely, he had no knowledge of what was going on with Gordon, but crumpled as soon as he found out. After two or three days in the French hospital Gordon was retrieved, brought home and sedated. He spent the next few weeks between Stratheden Hospital, near Cupar, and his parents' home in St Andrews. He was in a terrible state, almost a parody of someone losing his mind, talking about being Jesus and Hitler. He espoused conspiratorial pyramid theories and called his parents and brothers appalling names. He was almost unrecognisable from his month-long fasting.

The ordeal was incredibly disturbing to his whole family. Tears were shed, but Billy Anderson would console his sons by saying: 'That's not Gordon – he's saying things he doesn't mean.' He would flit in and out of reality, recognising people one minute and then not. Gordon had always had a wild streak, an ability to shock and to throw himself into dangerous situations, but this was on a completely new level. No one knew what to do or say. All the males in the family closed ranks. Suddenly earrings, haircuts and ripped jeans became unimportant. As with so many other families however, it was mum who managed to deal with it all. Eventually he recovered to a certain extent, but this was the start of a long-standing relationship between Gordon and the hospital.

In due course Gordon returned to Edinburgh College of Art. Although he had straight top grades for the work he'd done in France, he was unceremoniously booted out after a rambling, incoherent, stream-of-consciousness essay that made little sense to his tutors. It was of course crammed full of ideas and a work of art in itself, but unpalatable to the rigid structures of the education establishment. The art department fought to keep Gordon because he was such a great artist, but Humanities and Art History wanted shot of him. There followed an enormous hoo-ha, resulting in Gordon's expulsion as the institution threw the rulebook at him. 'It was a real shame. But he wasn't really happy there,' recalls John Maclean. 'It did seem like he was beginning to go a little crazy. He was writing about pyramid theories, outer space and Orion, plus the whole Jesus Christ complex was beginning to creep in. The way I see it is, Gordon was always heightened emotionally and that came out in his art and in his music. Sometimes the doors that shut for other people stayed open for him.'

Despite all this, Steve and Gordon began to meet up in St Andrews with a view to making music. Gordon remembers: 'I'd see Steve walking around and I thought he looked a bit like me. He seemed a little bit depressed and looked at the ground a lot. But I knew he was a great drummer.' They watched a documentary on the making of The Beatles' *Sgt Pepper's Lonely Hearts Club Band* and discovered it had been recorded on four-track. '*Sgt Pepper's* is like a big, lovely cake that you can maybe eat a couple of hundred times – but it's very sweet, tasty and colourful, just like the cover,' Gordon says. They knew nothing about recording, but they did know that Tascam made an affordable four-track recorder using ordinary cassette tapes. They had become obsessed with The Beatles, Steve proclaiming: 'They had the best songs and they almost invented being experimental. Along with The Beach Boys, they were the ones who started using the studio as a tool.'

They set about writing and recording their first compositions, doing everything themselves on the four-track. Initially they would record everything through a Quadraverb effects unit, playing live for hours at a time. Then they would listen back to everything while smoking a joint. Whether it was the drugs or sheer enthusiasm, they recognised they were making the exact music that they wanted to hear. Tracks from that time, all written by Gordon, include 'Waterfall' (now known as a Lone Pigeon track) and 'Silver Ship', among others. 'The reason we worked so well together is that I can sort out Gordon's shit,' Steve recalls.

Gordon encouraged Steve to sing for the first time. Steve reluctantly obliged and gradually built up his confidence. They soon realised their voices worked well together, although Steve maintains that: 'Gordon goes through stages of being other people. One minute he's Bob Dylan, then it's Neil Young or Bobby Gillespie. It's a real shame, because his own voice is the best of them all.' Commuting between the East Neuk and Edinburgh, where Gordon lived with Tomoko, they worked on their recordings and spent endless evenings in the pub discussing their plans. They tried to form a band in St Andrews but were unable to find the right people – if they had, Steve would almost certainly have been the drummer. They had to move. Steve took the first step and went to London with his girlfriend. The Edinburgh gang weren't far behind.

Aged only twenty-one, John Maclean graduated with first-class honours and was accepted into London's Royal College of Art. 'I was ridiculously young to be studying for an MA, but in a way I'm glad I did it. I got it out of the way,' he says. As his love of The KLF and hip-hop grew, he bought a sampler. It became his instrument immediately and he'd play it for hours. He adopted the whole philosophy of sampling and went on to write his MA thesis on the uses, history and progression of sampling and post-modernism in general. He remembers having a blazing row with Kenny Anderson about technology in music, with Kenny taking the 'Keep Music Live' angle. Reminded that Kenny now uses electronics and sampling in his own songs, he laughs and says: 'Well, I won!'

Steve moved in with his girlfriend in Streatham, dead set on making music again. He'd joined a 1960s-retro outfit, obsessed with the Yardbirds, the Jeff Beck Group and hard-rock circa 1968/69, called Knave. Kitted out in mod and psych regalia, Steve was uncomfortable wearing blazers, skinny ties and velvet trousers but involved himself heavily in the London mod scene. Outside this retro gang his musical interests widened as he rekindled his love of hip-hop, ragga and jungle. He loved playing 1960s music, though, and reckons this period was the peak of his drumming powers. He befriended bass player Steve Duffield, who played on the first Beta Band EP, 'Champion Versions'. John Maclean would occasionally see the band live or hang out with Steve at 1960s-revival clubs, but always felt out of place in his combat trousers, zipped-up sports jackets and trainers. He liked the music but also wanted to hear the Wu-Tang Clan, which the loon-panted DJs didn't play.

Gordon came and went from Scotland, still very much in touch with them all and continuing his music projects with Steve whenever possible. He rented a room near Steve in Streatham, where they wrote songs and went busking. They came up with a name for their duo, Chicken & Chips. 'We called ourselves that because that's all we could afford to eat after busking one day,' Steve laughs. 'We'd earned £1.99, and that was the exact price of a two-piece chicken dinner. Then we argued about who was going to be Chicken and who was going to be Chips.'

Outwith these exploits, their recording was coming on by leaps and bounds. Gordon's songs were improving fast with the help of Steve's arrangements, recording techniques and outstanding drumming. Steve's songs were gathering momentum too. They changed their name to The Pigeons (hence Gordon's Fence name, Lone Pigeon) as a homage to his brothers' 'dubhs' – 'doos', in Gaelic pronunciation – and with every tune their four-track efforts were sounding more expansive and mind-altering. One song that has taken on mythic proportions since is 'I Am the Unknown', their masterpiece of the time, resurrected by The Aliens many years later. It encapsulated their modern take on 1960s psychedelia, with Stone Roses affectations and transcendent, philosophical lyrics. Gordon and Steve's undeniable talent shone through so glaringly. No one was doing music like this in 1993, and to anyone lucky enough to hear it at the time it was nothing short of astonishing.

Sadly, the thread of declining mental health continued to run through the story. Gordon was becoming psychotic and progressively more deranged, while Steve was slipping further into manic depression. Problems that had haunted him from years before were returning, including his feelings about the bitter break-up of his parents when he was nineteen. Steve had looked after his mother in St Andrews while working as a car mechanic, and now his pent-up anger at his father came to the fore. 'I carried all this with me. I was like a roving ball of emotion going in a million different directions at a million different times,' Steve confesses. 'There were periods when I was taking a lot of hallucinogenic drugs, and that's never a good idea if you're predisposed to manic depression.'

On top of his own troubles, Gordon would then arrive with his own mental illness and the madness would increase all round. Steve recounts: 'I would take to my bed for two weeks, then get up and decide to see Gordon and make some amazing music. He would be sitting in the dark in front of a mirror with a candle, saying he could see the face of Jesus. That was our lives at the time, and it was pretty dark.' Steve could empathise with Gordon, but Gordon's psychosis was all-consuming. 'I was terrified for him. He was my best friend and we were incredibly close. Gordon and I are like brothers and have been since we met. There's a relationship there beyond anything I've had with anyone else.'

Soon the rest of the Edinburgh posse followed John and Steve to London. Robin went for want of anything better to do and moved into a now notorious flat in Shepherd's Bush with John. He got himself a dangerous job as a motorbike courier and bought a drum kit with £1,000 inherited from his grandmother. Steve split up with his girlfriend and approached the motley crew in their Shepherd's Bush gaff, using the immortal line: 'Can I stay for a week or so until I get a place?' before staying for a year. He slept in the tiny broom-and-gas-meter cupboard under the stairs, which could be entered only via Robin's room, and Robin was too shy to tell him to get out. But they got on well, sharing a cynicism and a darker worldview not always shared by John. They could rebel together.

The Shepherd's Bush flat was an asylum for creative thought, music and art. It was an open flat, too; there was no lock on the door and there were always broken windows. This didn't seem to bother the bohemian bunch as they worked and made a racket whenever possible. John remembers: 'I was playing on my sampler one day, just after Oasis's "Wonderwall" had come out. I looped the guitar intro and put a hip-hop beat under it. I'd been concentrating on it and listening for hours. When I turned around there was this massive Rasta behind me, nodding away. He started singing along, saying "Keep the beat going, man!" It was crazy.'

Steve and John were also talking about doing music together, usually over pints in the college bar in Kensington. Steve suggested that he, John, Robin and Gordon become an actual band. John liked the idea but insisted it be more avant-garde and atypical, rather than the guitar-bass-drums-vocals set up. He admired The KLF and wanted the creative freedom they'd had on *Chill Out*. His conceptual ideas and his passion for collage and sampling had to be in the mix too. As they were all growing to love electronic music as well as straight songs, nothing was rejected. Instead it was all to be added to the melting-pot. The next step was to try something together.

'Steve said: "I've got this song called 'Dry The Rain'," John remembers. 'He played it to me on the four-track and I immediately got a beat and got it to the right tempo, which is the beat that's on it. I had to speed it up a bit, but the song was as it was – it was instantaneous. Like Beck at the time, we were marrying hip-hop beats and acoustic songwriting, but I wanted our beats to sound more organic.' At this stage it didn't have Gordon's 'If there's something inside that you wanna say . . .' closing section; that came later, on the EP version. I recall Kenny Anderson handing me a copy of the demo and being mightily impressed. It wasn't labelled, and I remember slotting a track into a cassette compilation I was making for a friend. 'The Rain Song', as I called it then, was outstanding.

So there you have it – what is perhaps The Beta Band's best-known anthem was the result of Steve and John's first collaboration. The rest of the songs for their first EP, 'Champion Versions', came together quickly and easily. The idea was to use whatever was lying around, cut it up and stick it together. John wrote the first half of 'B+A' and stuck it on something that Gordon and Steve were doing. John then wrote 'I Know', while 'Dog's Got A Bone' was composed by Gordon, Steve and Robin writing alternate lines while John was out one night. The only other track from the time was an instrumental called 'Shepherd's Dub', put together by Robin and Steve. Unbelievably, none of the songs was completed with all four members in the room at the same time.

It was all recorded in the Shepherd's Bush flat on the four-track recorder, with Robin's drums set up in the living-room. 'I thought it was just fun and I didn't care,' John enthuses. 'I wasn't thinking about record companies or anything like that. I wasn't even thinking about being in a band! It was just us fooling around with my sampler and bits of Steve's songs. Gordon would come down every now and again, do a bit and then disappear back to Scotland. It was all very naturally chaotic.'

Gordon, who still saw his brothers Kenny and Een as the Dubhs, suggested the punning translation of that title into English as The Pigeons, his and Steve's post-Chicken & Chips identity, for the group name, but John kiboshed that. This was a new band, and if he was to be involved the name had to change. His suggestion, The Beta Band, harked back to Madras College, where the cleverest children were put in a top stream called the Alpha Band and the less academic were segregated into the Beta Band. It seemed perfect, somehow. 'I always liked the idea that Gordon and I were seen as the dunces,' says John, 'but I knew deep down that we were going to succeed somehow.' The name was agreed upon, although Steve remains adamant that he 'always hated that name'.

Perhaps John's mark was too obviously stamped on that first batch of songs, with his beats and melodies to the fore, or perhaps it was Steve's ego playing up, but the occasional harrumph was noted. One thing was certain, though: the music had been written, recorded and produced by a group of good friends in the name of fun and experimentation. Careers had never once been considered. The music came first, and petty arguments and jealousies would be swept aside by what was just around the corner. It had certainly been under strange circumstances, but The Beta Band was born.

3

Champion Versions

The Rise of the Beta Band

Riding around Shepherd's Bush on his bicycle, listening to the five-song demo on his Walkman, it dawned on John Maclean that this wonky collection of home-recorded tracks was actually really good. He duplicated ten cassettes and handed them to potential supporters. He gave one to Rough Trade – the shop, not the record label – and it disappeared without a trace. Heavenly Records threw their copy in the bin because Shepherd's Bush was spelt wrong, and now think of this as a *doh!* moment. Most significantly, he handed one to Nancy Tilbury, a friend of a friend of someone who knew Miles Leonard at Parlophone/EMI, and Nancy gave it to the Chemical Brothers' first manager, Phil Brown, who also knew Miles! Leonard was a hot young A & R man who had just set up Regal Records, a new EMI subsidiary, and was on the look-out for new talent. He listened to the cassette and liked it. 'We met Miles Leonard,' says Steve, 'right at the point that he was turning from an A & R man, with fresh ideas, innocence, dreams, passion and music in his heart, into a businessman. We caught him right on that cusp.' This was no bad thing, as Miles was brave and ambitious, as well as seeing a potentially lucrative opportunity in their music and attitude. He summoned the band to his office and suggested they rehearse their collection of songs and then record them properly in a studio.

They called Gordon down from Scotland and, with Steve Duffield from Knave on bass, they set up their ramshackle equipment and tried to play 'Dry The Rain' and 'Ionas: Look For Space', one of Gordon's songs, in an abandoned warehouse in Hammersmith. Egos clashed as Gordon insisted on being the frontman, with Steve as the drummer. Steve didn't want to be the drummer, but Robin perhaps wasn't yet quite skilled enough yet to hold the backbeat down. For Gordon and Steve, the racket they were making wasn't a patch on the demos they'd made as The Beta Band or The Pigeons.

Arguments followed and two complete days were wasted. The sessions were an utter disaster as Gordon's illness took control; he'd stand for hours in front of a mirror, adamant that he could see a demon trying to possess him. It was soon apparent that he was far too sick to continue with the rehearsals and should return to Scotland. Rumour has it that once, being wined and dined by Parlophone/EMI, Gordon jumped up on the table and kicked everyone's food and drink across the room, screaming at the 'suits' and storming out. He then referred to them as 'lizards' to Kenny on his return to Scotland. Truly disturbed, it was time for him to leave the band.

Although hesitant to carry on without Gordon, Steve was cajoled by the band and Miles to become the main singer and guitarist. 'I didn't want to be a band with a frontman. I wanted it to be more subversive, with no photos,' John maintains, but they decided to go for it and make the best of an unfortunate situation. They went back to Miles and proposed to record the EP without Gordon. Miles and Parlophone/EMI were still interested.

They were booked into a studio in Camden. John used the same samples as the demo and played a little piano on the end of 'Dog's Got A Bone'; Steve took on main vocals and guitar; Robin sat behind the drums and Steve Duffield played bass. 'Dry The Rain' was augmented with an end section by Gordon, including the famous trumpet line, at the request of Steve Mason but against John's wishes. John says: 'I felt the demo was quite evenly balanced and that section of 'Dry The Rain' was a little heavy at the end of what was a fairly lo-fi EP, but I wasn't part of the discussion. Gordon was fine with it.' A friend of John's performed the trumpet part and the rest is history – that closing crescendo is probably the most anthemic part of their catalogue, the refrain that fans sing at the top of their lungs.

John still maintains that the demo of 'B+A' is better than the version that made it on to 'Champion Versions', being more natural, funky, and lighter in touch than what he describes as a 'dirge' on the final EP – a little harsh, perhaps, but that's his prerogative. On the other hand, 'I Know' was taken straight from the demo and not re-recorded. John made the necessary pilgrimage to Gordon's hospital bed in Scotland to play him the finished EP, complete with the 'Dry The Rain' climax. Tears were shed, but the Lone Pigeon's approval was given. That was the first EP, an EP that fans and newcomers alike fell in love with and which paved the way for what was about to happen.

Hastily released on Regal with little fanfare, it caused a massive stir across the UK music press, especially the *NME*, surprising both label and band. As well as the inspired tunes, there was the reggae-influenced artwork, a collaboration between John and Steve, with the font stolen from an old King Tubby record and the banger and tiger images sourced from elsewhere. 'Because we didn't think it was going to take off, we thought we could just nick things and no one would ever know', John admits. Not only was the cover art bright, vibrant and explosive, it was a mash-up of aesthetics that suited the band's sample-a-delic music and magpie approach. Miles Leonard wanted all the bands on his new Regal imprint to use a generic record sleeve, but the band insisted on total control over artwork, aesthetics and videos. They knew what they wanted and they weren't overawed.

It had been a bumpy ride thus far, and now another bump came along. Steve Duffield, a consummate professional and stunning bass player, wanted out, much to the band's chagrin. He was low on money and didn't foresee a future with this shambling, unruly ensemble. His bass lines had helped define the colour and tone of the EP, with an organic, lolloping, funky feel. He had complemented their sound and fitted the vibe perfectly. 'We're still really good friends today, but at the time I asked Steve to join the band and he said no,' Mason laughs. 'He now bitterly regrets it . . . ha ha! He was trying to get his life back on track, and joining a band with me was not a good way to do that.' The band was extremely sorry to see him go. It was now a trio of Steve, John and Robin – the real core of The Beta Band.

Momentum was building behind the scenes, and the band were soon introduced to their first manager, Dave Halliwell, by Miles Leonard. Halliwell was part of a Wigan crew, good friends with Oasis, and had previously managed The Verve. 'He was a basically a football hooligan from Wigan. He was a great guy, he loved the music and would have died for the band at that time,' says Steve. Nick McCabe of The Verve had helped with post-production on the studio version of 'B+A' for the EP, and The Beta Band were soon welcomed into the inner circle of northern lad-rockers – who, though not exactly sympathetic to John's artistic visions, were friendly, enthusiastic and well-connected.

The next challenge was to play live, but they urgently needed another bass player and advertised in the music press to no avail. Out of the blue, a guitar-playing, weed-smoking, surf-loving carpenter, Richard Greentree, blagged his way into the rehearsal room. He was a friend of Halliwell's, and his mindset was laid-back and confident. As a guitarist he had the chops to handle bass duties, and, having a daft sense of humour, he fitted in perfectly. 'We all went for a drink on a boat on the Thames that had been converted into a pub. When we left by the gang-plank, I went last and watched the others in front of me. I distinctly remember thinking . . . "This is a band!".'

Their first gig was at the Water Rats in King's Cross, a scuzzy indie and rock venue frequented by determined and desperate bands. By this time they were using The Verve's rehearsal room and the lion's share of their backline equipment. They'd produced hand-made flyers for the gig and assumed that only a few friends would turn up for their live debut. Piled into a Transit van on the way to the gig, they heard 'Dry The Rain' on Radio 1. The pressure was on.

John Maclean says: 'It was the most petrifying experience of my life. I never wanted to be in a band, and suddenly I'm onstage. Two hundred people were jammed into a hundred-capacity venue. Richard Ashcroft was there and the UK music press were all there. The whole thing was so chaotic and mental I didn't really know what I was doing. "Dry The Rain", for example, took four floppy discs of samples to load, and they only worked half of the time. Steve hated it, but I was already sure we were on to something and we were a potentially great band.'

Having hardly even played in the same room together, holding the basics together was an achievement in itself. They'd borrowed a dining-room table to put all the keyboards and samplers on, and they only had five songs to play. 'It was a disaster' is Steve Mason's assessment. 'I had always been the drummer in bands, and now I was the frontman. It was beyond terrifying. Every single music journalist and A & R man in London was at that gig. Noel Gallagher was there. I broke a string and it delayed the gig by twenty minutes. It was awful.'

Although opinions differ, the gig created a huge buzz across London and the UK music industry. The *NME*'s review was negative, describing the show as 'a ship hitting an iceberg', but the band didn't care. They had more imagination than your average indie plodders. 'We already wanted projections behind us and we wanted to dress up,' John says. 'Robin suggested having plant-pots and foliage on stage too. We wanted to be The KLF meets Parliament or something. We certainly didn't want to be Menswear. And we didn't want to come across like roadies, which a lot of other bands looked like at the time.' Music was drifting away from Britpop, and here was a wild-eyed bunch of misfits who might herald a new dawn. They were ambitious and seriously over-hyped, but however rickety their entrance, The Beta Band had arrived and the world was taking notice.

Any group of musicians proclaimed as the saviours of rock 'n' roll are in for a crazy ride, whether they like it or not. The *NME* was saying such things in print, Radio 1 was playing tracks from 'Champion Versions', and the indie hordes, hungry for a new fix, were gathering *en masse* to catch sight of the new heroes of 1996. It was exhilarating and intoxicating, an adrenaline kick that would last for the next few years. Their second live engagement was in the *NME* tent at the Reading Festival and expectations were at fever pitch; a great day then, for the van to break down on the way. Making it with ten minutes to spare, they clambered onstage only for the sampler to pack up and delay them another five minutes. As the frontman, Steve was terrified, and freely admits that if it happened now he would play an acoustic song to bridge the gap, but at that point he had nothing to perform. When the sampler finally kicked into gear they played a blinding rendition of 'Dry The Rain' and walked off to rapturous applause. Yet again salvaging something from the fire, they ramped up their growing reputation as moody, uncompromising and antagonistic. Who would turn up to a massive festival at the peak of their hype and play one song before defiantly striding off ? The myth was building.

The first EP was out and the plaudits were flooding in as critics and new fans flocked towards the band. They had made a shaky but memorable start on the live scene, and now more was expected of this new gang of nonconformists. They were shaping music, and the iconography that went with it, as they saw fit. Laurence Bell of Domino Records says: 'I heard the first EP around 1996-97. They had a fresh sound. It was exciting to find someone doing something genuinely different out of Britain at the time. It was the middle of the Britpop period, and you could hear they had this original sound. It had this lazy shuffle to it and a charm. It was outside everything else. Great songs! I went to see them a few times, I bought the records. I was a fan.'

I remember going to see The Beta Band's first live show in Scotland at the now-defunct The Venue in Edinburgh. It was probably their third or fourth live show ever. The Venue was a legendary hole that had seen thousands of punk, rock and indie groups pass through its blackened doors over the decades and was firmly on any band's tour agenda. It had also become a techno mecca, housing clubs such as U.F.O. and Pure, where the cream of the world's DJs would astound the pilled-up crowds. It seemed like the perfect place for The Beta Band to subvert.

Attending the gig with Kenny and Gordon Anderson, I recall the evening being slightly fraught with tension. Gordon had obviously helped form the band's sound and identity and was close friends with them all. He was still very ill, but had managed to stay out of hospital. That evening he sported a tweed jacket and a moustache, looking like one of The Beatles circa 1968. He was utterly unaware that he looked a little odd. Kenny was on tenterhooks; here was a band from his home town that was actually having a massive impact. I was more than interested to see how they'd translate the carefree psychedelia of 'Champion Versions' live, and to see an old childhood acquaintance, Steve Mason, in action. Anticipation was high, to say the least. The three of us wanted them to be good.

With video screens erected behind the band, showing offbeat home-movies and artworks including magic carpet rides, crocodile wrestling and skateboarding policemen, and the stage bedecked with plant pots and vegetation, it was a totally different kind of live experience. There was no support band either, just DJs. Steve Mason says: 'Why do you want a support band? It was our night! Nobody wants to see a support band. You want to be immersed in the headliners' splendour from the moment you walk into the venue until the moment you leave. The DJ thing was us playing records that had influenced us and those that we thought were great at the time. The videos were a vehicle to get across the humour within the show. The music of the show was quite serious; the lyrics were dark and sad. It was also a vehicle to divert attention, as we were anti-rock-star. The whole thing is the show, and the audience are part of the show.'

Nevertheless, the venue wasn't completely packed and the jury was still out on the *NME*'s favourite new thing. Could they last the distance? Did they have the tunes? Were they just another flavour of the month for the desperate London music press? Colleagues from Edinburgh College of Art, friends from Fife and the occasional scooter boy were among the audience. The band played the entire first EP and a new, sprawling opus that I later learned was a nascent version of 'The House Song'. They then improvised on bongos and twin drum kits as the concert approached its climax. The crowd lapped it up. Edinburgh audiences were notoriously uptight then, with plenty of chin-stroking and little of the uproarious interaction that might happen in Glasgow. To see a band for the first time and actually dance was unknown. The band looked and behaved unlike anyone else. Instruments were swapped and a vague air of disdain for standard stagecraft was exercised. It wasn't yet musically polished, either.

Steve continues: 'We used to think of the music as cut 'n' paste. Like making collages, the way John and friends had done at art school. It was unlike anything else around and totally home-made. To me, we were a punk band! We were anti-establishment and we were against what was happening at the time. Oasis were utterly run-of-the-mill dad-rock – uninspiring, whining millionaires. That was not art, and not what music should be. We were anti-rock-star – that cigarettes, alcohol and cocaine thing.'

To say it was faultless would be a lie, but it was certainly a triumph and whetted everyone's appetite for more. Five songs and a drum freak-out wasn't completely convincing, but it was a lot of fun. Gordon, ever the perfectionist, was disappointed and thought they could do better. Kenny and I were more forgiving and recognised their huge potential. The world was potentially their oyster.

Although they're largely remembered for their recordings, from the 'Three EPs' through several albums and an exhaustive DVD collection, The Beta Band quickly became an impressive live act. Also crucially important were the films and the band's Dadaist sense of humour. The homemade films were pre-YouTube, and they had audiences laughing out loud and marvelling at their ingenuity. They'd add in-jokes to their cover art, with terrible photos of their manager on tour or comments about being late to rehearsals. 'There was definitely a Fife sense of humour that involved insulting each other and taking the piss,' says John. 'It was about going against the grain of the moody rock photos and videos with helicopters in them. I wasn't interested in any of the Britpop bands or the British art scene at the time either, Damien Hirst and Tracey Emin. It was all emperor's new clothes. I liked American artists like Mike Kelley, who made the knitted doll on the cover of *Dirty* by Sonic Youth. I liked German artists such as Gerhard Richter, Sigmar Polke and Joseph Beuys. And we watched a lot of films. I thought that one day we'd be making films and be some kind of collective.

'We had a serious point with The Beta Band, but there's no point in having a point unless you can laugh at yourself. The whole thing was a joke against Oasis, rock stars and the establishment in general. Yeah, we wrestle with crocodiles in a film, but we're a band and we make better music than you do! There was no sense of humour around in the bands at that time. The humour in The Beta Band was generated when the four of us came together. It was innocent and pure.'

They brought out a now collectible fanzine called *Flower Press*. This was mainly John's idea and again harked back to his art-school days. Most of his friends and fellow band members made some kind of art, and John's perception was that everything was art. Steve's doodles were as important as his songwriting, scribbled notes were as important as finished songs and there was no hierarchy in art – a very Dadaist concept. Three editions of *Flower Press* were sporadically released during the band's career. Here was something that their inner sanctum adored but the public knew nothing about. They pulled together artwork, sketches, doodles, photos, poems, cartoons and jokes into an A5 booklet. It was time-consuming and carefully arranged, hence the limited runs and issues.

You can't pin it on one band's influence, but since then I've watched as rock bands have embraced a more multi-media approach to live shows, incorporating visuals, lights, costumes and electronics. In my opinion, and in those you'll read later, The Beta Band had a profound effect on Fence, its aesthetic and its sound. *Flower Press* had also really connected with future Fence artists and fans. On top of this, with advances in home recording, filming and editing software on personal computers, musicians and bedroom artists have been able to produce far more elaborate and sophisticated music. The Beta Band realised this very early on, leading the way for others to follow. This must not be underestimated.

$$\oint$$

'Champion Versions' was a far bigger success than anyone expected and caused a commotion. Injecting a Jamaican influence into rock 'n' roll was uncommon, especially in the very white indie scene. 'I realised I was drawn to black music,' says John. Although reggae had been championed by artists as diverse as Keith Richards, Willie Nelson, The Clash and Madness over the decades, in the middle to late 1990s it felt fresh. From the artwork and imagery to the title, Steve remembers, he 'wanted something that sounded confident but also obscure, and had a direct reggae connection.' Original vinyl copies now change hands for serious money. However, they needed another offering to back up the hype and show everyone what they were made of. The title of the EP 'The Patty Patty Sound' was a direct steal from a U-Roy lyric: 'I just play my patty, patty sound . . .' Thematically and visually continuing themes from the first EP, it came together completely differently.

This EP was their first record as an official band. They were now living separately in their own London flats. Richard was permanent bass player, while Steve had loosely assumed the role of frontman and was the leading songwriter. Making the trip to Rockfield in Wales for their first session in a proper studio, their sights were set even higher than before. Yet it almost didn't happen at all, as on the way the band stopped at a pub and got trashed. Carrying a skinful, Steve jumped behind the wheel of their car, with the others in the back, to speed off around the country lanes. He then proceeded to play chicken with Mark Allison, the tour manager, driving the van containing their equipment. It shocked and scared the whole gang.

Steve now admits that he had a death wish at the time. Although he didn't know it, he was battling manic depression. He had acquired a samurai sword, and during the recording he smashed the drum kit and set fire to his Fender Twin amp outside. The pressure of being the front-man of the latest big thing, combined with his mood swings, made him destructive and out of control.

Musically, however, the band were firing on all cylinders and moving into uncharted territory. Steve says: 'We wanted to make music that felt like you were tripping . . . but you weren't! I've never, *ever* played a gig drunk or high. I hate this mindless thuggery and pretending to be stupid within music. There's a lot to be said for reading a book, having a decent conversation and appreciating a piece of artwork. That's what I was trying to get across in The Beta Band. Let's open the doors of percep-tion. I can't gather 2,000 people through the doors and hand them all a tab of acid, but I might be able to make them think differently through music – if I'm lucky.'

'It ended up being my favourite EP,' says John Maclean. 'We were at the height of our powers creatively and had a lot of ideas. I had this idea for us all going on the drums on "The House Song", and Steve had writ-ten "Inner Meet Me", which I loved. We wrote "Monolith", which Steve wasn't so keen on.' Steve says: 'The last time I listened to "Monolith" was around five years ago, and it made absolutely no sense to me what-soever. At the time, though, it made perfect sense, and we knew exactly when to come in at every section. We rehearsed it and, although it was always slightly different each time we played it, we recorded it live.'

With a budget of £2,000, John decided to direct the band's first offi-cial promo video, for 'Inner Meet Me', at his family's Highland retreat. He hired two cameramen and sent a message to all the band's old friends to make their own alien costumes and meet at a car park up north on 10 January 1998. Kenny, Gordon, Dave Halliwell and a further posse assembled to join in the madness. Steve, struggling with his demons, didn't make it. On release of the EP, the video did the rounds on MTV2, and 'Inner Meet Me' was seen as one of the hits of the EP, along with 'She's The One', with its Chipmunks-esque vocals and triumphant, almost Who-like finale. 'The Patty Patty Sound' is a hugely creative set of songs and soundscapes and still sounds refreshingly psychedelic and unhinged today. Now nobody was making music anything like The Beta Band. If they'd initially been compared to Beck or the Beastie Boys for fusing acoustic instruments with hip-hop and electronica, now they were far away on their own outer limits.

With more scattershot live shows and a growing profile in the music press, the band were keen to get back into the studio as soon as possible while on a creative streak and enjoying the spoils of being on a major label. The third EP was called 'Los Amigos del Beta Banditos', and its release coincided with an *NME* cover featuring the band dressed as Mexican bandits. I remember feeling so proud when I saw it. What contrary bastards! Here was a band who were utterly self-aware and having a laugh along the way. Their music was deadly serious, but they knew something ridiculous was going on. Everyone conceives dream projects in the pub, but rarely ends up realising them. The Beta Band could. With an almost endless flow of record-company money, anything could be bought or hired and lunatic ideas would happen.

All was not well behind the scenes, though. John remembers Steve being in a black mood throughout the recording of this EP and into that of their debut album. It was probably for a combination of reasons. He was feeling the 'frontman and songwriter' pressure, something he had foisted upon himself against the wishes of his bandmates, who were just enjoying themselves. 'I'd been working towards this for the previous four or five years,' says Steve, 'and I'd been making music pretty much all my adult life. Maybe the others were along for the ride a little bit, I don't know. John had the potential to become a really great visual artist, but I remember saying to him: "Give me a couple of years of your life and I think we can do something great here." He did, but it lasted a few more years than that.' Perhaps he felt he still had to prove he was capable of some kind of greatness.

Gordon was becoming a Syd Barrett figure, and Steve's subconscious was possibly whispering that the band had to survive without him. The Beta Band's most anthemic moment had been written by Gordon, and that may have irked Steve. John tried to take the pressure off by making beats and constantly coming out with ideas, but Steve began to retire to his bedroom, excluding himself from the gang. He was short-tempered and mean at times, and Richard and he were not seeing eye to eye at all. In retrospect, Mason's own mental illness was encroaching.

Against the odds, they were still good mates and continued to spend almost all their time together, whether drinking, partying, making videos, rehearsing, touring or coming up with ideas. 'Los Amigos . . .' was another triumph, adored by critics and fans alike. 'Dr Baker' and

'Needles In My Eye' were stand-outs and became live favourites almost immediately. Today, some would say that the 'Three EPs' marked The Beta Band's finest period. Steve says: 'It's not for me to decide. When you put a record out, it's in the public domain and it sits in their life. I don't really have an opinion on that.' John adds: 'We never repeated ourselves and we were always being experimental. We used up a lot of ideas, and maybe we did drop off a little. We had done a lot: classic singer-songwriting, sixteen-minute odysseys, dance music. We swapped instruments, smashed up washing machines, recorded inside and outside and so on. It was difficult to keep coming up with new concepts.' When asked today about the reaction the band received at the time, Steve says candidly: 'Of course they liked us and thought we were amazing! It was better than anything else out at the time. I had that confidence.'

𝄞

As the hype machine went into overdrive, they coped with it by reacting with in-jokes and a notoriously difficult public stance. 'We became this insular gang,' John remembers. 'Although we were all quite different, we shared a common sense of humour. We used to reduce journalists to blubbering wrecks! I met a journalist six months ago who worked for *Select* magazine at that time, and he admitted that we were the hardest and most horrible band he'd ever had to interview.' Steve maintains that 'if you're a journalist, it's your job to make a good interview. You can't just stick a microphone in front of me. Journalists have to do some work and ask me some questions – ask me what I like, what I don't like etc. At that time London journalists didn't have any questions. They were used to coked-up, arrogant loudmouths with no talent talking about themselves. We weren't prepared to do that. We're artists, and if you want to engage with us, do your fucking job!'

'I did think we could be a bit mean sometimes,' says John. 'Steve would occasionally go for the jugular.' Often the band were misunderstood, or wires got crossed. Once their new press officer forgot to tell the band that Alexis Petridis of the *Guardian* was flying over to Atlanta to cover the opening nights of an American tour and spend a few days with them. They had no idea he had been on their flight, or who he was, so they didn't introduce themselves or befriend him. When he came backstage after the first show, they told him to get lost. When he finally managed to sneak some time with the band, they gave him just an hour. He thought they were rude, arrogant and dismissive, and his published piece was vitriolic. 'I thought "Who is this twit, anyway?",' John recalls.

I remember my first live link on Radio 1 as part of a *Lamacq Live* special from Glasgow in 1999. I was excited and nervous. Steve Lamacq had The Beta Band playing live on the show just before our big moment, and they behaved dreadfully. When asked what they were going to play first, they said they'd do a version of the record Lamacq had just played (by Ash or someone like that) and sniggered. Steve called Lamacq an old punk, annoying him further. I thought it was funny and playful then, although the cringe factor was immense, but as a presenter I realise now that it's extremely tough when a band won't play ball. That was the last time for many years that Lamacq so much as mentioned the band, much to their chagrin and the dismay of Regal/Parlophone, who knew how important he and the *Evening Session* show were then.

It was a classic foot-shooting moment that would come to haunt the band, but it boosted the uncompromising outsider myth that surrounded them. Although they wanted to sell records and become more mainstream, they were becoming a cult band and gaining a surly reputation. Steve now says: 'It's easy for others to see intelligent people as difficult. We were four interesting individuals who came together to form something original. If we were asked an interesting question, we had the tools to give an educated answer. I can engage with journalists now, but back then I wasn't interested in playing their game. I was a little naive, I suppose.' John adds: 'We didn't particularly like the music industry and the press. *The Face* had a lot of power and their music writing was awful. Everything was about "cool" and image. But the coolest thing is . . . not trying to be cool! Fashion always seemed to be against us. Journalists didn't know how to react when we said we liked Santana and the Wu-Tang Clan.'

The studios where they recorded loved them, for the most part, until they became drunk and mischievious. There are many stories of studio and tour debauchery and mayhem. Back then, these tales never made it to the press. John recalls: 'The music press thought we were nerdy types in hill-walking clothes. Their version of rock 'n' roll was snorting coke in Camden, which we wanted no part of. Meanwhile we were smashing stuff up in the countryside.' All band members are reluctant to relinquish these secrets, but I know they put a sandwich in a studio's microwave and set it for five hours until it blew up. They spun 'doughnuts' on the grass in a car in front of one studio, then drove it into a lamp-post. Robin and Richard in particular enjoyed trashing hotel rooms and, yes, throwing the odd TV set out of windows. One of their most dangerous escapades entailed climbing through the pipes of a china-clay factory. Had someone turned on the furnaces, they would have been incinerated. At times they were very naughty boys indeed.

♪

With three ground-breaking EPs (repackaged today as a CD) out, fans and critics were hungry for a full-length album. Here was a band with pop songs, experimental pieces, stunning artwork and a stubbornly DIY approach. Surely they could record something that would enter the pantheon of classic debuts? What was to come would be remembered for slightly different reasons.

'I think we ran out of steam a little bit,' says Steve. 'We wanted to compile the "Three EPs" and put it out as an album, but we hadn't thought much beyond that. I had some songs. I had "The Hard One", "Around The Bend" and "Broken Up A Ding Dong"), but that was it. We told the record company we wanted to record the album on three different continents – South America, Africa and India. Someone did a budget and it was £1 million. Ha-ha! So it got whittled down to three studios in the UK.'

Robin says: 'The first album was a great example of a band surfing the crest of a wave and thinking: "We can't do anything wrong." What happened was, we turned up in an expensive studio for a six-week stretch with no songs. We blew the budget hiring every instrument under the sun. Which is why I think it's a great piece, a great historical document. We were riding high on confidence and they were daft enough to put us in a studio, so we'll do something!'

Mason was still in a dark place and spending most of his time alone. He felt scared and pressured, and he was more and more self-destructive. He insisted that the first real album be amazing, but the others struggled to get by without him as he skulked in his room for days at a time. Robin remembers: 'We all had our moods occasion-ally . . . but without victimising him, it was mainly Steve. He took it upon his shoulders that he was responsible for everything, when clearly he wasn't. We were doing just fine. He felt like he was shoved out into the spotlight, when he wasn't. Someone has to feel like they're the dad . . . saying things like "You're just getting drunk and laughing, and I'm doing all the work." Well, join us! It's going to be all right.' There were a lot of dark rehearsal days, dark gigs and even dark tours around this time.

After brief rehearsals near Brighton, where they spent most of the time getting drunk and skimming across a flooded lawn on a tractor inner tube, they were about to re-enter three expensive studios with only three or four songs. They were confident in their own talents and felt they could get away with it, as they had done on the EPs. They wanted to use more digital recording technology to create loops and do some drum programming, but the technology available wasn't user-friendly enough for them to move forward at a pace that suited them. It would take at least half a day to make a single loop, and it all felt deeply frus-trating. This affected the mood and the band's confidence. John says: 'Some of the stuff we threw down was too raw, and some of it was really fresh. It's getting that fine line between the two.'

The Beta Band is a sprawling psychedelic mess. From the jokey chaos of 'The Beta Band Rap' to 'It's Not Too Beautiful', here was a band that sounded visionary but unprepared. There were rickety acoustic textures, wonky electronics, *Black Hole* film soundtrack samples, choral sections, lots of larking about, and the notorious 'Total Eclipse of the Heart' lyrical steal. It sounded playful and buoyant, morose and sombre, often in the same song.

Those were excessive times, and the record company pandered to their every whim. John recalls: 'We had a £10,000 percussion budget and went to this percussion warehouse where they had tuned tubular bells. We hired them for eight weeks and used them once. A mental amount of money was getting wasted.' When asked what EMI/Parlo-phone's reaction was, John says: 'Miles Leonard was in control and said "Let them have what they want, when they want" for the entire dura-tion of the record deal. Hence the million-pound debt we accrued.' The record company was actually more worried that Radio 1 wasn't interested and magazines like *Q* were still putting U2 on the cover. They spent their time schmoozing the right people while the band were left to their own devices.

When left alone with time and money on their hands, bands get up to all kinds of mischief. The Sawmills studio, where they had recorded 'Los Amigos Del Beta Banditos', is situated up an estuary and accessible only by boat when carrying equipment. One night Steve, Robin and Richard got drunk and found a small motorboat with the key in the starter. Obviously now was the right time to venture down the estuary, not knowing that it went all the way to the English Channel. Robin was angry about something and had kicked the navigation lights off the boat. As they approached the Channel, they realised things were getting dangerous. Trying to turn the boat, they almost capsized several times and began to panic as they bobbed about among much larger vessels. Eventually managing to turn around, they moored next to a Russian trawler, climbed aboard and stole an engraved bell. Unbelievably, they made their way back to the studio and kept the whole episode hushed up. What's more, the bell was used at every single Beta Band gig thereafter!

At their beloved Rockfield in Wales, their engineer, Mick, fell ill and sessions were halted for a day or two. During this downtime Kingsley, the owner of the studio, took them out in his Rolls-Royce, driving around the countryside. He claimed the studio was down on its luck and needed some serious financial input. The next day Steve rang up, pretending to be Michael Jackson's manager in a fake American accent. He said Michael wanted to use the same studio that The Beta Band was in, and would Kingsley kick them out? Steve told him that Michael loved 'Bohemian Rhapsody', knew it was recorded at Rockfield and wanted to move to Wales. Steve ended up offering hundreds of thousands of pounds a day, but Kingsley retorted: 'Sorry, we've got a band in just now.'

To seal the deal, 'Michael' would have to visit the studio, so the band hired a limo and dressed Robin up for the role. 'Michael', of course, was ultra-sensitive to sunlight and carried an umbrella with him, obscuring his face at all times. On top of that, he wanted only Mick the engineer to show him around, and Mick was now in on the gag. The visit took place and the band got away with it, eventually phoning back to say 'Michael' didn't want to use the studio after all. What shenanigans!

There *are* some moments of greatness on the album. Take 'The Hard One': the band recorded it ten different ways – once using bells, once as a live song, once using computers and so on. They then took the tape, cut it into pieces and stuck it all back together by hand. 'It's Not Too Beautiful', 'The Cow's Wrong' and 'The Hard One' are all good songs. 'Smiling' and 'Number 15' outstay their welcome, and 'The Beta Band Rap' was probably a mistake. John says: 'We went too far with "The Beta Band Rap". You don't want to be Frank Zappa at his worst. You don't want to be whacky or zany, although annoyingly we got called both those things.' In Steve's words: '"The Beta Band Rap" is our "Frigging In The Rigging", and should be obliterated from human existence.'

In their defence, as techno-boffins they were ill-equipped. Editing was almost impossible as the computers were too complicated and slow to use. Songs were left on the album that were plainly far too long. 'There was probably a great EP in there somewhere,' Robin announced when leaving the studio, but an EP would not have justified the expenses incurred, far more than most bands would spend on a full album, or possibly two. So their self-titled debut album was released.

Never one for self-aggrandising statements, Steve declared that it was 'fucking awful'. Perhaps it was too arty and unfocused; perhaps he thought it was uncool. Whatever the reason, he said it, and in a weird way the release went down in history as a result. John is more upbeat: 'That's what we sounded like at the time, that's where we were and that's what we put on tape. You shouldn't regret anything.' The others were affronted by Steve's comment, but they learned to live with it, and it earned a lot of publicity, inciting fans and curious onlookers to investigate further.

Commercially, though, it was suicidal, and it knocked the wind out of the band's sails. Steve says: 'I wasn't pleased with it, and I suppose I wanted to destroy it before someone else got the chance to. It was my depression to blame. I felt the fear of expectation and a huge weight on my shoulders. Maybe I should have brought these feelings up while recording the album, rather than when doing interviews to promote it. But I have no regrets. I'm glad I did what I did, rather than being swept along in all the hype. I would have felt like an absolute fraud.'

Those who 'got' the band and their whole worldview took the album to their hearts, while naysayers used it as a stick to beat them with. It had some good reviews, but soon disappeared from view. To this day, it remains much loved among fans. Band devotee Johnny Lynch, alias The Pictish Trail, insists it's his favourite Beta Band album and that it blows his mind every time he listens to it. Robin says: 'It's not bad. I totally love it! It's mental, and as a piece of art, it's exemplary!'

A little-known secret is that The Beta Band recorded another whole album around the same time. Recorded in the north of Scotland, *The Hut* was a homage to their heroes, The KLF. It was a continuous chill-out ambient piece that involved wave and seagull sounds, speeded-up songs, samples, found sounds and the band giggling a lot. Like 'Monolith', but two hours long, it was never released and remains a curio. Not even I have heard the complete version. Without the right songs and decent technology to record it, John says it isn't as good as he wanted it to be, so only a select few have heard it. Robin has one of only two acetate dubplates in existence, and recently he emigrated to Australia. Let's hope it sees the light of day some time.

Although critically acclaimed, loved by their fans and lauded by their peers, the band had taken a meandering detour with the debut album. It reached number eighteen in the UK album chart in 1999, but perhaps they should have interrupted the sessions, taken some time off, regrouped and rewritten some songs. It's hard to stop the momentum, though, when dates are planned, studios are booked and money put in place. All major-label artists get swept along on that kind of rollercoaster. But that wouldn't have made such an interesting story, or such a bizarre and deranged album. All said and done, The Beta Band had made their mark.

4

Moving Up Country

The Early Life of James Yorkston

Childhood in the East Neuk was fairly idyllic, as I remember. There were no distractions and very little danger. In fact, most of the time there was absolutely nothing to do. That may have been why some children gravitated towards music, art and creativity in general. If we weren't riding our bikes across the neighbouring Cambo estate or mucking about at the beach, we were making stuff up. Soon that stuff would be music, and soon that music would become an obsession that survives to this day.

James Patrick Yorkston Wright was born on 21 December 1971, and in 1974 he and his large Catholic family moved from Stratford-upon-Avon into the big house across the road from my family in the tranquil farming village of Kingsbarns. There was his mother, Clare, and his father, Andrew, alongside brothers John, Tom, Dominic and Harry, with soon-to-be-born sisters Mary-Anne and Sarah waiting in the wings. 'My dad always describes us as British mongrels. I don't feel particularly Scottish at all. I only become slightly patriotic when these things are put under a microscope,' James admits. His parents had met at St Andrews University, which they loved, in the 1960s, deciding to return to the area when an accountancy firm offered Andrew the right job. It was time to put down roots as their family grew larger. For me, it was amazing: suddenly there were lots of different children to play with. Growing up across from the Wright family would have a profound effect on me.

James and I gravitated towards each other. He is my oldest friend in the world; I've known him longer than I've known my own brother, who was born in 1975. James is eight months older than me and was in the year above at school, but we immediately shared a sense of humour and a creative, inventive streak. I was good friends with his brother Harry, who was a few months younger than me, but James and I just clicked. The usual childhood games were soon superseded by our *Star Wars* addiction as we watched the films incessantly and began to collect the toys. Although we weren't into science fiction as such, I'm sure that between us we could recite almost every line from the initial trilogy. Hours would pass as we played at his house or mine, making up new worlds and scenarios for these cheap plastic alien figurines. I'm sure his parents and mine were delighted. It kept us out of trouble, away from vandalising the village bus shelter or antagonising the neighbours. A future Beta Band member, Steve Mason, whom James had befriended at Greyfriars primary school in St Andrews, joined the *Star Wars* games one summer weekend. Who would think that, more than thirty years later, we would all still be friends and making music?

Other than hearing mass every Sunday in Crail, where the Wrights would take up an entire wing of the small church, James's earliest musical epiphany was Adam and the Ants. In 1981 I introduced him to the dandy highwayman and he was smitten. We would collect the records when pocket-money allowed, learn the moves and, yes, paint the white stripe across our noses and yodel along to those hilarious, heroic anthems. 'A new royal family, a wild nobility – we are the family!' It was music, fashion, art, sex and pantomime rolled into one. Everyone else seemed utterly redundant. To not like Adam Ant seemed like a betrayal at the time. Only Steve Mason matched our devotion. James recently acquired an Adam Ant T-shirt again and wears it proudly. *Star Wars*, riding bikes, playing tig and hide-and-seek all paled beside this new interest, pop music.

Aside from Adam Ant, the other key early influence was 1950s rock 'n' roll. This had been my father's pop music, and although he now enjoyed classical music, with occasional forays into Scottish, Greek and Italian folk, he still enjoyed the wild-man sounds of Little Richard, Fats Domino, Jerry Lee Lewis and Carl Perkins. They reminded him of his youth, and he'd happily sing along to the compilation tapes he gave me. James and I would also listen to them incessantly. They sounded exotic and untamed. And they were instantly accessible and gratifying on a first listen, bearing up to repeated plays. When trying to learn the basic guitar chords and song structures, those tracks were soon almost within your grasp, which was incredibly satisfying. I still think that early blast of original 1950s rock 'n' roll is the most exciting music of all time.

James's own family had a selection of crackly 1950s and 1960s 7-inch singles that we would spin on a buckled Dansette. There were a few saucy rock 'n' roll numbers in there, as well as a record of Italian nuns singing and a few *Black and White Minstrel Show* albums. Popular music was not necessarily encouraged in the Wright household, and *Top of the Pops* was largely banned. Even the soundtrack to *Grease* was a no-no. 'I didn't mind that, though – I thought *Grease* was rubbish even then,' James says. 'The first record I bought was *20 Rock 'n' Roll Greatest Hits*, which featured Bill Haley, Johnny Cash and Roy Orbison. It was full of energy and I still use it to DJ with today.'

Soon we discovered Adam Ant had once been a punk, so sideways, backwards and off into that netherworld we went. To children of our generation, born in 1971 or 1972, punks were little more than thugs with ridiculous haircuts and shabby leather jackets – an opinion shared with the tabloid press and its readers. Sneakily watching *Top of the Pops* in the late 1970s, one of James's brothers commented on Sham 69, playing 'Hurry Up Harry' – 'Hey, you have to watch this. It's one of those bands who make it up as they go along!' This was punk to us: making it up as you went along.

As we investigated further, however, we realised punk had a labyrinthine back catalogue of musicians, thinkers and fashionistas, spawned in New York, London, Manchester and even Scotland. It cast a critical eye over politics, art, music, philosophy and life in general. It questioned cliché and mainstream opinion and asked you to think for yourself. Although James and I were middle-class, from a young age we had an inbuilt scorn for the cheesiness of most pop culture. We were only ten and eleven, but increasingly advanced in our tastes. We hated *Smash Hits* and the formation choreography of Michael Jackson and his copycats (though I must confess to buying the occasional Kajagoogoo single at the time). One day James brought a cassette of the Sex Pistols' *Never Mind The Bollocks* album back from school, and we listened intently as my mother cooked tea downstairs. We were staggered at the ferocity and the danger. These so-called punks were expressing themselves and screaming away in a primitive style that we could easily imitate. There was rage in there, but also a sense of humour and of the absurd. This was definitely our thing and we dived in head first. We became the only punks in the village.

$\oint$

For the record, James's first musical outings were with me, recorded in the games room above his parents' garage with a Casio VL-Tone keyboard, an extremely cheap microphone and some crap guitars. We called ourselves The Cows. 'Bah Bah Bah Went the Cow, Moo Moo Moo Went the Dog, Woof Woof Woof Went the Hippopotamus . . . and They All Went to Sleep', was our first composition. We'd record ourselves on a cassette player/recorder via its built-in microphone. It was basic, but it opened up a world of possibilities. Songs, storytelling and silly noises were recorded in endless hours of hilarity after school and at weekends.

This was actually before we'd even stumbled upon punk. Things slowly gathered pace as we became a succession of daftly named duos, my favourite of which was Sid Steamer and the Chemical Toilets, making inept, tuneless music for our own enjoyment. I still have cassettes of those early recordings. Our voices hadn't broken and we could only play guitar with one finger on the fretboard. We'd cover 'Boredom' by Buzzcocks and make up songs about French teachers, 'Willis the Sad Song' being one of James's early numbers. I hate to imagine what my mother used to think when I returned for dinner armed with cassettes of this primitive, atonal nonsense, insisting she listen. 'Very good, son,' she would say, little knowing we were laying the groundwork for the rest of our lives.

At that time James and I were an inseparable duo. We'd share all our musical discoveries together, often disagreeing vehemently and venturing off on our own journeys as we foraged further into goth, post-punk, psychobilly and indie-pop. Every weird, underground subculture was there for the plundering. It was now the mid-1980s, and the C86 compilation given away with the NME had a huge impact on James in particular. He also began to listen to John Peel on Radio 1 and immerse himself in Peel's more outlandish selections. This was perhaps the high point of Peel's broadcasting career as he investigated the hugely adventurous and diverse sounds of the post-punk years. James turned me on to the *John Peel Show*, and I soon had my mind duly blown by the man.

So we had some records, we'd read some books, we dressed in drainpipe jeans and unfeasibly pointy shoes, and we were John Peel fans: it was now definitely time to actually witness a live gig. On a record-buying mission to Dundee we looked in the window of Groucho's (still in business) and saw that Adam Ant was playing Dundee and The Damned were playing Edinburgh. We were now punks of course, aged twelve and thirteen, so the coin was flipped and our allegiance swapped. With the help of my long-suffering mother, James and I, accompanied by friends John Cummins and Dick Petrie, attended our first concert – The Damned, Edinburgh Playhouse, 1 June 1985. It was astounding in every possible way and sealed our fate forever. My mother still talks of how euphorically happy we looked when we met her after the show. The place was filled with real punks, the stage was dressed as a graveyard and the band played fast and loud. We were shocked, stunned and over-awed. This was what we had to do . . . or try to.

At this point, however, James and I went our separate ways for a few years as my mother moved to Haddington in East Lothian to be nearer my brother and me at Loretto school in Musselburgh, where we'd been sent after my father left home. Parted only by the Firth of Forth, James and I remained in touch and saw each other at holidays. We maintained our passion for music, defiant teenage fashion sense, distrust of authority and acute cynicism.

James cut a striking but strange figure as a teenager. Over six feet tall, skinny and gangly, he was an uncompromising vegetarian, wore glasses, dressed solely in black and had a shock of ginger hair. After Greyfriars Catholic primary school, James went to Madras College in St Andrews. Though intelligent and adept, he didn't take to school. 'I didn't like the teachers, I didn't like the subjects and I didn't like the pupils, so all in all I was on a losing streak,' he recalls. A progressively more difficult and contrary teenager, he grew apart from many of his school friends and even his own brothers at times, seeking refuge in alternative music, fashion and culture. Adopting the nickname of 'Commie' for his red hair, and making new friends such as music fanatics Ricky Gould and Ally Fox, he listened to albums such as The Jesus and Mary Chain's *Psychocandy* and *Night Time* by Killing Joke.

School bands were duly formed and an unlistenable clatter was played at extreme volume to school buddies and girlfriends. It wasn't pleasant, but it was fun, and it became his solace. James's first public performance was with the band Verkrampte, swiftly renamed Nicht Verkrampte to avoid right-wing Afrikaner connotations unknown to the young upsetter. They played school gigs and annoyed everyone in earshot with an irritable psychobilly-punk racket that bore little resemblance to music. Reappearing again in our story, Steve Mason played drums for them at one point. What a start! What a horrible noise! James recalls a memorable gig at the Younger Hall in St Andrews alongside other school combos. 'We were supposed to go on second-last, but after our soundcheck we were asked to go on first. We were utter shite!' It wasn't long before they disbanded.

James's next project was the decidedly goth Orchid Segura, teaming up with face-painted girlfriend Adrienne McGillycuddy. Pitched somewhere between The Hook and Pull Gang, The Bolshoi and All About Eve, they were a relatively serious proposition and had vague ambitions to play in tune and in time. James wrote his first real songs, rather than jokes about teachers set to music. Was there a serious possibility of doing this properly? Of course there wasn't. He was a lanky ginger post-punk from the East Neuk with a black trenchcoat and a bad attitude. The world was not his oyster.

School came and went, limited qualifications were acquired, cider was imbibed and glue sniffed. James was delighted to leave, but misguidedly went on a computing course in Edinburgh, not knowing what else to do. Napier College was unceremoniously dumped soon after, and he rejoined forces with me. With drummer Stuart Bastiman and guitarist Andrew Burdall, James picked up his Epiphone Rivoli bass alongside me on guitar and vocals and we formed our first proper band. Soon Burdall left and the super-talented frontman and babe-magnet(!) Clifford Simms joined. It was 1991, and we'd formed Miraclehead to play an unholy mixture of punk, funk and indie-rock. We ended up sounding like a cross between Nomeansno, Madness, Elvis Costello and Faith No

More. We played the length and breadth of Scotland in every toilet that contained two men and a dog. People liked us, though, and we built a following, rapidly improving as musicians and writers.

'I remember feeling that these were great times, and it was an incredible period of my life,' James says. We must have been a fairly intimidating prospect: James was six feet tall, with dyed-black dreadlocks, jackboots and a low-slung bass guitar, Peter Hook style; Stu Bastiman was an octopus-like, ambidextrous drummer with boyish good looks and hair to his waist; I was a tank-top-wearing, gurning, guitar-wielding maniac with bleached hair, and Cliff resembled a Ninja-Elvis Mike Patton, singing like a bird and blowing a mean harmonica. We played with metal bands, funk ensembles, punks and indie bands, blowing pretty much everyone offstage, if I do say so myself. We even supported Radiohead as they toured their *Pablo Honey* album, outdrawing and outperforming the headline act. They're not bad nowadays though. Didn't they do well?

We scorned most other bands, with the exception of a raggle-taggle bluegrass band from Fife called The Skuobhie Dubh Orchestra. Although miles apart musically, they shared some kind of attitude with us and we were mutually appreciative. We asked them to play our club night, Garbage and Honey, which they did, impressing all in attendance at the Subway. We next hooked up and got drunk with them when appearing at the inaugural Cupar Festival on the back of an articulated lorry.

Inevitably, as Miraclehead were getting good – selling-out shows, beginning to tour and shifting T-shirts – we recorded our finest EP and collection of songs to date, then split up. Cliff was submerging himself in the Edinburgh techno scene and dropping ecstasy at club nights such as Pure and Sativa. He wanted to be anonymous and escape the world of the lead singer. James was also having doubts and was often at loggerheads with me over the songwriting. Our manager Paul Mustarde was livid, as he was just about to plough some serious money and energy into the band.

In 1994 Stu and I joined forces with Kenny Anderson, alias King Creosote of the Dubhs, to form another daft band, Khartoum Heroes (see Chapter 1). A folk element was introduced and James began to dabble in acoustic music, drawn in by the white-magic ramblings of

Swans and Current 93 as well as the tragic melancholia of Nick Drake. He still loved punk rock and noise, but was also drawn to more sensitive music informed by country, world and folk. His next endeavour was the little-heard and seldom-seen Agapapa, whose music resembled an up-tempo mixture of The Pogues, Bad Religion and Violent Femmes. It was fast, tight, heartfelt music with a rhythmic swing that was missing from a lot of acoustic bands. 'It was basically what I'm still trying to do now – acoustic pop music. Except back then, when the song wasn't that great, I'd just make it fast as fuck!', James says. He wrote the songs, and though he didn't sing them you could see him striding forward as a songwriter, writing lyrics and melodies that were increasingly his own. Agapapa lasted a year and played around Edinburgh, accruing a following and making some decent recordings.

Khartoum Heroes and Agapapa ground to a halt simultaneously, and our fates would cross once more. In 1995 James and I joined forces to embellish his acoustic work and started a new outfit called, for some reason, Huckleberry, a name neither of us liked. We played our first gig in a small town called Insch, near Aberdeen. However, with a remit to continue the amped-up busking-band idea, distortion pedals were soon added and an incredible organ player, Reuben Taylor, augmented the line-up. Soon Huckleberry were a full-fledged punk-rocking garage band with prog flourishes and pop melodies. We thought we'd struck gold and took to the UK and European circuit like a Toilet Duck to porcelain.

Picking up where Miraclehead and Khartoum Heroes left off, the generous and optimistic Paul Mustarde decided to start a record label. Due to the colour of his hair it was called Copper Records, and he proceeded to bankroll the band and finance a string of independent releases. The 'Halo Jones' EP was followed by the 'Idiot Listening' EP, followed by a couple of singles, 'Morocco' and 'The Lives Of The Saints' before an album, *Hard Luck Stories*, was released to a wholly underwhelming response. We didn't quite fit in anywhere; we didn't particularly want to, either. However, post-Britpop and pre-Strokes, no one was interested in a full-throttle guitar band with lead Hammond organ. It was all nu-metal and soundalike indie back then. We had some radio play from Steve Lamacq and John Peel, and the occasional review. *Scootering Monthly* loved the album . . .

Paul was truly dedicated to that band and our bizarre songs. He was a committed guy, and still is, in whatever he does. However, he sided with me in a lot of decision-making, alienating James at every turn. There was a widening divide between James and me, both as songwriters and in the way we approached live shows. To our credit, we worked as hard as we could. The band toured the UK, usually to nobody, and played some big festivals including Reading, T in the Park and the Transmusicales in Brittany. Increasingly, though, James felt left out. After a good few years slogging away, diversifying and extending the music, the cracks became visible. I wanted to write brash, quirky rock songs, while James preferred a more subtle acoustic approach. He says: 'The thing I enjoyed the most was jamming, when we'd turn up to rehearsal one by one and just play for half an hour before we did the set. I wanted to keep that freedom in my next stuff.' As musical differences rankled and egos clashed, James left the fold in 1999 at the age of twenty-eight.

This is the point where James Wright, the dreadlocked, black-wearing punk rocker, slowly transformed into James Yorkston, the soulful acoustic songwriter you know and love today. He'd always written solo, and was increasingly attracted to 1960s folk revivalists such as Anne Briggs and Shirley Collins as well as enjoying the skewed sounds of Can, Michael Hurley, Jacques Brel, dub reggae and guitarist D'Gary of Madagascar. 'A good unaccompanied singer like Anne Briggs or Bess Cronan is just incredible,' he says. 'Before I heard Anne Briggs, I thought all English folk was very staid, precise and court-like. Then I got a CD out of the library, because she looked bonnie on the cover, and I fell in love with it. Just the silence between the notes – it sounded like winter. The way she sang was so unornamented and pure.' In other styles, he now realises it was the rawness that attracted him. 'The dub that I like sounds man-made. You can hear the switches being pressed or Lee Perry jumping out at you. The panning's not quite right, or certain bits are too loud. That's the stuff I like.' He's also very candid about the influence of folk. 'When my family went to our house in Ireland on holiday, I heard traditional music in the pubs.

When I started listening to folk music later in life, it probably reminded me of that. Certainly my parents never went to folk clubs or had singers around the house. The reason I latched on to it was probably that it reminded me of being a kid.'

In 2000 James was almost thirty and had had enough of loud guitars and flogging the dying pop-star dream. To add insult to injury, others he'd grown up with were making inroads into music and the media. 'I remember back in the day we'd make each other compilation tapes, and one you gave me had "Dry The Rain" on it. It was the demo version without the big bit of Gordon's at the end, and you said it was Steve Mason's band. Then a couple of years later The Beta Band got really big, and you got your job on the radio. You and Steve were my old school pals and I was working in a bookshop, not getting anywhere. I remember you interviewing Steve on the radio around then, and my girlfriend said: "This must make you feel really sick!" But I thought no, they both deserve it.'

Soon the long-term relationship with his girlfriend came to an end, and without a band he began to feel like giving the whole thing up. He'd studied at the Open University and acquired some extra Highers, having flunked school. With these qualifications he could go to university. With his growing love of world music, he applied to study ethnomusicology at Belfast University. He was accepted, but postponed it at the last minute to have one final bash at songwriting. The break-up with his girlfriend had one positive outcome: pouring out of him were the songs that would make up his debut solo album, including 'St Patrick' and 'Tender To The Blues'. He was offered a support slot with ex-Pentangle guitar virtuoso Bert Jansch and, though petrified of taking to the stage on his own, took it up. Afterwards he thought this could be the beginning of something.

It was time to record a collection of songs he could be proud of. In his own mind it was a last-gasp attempt, and it would be solely on his own terms. Armed with a Tascam four-track tape machine, he recorded his material in a very rudimentary fashion. He'd experimented on the machine before as Heehaw Hairhead, a jokey experimental project with his brother John, and as Huckleberry we'd recorded on four-track in our practice room. These songs were serious, though, and performed for the most part by James himself. They included 'A Man With My

Skills', 'Blue Madonnas', 'My Distance Travelled', 'Catching Eyes' and 'Saviour A Saving'. ('Easily Led' and 'The Patience Song' were written and recorded with Huckleberry.)

From his base in Edinburgh he began to revisit his childhood haunts in Fife and realised that former Skuobhie Dubh Orchestra frontman Kenny Anderson was a kindred spirit. Kenny had started a record shop, label and outlet for his outsider art in St Andrews, called Fence, and James was intrigued. This was a key moment for both artists. Miraclehead and the Dubhs had shared a stage or two, and they'd met through me when Khartoum Heroes were still going, but they hardly knew each other. They developed a friendship out of now doing music entirely for themselves.

With visiting mutual friend David 'Wearie' Waters, James found himself enjoying the daft St Andrews Citizens Band and the impromptu live events organised by Kenny in the ever-hospitable Aikman's pub or the local student union. He remembers the gigs: 'Some of them were cold, dank and atmosphereless, with maybe just Kenny and Pete Macleod and a couple of folk watching. But most of them were quite full, with Kenny playing his music to people who loved it. Then there were the extreme ones which were amazing – the fancy-dress ones, the all-dayers, or when Steve Mason turned up and did a Chicken & Chips set with Gordon Anderson. Some of those were pretty special.' Asked about Kenny himself, James says: 'Kenny has always been amazing. I've seldom seen a duff show from him. He's an intuitive musician. He's consistently good, he's innovative and lyrically he's astonishing. He has a great voice and a great way with melodies. I love his acoustic stuff and his crazy stuff with samples. He has a full head of hair too!'

Before long it felt like a collective was developing, with no pressure or outside interference, under the umbrella of Kenny's Fence shop and label. James had escaped the ambitious, competitive world of indie rock. 'At gigs I'd feel like the old baldy guy surrounded by students,' he says of playing with Huckleberry. Now he wanted somewhere to play free-form, away from rigid structures and set-lists. This was the perfect place to do it; anything felt possible at those Aikman's gigs. 'Kenny let me play some of my songs and it was amazing. The open-mic nights in Edinburgh were terrible, with everyone playing "Brown Eyed Girl" and so on. There was none of that there. Kenny also gave me the confidence to sing onstage and just go for it.' As well as King Creosote (Kenny), James began to share the bill with Pip Dylan, Billy Pilgrim, HMS Ginafore, Pictish Trail, Gummi Bako, The Abrahams and a whole cast of bizarrely named musicians. Fence suited James and James suited Fence. He ended up playing, singing and joining in with whatever was going on, when he was needed or simply when he felt like it. 'It was so open, honest and free. There was always an energy and enthusiasm.' Those were special shows for all concerned, and James began to feel part of the gang. 'Eventually, when things started going better for me, I felt like I could bring something to the pot as well.'

On a whim he sent some basic recordings of his new songs to people he hoped might share his intimate acoustic vision. One was John Peel. Under the name J Wright Presents, a CD of 'Moving Up Country (Roaring The Gospel)' was played on Peel's show, and to James's delight Peel proclaimed his love of the title – 'Song title of the year!' – and the music. A young music obsessive, Joff Gladwell, contacted him via Peel's producer, asking if James might want to release something on his fledgling Bad Jazz label. His debut release was an original, home-made recording of the same song, and Peel picked it up again. Suddenly James was on a roll. Around this time he set up his own website for Whoppit Records, named after his cat, to sell releases by King Creosote, UNPOC, Lone Pigeon and himself, but let the practical side slip. 'I never had any stock, so I always pointed people towards other places to buy stuff,' he admits.

James's star, however, was now rising, and he released another single, 'St Patrick', on Bad Jazz, a split 7-inch with Kenny's brother, Gordon Anderson, alias Lone Pigeon. He played his first live band show as J Wright Presents with help of Fence Collective chums Kenny Anderson and Pete 'Uncle Beesly' Macleod as well as drummer Faisal Rahman, later of The Athletes. A young and hungry management and production company, Electric Stew, began to book solo shows for him in London. They wanted to take him to the next level, as they say in showbiz, trotting out superlatives along the lines of 'Your songs are better than the Beach Boys!' James was flattered, liked the people involved and was pleased that anyone was enjoying his music outwith his Fife pals, John Peel and Joff. They promised the earth, and at first things started to happen for him. After the struggles of Miraclehead, Agapapa and Huckleberry, it all seemed effortless and organic.

As a live act, James's baptism of fire came when asked to support revered songwriter John Martyn on a twenty-nine-date tour of the UK and Ireland. He'd inquired about supporting Martyn when the latter played Edinburgh, but was offered the entire tour when Martyn heard his recordings, thanks to Electric Stew. It was a daunting prospect, but an opportunity too good to miss. It also taught him a lesson in stage-craft that has carried him through to the present day. He admits: 'Every night was terrifying until the last eight dates in Ireland. As soon as I realised I had to look after myself and had to do everything myself, which was after gig three, it became a lot easier.' The audiences were largely polite and appreciative, with only Manchester warranting a minor onstage panic attack. He says: 'By the time I signed with Domino, I didn't really give a fuck on stage, because I knew how bad it could get and it would never get that bad again.' His confidence grew and things went well, considering he'd only ever played a few solo shows before setting off around the country. 'It was a strange few weeks. In Gates-head I remember seeing John Martyn lamp the promoter after some communication breakdown with his manager backstage. It was an odd tour. I learned a lot, but I was glad when it was over.' Terrified but exhilarated throughout, he drank a lot of whisky to console himself each night. And so began another long-standing love affair, this time with the single-malt firewater.

$$\text{\Large\symbol{"266D}}$$

Though things were looking positive, James was still penniless, working in an Edinburgh bookshop and spending huge amounts of energy, time and money travelling to and from London. One-off gigs at the enormous Great Eastern Hotel for Electric Stew were fun, but weren't leading to much more. Once he'd been booked to play the Heavenly Social in London, accompanied by Faisal, only to have a table of rude lads talk through the first three numbers. After starting the fourth, he stopped and told them: 'My music's quiet, and if you don't want to hear it, why don't you just fuck off to McDonald's?' James being a vegan, this was meant in the most insulting way possible. The group were silenced and listened for the rest of the performance, leaving quickly at the end. Congratulating him after the set, the promoter mentioned that the lads he'd insulted were all A & R men. Bad luck, perhaps, but with friends like that, who needs enemies? Even when playing quietly, James was uncompromising.

James needed a serious record deal and some investment if he was to take this any further. Joff and Bad Jazz offered to release an album, and Rough Trade and 4AD had sniffed about and offered paltry publishing deals, which James turned down, but nothing else had materialised. Electric Stew were enthusiastic and promised a lot, but couldn't deliver what was required. James was releasing occasional tracks under the radar on Kenny's new Fence imprint, but nothing of any significance was happening. Where to next? Chance and coincidence played a deciding role.

In April 2000 the sadly missed, eclectic and purposefully *outré* Triptych festival was happening across Glasgow, Aberdeen and Edinburgh. As I was now a Radio 1 DJ, out reviewing gigs and festivals whenever possible, I invited James to a Geographic Records night at the Attic in Edinburgh. Future Pilot AKA played live and the Pastels did a DJ set. As the gig finished I approached and spoke briefly with Stephen and Katrina Pastel, who were accompanied by a lanky bloke in a duffel coat. James and I were heading out for more music and beer, and invited them to join us. The Pastels declined, but the lanky bloke came along. His name was Laurence Bell, and he seemed very affable and down-to-earth. He liked talking about music, and later told me he owned and ran Domino Records. I was encouraged by the fact that this genuine enthusiast was running a label, and an important, ground-breaking label at that. The music industry seemed to be full of people who didn't like music, just the lifestyle, but this chap had his priorities in order and was devoted to and knowledgeable about music across genres and eras.

Laurence remembers: 'I went up to Edinburgh to see Future Pilot AKA and met Stephen and Katrina from The Pastels. The Pastels were going home and they introduced me to you. And you were with James Yorkston. One thing led to another and it got quite late. During the night I got into a conversation with James and asked him what he did. He said he was a singer and I asked what kind of songs he sang. He said: "Well, I suppose they're kind of folk songs." I said I liked folk music and we found some common ground in Anne Briggs and Shirley Collins. I mentioned Fairport Convention, but he wasn't having any of that. He's got very singular taste. I was devouring it all, right in the middle of a little folk epiphany. He'd had this punk-rock route, and I knew a lot about that. He was into DC hardcore and we talked about that. It was funny to meet a folk-singer with a strong punk-rock background, but I suppose it makes sense.'

James didn't have a clue who Domino Records were or what music they released, so he was unfazed by the meeting, simply asking for advice about contracts and legalities. As the night continued we all bonded with Laurence about punk, hardcore and psychedelia, while James and he chatted endlessly about folk, traditional and acoustic. After some whisky, singing and falling over, to the soundtrack of Riley Briggs from Aberfeldy playing Beatles and Neil Young songs on a piano, we went our separate ways, swapping contact details. James says: 'I just remember it was three music heads talking about music and getting drunk. I didn't think I'd hear from him again.'

But James and Laurence did keep in touch. Laurence posted James a selection of Domino's recent output, including Smog, Bonnie Prince Billy, Woodbine, Pavement, Elliott Smith, Papa M and more. Now calling himself James Yorkston to avoid confusion with singer-songwriter Jimmy Wright, he sent Laurence a compilation of Fence artists such as King Creosote, Lone Pigeon and UNPOC, adding a few of his own songs. Laurence said he loved the CD – but were those songs at the end James's? When James answered yes, Laurence was sold. He explains: 'That's when I first heard it all. I put the CD on and couldn't believe how good the music was. It was lo-fi, but that's never been a problem for me. It was the quality of the songwriting and the originality of the presentation. It was out of nowhere. I've always been fascinated by music that comes from places you don't expect it to come from. That song "The Lang Toun" was the one I jumped on first. I couldn't believe it – it was one of the most intense, brilliant, unbelievable tracks I'd ever heard. This ten-minute epic with this almost scary emotional power, over this Krautrock rhythm – it was an extraordinary piece of music.'

The stakes were now raised, and Electric Stew were keen to match the deal, proposing a new label with James as a priority act. It was a tough call: James had known little about Domino until Laurence had sent him their recent releases, while Electric Stew had been supporting him as a complete unknown for a year or so. James remembers: 'I'd been waiting for the Electric Stew contract for about a year, and when I got it my lawyer said it was utter shit. I'd been banking on it, so when it came through it was soul-destroying. There were some really distressing and abusive phone-calls at the time, but they hadn't come up with their side of the bargain. My lawyer asked if there was anyone else, and when I mentioned Domino he said: "*They* are the label for you!"'

James emailed Laurence, asking if he was still interested. He was, and came to Edinburgh to talk basics. He wanted to hear more and see James and band live. Laurence clarifies: 'I loved James's songs and was very into what he was doing. He told me he'd had a record offer of some kind, but it had been very slow and wasn't really working out: I said: "If it doesn't work out, let me know. I really love this stuff." He came back to me not long after and said he'd be up for talking about me doing it. So we started talking more seriously.' The tiny Bar Fez in Edinburgh was booked for the first live outing of James Yorkston and the Athletes, with King Creosote on occasional backing vocals. I was in that small audience too. Bowled over by the songs and the musicianship, Laurence offered James a deal. 'We made a deal and I borrowed some money, because we were skint,' Laurence recalls, 'and we made this beautiful record that became his first album.'

The decision was made on the advice of James's lawyer, Gavin Maude. Electric Stew were not at all happy, but it was the right thing to do; in many ways, it was the only thing to do. This was before Franz Ferdinand, Arctic Monkeys, The Last Shadow Puppets and the forthcoming Domino beanfeast, yet the label was well respected and well connected, and, most importantly, believed in all its artists. Asked what he liked so much about James's music, Laurence says: 'I thought the lyrics were brilliant, and I've always been interested in lyrics. It had a real soul to it and a real poetry. Melodically it was really strong. I've worked with some great American singer-songwriters through the 1990s, and James was the first British singer-songwriter I thought stood up to some of the great talents out of America, like Elliott Smith, Smog, Will Oldham etc. It was something that I wanted to listen to at home.' James says: 'When Laurence said he'd been listening to my songs almost every day for a year, that was the clincher.' He had found the right home for his music and his off-kilter character. Here was a label that wouldn't ask him to water down his ideas, where he would be encouraged to develop as an artist, not as a commodity. By September 2001 James had signed a deal with the label he is still with today.

$$\oint$$

In November, with £10,000 of Domino's money to invest, James and the far from athletic Athletes went to a small country house outside Hawick that could be converted into a makeshift recording studio. The line-up was James, Reuben Taylor on keyboards, Dougie Paul on bass, Faisal Rahman on drums and Wendy Chan on violin, with help from Rob Armstrong on cittern and Holly Taylor on small pipes and whistle. Rather than spending their advance on a proper studio, they'd bought a ton of new computer equipment that at the outset simply wouldn't work. Electronics whizz Reuben Taylor took ten days to fix it. At last they began to record their debut album, *Moving Up Country*.

Working hours began as 10 a.m. to 6 p.m., gradually becoming midday to 8 p.m., then 4 p.m. to midnight and eventually any time at all. Dougie and Faisal would often sleep in the control room, as their digs in the house were too damp. The cottage was on a pheasant estate, so band members, other than James the vegan, would hunt, shoot, pluck and eat the birds as often as possible, which kept the album's food budget down. Weirdly, there was a forest nearby full of mannequins set up to scare away woodland predators. If you took a stroll between sessions, a showroom dummy with an orange head might be there to greet you and freak you out.

Despite cabin fever and a chaotic feel to proceedings, the planned three weeks overran by only a week. 'It was all a bit of a panic, and we ended up recording almost the entire album in the last five days or so,' says James. 'We only got the equipment working towards the end, so it was a struggle. But in a way it was good, as we could use the demos for "Sweet Jesus" – recorded at Kenny Anderson's house in Crail with his brother Gordon – "St Patrick" and "Tender To The Blues" – recorded at Reuben's flat in Edinburgh – which were all better than the newer recorded versions. If we had invested a month in recording those songs, rather than doing them quickly after two weeks of drinking and panicking, they probably wouldn't have been as strong. My only regret with that album was not including "The Lang Toun".' In 2012, when the album was re-released, that mistake was corrected and the Kraut-folk epic was added to the track listing. Explaining the genesis of the track, James says: 'I was working in the James Thin Bookshop at the time and there was a traffic jam outside with everyone blowing their horns. I thought it would be great to have a song with that big, angry drone going through it. We did it really quickly, adding the different parts one by one, then in the middle I added a sample by Hukwe Zawosi, a Tanzanian thumb-piano player, and at the end added a Galician dance tune I learned from Andrew Cronshaw.'

The finished article was a combination of the Borders sessions and some solo demos of James's, mixed by former Cocteau Twin (now Bella Union label boss) Simon Raymonde, who also takes a production credit. It was recorded and produced by James and Reuben Taylor with no grander ambition than a true representation of these raw, personal and intimate songs, though with some mastering wizardry in post-production. Alongside the single release of the 'The Lang Toun', the album was released with little fanfare in June 2002. The response eclipsed anything James or the label ever imagined, press and radio going overboard with praise. There had been a sea-change, and music fans and media wanted roots and authenticity. Sidestepping such horrendous tags as 'new acoustic movement' and 'nu-folk', here was an unpretentious, soulful songwriter with a collection of timeless, poetic, heartfelt songs that rang true in an age of fakery, career rock and vacuous celebrity. In relinquishing his ambition to be a pop star, James had found his own voice and his own audience. 'We were all surprised by the reaction,' James recalls, 'and I ended up doing huge interviews with all the national papers. The album just sold and sold and sold.'

With the smooth comes the rough. Horrendous tabloid interviews were happening more often, one conducted by a journalist who, having misread another article, thought James was the violinist with Pulp. That aside, apart from an ill-fitting tour supporting McAlmont & Butler, everything went swimmingly. The singles 'St Patrick', 'Sweet Jesus' and 'Tender To The Blues' were widely applauded. Appropriate tours were undertaken, supporting Tindersticks and David Gray in the UK and

Beth Orton and Turin Brakes in the US, and a small but loyal fan base steadily grew. One highpoint was touring France supporting Lambchop. 'They were really great guys to hang out with, and when you're outside Britain you're always treated better. I have a lot of affection for Scandinavia too. There was always an audience, and people were genuinely pleased to see you,' James says.

'David Gray gave me the best piece of advice ever. He said the audience don't really care if you're good or bad – all they want is to experience something unique for that night. I always try to give an audience a special experience.' For James this tour was a life-saver. He'd also been invited on a European tour of smaller venues supporting John Parish, but the David Gray tour was to audiences of 3,000 to 12,000 a night across the UK and Ireland, and Gray's audiences were responsive to The Athletes. The year 2002 was a stressful one with a packed schedule, but unbelievably exciting. Some of those gigs were with a full band, some solo, and some as a duo with Faisal on drums and harmonium. Whatever the combination, James was much in demand, but he was exhausting himself, and eventually he took a break. He looks back and says: 'Maybe that wasn't the best move. I should have taken on everything going!'

The album became Rough Trade's Album of the Year for 2002 and received plaudits across the board. *NME* said: 'Yorkston has talent as deep as a mineshaft.' He was invited to play a John Peel session, and Peel called him 'the finest songwriter of his generation'. Laurence Bell says: 'I was really pleased when *Moving Up Country* was properly received, and I still feel it should have done a lot better than it did. It's a travesty that it wasn't nominated for the Mercury awards. It should have gone deeper, but it was a great start.' James says: 'I felt very lucky: lucky to have worked so hard, lucky to bump into Laurence, lucky to have had those two years of songs ready. I'd been given a second chance. The depression that had blighted my twenties was gone. I could walk down the street with my head held high – not in an arrogant way, but in a "Thank fuck for that!" way. I remember bumping into an ex-girlfriend and telling her what had happened. She said: "All your dreams have come true." And I suppose she was right; all my dreams *had* come true.'

5

Eye to the Telescope

The Early Life of KT Tunstall

Some people light up a room. Whether on account of their raw talent, their good looks, or their sheer energy, people are drawn to them like moths to a naked lightbulb. Few have all three. KT Tunstall, or Kate Tunstall as she was known then, always did and still does. Her intelligence, rakish sense of humour and boundless enthusiasm were noted by everyone who crossed her path, myself included. When I first met her she was a gregarious tomboy with cute dimples, scuffed jeans and an obvious desire to be liked. Constantly carrying a guitar, she was gifted as a singer, songwriter and multi-instrumentalist, the first to join the jam session, provide a backing harmony or simply mess about. She was also able to keep up with the boys when humour took a turn for the worse or one-upmanship set in.

Unsurprisingly, she seemed to drift into the lives of anyone who played music or had an artistic bone in their bodies in St Andrews in the early to mid-1990s. Onstage or off, Kate had the ability to show warmth and make others feel good about themselves, whether she meant it or not. She was an immediately comforting force, with a knack of assuming the role of girlfriend, sister or best buddy. The rock 'n' roll world has fewer forthcoming, confident female extroverts than it has male, so when you meet someone like Kate Tunstall you know all about it.

Adopted at eighteen days old, she was brought up in a household that played virtually no music. Her mother, Rosemary, was a primary-school teacher, teaching a young John Maclean in Tayport (her school reports said John drew a lot and didn't listen, which his parents were probably secretly proud of), and her father David was a physics lecturer at St Andrews. Both were English, and they had moved to Fife a few years before Kate was adopted. Their only records were a live album by the American musical satirist Tom Lehrer and a handful of classical discs. Her mother had played the piano but for no particular reason gave it up. Her younger brother, Dan, was born profoundly deaf and had to use a rudimentary phonic ear, which didn't work properly if there was any loud background noise. Music rarely featured in the house at all.

It was hardly the background for a musician and performer, but music was obviously in her genes via her biological parents, her Scottish/Chinese mother and Irish father. Her adoptive parents didn't know what she'd be good at, but they encouraged her and let her try the things she wanted. A former teacher at Greyfriars nursery proudly displays a certain guitar today. Kate says: 'I remember wanting to make noise and being able to do stuff. I found it easy to get a cool noise out of something. Musical instruments were interesting and I really enjoyed mucking about with them. At Lawhead Primary I remember a brilliant music teacher, Mrs Kingsley, playing piano. We had to sing along with her, but I remember feeling slightly envious and wanting to get up and play the piano too.' At a very early age she cajoled her parents into buying her a piano and took to the instrument instantly, taking lessons and passing exams with exceptional grades. Playing the flute followed at eleven and she scored more outstanding grades, increasing her theoretical and instinctive musical knowledge.

Like most children, she was enthralled by the music in TV programmes and adverts. Animated children's shows like *Mr Benn*, *Bagpuss*, *The Moomins* and *Sesame Street* had the first impact. She tried to imitate their clunky, DIY, junkyard-but-folksy melodies, loving the rhymes and songs. Soon she was acting in school plays and joining the local Byre Theatre youth group Stage One. 'It wasn't too pretentious and thankfully quite non-Disney. I wanted to be an actress until I was about sixteen.' She and her friends would record skits, sketches and comedy routines on tape, and it was obvious she was focused on performing. Her parents and school encouraged her flair for the stage.

'My introduction to pop music was probably through my brother Joe's love for hair metal. Bands like Bon Jovi, Def Leppard, Van Halen, Guns 'n' Roses . . . and I'm totally unashamed to say I still love that stuff today. I had the honour of playing alongside Bon Jovi at a Live Earth concert and they were fuckin' awesome.' More than anything she was pulled towards the melodies and pop arrangements of those rock songs. It was the huge choruses and plentiful hooks that attracted her. In addition to poodle-rock and Joe's record collection, Kate also became fixated on Vangelis's soundtrack to *Chariots of Fire*, which was filmed largely in St Andrews. 'I specifically liked the B-side to the soundtrack. It had this weird underwater-type section on it which I loved.'

Her improving skills on the piano came to a halt when she rediscovered the guitar in her early teens. She realised she could express herself on it in a way she couldn't using keys alone. She became obsessed with classical guitarist John Williams. In the years above her at Madras College she saw characters like Steve Mason and Gordon Anderson, all wrapped up in music and pop culture, but her own peer group weren't interested. Musically she was out on a limb. It was all about playing, not buying into a scene or fashion. She didn't buy Madonna or Bananarama records, or soak up the retro sounds of the 1960s and 1970s as those older than her were doing. She had an ear for music, pure and simple. She had an innate ability to hear something and play it back. 'Everything was going in,' she says. 'I remember all kinds of music from that time.'

Although intimidated by the size and anonymity of Madras College, she quickly took to her secondary school and her fears subsided. She began to have boyfriends, including local skater Kyle Martin, who had scuzzy punk and indie bands such as Dead Kennedys and Sebadoh on his playlist. She breathed it all in and took notes. When her father signed up for a satellite dish in 1990 she was exposed, aged fifteen, to MTV, and became acutely aware of the worlds of pop, indie and dance. She heard The Stone Roses and Beck for the first time and was further intrigued. She looks back and says: 'This was the music boys made! It was different from the girl music I'd been hearing, such as Whitney Houston and Madonna. To this day I probably know Beck's music better than any other.'

She auditioned for and joined the Scottish Youth Theatre in Glasgow, yearning to explore and experience something else. 'I was there for five weeks in student digs and it completely blew my mind. Leaving St Andrews for a start, where I'd lived all my life. It's a small town and I'm completely grateful for having grown up there. It's safe, somewhere you can stay young longer than people in other parts of the country. My childhood seemed to last forever.' As well as acting and interacting with a huge cross-section of other walks of life, she heard new artists who connected with her growing pop sensibilities. 'In Glasgow I was exposed to PJ Harvey and the Cocteau Twins, and became a lifelong fan of both. I also went to a proper Glaswegian soul party, where all they played was James Brown. I was smitten with him and probably listened to him every day for the year after.'

On her return to St Andrews at the age of fifteen, she was moved to Dundee High School. She was having too much fun at Madras and her school work was suffering. On top of that, the curriculum didn't allow pupils to study art and music at the same time; she excelled in both, and was weaker at maths and science. Her parents convinced her that Dundee High would suit her better. She missed Madras and her friends, however, and thought the new school was a little uptight. Soon, though, she befriended the guitar teacher. He never gave her a lesson, but allowed her to muck about in free periods and breaks. With oddball influences from *Sesame Street* and Tom Lehrer to John Williams, Vangelis and Bon Jovi, via skater-punk, PJ Harvey, James Brown, The Stone Roses and Beck, her musical mind was beginning to tick over and soon she would write songs of her own. Her first songs were composed on the piano before she shifted to her new love, the guitar. 'They were shocking. Really bad, predictable lyrics. I wasn't even particularly pleasing myself – it was just fun to write something. But when I started on the guitar, it sounded more like me.'

Up to this point hell-bent on acting, strangely it was the Scottish Youth Theatre, which she had enjoyed so much, that was the turning point. She found herself playing guitar more and more, on her own and for others. 'I was definitely morphing into a wannabe musician rather than a wannabe actress,' she says. Asked whether she was aware of being a 'female' songwriter at this point, she says: 'Only in a positive way. At the end of SYT, I played a song instead of acting a solo sketch and realised: "Every girl here wants to be an actress, and I want to be a musician." It was a Darwin moment.' She continued acting for a while, joining a youth ensemble at the Royal Shakespeare Company, but quickly realised it probably wasn't for her any more, even though she would go on to study theatre at Royal Holloway in London in the not too distant future.

Between school and university, Kate was about to experience a life-changing year. On her seventeenth birthday she left school with all the Highers she wanted. Believing she was too young to go straight to university or take a gap year abroad, her mother spotted an ad in a newspaper for a year-long scholarship to the expensive Kent boarding-school in Connecticut. Unexpectedly, Kate was accepted, and now enthuses: 'If I hadn't met many people of my own age who were obsessed with music before, I certainly did there.'

Fitting in immediately, she soon met and fell in love with a young hippie called Ethan Kramer, from Fairfield, Vermont. His mother had built her own house in the woods and had lived in a commune since the 1960s. Living so close to an alternative lifestyle, Kate was shown a different set of values and welcomed into a bohemian circle. Here people made art using garbage, they recycled everything and used all manner of eco-friendly household objects. They washed with biode-gradable soap, jumped in the pond during the summer and struck up the generator only for a few hours in the evening before the candles were brought out. In the early 1990s the UK was a mile behind the US eco-boom and Kate saw this as a magical new way of living. 'It had a massive effect on me and resonated with me as a way of life I respected and enjoyed,' she says.

By all accounts Ethan was a fairly subversive guy, a talented poet who introduced her to Charles Bukowski and other Beats. Kate recalls: 'I was immersed in a passionate affair with being creative.' It wasn't just Ethan who captured her heart; Kate also fell in love with the blues. Ethan had loads of old blues vinyl which he played incessantly, including records by a female-fronted outfit called Sweet Emma. She was besotted and started writing more bluesy material, including 'Sweet Emma', a tribute to the band. 'It was just being in America, where there are genuine seams of musical culture entering into the consciousness of the country. In Britain it feels borrowed.'

She was soon introduced to psychedelic rock, seeing Phish on a few occasions, as well as the penultimate Grateful Dead concert in Chicago. Best of all, she bonded with like-minded souls and formed her first band, The Happy Campers. The band's guitarist was a massive stoner and wanted to call them THC after the active ingredient of his beloved weed, but Kate, showing her ambitious side for the first time, vetoed it as too likely to get them into trouble. As they only played at school, she probably had a point. As a compromise the letters became the initials of the band name. The Happy Campers were kind of prog-pop, with long sections of guitar noodling followed by massive choruses. 'Lots of people liked us,' she says, 'but said my between-song chat was diabolical. I'm a hugely optimistic, trusting and slightly naive person who's always going to walk onstage and say "Hiya!"' She loved being in the band and even started playing electric guitar for the first time.

It was tough on the young lovers, but Kate had to return to the UK after her time at Kent. Tellingly, when interviewed about her first trip to Connecticut, she said nothing about classes, subjects or teaching. She was getting a different kind of education, one that would drastically change her life. The following summer she made a return visit to the US, spending the time with Ethan and his mum again. As an artist and songwriter her self-belief was increasing. A friend started to record her songs for the first time, and she plucked up the confidence to play local open-mic nights and go busking in nearby Burlington. She did well, often making eighty to a hundred dollars in an afternoon. 'When I went back to play there, there were people in the audience who claimed to remember me busking. I'm a terrible busker, though. I can't really play covers, as I always forget the words. I just play my own stuff, and it often becomes a barometer for which songs should become singles, as you can tell immediately which ones are getting attention.' In Vermont she was busking a few hours every day, becoming more self-assured on the guitar by the minute. When she first picked up the instrument she had tried finger-picking, but soon realised that style wouldn't work for busking, so she developed a knack for whacking out a potent rhythm on her acoustic six-string.

It cannot be overstated how important a time this was for Kate. She was finding herself; she had gone a teenager and come back an adult. She had entered a world of limitless possibilities, but also one of drug problems, absent fathers, family issues and financial worries. She saw the positive and negative sides of alternative living in the Fairfield commune, though Ethan had protected her as much as he could, so she came away with a largely optimistic view of the life/art collision she had just been thrown into. 'At the time I had this completely utopian idea of it all, and I'd largely put it down to growing up in St Andrews,' she says.

It was almost inevitable that her relationship with Ethan would lead to heartache, if for no other reason than distance. Across thousands of miles they wrote poems and letters to each other, but ultimately their lives had to go in separate directions.

$$\oint$$

Back in St Andrews and working at the ice-cream parlour Luvians, Kate was good friends with a girl called Siobhan Grundy, who worked at the Woollen Mill with Kenny Anderson. After her Scottish Youth Theatre success and her musical forays in the US, Kate decided to put on a debut gig in her hometown. She discovered the Oval Room in the Vic Café, and it seemed perfect. 'Why are people creative in St Andrews? Well, by the time you become a teenager, it's boring! There's no nightclub. There are pubs, but they're for young farmers. There's very little to do. You're not living in a city, so putting on a gig is great – you 're creating a night out. A lot of pleasure comes from being the creator of someone else's night out. I still get a huge amount of pleasure from that.'

As she played to an almost exclusively female audience of about eight friends, along came Kenny, possibly to further his friendship with his workmate. You may remember Kenny's words about the experience from Chapter 1. Kate says: 'I remember being really impressed. This guy was a real musician. He was bearded and colourful, an attractive, mischievous guy with an infectious personality. He said he liked my voice and asked me if I'd like to do some backing vocals with his band. Of course I would!' The way Kenny looked and his wide-eyed worldview took Kate straight back to her time with Ethan and Vermont. Could it be possible to live a similar life in the UK?

Kate's life would become inextricably intertwined with the Anderson brothers. Although she went to London to study for three years, she always kept in touch with them and saw them at holidays and any other times possible. The bond, however, was initially forged after her time in the US and before going to university. They began to play music together and make their own fun. 'Kenny is pivotal to the whole thing,' she says. 'He seems to be the central pin on a map that connects a lot of different people. Of everyone I knew, his was the only family that had a professional musician in it, his dad. Kenny was very determined. There was no way he was going to be doing anything else.'

As she got to know the brothers and saw them play live, she was startled. 'I was blown away by their musicianship, and Een in particular – he was so amazing on the banjo, double bass and guitar. They were great harmony singers and I remember the rhythm in the music. They were playing up-tempo skiffle and bluegrass, and because it's so fast it has to be tight. They were *so* good!'

Kate would sing backing vocals and play bits of percussion. She became an auxiliary member of The Skuobhie Dubh Orchestra and spent a lot of her time in the band's van, travelling across Scotland to venues such as The Twa Tams in Perth and The Lemon Tree in Aberdeen, where the band was building a sizeable following. 'They had this hardcore female following – Rosy, Shona, Sheena, Iona and others – and the girls seemed really fucked off that there was a girl in the band. I was quite resilient about it, though. I was more than happy to be the only girl on stage.' Asked about being the only girl in a gang of boys, she says: 'The musician side of it is great. You're often the only woman there, and you get treated like a little princess. Often men appreciate having a female around. When there's a folk edge to the music, a female voice is always appreciated, especially with harmonising.' She wasn't intimidated by the music either. 'Not at all. I've got a good sense of rhythm and a good sense of harmony, and I think Kenny was delighted to find someone who could harmonise with him and stay in tune! The minute we sang together we thought: "Fuckin' hell – that works really well!" Our voices sounded great, and I would always sing a little more in Kenny's accent.'

She started falling for Een and soon they became an item. They'd snog in the back of the van, thinking no one else knew. Everyone knew, but it didn't seem to matter too much at first. She wasn't a Yoko Ono figure, but 'Kenny was probably a bit pissed off that I'd got together with his brother –sibling rivalry and all that. He and Een would definitely spar. Een was sometimes difficult on purpose, but he was a cheeky chappie and he was really good fun. We had a really good time a lot of the time. He was such a brilliant musician. He also had a great record collection, so I stole a lot of his interests in music, such as Johnny Cash, Loudon Wainwright III, Bill Munro, Django Reinhardt and others.' But the time had arrived for her to go to university, so young love was put on hold.

Kate was now determined to become a musician and use her time in London to the best of her ability. At the Royal Holloway, though, she again found herself in a stiff and clinical environment. Her campus was in Egham, outside Staines, hardly a cultural epicentre. Royal Holloway was a second choice: she had wanted to go to Goldsmiths College, famous for its bohemian nature. On her Music and Theatre course the music was almost exclusively classical, and the department was uptight about her excursions into folk, roots and Americana. Her playlist at the time consisted of Muddy Waters, The Rolling Stones' *Sticky Fingers*, Joni Mitchell's *Blue* and Tom Waits's *Bone Machine*. The last was a big album for her. Finding that Waits wasn't, as she had assumed, black, she thought: 'Well, I can sing like that. I'd thought you shouldn't sing bluesy unless you're black. I thought, I'm going to go for it.'

She should have dropped the music side of her course and studied theatre on its own; she believes she'd have learned more. She could have made music as a side project outwith her college work. In fact she did drop the music course before her final year. She says now: 'I'd love to go back to uni and do it all again, properly.' Not that she performed badly, leaving with a 2:1.

'I made great friends and had a great time,' Kate recalls. 'I got lashed almost every night and had brilliant fun, but I was a big fish in a little pond as far as music went. I asked the student union if I could put a gig on there every two weeks, and they said yes. So I was in the diary twice a month, every month: "Katie".' This was the first time her name had two syllables. 'I'd always been Kate back home, but when I went to uni everyone started calling me Katie. Maybe it's an English thing.'

She trawled for musicians, who were thin on the ground, and connected with a talented guy called Jay, who played the mandolin. Then they searched for anyone who could augment their sound. 'It wasn't electric in any way,' she says. 'It was pretty folksy, with violins and mandolins on top of my songs.' She and her friends soon won a campus Battle of the Bands, grabbing the star prize of £100 and a head-lining gig at the student union.

As her musical dreams hadn't been realised in any way during her three years at university, she tried to be pro-active by playing acoustic in

London city centre. Her ties with her old Fife comrades were still strong too, and she would sporadically play gigs with the Skuobhie Dubhs. She remembers a doomed mission to get to Bath to sing with them on tour, which she missed because of a train delay. 'I remember feeling gutted. I really wanted to see them and play music with them.' It wouldn't be too long before she would do so again.

Back in St Andrews after university, Kate says: 'There was no question in my mind where I wanted to be. I'd had dreams of staying down in London, but I needed to be with other musicians and people who knew me. And I wanted to be back with Een. I'd not had a proper relationship at university, and missed the more solid thing I'd had at home.' Their relationship fired up as before and they moved in together, living in a cottage near Kincaple and the Hungry Horse roadside café. They were on the dole and extremely hard up, and at first there was some tension between them, as she'd been to university. This was not Een's scene, and he probably thought of her as the posh girl and him as the bit of rough. She says: 'I didn't see it as that. It was just deciding how you wanted to live your life, and realising you didn't want to live the same as your parents.'

Although more or less penniless, she was living the dream. She was with her boyfriend, writing music and playing all the time. The lack of stimulation at Royal Holloway was replaced by a great splurge of creativity. 'The thing about Kenny, Gordon and Een is that they could keep me mesmerised with one chord. They had these really simple melodies, but a real grasp on being tasteful. They'd never do anything that would make you go: "Oh that's really cheesy!" It would always keep me guessing what would happen next. It was so different from the music I'd grown up with, so refreshing,' she says. 'There was a lot of support. I don't remember any jealousy. If one of us wanted to put on a gig, everyone else would turn up to play in the band. The Fence Collective has that incredible spirit now, where everyone plays on and knows each other's songs. It's amazing.'

One of her first gigs back with them was in the Ceilidh Tent at T in the Park in 1996, in a last hurrah with The Skuobhie Dubh Orchestra.

She was twenty-one years old and spent the weekend dancing with Een to Cocteau Twins, Beck and Radiohead. 'It was the first festival I'd ever been to and it completely blew my mind. I made a pact with myself: "I'm not coming back to one of these things unless I've got the gig." And I never went to another festival until I played Glastonbury.'

All was not well with Kenny. He had hit a wall and was spiralling out of control. He was losing faith in being a band-leader, and in many ways losing his mind. Kate recalls: 'He was at the start of a really big "Fuck the Man" phase. He had tried going down regular music industry routes and been let down. He was vehemently on a backlash against the London music industry and getting signed. He was pretty fiercely independent by the time I got involved in The Skuobhie Dubh Orchestra. I just wanted to copy him; I thought he was really cool. He would badmouth the industry and say it was unfair that they took eighty per cent of what you made, and it all made sense to me. That's why I didn't try to chase a record deal for six years or so, and I remained in Scotland. I was dead-set on trying to do things independently.' Kenny is now celebrated for this viewpoint, and rightly so, but at the time it wasn't necessarily the most attractive prospect.

In my timeline, this was the period after Khartoum Heroes and my collaboration with Kenny and Een. There had been a sense of hope and positivity, but Kenny was beginning to break down. I had set up a new band called Huckleberry with James 'Yorkston' Wright, and was based in Edinburgh. The ex-drummer of Khartoum Heroes and Miraclehead, Stu Bastiman, had stayed in Fife and taught himself bluegrass drumming. He was comfortable with basic cottage living and ended up playing with Een every day. Soon he would be part of the close-knit gang, and he turned his attentions to Kate's songs. I'd met Kate before her degree and got to know her a little better when she returned to Fife. She was affable and sparkled with wit, good humour and drive. It was easy to see how skilled musicians would be drawn to her and her songs.

Sharing a cottage with Een and Stu, and continuing to sign on the dole, she set to work on bands of her own, such as Tomoko (named after a Japanese girlfriend of Gordon's), with the brothers and the rock-solid bass of Pete 'Uncle Beesly' Macleod. That morphed into the psych-folk band Elia Drew with Een and a revolving cast of musicians, with Kate's songs centre-stage. Pete Macleod recalls: 'Kate struck me as ambitious and highly driven, but also really easy-going. She was extremely musical and great at arranging songs. When I played bass for her, she could write people's parts for them and had the music in her head. I always thought she was a musical chameleon and could be very much influenced by people she was with, whether it was making dance music or playing in a hippie-folk duo. She would assume the role and the lifestyle that went with it.'

At university Kate had taken part in open-mic nights in London, including a spot upstairs at the Highbury Garage where Simon Banks, now her manager, saw her. He then called her every six months for six years, asking her to relocate to London, but Kate insisted on staying independent and in Scotland. He came to Scotland and stayed with Kate and Een in their cottage, trying to persuade her to come to London, but still she refused. This was in no small part due to Kenny's influence. However, Kenny now felt betrayed as members of his own band, including Een, had prioritised Kate's music over his. Perhaps they felt Kenny was washed up, perhaps it was simply the feeling of doing something completely new, but their allegiances had switched.

Kate wasn't totally averse to this. Having a group of stunning musicians couldn't hurt her chances. Friends, colleagues, fellow musicians and onlookers were now beginning to see another change in Kate. She was becoming more ambitious, some would say ruthlessly so. She admits her ambition kicked in after university. 'The driving force was not getting another job. Kenny was almost at the point where he could make the books work and be a working musician. He still had to juggle stuff and do a little job sometimes, but he was almost there. That's all I wanted, to not need to do another job.' Her determination and focus would propel her to stardom, but it was a tortuous path with many casualties along the way. To get her way and move forward, she would have to make some hard-nosed decisions about band members and collaborators along the way.

Soon Stu would weigh up his bets and leave Fife. He joined James and me in Huckleberry, thinking it was a better meal ticket than what was on offer in Fife. The bohemian living was getting harder and the paying gigs were getting fewer. Kenny had dislocated himself from music for the time being, and Stu's heart wasn't in Kate's songs. All bands need a sprinkling of lucky magic dust, and it looked as though Huckleberry had the brighter future, with a record deal, a promotions company, festival dates and a European tour. The music perhaps seemed more of the time too, with loud guitars, Hammond organ and brattish punk spirit. In hindsight we were all a little misguided, a little too optimistic. Huckleberry, like so many other bands, faded away over the years. We wrote some good songs, released some interesting records and had a good laugh, though.

Kate and Een moved into another cottage with Gordon at 1 Tinker Row, Denhead. 'Tinker Row – my mum was so proud!', Kate laughs. Living with Gordon, however, was a whole new ball game. He was energised and super-creative but also increasingly unstable. Kate says: 'I got on very well with Gordon; he was bonkers, unhinged and a lot of fun. It hadn't got dark yet. It started to go downhill quickly, though.' Gordon would write volumes and volumes of journals filled with disturbing artwork, geometric formulae and philosophies. He had psychotic episodes, heard voices and displayed messianic delusions, ranting about Jesus, the devil, good, evil, right and wrong. He was very ill.

Kate remembers it all clearly: 'He got sectioned when he was living in that house with us. It was very sad, but he revelled in going nuts – he used every minute of it. He definitely took some form of pleasure out of going mad and being mad. It gave him licence to ill! He would strip off in the middle of the street after the pub, throw stuff out of the windows and say whatever he wanted to people. But most of the time he would be away in his room writing. He would play one chord for hours and just chant over the top of it, but I could listen to it for three hours. I don't know what he was doing, and I don't know why it was interesting, but he's a very musical guy.'

To say life was tumultuous would be an understatement. This motley crew of creative spirits was splintering. Though all were friends, they were following their own paths. Some wanted the big-time, while others were simply trying to hold their minds together. It was increasingly obvious what Kate wanted. She says: 'It's all very humbling now, coming back to Fife and Fence events as a black sheep after pop stardom. But I write very different music from them. It was becoming obvious early on that the stuff I was writing was a lot more mainstream.'

To further fuel her fire, members of The Beta Band turned up soon after they'd signed to EMI. She heard what would become their

'Champion Versions' EP and now says: 'They sounded like Beck, but they were from Fife! It was a really big deal for me. Kenny had been so anti-industry, but I thought: "Hang on a minute, they've signed a record deal and they sound really good. Maybe I should look further into this. It's doable."' Kate and Een went to London to play a gig and do some busking, and ended up helping John Maclean move house. When Kate saw his flat and all its artwork, she remembers: 'It all seemed really attractive to me. All this creativity in an urban environment; it was inspiring. I went to see them at the Electric Ballroom in Camden, and they were stunning that night. They had a record deal, they lived in nicer flats, and I thought: "Hmm, I need to embrace this!"'

As Kate's determination grew and her focus sharpened, things started unravelling with Een. She says now: 'We didn't have a huge amount in common. It was music that we shared and little else.' They were growing apart and she moved back to St Andrews. She started a relationship with Andy Cook, who was a massive music fan, latterly into Fence and then into electronica. He ran the wine merchants Luvians Bottle Shop and was in a band with Pete Rankin, who would later set up the seminal Old Jock Radio. She saw less of Een and his brothers and played lots of gigs at the West Port Bar and worked at the Bottle Shop, where as a teenager she had served in the ice-cream parlour. It was all a bit of a step back, and it was time for a change.

She formed a new band with a percussionist and programmer from Newburgh called Fenton Iddins. Along with Fenton's girlfriend Aline Hill (whose sister had gone out with James Yorkston), they lived in a quirky little house down a lane where they hosted many a mad party despite being strapped for cash. It was at this point that Kate started in earnest to make a go of it. She hit the phone and booked as many gigs as possible wherever and whenever, making constant trips to London. The group featured Kate, Fenton, Pete 'Uncle Beesly' Macleod and a cellist called Helen, and they were called Red Light Stylus. 'I was always terrible at naming bands,' she admits. Soon a drummer called Chris joined the ranks. Combining Kate's free-flowing melodies and acoustic guitar with Pete's syncopated bass, with live drums, turntable cuts and elements of electronica, it was fresher and more contemporary than her previous stuff but still lacked a propulsive edge. Fenton wasn't advanced enough at programming. 'I'd write an album's worth of material as he'd finish programming one tune. I knew I had to kibosh it and change my situation, and that went down really badly. He and Aline stopped speaking to me, and haven't done to this day. I probably didn't handle it well, but how do you tell someone you don't want to work with them? It's never easy.'

Having spent two years with Een, followed by a year or two in St Andrews, Kate felt the need to hit the bright lights of Edinburgh. Taking the Red Light Stylus name forward, she wangled an amazing flat on the Royal Mile and set out to connect with the city's music scene. They played venues such as the 369 Gallery, Medina and La Belle Angele, and soon realised there wasn't a coherent music scene in Edinburgh at all. 'Everywhere I went I was always looking for a music scene. I didn't find one at school, at university or in Edinburgh. At that time it was all indie-boy rock. Bands like Idlewild were popular, and I remember thinking it was going to be harder being a girl playing "nicer" music, but it didn't deter me.' She also saw corruption in the city's small venues. 'Paying to play is bullshit. It's disgusting that places were making money out of musicians with nothing.'

As at St Andrews, she felt the need to put on her own shows. One Hogmanay a friend suggested she go down to the Gilded Balloon in the Cowgate and knock on the door. She did just that and entered at 2 a.m. for a New Year's Day lock-in. High on Dutch courage, she chanced her arm and asked the owners and organisers if she could put on regular gigs. They said yes and she started the bi-weekly Acoustic Extravaganza night soon after. It's still going as Acoustic Edinburgh. Here was a little light at the end of the tunnel. The premise was simple: it was free to get in, but your fee was to be quiet. It worked, and it turned into a great spot for local singer-songwriters. Even Kenny came through from Fife a couple of times.

Another important character for Kate in Edinburgh was Bobby Heatlie from Coloursound rehearsal studios. On hearing her voice and songs he became her greatest cheer-leader so far. He put his money where his mouth was too, giving her unlimited rehearsal time and occasional recording time. Kate says: 'He was amazing! He gave me so much advice.

His dad had been a songwriter and had been diddled out of quite a lot of money. He said: "Get your publishing deal first and don't sign your record deal for money." He was right, too!' Today they're still great friends. Bobby loaned her money to make demos and is incredibly proud of her career. 'He couldn't have been more helpful, and I've finally been able to pay him back for all the years of money and support. There are whispers that I took the piss out of him, but I paid him back when I could. Anyway, I can't thank him enough.'

Another crucial supporter was Karen Koren, who ran the Gilded Balloon comedy and entertainments venue at the Edinburgh Festival Fringe. Impressed, she gave Kate and the band a paid gig every night for a month in August 2000. Although they were paid and had a guaranteed audience, those small-hours gigs took place at the notorious Bear Pit at the student union in Teviot Row. It was terrifying. Looking hesitantly back, Kate says: 'Cocaine started creeping in too. My drummer, Chris, was into it and I thought: "What a shame!" I was a drinker, but I didn't do anything else. I was hell-bent on getting somewhere with the music, and I didn't feel the need to get fucked up. I was taking things seriously.' After the Festival and the brutal, drunken audiences they'd performed to, she realised they'd have been better off playing covers, which was not why she had started. Disheartened, she broke up Red Light Stylus. 'Chris never spoke to me again, despite having once told me he preferred his other band. I was learning it was very difficult to stop working with people.'

Ever hungrier for success yet just as far away, Kate tried another tactic. 'Trying to get anywhere with my own stuff wasn't working, so I decided to try something different and hook up with someone else. I was getting into the Ninja Tune label at the time, and I loved Nightmares on Wax and DJ Shadow, among others.' AJ Nuttal, a local bad-boy producer and former rapper in Edinburgh hip-hop crew Zulu Syndicate, asked if she wanted to add some vocal lines to his backing tracks. He'd had some success with his Yush 2K label and the Blackanized project, putting Scottish urban music on the musical map. Kate recalls: 'It was a great time and a real education in music I knew little about. It started my love affair with electronica and really widened my musical horizons.' As well as studio sessions when Kate would write lyrics and melodies to AJ's beats, she started doing live nights with AJ at La Belle Angele, playing jazz/blues flute along to sequenced beats and breaks. The collaboration went nowhere, and the tracks they'd worked on sank without a trace. AJ tried to sue her for £90,000 worth of studio time a few years later, when Kate was a proper pop star. It didn't go to court. He also wanted fifty per cent of a publishing deal she'd just signed. Astonished, Kate says: 'I asked a friend, Lenny, who'd played keyboards for AJ, "Have you ever been paid?" He said no, and I told him I was being charged for his time. AJ charged me for a flautist . . . and it was me!'

Whether super-ambitious, pushy or ruthless, the young Tunstall could not be faulted for not trying new things. She threw herself into various projects and spread her talent far and wide. All the while she was sending her own songs out to publishers and record companies, then suddenly came an offer that would change the game and accelerate her down the road. On the table was a £12,000 publishing offer for everything that she'd written so far and would write in the near future. For a penniless musician it looked like a reasonable deal but, heeding old advice, she was wary. She phoned Simon Banks after his six years of constant pursuit. 'I said: "I think I might need your help here." He said "Give me six months – we won't sign anything and see what happens." In three months he had Sony, Chrysalis and Warners bidding for me as a writer and got me an amazing deal.'

Going with Sony, she moved to London soon after. 'I remember not wanting to do it all on my own, but you can't expect everyone else to be as passionate about your music. So you end up doing everything your-self.' Finally, at twenty-seven, Kate was edging towards the success she so desired.

After signing her publishing deal with Sony, Kate was persuaded to co-write with others. Having played music with so many people over the past twelve years, she was surprised she hadn't done it before. Companies possibly think two talents are better than one, but she says: 'From a cynical point of view, it's probably to gain some kind of control of your output.' At the outset she was teamed up with a producer and writer called Jimmy Hogarth. Originally from Orkney, he'd won a Grammy for a Suzanne Vega album and worked with James Blunt, Amy Winehouse, Paloma Faith and many more. He was seen as a go-to guy for new artists to achieve lift-off.

Later she was teamed with Martin Slattery, latterly frontman with The Hours, and a Glaswegian, Scott Shields, who had been the drummer in Scottish rockers Gun. As well as being writers, musicians and producers, they were in the Mescaleros, Joe Strummer's comeback vehicle, and were producing the Mescaleros' second album. Former Catatonia singer Cerys Matthews was around in the same studio too. Kate remembers: 'It was all very exciting, but I was on a mission. I wasn't wildly interested in anything but getting some good music down. I didn't feel part of it.'

Kate spent almost the next two years developing as a writer and an artist. Though frustrating at times, it did her a power of good. Many of the songs on her first album were written in that spell in London, with a handful from her Edinburgh and Fife years. With material coming thick and fast, she needed to make some demos. She hooked up with an Austrian bassist called Arnie Lindner and hit it off immediately. For a drummer she was introduced to Luke Bullen, soon to become her husband, who was playing with the Mescaleros. She recalls: 'With Luke, we'd played together for about a year. My relationship had gone down the pan and he was single. I'd had months of full-tilt hedonism. I was a little out of control, but I knew I couldn't do it for very long. It was just a bit mental. Then I got together with him, which was great – definitely worth jacking in getting wasted for. Our first date was on the anti-Iraq War march. It probably says quite a lot about our relationship. It's about doing stuff that actually means something to you, instead of frittering things away. However, just after we met, Joe Strummer died. It was traumatic. But if it hadn't happened, we probably wouldn't have played together and wouldn't have got married.'

The trio built up a solid friendship and musical bond, with Martin on occasional keys. She says: 'I still wasn't totally comfortable going out on my own and I wanted to be in a band. These guys were the people I wanted to play with.' Although not entirely comfortable about the business, she knew how important it was to be a writer. 'You can look great, you can get your tits out, and you can get pissed and end up in the paper . . . but you have to write songs!'

Manager Simon Banks was working his magic, and the publishing deal kept her afloat for the two years before she got a record deal. 'I couldn't get arrested,' she says. 'The Norah Jones effect had just happened and every label wanted a female singer-songwriter. A lot of labels said "We've got our girl and we don't need another one." I don't feel any bitterness, though. I was a female Scottish folk-singer and it doesn't shout "goer", does it?' Soon, however, the band started playing gigs, billed as 'Katie', drumming up interest in the songs, and Simon started getting her meetings and auditions at record companies. The first label they tried was Independiente. Arriving in an unnamed A & R man's office, she was asked to play three songs for this guy who 'loved Stevie Wonder' and was clearly off his face. He said: 'I want you to go home and write a song with just three chords in it.' He then went out to eat with Simon, and Kate wasn't invited. She found the experience humiliating, confirming what Kenny had said and what she'd felt when living in Fife. More auditions followed, slightly less traumatic but with the same results. Although the word was spreading, it became soul-destroying.

In a detour from standard procedure, a small major-label offshoot, Relentless Records, offered her a deal. The head of A & R, Shabs Jobanputra, a pioneer of the Asian club scene, had signed Nitin Sawh-ney and Outkast. Kate felt it wasn't the right label for her music, but she wasn't totally against the idea. They asked her to go on a Euro-pean tour with Oi Va Voi, a klezmer hip-hop band on their roster, to see what it was like being signed to the label. It was an amazing experi-ence. She raves: 'I knew nothing about Jewish culture and I learned so much. It was loads of fun.' She spent the best part of a year touring with them as a backing singer.

In November 2002 her luck began to change as US giants Atlantic and Columbia flew her to New York with a view to signing her up. She and Simon were put in a seriously upmarket hotel, and then she played on the twenty-fifth floor of the Atlantic Records building. Singer-song-writer Jewel was there and Phil Collins was in the room next door. She also saw a friend from Kent school, Amanda 'Mandi' Stein, who turned out to be Sire Records supremo Seymour Stein's daughter. She'd had no idea! But Atlantic were reluctant to sign her on the spot, and she and Simon were flown over again a week later by Columbia, who made an amazing offer almost immediately. It was going through when Columbia's head of A & R was fired and all bets were off.

Kate and Simon took the Relentless deal. 'I felt a bit shit, actually,' she says. 'Not because it was a bad deal. It just felt scary signing a record deal. I thought, what am I doing?' It was the right thing to do, but the wheels turned slowly. She recalls: 'I thought it was bam, bam, bam and out comes your record . . . but it took so long!' It took another year of writing and co-writing. Although she felt hassled, she wrote 'Suddenly I See' just before the sessions began, and 'Black Horse And The Cherry Tree' just after. Perhaps the pushing by the label had done some good. 'I was very glad to have had the two years in London before signing my record deal. But I still didn't have my sound.'

Her sound came from working with Steve Osbourne on *Eye To The Telescope*. Martin Moralis at Relentless suggested Steve, and Kate trusted him from the off. She says: 'Everyone up to that point had said: "Your guitar-playing is too crazy", but he was the first to say: "It's all about your guitar-playing and your right-hand."' The whole album was to be made on £15,000, even then a minuscule sum by major-label standards. They didn't go into a fancy studio either, having tried Peter Gabriel's Real World and not felt comfortable. They eventually went to Bradford-on-Avon's NAM studio. This was a house where a disabled ex-crew guy, who lived with his mum, had created a ramshackle studio with a lovely old analogue desk. For the sessions it was just Luke, Kate and Steve and they focused on the guitars and drums for what was on the whole an enjoyable experience. Having said that, Kate maintains: "I didn't enjoy doing the vocals. I didn't like singing in the studio. I couldn't really muster the self-expression that I get when I'm on stage.'

It sounds like a fairly homespun affair. As well as producing, Steve acted as the group chauffeur and on some nights housed Kate and Luke in his children's bunk beds. He put his heart and soul into the record, albeit with difficulties at times. Kate says: 'It was a difficult relationship. Steve's quite an eccentric guy and I'm an artist who wants control. But I like having a producer, and I still feel like I need the direction. We locked horns quite a bit about how much control each of us had. I'm so lazy, though. I'll record something and say it's great, whereas Steve will go: "No, no! We're spending three days getting that right," and that was good for me.' Although they'd recorded in a weird studio and stayed in a strange, haunted B & B, or often in Steve's kids' bedroom, they got the job done.

The process was tainted, however, by what happened after the album was recorded. Kate recounts: 'My boss at the company was a real control freak and I wasn't invited to my own mix. It got mixed without me. Just because it was taken away from me, I hated that mix. Nowadays I rarely listen to my own stuff, but when I do occasionally hear something, I'm always very pleasantly surprised.' She also insists: 'It started as a really raw, DIY, indie-sounding record, and the mix smoothed all that out. There's still edge and attitude in it, but it's not as it was. That was my first experience of a major label stepping in, I suppose.' In the long run it worked, because *Eye To The Telescope* became an enormous success. 'Yes, I learned another lesson. I realised how enjoyable it is when you've had a fucking massive hit record – I had the best time of my life.' But that was still to come. Two more life-changing experiences were to materialise first.

First she was asked to tour with the band Half Cousin, fronted by Orcadian Kevin Cormack. His wonky brand of Tom Waits-inspired junkyard indie was a thing of idiosyncratic beauty and he needed musicians to play live with him. Kate, Arnie and Luke volunteered and hit the road, supporting Manchester band The Earlies and US songwriter Micah P Hinson. Half Cousin's music was the antithesis of Kate's polished acoustic-pop, and in the touring group she ended up playing clarinet, keyboards and flute and banging a metal box with a hammer. She fondly recalls: 'It's one of the happiest musical memories of my life. I loved the music and loved not being the front-person. It wasn't about getting it perfectly right; it was about getting it to feel right. As a classical musician, it was massively liberating.' With sixteen people sharing a tour-bus for three weeks, everyone had a ball.

Second, halfway through the tour she received a call from her label company telling her to get back to London right away for a last-minute spot on BBC2's flagship music TV show *Later . . . With Jools Holland*. US rapper NAS had pulled out and the show was to be filmed the following night. It was too good an opportunity to miss, so she raced back to London the next day. Oddly, though, the label wanted her to perform a non-album song, 'Black Horse And The Cherry Tree', which had been written after the album had been mastered. 'Trust us,' Kate remembers them saying. 'But I screamed: "It's not on the album – you're mental!"'

She didn't have time to practise, but she had played it a lot, having performed a handful of Scottish shows at Bean Scene cafés earlier that year, and she knocked out the tune as part of the pre-recorded show. Also appearing was a stellar line-up of The Cure, Anita Baker, Jackson Brown and The Futureheads. After playing, she got drunk with Robert Smith of The Cure ('a total thrill!') and went back to the tour. 'I was over the moon to get the chance,' she says.

Kate not having told anyone what she did as a solo artist, the sixteen musicians on the Half Cousin tour were watching TV in York venue Fibbers after their gig that night when they saw her on *Later*. Everyone was astonished. Luke and her own bandmates knew she'd nailed it, while The Earlies said they didn't know she even played guitar. 'Even though it was recorded, I was convinced I was going to fuck up . . . and of course I didn't. But every time I watched it for months after, I got the same fear!'

This TV performance was Kate's breakthrough moment. Not everyone gets one, but she did and she shone. 'My parents phoned me up and said they danced around the living-room to it. It was the first time they could see that I was any good. They didn't listen to music, you see.' After sending her to tap and ballet classes, getting her piano and flute lessons and sending her to university to study music and theatre, they were still surprised she wanted to perform. Kate remembers her mum saying: 'You don't do that, The Beatles do that. You don't get to do what you love for a living, you get a job and use your spare time to do what you love.' Her mother had even sent her a job application for an airline cabin crew job at one point, and her father had said: 'You don't sound any different to anyone else on the radio.' This had made her even more determined, and now she was well on her way.

By the age of twenty-eight, she had been a songwriter for thirteen years, studied at university, signed on the dole and lived as a poor musician in Fife, Edinburgh and London. She wanted success so badly and finally it was about to happen. 'It totally surpassed anything that I thought was going to be possible. It was insane!'

6

Rocket DIY

King Creosote and the Start of Fence Records

In the spring of 1996, Kenny Anderson felt like a broken man. He moved back into his parents' house in St Andrews and took on a more permanent job at the Woollen Mill. He was cracking up and would often hear his mother and father discussing his mental state as he sat alone in his bedroom. 'I fantasised about driving my car into a tree at sixty miles an hour,' he admits today. 'It was awful. I was having thoughts I'd never had before. I confided in my parents, but they didn't know what to do. Eventually my mum said: "You need to get some help. We can't help you."' The eldest son, he felt he had to cope with everything and get on with things, but was finding life extremely hard to deal with. He would burst into tears as he returned home from work, and the slightest problem would send him over the edge. He couldn't take any stress or criticism, and his old mate Stevie Paul would regularly clock him out and send him home. His mother worried incessantly, but Kenny couldn't reason with her or with himself. Not only was Gordon having serious mental health problems, but the older, 'more sensible' brother was in a similar boat. Strangest of all, he put down his guitar and accordion and refused to play. He stepped away from music for months. He did nothing.

At last he visited his GP, Dr Clark, who happened to be a Skuobhie Dubh Orchestra fan, and blurted it all out – every worry, every issue, every problem eating away at him. Immediately the doctor said: 'Why are you thinking about all these other people? They're all fine. They're not in here. You have to start enjoying yourself.' Kenny was prescribed a small dose of a new anti-depressant, Seroxat, for the coming year. He had to start with a quarter of a pill and slowly increase the dose until he was taking the full amount. His appointments with the doctor would be weekly at first, decreasing to monthly. In the meantime he was instructed to take the next week off work and go to Turkey with his parents. And that was that: at the grand old age of twenty-nine, Kenny went on holiday with his folks and had a good time.

On his return, at his mother's behest, Kenny moved into a new cottage on the outskirts of St Andrews with Gordon, just released from Stratheden Hospital. It would be good for them to live together and help each other make sense of the world and their own troubles, she thought. Gordon had been living a parallel nightmare far worse than his older brother's. 'In hindsight, I should have been a man about it and helped out my folks,' Kenny considers now when looking back to May 1996 and thinking about Gordon's hell on earth. 'It was like "Let's put the crying one together with the holy one, Gordon, and see what happens." But I had an amazing summer with Gordon in that cottage. Talk about a hoot!' The cottage was on the Brigton estate, well out of the way. It was well restored and in very good condition. The first thing they did was to invite two girls to live with them for a week, and then they bought two kittens. Rather than a calm and collected time together, it quickly turned into a summer of parties and wild abandon.

It was the last hurrah for The Skuobhie Dubh Orchestra. Ever the stickler for honouring engagements, Kenny had committed himself, the remains of the band, and the young Kate Tunstall, freshly returned from university in London, to play two sets at the T in the Park festival. Then in its third year, it was still based at its original home of Strathclyde Park. My new band, Huckleberry, with James 'Yorkston' Wright, also played. I hooked up with Kenny, Gordon and Pete 'Uncle Beesly' Macleod over the weekend. They came to see us perform at the PRS tent (now the T Break tent), and we returned the favour, watching them thrash through those classic bluegrass numbers in the Comedy/Ceilidh tent. It was almost an out-of-body experience simply to stand in the audience and enjoy the show.

Much hilarity and chaos ensued for the Anderson brothers at the festival. In a story legendary among the inner circle of Fence friends, Kenny and Gordon stumbled across a bag of misshapen, multi-coloured hand-made pills while watching Beth Orton. They looked at each other and gobbled a handful each. At first nothing happened. An hour or so later, in the crowd for the Cocteau Twins . . . *bam!* The full effects took hold and the next twenty-four hours were a random, psychedelic blur. The brothers found themselves swimming in the Clyde, and Kenny awoke the next day wearing boots but no socks. He had also managed to get a cross branded on his head; Gordon, of course, read far too much into this. That bag of pills lasted them the rest of the summer. They had no idea what was in there, but Kenny assumes it was a combination of home-made ecstasy, amphetamines and God knows what else. Every time you took one it was Russian roulette. They counted forty-four in the stash after T in the Park, and energised a couple of great weekends. Kenny maintains that he 'never had a bad experience'.

Under doctor's orders to enjoy himself, Kenny duly spent the rest of the year drinking to excess and befriending and dancing with complete strangers, regularly walking home to the Brigton cottage in a stupor. It might sound like a man losing his marbles and making a cry for help, but it was lots of fun, precisely what he needed to do in order to break from the past ten years of hard slog and little reward. He joined a comedy funk band called Nat's Chuff, which played student balls and parties around St Andrews and misbehaved at every opportunity. He ended the year playing Orkney in a ceilidh band with friends including Stew Ross. The months from May 1996 to January 1997 were like a breath of fresh air, and although he was at his lowest ebb he reminisces fondly about them now.

Due to the Seroxat, he was celibate too. He would befriend girls but never take it any further. This intrigued interested female parties, but frustrated them as he staggered off on his own at the end of the night. Most importantly, although his sex drive had been diminished by the anti-depressants, he began to play and compose again. As momentum built and his mood became more positive, it turned into a very productive time. Songs of Kenny's written in 1996 include 'Meantime', 'Counselling', 'Visiting Hours', 'Outback Self-Abuse', 'You Are, Could I', 'Casino Clubbing', 'Little Death', 'Advice', 'Eggshell Revenge' (a break-up riposte to 'Eggshell Miles'), 'Nooks', 'Space In Jerusalem' (about Gordon) and 'Russian Sailor's Shirts', among others. Most of these would later appear on self-released King Creosote albums on Fence, and some made it on to larger-scale releases by Domino and 679, such as *Kenny and Beth's Musikal Boat Rides* and *KC Rules OK*, almost ten years later. It's amazing to see how far back many of Kenny's songs date. In his song diaries and lyric books, all of which he still has, Kenny also notes that he helped write two of Gordon's songs, 'Summertime Beeswing' and 'Let It Come' in 1996 too. Many of these songs are still Fence classics.

During the summer and autumn, Gordon travelled to and from London when health allowed, demoing and contributing to the songs that would become The Beta Band's first EP, 'Champion Versions'. Back in Fife the two brothers would play four-track recordings to each other, inspiring each other's creativity. When Kenny heard the first five songs sent by Gordon from London on a cassette labelled 'you might like it a little', he was blown away. These were the songs that kick-started The Beta Band's career. It can't be overstated how important this period was to Kenny. The Beta Band was like a beacon of hope. Without compromise, they had expressed themselves without pretension and made the music they enjoyed with no recognition of fashion or fads. Moreover, they soon signed a deal, insisting on complete artistic control.

Kenny was realising that there was no set way of making music and getting it out to the world. He saw there was no justice in the world either. Here was a guy who had done everything by the book, worked hard, written prolifically and surrounded himself with great musicians. Nothing had happened for him, while a haphazard group of chancers had recorded five songs on a four-track and the demo had gone straight to the head of A & R at EMI/Parlophone. Kenny now insists: 'You can try as hard as you like and go absolutely nowhere. You might as well do what the hell you like. It took me a year in the doldrums to realise that. Going into 1997, that basically became the Fence manifesto.'

𝄞

Looking back on his time in the Brigton cottage with Gordon, Kenny believes it was one of the best years of his life. Whether it was the anti-depressant drugs or the freedom to do what he liked without pressure from band members and employers, he did as Dr Clark had ordered, relaxed and enjoyed himself again. He loved the house and its spirit and had rediscovered his creative mojo. Gordon was around, often acting as a stimulus or a hindrance to his writing. Either way, it was inspiring. Gordon would disappear to London, then return, then live at his parents' for a night or two, then return, then go back to London . . . Gordon was wild and restless. Somehow, however, Kenny had taken stock of his own situation and was back on the road to recovery.

He felt he'd dedicated too much of himself to 'doing the right thing' concerning music, bandmates and his approach to the business. Around his thirtieth birthday, in 1997, he looked back on a decade of toilet gigs, albums that disappeared without a trace, and playing with talented bands that imploded. He tried to analyse what he should do next. He soul-searched and recognised that the key lay in self-fulfilment. If he enjoyed writing songs, recording them and occasionally playing them live, he should continue to do exactly that, but under his own steam and only if he wanted to. It would make his life as legitimate as those of school friends who were now professionals and entrepreneurs, even if no one liked his music. It was time to zone in on what made him happy. After playing a festival on the banks of Loch Laggan, he had conversed with a guy who had advised him to flip all his negativity into positivity and fully apprehend that he was an extremely talented thirty-year-old who still made music, with initiative and determination to continue while most others had given up. It was what he needed to hear, because it was what he already knew. On the journey back to Fife, he made the decision to focus on the thing he liked best: recording.

He bought a new eight-track machine in 1997, and a CD burner, some microphones and other equipment in 1998, and began to put his ideas down. A few close friends and confidants supported and encouraged him. MC Quake in the US was one of them. As a fan, especially of Khartoum Heroes, he pushed Kenny to do more of his own thing and stray down any musical path he fancied. Kenny also decided that if he was going to play gigs, it would be in St Andrews. If anyone outside town showed any interest, he'd gladly talk about the music, or play, but only on his terms.

His aim was to start a new label and record albums whenever he wanted. It would primarily be a vehicle for him to catalogue his own music. The new imprint was given a name, Fence. The premise was simple. Kenny, now King Creosote, recorded material, compiled it on CD albums, duplicated them one by one and distributed them locally, by hand, to anyone who was interested. He'd been using the pseudonym in private since around 1994 for his own recording purposes during the

Skuobhie Dubh and Khartoum Heroes days. Kenny says: 'I think it's essential for someone who is shy, and for someone who's always hidden in a band. I had "Fence", and creosote on the fence seemed to fit. I liked the "King" label as setting myself up high, and the combination with creosote, this foul substance – it's actually banned now. I wrote it down and it looked like King Crimson, Kid Creole, King Creole, and even had associations with the Kingdom of Fife . . . but then I got used to it.'

He approached the CD Outlet shop in St Andrews and asked if they would stock his new titles. They said yes. The staff had been fans of The Skuobhie Dubh Orchestra and loved Kenny's new alter ego. When he released the first album, *Inner Crail to Outer Space*, they played it incessantly in the shop, selling copies every time it was aired. Every batch he gave them they played in the shop, selling out before the album ended – and that was the start. That was FNC01, the first official Fence release. Anyone who has a copy should treasure it. Inadvertently, I became a Radio 1 DJ in 1999, promoting new music across genres. I'd remained friends with Kenny and investigated his new music and the whole Fence ethos. I'm proud to say I played 'Dressing Up As Girls' from *Inner Crail to Outer Space* on one of my shows, giving KC his first national airplay.

Things took shape rapidly. Een and Kate Tunstall had split up and he was reeling in the aftermath. He came to Kenny with a solo album, asking him to put it out on Fence. Gordon handed in a ton of demos and self-recorded odysseys, saying 'Release what you like.' By 1998 there was a micro-indie releasing material by the brothers, including *Travelling Country Crops* by Pip Dylan (Een) and *Moses* and *28 Secret Tracks* by Lone Pigeon, as well as a large catalogue of King Creosote albums.

Remember, there was no distribution other than Kenny handing the occasional box of CDs to a few local shops. There was hardly a huge audience for the music either. All the CDs were burned one by one, the artwork done individually by hand. This was the true definition of a cottage industry (they all lived in cottages, after all) and barely covered the cost of blank discs, cardboard, Sellotape, crayons, photocopying etc. That wasn't the point; the point was to do your own thing and to have fun doing it. But person by person, CD by CD, people were starting to take notice. It was hardly a rollercoaster ride to superstardom, but things were starting to move forward and Kenny was taking some encouragement from the process. There was a feeling of vindication, but far more importantly, he was enjoying himself again.

Kenny stresses that 'King Creosote is not a band. I didn't want a band again. I'd made an arse of it so many times before, so now I was a singer-songwriter and that's it. If people want to play with me, brilliant, but I'm not their leader or their chief or their provider.' The mysterious name began a trend within what would become the Fence Collective. Almost everyone would have a pseudonym, whether they liked it or not. Kenny says: 'I thought it was important to have this alter ego that could be whatever you wanted it be.' This arrived hand in hand with the rise of the internet, where people have online aliases anyway. It also brought intrigue to what they were doing. Who was King Creosote? Pip Dylan? Lone Pigeon? Looking back at it now, people were perhaps drawn to these strange names alone. Here was an unlikely bunch of new superheroes whose music you could explore away from the glare of the media. Just as punks had exotic names like Johnny Rotten, Sid Vicious or Captain Sensible, now these masked musicians were unveiling their wares to an unsuspecting public. Kenny says: 'None of us wanted our photos online or on artwork. The music has to stand for itself – it doesn't matter who we are and what we think.'

One could see Fence as continuing the homespun cut-and-paste philosophy that The Beta Band had begun to inspire. There seems a united ethos to the collective, the songs and the artwork that is perhaps rooted in The Beta Band's psychedelic collage world. Fence mixes up electronics and guitars, acoustic instruments, hip-hop beats, electronica and samples, continuing the 'anything goes' ethos of The Beta Band. 'I saw The Beta Band as a green light for whatever I wanted to do,' Kenny recalls. 'But I was still very much of the Skuobhie Dubh ilk. I still had the same rhythms on guitar and accordion.' Though inspired by the aesthetics and feel of the Betas, the brothers' music was very different. Kenny was on his own path that had started with the Dubhs and the Heroes, singing in his own accent and incorporating folk and traditional elements. Een had devised a new world as Pip Dylan, singing in a Deep South accent and recording rootsy Americana on solely acoustic instruments, developing a gypsy-troubadour persona. Gordon, with his ever-growing Beatles, Neil Young and Beach Boys obsessions, was the most obviously enamoured of pop culture and the classic lineage of rock 'n' roll. The brothers all had music flowing from them, and their characters complemented each other. This added an extra level of fascination. Soon people were talking about the Anderson brothers in the same breath when referring to Fence and music from St Andrews.

Basic living and day-to-day reality were looking up for Kenny. Throughout 1997 he was working at the Woollen Mill and playing for money with his ceilidh band, and Fence was up and running. Mentally, he was doing far better; financially, he was out of the doldrums and earning enough to get a mortgage and buy a little house in Crail, underneath the flat in which his grandmother lived. He set to work doing up his new digs and driving his father's cast-off cars. It dawned on him that he wasn't in any rush. The world didn't end at thirty and people weren't laughing at him in the street. He relaxed.

As the 1990s drew to a close Kenny's life was more settled. He met Lindsay, who became the mother of his daughter, Beth, and in 1998 he started working part-time in the CD Outlet as well as at the Woollen Mill. Fence was less a label, more a hobby. It occupied a corner of the room, with a handful of blank CDs, piles of cardboard, glue and photocopied sheets of artwork. His microscopic DIY sideline ticked over whenever he or his brothers decided to record something new. Until now it had been a recording project and Fence had yet to mount a stage. That was to change.

At the invitation of Malcolm and Barbara Ritchie, the owners of a small pub in St Andrews called Aikman's, Een and Kenny played at the twenty-first birthday of one of their daughters. It wasn't just a knees-up, but a fuss-free, relaxed space to play music in with no overheads or pressure. It had taken place on a Wednesday night and everyone had enjoyed it. Two weeks later they decided to do it again, without the excuse of a birthday. Kenny secured a fortnightly residency, ensuring it would bring in punters to drink the craft beers and keep the place busy on a weekday night.

Every second Wednesday for the next couple of years, they would put on a unique live event that gained a reputation as St Andrews' best live music night. With Kenny as the instigator, Een as his accomplice and Gordon occasionally joining the throng, more of the usual suspects were drawn to the party. Pete 'Uncle Beesly' Macleod would show up with his bass. Andy 'Captain Geeko' Robinson had returned to St

Andrews and would arrive with a djembe or other percussive knick-knack to rattle, and other singer-songwriters and musicians began to muster. Jason Kavanagh, who worked at the CD Outlet, would inject a further element of experimentalism by playing percussion or tape loops. The gigs took on an air of chaotic invention and unbridled lack of inhibition as costumes and comedy sketches were added. They had free rein to do what the hell they wanted.

As the Wednesdays grew in stature and in number of performers, they mutated into the Sunday Socials, all-day events where anything was possible. If you attended one of those now legendary shows, you could watch a heartbreaking solo lament in front of a silenced room one minute, and then the Anderson brothers and friends would be dressed as women, chattering away in falsetto like a surrealist Monty Python sketch. One memorable night had Kenny, Jason, Een and new friend Alan 'Gummi Bako' Stewart performing the whole event as caricatures of their own dads, calling themselves The Four Daveys. Humour, musicianship, art and play-acting all began to fuse into one. Locals loved it, and fans from the nearby village of Anstruther, quickly dubbed the Ainster Heroes, would come along. There was now a specific focus for Fence and its friends to gather around and impress or depress each other. New recordings were sold, new songs were tried out and endless collaborations began to take place, further shaping the attitude and philosophy of Fence.

In 1999 the news came that the St Andrews Woollen Mill was to shut down. Not only was it a local institution, it employed a fair number of people, including Kenny Anderson. Suddenly redundant, he went to work full-time at CD Outlet with Jason Kavanagh. There was change in the air, and Kenny felt a palpable sense of excitement as he slowly overcame his demons. The new millennium was approaching, and there really was a feeling that a new set of circumstances was about to unfold. Kenny says: 'It was the start of a brand new everything. Sometimes you need that artificial new start, like at the beginning of a new year. But I suppose it was that I felt like I was shrugging off the 1990s.'

Kenny and Jason took a leap into the unknown and a serious gamble. In May 2000 they took over the CD Outlet lease and re-opened the shop as Fence. Never one to walk the easy route, Kenny was taking on the day-to-day running of a business. However, using his mathematical skills from school and university, combined with those of balancing the books in a band, he felt equipped to deal with the challenge. As Jason and he had worked behind the scenes in the shop for years, they knew the distributors by name and the way a record shop worked. Surely they could make a go of it?

Along with a £10,000 loan from the bank, Kenny invested his savings into it, using his redundancy money from the Woollen Mill. With a three-year term on the loan, they did the sums and went ahead. Immediately a set of carved wooden letters adorned the shop's awning with the immortal FENCE. I went to Fife to visit Kenny not long after he'd opened the shop, and was hugely impressed. I thought he'd cracked it. Now he had a base, an income and an umbrella brand under which he could slowly spread the word about his and other people's music.

With a shop and a label at Kenny's fingertips, the future looked brighter by the second. Within a month a girl walked in and offered to make them a website. They wondered what on earth that was. She said it was the way of the future and a way of selling music by mail. As a fan of The Skuobhie Dubh Orchestra, she promised to do it for nothing. These were the early days of the internet and the majority still viewed it with suspicion, but the Fence website looked odd and strangely appealing. Although Kenny is extremely wary of the internet today, it's difficult to undervalue its importance in Fence's early days.

As rumours spread, Beta Band fans began to follow the path back to Fife and St Andrews in particular. With reference to Gordon, the question: 'Who's this fifth Beta Band guy?' hung in the air. When the inquisitive discovered Lone Pigeon albums, they were further intrigued. When they found his brothers' records, and those of a host of other characters with bizarre pseudonyms, they were hooked. Among those early investigators were Stu 'Arab' Paterson, Rich Amino and Adam Ogilvie. Stu would text and email my Radio 1 shows, requesting tracks by artists such as Orange Can and Simian. I deduced he was a Beta Band fan and wanted music that reminded him of them. Eventually he became a Fence aficionado and still is one today. Rich Amino became a Fence Collective member after sending his Amino People music to Kenny for release on the burgeoning label. The interest of people from London and further afield phoning up the shop and ordering music gradually became that of a growing fan base. There was a community of like-minded, DIY music enthusiasts who wanted something that mainstream pop culture wasn't offering.

Local musicians were soon drawn to the shop and the live spectacles at Aikman's. Jason started writing and performing as Billy Pilgrim, and Johnny Lynch was calling himself Pictish Trail. A young local band called The Jose, who had walked into the shop and made friends, were on board as well. Soon a sonically polarised but mutually admiring group of eccentrics had assembled around Kenny and his hare-brained musical whims, calling themselves the St Andrews Citizens. (*The Citizen* is the name of the St Andrews local paper and bookshop.) Although not yet called the Fence Collective, this could well have been the first Fence band. Alongside Kenny were Billy Pilgrim, Gummi Bako, the Bosnians Dragan and Boyan, Alan 'Cheehee' Reid of local shockabilly band Bone Daddy, and skinhead David 'Wearie' Waters. Basically, anyone who befriended Kenny and his merry men could be in the band.

Striking a chord with open-minded and fun-loving students and locals, the Citizens and the regular nights at Aikman's, and now at the West Port Bar, grew apace. The nights were often themed. Ideas included fancy dress, puppet shows, board games and Scalextric layouts. These were anarchic evenings devised solely for the fun of those performing, taking part and watching. With no concept of making large sums of money, the posters were almost like anti-advertisements, with cryptic pieces of photocopied art. 'One year we had the year of February,' Kenny recalls. 'I thought "February's too short", so all the gigs had February dates on them. It went up to the eighty-somethingth of February towards the end of the year.'

The stunts and themes got more outrageous with every show. They'd invite the audience to bring the vinyl they hated and smash it on the dancefloor, pass instruments around the crowd and pretend to record them for an album, and notoriously had random girls from the crowd cut the seats out of the musicians' jeans while they played. The nights gathered huge momentum and audiences expanded, even attracting Steve Mason and John Maclean to have a look and a laugh when they were back home between Beta Band duties. Rising local indie stars Dogs

Die in Hot Cars would turn up and ask to be involved. It was the talk of the town, and it was here that the Fence Collective ethos developed and the concept of collaboration and community took shape.

As the Fence label, shop and collective had grown so naturally, it seemed impulsive and pure. This attitude attracted others who had been burned by the business and wanted something more real and untainted. Enter a jaded James 'Yorkston' Wright. Returning frequently from Edinburgh to visit family and friends, he'd heard of the gatherings at Aikman's and decided to take a look. Having quit Huckleberry and embarked on solo acoustic songwriting, he found these nights the perfect platform to try out new songs and indulge his growing love of acoustic instruments. He'd turn up with a mandolin, bass or guitar and join in. He vaguely knew Kenny from Skuobhie Dubh days and even Madras College. He embraced the chaos and loved the unruly jam sessions. Having been tied into the garage/punk/pop rigidity of Huckleberry, he wanted something more freewheeling. He found it in Fife and started to forge a friendship with Kenny and his brothers. There was no pressure to play perfectly, and if you forgot the words or the harmonies it was instantly forgiven and laughed off.

James decided to go for one more push and give his own music another go, and his songs would be the first to attract serious interest from London and the behemoth music business they'd all but forsaken. Soon his J Wright Presents project was turning heads, thanks to some John Peel radio play and occasional gigs down south. A micro-indie label, Bad Jazz, run by an enthusiast called Joff Gladwell, had taken a leap of faith and released a single, 'Moving Up Country (Roaring The Gospel)', as mentioned earlier. The deal was that Joff pressed five hundred singles and the artist got thirty to forty per cent of the stock to sell at gigs and online. It was nowhere near enough to earn a living, but it was acknowledgement of the artistry in the songs and a way to achieve some small notoriety. Interviewed about his heritage and inspiration, increasingly James mentioned this mythical new group of troubadours under the banner of Fence. When he needed a band, members of the collective, including Kenny, would accompany him at gigs, and when he wanted to showcase talented friends to his London contacts, he pointed them towards King Creosote, Pip Dylan and Lone Pigeon. His next single, 'St Patrick', was shared, one side apiece, with Lone Pigeon.

Soon the cat got out of the bag as London labels and publishers took heed and investigated further. Bad Jazz flew the flag for King Creosote and released 'So Forlorn' on 7-inch vinyl. It showed the London scenesters that there were untapped riches in this rural backwater. Who were these talented, psychedelic eccentrics living in this remote part of Scotland? Not only was the music outstanding, but the story was fascinating too. People wanted a piece of the action. Lone Pigeon's superb 'Touched by Tomoko' 7-inch EP followed shortly, and soon Domino came sniffing alongside 4AD, Mute and Chrysalis. As documented before, James famously tied his colours to the Domino flag and is still there to this day. Laurence Bell, head of Domino, recalls: 'He told me about the Fence scene, and that he was from a little village up in Fife near St Andrews. He told me about the shop and a great little scene up there that was putting out music on CD and writing brilliant songs. I said I'd love to hear some of it. I'd heard a little whisper or read somewhere about Lone Pigeon and I was very intrigued by that, but I hadn't heard any music. I wanted to know more.'

James's early support for Kenny, Een and Gordon should not be underestimated. Aside from a handful of local supporters including myself, he put the first spotlight on Fence and they owe a lot to his patronage. His career was on the up and he wanted to bring a few friends along. Laurence continues: 'It was a time when I was a bit disillusioned with everything in terms of running the label. It was a very difficult time financially and a period of transition for the label, and I wasn't enjoying it. I was so energised to discover all these people just doing something on their own, it seemed without any knowledge of the music industry. It was so pure, and it struck an enormous chord in me. London can be very depressing, with people chasing what's going to be successful. So when you find something going on without any concern for all that stuff, it strikes you on quite a deep level.'

In 2001 the Fence shop threw a party for its first anniversary. More elaborate than anything they'd done before yet just as home-grown, the concert took place in the Cosmos Centre. The converted sports hall was awash with oil projections, lava lamps and home-made decorations.

King Creosote, Lone Pigeon, James Yorkston (as he was now known), Billy Pilgrim, The Jose and Gummi Bako played to a mainly local gang of supporters, customers, fellow musicians and friends. Laurence Bell from Domino came up to be there too.

This was a big deal for the collective, vindication for having built something up away from the big cities and established scenes. Domino hadn't yet signed Franz Ferdinand or Arctic Monkeys and weren't as muscular or as financially liquid as they are now, but they were loved and respected amongst leftfield music fans and media. If a new Domino release arrived in my pigeonhole at work, it would get special attention. For Fence, a label like this could be extremely helpful. Laurence got firmly stuck into the evening and enjoyed the boozy Fife hospitality. I remember sitting next to him by a bonfire on the East Sands at an after-show get-together. Instruments were swapped and songs sung as the warm, flat beer flowed. When Gordon 'Lone Pigeon' Anderson picked up his favourite acoustic guitar and asked who would like to hear 'the greatest song ever written', we all hollered in affirmation. He then smashed the guitar into a thousand pieces and tossed it onto the fire. We were all appalled and sat in silence . . . before breaking into hysterical laughter.

Laurence recalls: 'We all ended up on the beach for a party afterwards and a fire was built. The Lone Pigeon appeared. He was supposed to have played in the hall earlier, but didn't, so there was a rumour he might play as we sat around the bonfire. When the moment came for him to play, he put the guitar on the fire! It was painted in bright psychedelic colours and went up in flames very quickly. It was like this profound moment at 2 a.m. It was pretty mind-blowing, actually. But we got over this and the party carried on. I had a fantastic time, and I got a sense of evangelism for what I'd seen. I was running around telling everyone about this amazing thing that was going on up there.' It wouldn't be long before a more solid relationship between the two labels would be founded.

You probably think all this sounds fast-moving, but things often move slowly within the music business, independent or otherwise. Musicians need some kind of momentum or they can lose confidence and hope, and that black cloud was never too far away. As links were being forged between Fence, its key artists and the industry at large, all was not hunky-dory at the shop, where Kenny and Jason soon drifted into stormy waters. Problems were arising that were outside their control. The local rates were hiked sky-high as Prince William came to study at St Andrews. Discount CD and vinyl store Fopp in Dundee and the local Tesco supermarket were selling chart albums and singles cheaper. Illegal downloading had arrived and CD copying was rife. It was commonplace for student customers to buy blank CDs and covers, then invest in one original CD title and copy it. Kenny now estimates that there were fifteen or sixteen copies made per album sold. They looked at the books and realised they were losing around £1,000 a month. It seemed that the shop could have paid one person a fairly bad wage at a push, but not two. It wasn't looking good.

Finally the worst of all situations developed. As the shop slipped further into financial woe, Jason Kavanagh bailed out forever. He met a girl and left town, insisting that he wasn't well and had to move to Glasgow for health reasons. Whatever the reason, he left Kenny with an enormous debt and personal overdraft. Kenny had no option but to shut up shop. There were twenty-one months left on their bank loan and roughly £6,000 to repay. Kenny had to shoulder the whole burden on his own when Jason vanished, never to be seen or heard from again.

Unbelievably, Kenny managed. For two years he lived hand-to-mouth. His savings had been tied up in the business and now he was penniless. Somehow he survived. He'd sold everything of his own that he possibly could, including his car. Whenever he got a bill, a random customer or friend would come into the shop and offer to buy the racks, which would pay off another small debt. An insurance policy his dad had taken out for him twenty-five years earlier matured, paying him £1,000. It was tough, but he kept going until the loan was paid off in 2003.

King Creosote's 'So Forlorn' had come out on Bad Jazz, and, as Kenny recalls, 'There was always a light at the end of the tunnel.' Things were moving forward, and so far all on Kenny's terms. Joff had started a label called Sketchbook and wanted to sign King Creosote immediately. With the help of some industry insiders, Kenny looked at the contract and said no. Mute (with Joff Gladwell in a new job at the company) then tried to sign Fence publishing, while 4AD and Chrysalis hovered around the edges, offering small amounts of money. It seemed that everyone wanted to sign the Anderson brothers' publishing. It was tempting: surely a little money and some distribution and marketing was better than nothing? Then Laurence Bell stepped in and said: 'Why are you signing with anybody? Your strength is in staying independent and staying together as a collective.'

Domino were now genuinely interested. They saw the talent on tap in Fife and wanted to associate themselves with it. As an eclectic label and champions of new, leftfield music, they felt some affinity with the collective and possibly saw some of their younger selves in Fence. Laurence offered to funnel Fence releases through the larger company and distribute their albums. A percentage would come back and Fence would stay in control of the rights. Laurence recalls: 'It wasn't very complicated. I was getting more into what they were doing. I was getting to know Kenny quite well and I just wanted to help them. I didn't want to sign everyone on Fence. There are only so many people Domino should be signing, and I didn't want the whole roster anyway. I suggested this joint venture where we paid for it and did what we did with proper distribution, press etc. It started to spread the Fence identity, and the more people who knew about Fence the more people would buy into it. We did a deal on a napkin and that was that.'

As pressure mounted, Kenny looked at James's growing profile and budding solo career and went with Laurence. He says: 'It was because he was keen on keeping the collective as it was, and not messing with what we already had. I signed a small publishing deal with Domino, which gave me a little bit of money for myself and Een. It helped pay for what would become *Kenny And Beth's Musikal Boat Rides* and Pip Dylan's *Of The Things I Can Eat I'm Always Pleased With A Piece of Cheese* albums.' Laurence adds: 'People would say "You should hear them sing together!" When I finally did, I almost fainted. It was such an angelic, glorious bunch of harmonies. They're all unique characters and utterly fascinating. I saw an amazing spirit that I loved. It was outside everything, and I just wanted to help them and be part of it.'

But it was Lone Pigeon that Domino really wanted. Of the three brothers, Laurence liked Gordon's music best, finding comparisons with 1960s pop outsiders like Brian Wilson, Syd Barrett and Roky Erickson. Gordon's music was steeped in nostalgia, with a poignancy and hopefulness that touched hearts. His Bad Jazz singles had been well received, alerting the London industry and intriguing Beta Band fans. Laurence wanted to release a Lone Pigeon album. Kenny still maintains that Laurence wasn't a big King Creosote fan (although he's now on his label) and was more interested in the collective idea, needing access to Gordon's material. Nevertheless, the history between Fence and Domino is tight and trusting, if a little fraught. Starting with James Yorkston and then going deeper into the works of the Anderson brothers, Domino began a relationship with Fence that was mutually beneficial but of crucial importance to Fence. Kenny, Een and Gordon didn't sign to Domino, but they received financial and logistical help. 'I remember Laurence turned to me and said "What do you want?",' Kenny recalls, 'and I said "I don't actually know . . . " Even though Mute, 4AD and others had offers on the table, we went with Laurence.'

Domino were also starting to circle a young Edinburgh-based song-writer called Tom Beauchop, originally from the Crook of Devon in Kinross. His UNPOC (United Nations Peacekeepers of Cool, or Unable to Navigate Properly on Course) guise was another 1960s-influenced, lo-fi, bedroom-recording project with a pop classicism that appealed to Laurence. His big influences were The Beach Boys, The Velvet Underground, epic pop and modern indie-rock. I had shared a flat with Tom for years and heard the songs at their birth, and when he became involved with Domino, through James Yorkston's patronage, it seemed like his natural home. Here was another secretive character whose connection to Fence would reinforce the Fence/Domino bond. His soon-to-be-released album *Fifth Column* was another helping hand to the collective.

This was when the world started to become aware of Fence. Kenny was working hard as a live act on the Three for the Road package tour with Aidan Smith and The Hokum Clones as well as solo gigs and Fence events. The newest compilation, *Fence Sampler 3*, was released to inde-pendent record shops within a small radius of St Andrews and a network of like-minded shops in Edinburgh, Glasgow, Leeds, Manchester and London.

Through Domino, Fence negotiated a small distribution deal through Vital and soon released new compilations *Let's Get This Ship On The Road* and *Fence Reunited*. Possibly the most adventurous and collective-minded albums so far, they saw an array of Fence artists remix and collaborate on each other's material. These were Kenny's brainchildren, with new members reworking songs they wouldn't have had access to otherwise. Names like UNPOC, HMS Ginafore, Onthefly, Pinkie Maclure and John Wills (former drummer of Loop and The Hair and Skin Trading Company), Reporter, Deaf Mutes (featuring myself and ex-Huckleberry organist and current Athlete Reuben Taylor), Amino People, Immigrant and Gummi Bako, as well as the Anderson brothers, were now exposed to a small but inquisitive fan base. Everyone brought a unique flavour to the collective and conveyed their own vision to the DIY aesthetic, and there was nothing like it in Fife – or anywhere else, for that matter.

Sporadically and unconventionally, Fence was making a name for itself with every new release. Outwith official CD albums in hard cases, distributed nationally by Vital, the cottage industry was growing apace behind the scenes. 'In the early days of Fence,' Kenny recalls, 'the whole idea was to dissuade people from coming to us as a label. We weren't a proper record label, so don't come to us thinking we're going to do this, that or the other. But that's what sold us as the label for them! The selling point was not doing it like everyone else. That's what attracted everybody.'

Short runs of hand-made mini-albums were knocked out in Kenny's house under the rubric of Picket Fence, with artists across Fife, Scotland and further-flung parts submitting their newest recordings. These albums would be burned one by one on Kenny's CD duplicator and placed in heavy brown card sleeves with individual catalogue numbers and hand-drawn artwork. These have become collector's items, though occasional re-pressings are still made when time and demand allow. Almost all of the names above, including James Yorkston and the Athletes and UNPOC, recorded and released Picket Fence CDs, made up of material that wouldn't always make a full-scale release on another label or through Fence/Domino. That's not to say these are lesser pieces of work. Far from it: in many ways, these extraordinary recordings are the true essence of what Fence is about. Another stroke of genius was to do individual samplers for record shops that people couldn't buy from the Fence site. This set up an exclusivity that appealed to the mind of the collector.

Fans across the country were cottoning on to the collective and lapping up these limited-edition albums, bolstering Fence's coffers, confidence and creative spirit. And it was all masterminded from Kenny's front room, with help from Allan 'Gummi Bako' Stewart. Unbelievable!

$$\oint$$

Around this time Johnny Lynch stepped into the picture. A fan and a regular customer at the Fence shop, he had helped run the Alternative Society (Altsoc) at the university. He'd put on gigs, club and comedy nights for a tiny minority of alternative and indie music fans in the town and had his own gear, the Prince William Golf Band. He'd attend the Aikman's gigs, the Sunday Socials and the St Andrews Citizens Band shows, and had booked Kenny and the gang to play the student union. Their friendship was developing, and his ambition and indie-pop-suss would play a major part in Fence's progress. Whereas Kenny admits to not knowing or caring about the cliquish scenes, labels and movements within the UK music world, Johnny was well versed in who was involved and how things worked. He read music magazines, fanzines and papers; he listened to John Peel and the *Evening Session*; he had researched the DIY culture and was knowledgeable about its origins.

He would soon be Kenny's right-hand man, and it was useful for Fence to have such a funny, friendly, motivated and tasteful individual to take things in different directions. His own music, as The Pictish Trail, was also fast becoming central to Fence events and releases. Leaving university in 2003, he saw the potential in staying in St Andrews and working on something honest and independent with compatible song-writers and friends. Why move elsewhere when everything you want is right in front of you? He knew Kenny was on to something and wanted to be a key part of it. His first job was to start booking live gigs and events for Fence artists.

With every move Fence was reaching out and connecting with more disenfranchised music lovers. In Johnny Bradshaw, whom Kenny calls his point man at Domino, Kenny met a true fan of King Creosote and the Fence aesthetic and manifesto. It was soon time to let the world hear his most high-profile release yet. Planned as a Fence/Domino co-release,

Rocket DIY was to be a gateway album to help King Creosote reach a far wider audience, graze the mainstream and eventually sign with a major label.

Kenny And Beth's Musikal Boat Rides and *Of All The Things I Can Eat, I'm Always Pleased With A Piece of Cheese* had just been issued, and a tour was booked for King Creosote and Pip Dylan. Een looked at the dates and the money and point-blank refused. In some ways this was the beginning of the end of Een's involvement with the bigger Fence picture. He would never fully commit himself to the collective again. He wasn't that interested, and although additional Pip releases would come out via the label and he'd play at festivals and shows, he began to distance himself from Kenny and the others. Early fans of the label, the collective and Een's music are disappointed, of course, and even today his reticence about being more involved is discussed and mourned. It's sad that such a talent feels this way, but maybe one day he will change his mind.

Johnny volunteered to accompany Kenny on the tour under his Pictish Trail alias, playing his own material and accompanying Kenny's set. This would become an extremely steep learning curve for Johnny, his first proper touring experience. They hit the road, fulfilled their duties and bonded further as friends and collaborators. Today you can see a certain chemistry between the two that harks back to this period in their lives. Een's loss was Johnny's gain, especially when they contributed to and played at Domino's tenth-anniversary celebrations in London on a bill headlined by James Yorkston. The London indie media were there in droves as the bedraggled trio impressed with their direct, emotive song-writing and sweet melodies. Domino had gambled and Fence had won, further cementing their reputation as quality performers.

Fence events began to gather more and more kudos among the media and musicians desperate to visit this bizarre little area of Scotland, and the 2003 Hallowe'en bash had more than its fair share of newcomers, keen to be part of something fresh and new. The chaotic, non-corporate nature of the event added to the mystery and enjoyment. It hadn't entirely been planned, but things were beginning to swing in Kenny's favour. Word was spreading, and so were the Sunday Social events that had grown out of their Aikman's residency. Gav 'Onthefly' Brown invited the collective to play his Falkirk local, the Rialto, David Love was booking them for events at Nice 'n' Sleazy and The 13th Note in

Glasgow, and Andy Kelly had them on in Hartlepool and Stockton-on-Tees. The inaugural Green Man festival in Wales, (now a major festival on the calendar) had booked James Yorkston to play high up on the bill, and Kenny, Een and Johnny jumped aboard and played various sets to great acclaim. Kenny would go on to play the first seven Green Man festivals. Out-of-town fans wanted the music to come to them, and the word spread organically. Music fans were booking musicians who made music solely for those fans! A network of believers and supporters was building throughout Fife and way beyond.

Continuing to record at home, Kenny had clocked his biggest success so far with 2003's *Kenny And Beth's Musikal Boat Rides*, gaining a substantial amount of airplay for the track 'Homeboy'. Not only were specialist DJs like myself playing it, but more leftfield daytime shows too. To those not in the know, *Kenny And Beth's* was Kenny's first album. That couldn't be further from the truth, of course. It had been a collection of KC songs hand-picked by Joff Gladwell to be released on his label Sketchbook. Kenny decided against it, preferring to do it through Fence, and Domino put some of their weight behind it. Though it earned Kenny no hard cash, it felt amazing to have a proper album out. 'It was the real deal,' says Kenny. Tracks like 'Homeboy', 'Missionary' and 'Friday Night In New York' became fan favourites and still appear in the King Creosote live set.

Rumours of Kenny's back catalogue of fifty-odd albums, and of his contrary, outsider status, enthralled and enticed. When they heard the music it was tuneful, lyrical and full of ideas. It wasn't unlistenable thrash or DIY punk. Here was a songwriter who was, in his idiosyncratic way, speaking to hearts and minds. These were melodic songs that didn't adhere to clichés and, although modern and contemporary, had a timeless quality. It was just that he wasn't going to play the game, or toe the industry line. Indie and DIY music had always been seen as uncompromising and often marginal. With Fence, music lovers of all ages and dispositions could enjoy what was on offer.

Soon Fence's first Homegame festival, now their signature event, would take shape for spring 2004. Having visited a site in the middle of nowhere on the insistence of über-fan Stuart 'Arab' Paterson, the four-hour drive and the remoteness of the location struck fear into even Kenny and Johnny's hearts. It was then suggested they should do it on their own patch, Anstruther. If it couldn't work there, it wouldn't work anywhere. A hundred and fifteen tickets were sold for what was little more than an extended Sunday Social, adding a Saturday night to show-case more music and give added value. Homegame No. 1 is still mentioned in reverent tones by those lucky enough to have attended.

As 2004 arrived on the horizon, Kenny decided to take a year out from serious touring and recording. It seems crazy now, but it had to be done. His daughter, Beth, was about to go to school for the first time and he wanted to take at least a year out to be dad. He could only be so busy, and he had to put a cap on playing live, apart from one-off Fence shows, occasional festivals and mini-tours. Back home in Crail he industriously assembled box sets (cutting the wood by hand, with individual artwork and numbers) and taking orders through the website, all while Beth was at school during the day. It was labour-intensive and time-consuming work, but it kept the fan base dedicated, and Kenny loved, and still loves, the process of putting these hand-crafted items together. Now on eBay for sums like £300, he would sell them for a paltry £60. 'But that is a Fence thing . . . it wasn't about the money,' Kenny attests today.

His next album, *Rocket DIY*, would have an even bigger impact. As he busied himself in Crail, Johnny Bradshaw inquired about his next batch of tunes. Kenny sent him fifteen tracks, prompting an immediate response. Whittling it down to a tighter twelve tracks, this *had* to go out on Domino. Johnny loved the collection, hearing the improved sound quality with piano and banjo augmentations. It was a step up sonically. A March 2005 release was planned. However, it wasn't long before other labels got wind of it and wanted to get involved. The year 2005 was going to be a big one, with two King Creosote albums within months of each other, more of which later.

Rocket DIY was a quintessential release for Kenny and Fence. It had all the hallmarks of home recording and another superb set of songs. From the artwork, featuring Kenny and Beth in a rocket painted on a strip of skirting board, to superb tracks such as 'Twin Tub Twin', 'Saffy Nool', 'Circle My Demise' and 'King Bubbles In Sand', this was and is a classic Fence release and one of the fans' favourite albums. Johnny 'Pictish Trail' Lynch told *The Skinny* magazine: 'Yes, this was a Fence Records release, and yes, I'm fully aware that I am a member of King Creosote's band. But I genuinely think from start to finish that this is the best album Scotland has produced in the first decade of the 2000s.' Listen back and see what he means. Kenny was now in a league of his own. Huge respect must go to Domino, and Johnny Bradshaw in particular, for getting behind him and this album.

In the early 2000s there was a revival in acoustic and folk-influenced music across the UK, US and Europe, abetted by odious acronyms, such as NAM (New Acoustic Movement), cooked up by the music press. 'Instead of always being the wrong thing at the wrong time,' Kenny says, 'now we were one of the right things at the right time.' Having gone back to basics after years of slog and dwindling success, Kenny now had some of the key players in the music industry begging to come to the East Neuk. He'd somehow done it all on his own terms, against all odds, albeit with a stroke or two of luck. With the most unlikely of compatriots at his side, he was coming out the other side victorious.

7

Heroes to Zeroes

The Life, Times, Decline and End of The Beta Band

With what some, including their lead singer and record company, thought of as a disastrous debut album just behind them, The Beta Band had to salvage their reputation. Having burst on to the UK scene four years earlier with their contrary humour, experimentation and melting-pot of ideas, their seemingly unstoppable momentum had been dented. The 'Three EPs' were much loved by fans and critics, but what was next? Touring, and lots of it! 'We were put out across Europe in these horrible buses,' says John Maclean. 'It was cold and a lot of the venues were quite empty. Steve thought the record company was doing it to punish us after we'd spent so much money on the album and called it shit.' This can't be proven either way, but it toughened the band and tightened them up. If they were seen as slackers, stoners and media darlings (which they weren't), they started to revel in the touring lifestyle. This heavy schedule reaped benefits for the band in the long term, especially in the US.

Despite their reputation in the media and the mixed reviews for their album, the band were coming into their own as a live act. They cherry-picked the finest tunes from their sizeable back catalogue and took to the road with a multi-media show. No expense was spared with screens, back-drops, instrumentation and entourage. If the band didn't want to play ball in radio and press interviews, they impressed onstage. Creating their own world in soundscapes and songs, they swapped instruments and disobeyed all rock 'n' roll rules and regulations. Occasionally chaotic, their shows were unique and frequently astounding.

I remember a gig in the Edinburgh Liquid Room, packed out with expectant fans and old friends. They played the key tracks from the 'Three EPs' and peppered the set with the more conventional numbers from the album. To this day I've never seen so many banks of keyboards, guitar pedals, drums and effects units cluttering up a stage. Somehow they managed to circumnavigate any technical difficulties and come across as strong and confident in their psychedelic message. The recorded songs weren't replicated, they took on a new life and soared.

Soon it would be time to prepare for their second album. Before the album itself, the band released a stand-alone single, 'To You Alone'/'Sequinsizer', recorded with producer Gareth Parton of Go! Team fame. 'To You Alone' was a tremendous song, one of their most focused pieces to date. It was also the first time the band had used their recording device of choice, ProTools. The label company wanted it on the album, but the band insisted it should stand on its own feet. In fact, Steve asked Beta Band fans to lobby Regal/Parlophone to have it released. In the single/album/ single/tour culture of the industry, it was another move that didn't make commercial sense or please their paymasters. However, it was seen as a return to form by fans and critics. *NME* made it Single of the Week in January 2000 and it gained a fair amount of Radio 1 play, but then disappeared. 'It was good,' John says. 'It was a song and yet it had the right amount of experimentation in there too.'

In even better news for the band, Steve started taking anti-depressants, practising kung fu and training in the gym. His darker moods began to recede and he even relaxed a little. Although by no means cured of his depression, his more regimented day-to-day living improved band relations and spurred on his creativity. Meanwhile Steve had begun to release music as King Biscuit Time, a name appropriated from an Arkansas blues radio show of the 1940s (all archived online today, if you want to listen). Regal issued his first EP, 'Sings Nelly Foggit's Blues in "Me And The Pharaohs"', which had been recorded on a Tascam four-track in December 1998. It had four short songs including 'Eye O' The Dug', which years later would be used as a name for a Fence Records festival in St Andrews. Released before the first Beta Band album, it had an undiluted purity to it. These songs were seen by Mason as more focused and not suitable for The Beta Band. 'I simply wanted to make a record on my own. I was finding big studios a bit stifling,' he says. Now he was writing again, which was a good sign after the obvious problems with the first album. His next EP, 'No Style', appeared in June 2000 and included a brilliant single, 'I Walk The Earth', which had quite a bit of radio play and showed he could still write catchy hooks and melodies in among the more scatterbrained Beta Band epics.

When asked about the King Biscuit Time project now, Robin Jones exclaims: 'I just thought: "Why? Why can't you just be part of the band and enjoy it?" Was it a feeling of superiority? Musically it was good, though.' John Maclean says: 'Maybe he wanted to show the world he could do it on his own. On the other hand, Robin and I would do the artwork and videos on our own too. It wasn't like he kept all the best songs for himself and chucked us a bunch of crappy songs. It wasn't a big thing.'

$\flat$

In the lead-up to the second album, the band regrouped in London's East End and holed themselves up in Garden Studios on Old Street. Here they spent months working out how to use the ProTools software. Their creativity and freedom returned after their time on the road. Bizarrely, they'd sit at separate workstations with headphones on, working on separate songs. Occasionally they'd practise and record a full song with the band set-up of bass, drums, guitar and keys. They'd then chop it up and experiment with the radical new technology. Their impish sense of humour returned too. When their A & R man, Miles Leonard, arrived to check on progress, they recorded him with a hidden mic. Then they chopped up the audio and re-edited it so that he sounded ridiculous, using his catchphrase 'Just great!' all the way through. Apparently he heard it later and didn't quite get it.

Having learned lessons from the previous album, and being a band who never wanted to repeat themselves, they set themselves new boundaries and limitations. 'We wanted to get organised before we hit the studio,' says Robin. 'There was a big emphasis on that. We felt like we'd really arsed it the last time, so this time we'd make sure there were twelve songs demo'd before we went into the studio.' John says: 'There was a definite effort to make more concise songs, unlike the long ramblings of the first album. We weren't lo-fi and we wanted to be a big band. In that way we weren't like the Fence Collective today. That's why we hired an R 'n' B producer.'

The group were now listening to Timbaland, Brandy, Aaliyah and other R 'n' B artists, but they embraced all forms of modern music. To their ears, the main progressive forces in pushing music production forward were to be found in Jamaican ragga and dancehall and American R' n' B. It became their mission to incorporate these sounds and get away from the wigged-out stylings of before. They wanted to make a tight and precise-sounding record. Steve says: 'I saw every record we put out as a complete reinvention. I wanted the second album to be like a modern R 'n' B record. If it had been a King Biscuit Time record, it probably would have been like that.' John continues: 'Steve instigated getting Colin Emmanuel (C Swing) involved. We wanted a pop producer to rein us in and give us a more contemporary sound. But looking back, it's difficult to know which bits are his and which are ours. We did a lot of beats and production ourselves that he changed subtly. He was there to make it sound good on a big stereo.'

The band ploughed on and step by step laid down the groundwork. Rumours emerged that they were making an urban album in a radical departure from their previous work. Some fans were scared, others waited with bated breath. Though seen as an indie band, they never saw themselves like that. They had already proved they were into hip-hop and R 'n' B, and were serious about combining those genres with their own sound. They wanted to encompass all the artists they liked. They just happened to like modern, ultra-slick, super-produced music. Contrary to what many may think, they never sat around getting stoned listening to Pink Floyd.

They decided on a title to rival those on the 'Three EPs' – *Hotshots II*. Steve says: 'Yeah, it was self-deprecating. We wanted this big, boombastic, American-sounding title like a film, but not the original. The sequel's always worse than the original. It was a giant joke.' Robin continues: 'It was our second album and it felt like four heroes stepping out and taking on the world, whereas we were actually skinny Scottish guys. It just looked and sounded great.' Now writing, recording and co-producing their own material, their love of films both classy and tacky came to the fore. During the sessions they watched a different film every lunchtime and wanted a title that reflected their new obsession and tongue-in-cheek sense of humour. John Maclean had been making videos for the band for some time, and would make films in his own right in the future.

The cover was always important too. For *Hotshots II* they wanted a breathtaking explosion – but in space, where no one could hear or see it. Their conceptual thinking was mischievous and self-mocking. To most eyes it looked striking, but John is disparaging of the cover today, 'It was yet again technology out of our hands. I just see it as a bad Photoshop job. It looks more like a muffin than a huge explosion.' The photo-shoot took place in a futuristic house and the band wore illuminated spacesuits, made by a fashion designer friend, reminiscent of characters from the film *Tron*, which all added to the new aesthetic and the sci-fi theme. On the back cover the band laid out everything they used on the album, from the pots and pans they'd used as percussion to their spacesuits.

The album, though by no means an urban or R 'n' B record as rumoured, was far more streamlined and focused. It clicked, bleeped and rumbled in all the right places and contained an array of potential singles. Though it wasn't lowest-common-denominator pop, it had all the hallmarks of a record that could break them to a wider audience. The Beta Band trademarks were there in Mason's semi-whispered vocals, Robin and Richard's lolloping grooves, John's keyboard effects and the all-important catchy choruses. There was a healthy amount of experimentation and a further nod to their beloved electronica, and the songs seemed more personal and concise than ever before. It didn't scream *Revolution!* or reinvent the wheel, but it showed the Beta Band were back on track after their lambasted debut album.

Leading the charge and crying out to be a single was 'Squares'. Sampling the 1960s track 'Daydream' by Gunther Kallman, Mason had constructed a pop-song that harked back to flower power but sounded utterly modern. It was potentially what Beta Band fans were waiting for. It struck a balance between 1960s pop art, shuffling baggy beats and hip-hop culture with a melodic twist and acerbic lyrics all of its own. However, their moment of glory was snatched by a one-hit-wonder from studio outfit I-Monster. Unknown to The Beta Band or their record company, I-Monster had used the same sample and made a far more chart-friendly and less inventive track for mass consumption. 'It was frustrating,' says Steve, 'because I-Monster put beats behind the whole record. I sampled three or four seconds of "Daydream" and built a song around it. It's a very different thing.'

Undeterred, Parlophone built up their hopes and thought 'Squares' would be a huge hit. Radio 1, however, decided they would only play one record with that particular hook, and they went for I-Monster. The record company buckled. Steve says: 'At that point I realised I'd had enough of the record company. When they caved in, I thought it was unbelievably weak. There are a million ways you could have twisted that to promote the record – "the record Radio 1 banned" etc.' Robin adds: 'We had the song done and were ready to release it before I-Monster, but the record company said: "You can't put out singles before Christmas," so we waited until January and then February, by which time it was too late.' John maintains: 'The record company hummed and hawed and eventually decided to go for it. Radio 1 was all-powerful then, and they went with I-Monster instead. Years later I met the guy from I-Monster and even he was apologetic. He said: "You were a career band and we did a one-hit-wonder single, and we feel bad we scuppered that for you." Because it did fuck us at the time.'

'Squares' was quickly withdrawn, much to the band's chagrin. It seemed to them that Parlophone almost gave up on promoting the album, apart from sending them out on tour. Other excellent singles such as 'Broke' and 'Human Being' were released, but the wind had been knocked out of their sails. In a last gasp effort they put out 'Squares' again. While all charted modestly, the *zeitgeist* had shifted. The Beta Band had been seen as pioneers and revolutionaries, but now they were a band like any other, putting out singles, touring and developing their niche. They were being bracketed and sidelined with music-industry-invented genres such as the dreaded folktronica.

Steve says: 'It all depends on what your reference points are. If you're into folk and intelligent electronic music, you'll find that in The Beta Band. If you're into hip-hop, you'll find that. If you're into indie, you'll hear that, and so on.' John elaborates: 'We got knocked for the record sounding too straight. It did sound more straight, but it was about not repeating yourself. The thing about not repeating yourself is that people have expectations of you. Some people want "Dry The Rain" again and again, but if you did that, others would say: "Wait a minute, it just sounds like 'Dry The Rain'", so ultimately you can't listen to them.'

Behind the scenes, however, the band were increasingly ambitious. They'd parted company with their management and were searching for someone new, finally settling with a manager in Los Angeles called Frank Gironda, who worked for Lookout Management. Their roster included Neil Young, Mazzy Star, Fishbone, and even Bob Dylan for a while. Steve says: 'We only liked him because he had eyes like a great white shark when he went in for the attack. That was very appealing to us.' By all accounts he was an odd guy. He'd been a hippie in the 1960s but, as so many of them did, had become a businessman in the 1980s. The trouble was, they were to find out, that Gironda was a terrible businessman. 'It was typical Beta Band, "Let's go for the craziest guy!",' says John. According to Mason: 'He didn't do anything and he made no decisions. The time difference of eight hours between us and him was a problem. He'd repeat over the phone: "I'll take all that worry off your shoulders, just stop worrying about that", and then do nothing. How did he keep getting employed? There are so many people in the music industry like that.'

Hotshots II wasn't as big a success as anyone had hoped. It managed to reach number thirteen in the UK charts in 2001, which was no mean feat, but they were seen as under-achievers not delivering on their early promise. However, as the blasé UK music scene was moving on to the next flavour of the month, The Beta Band were starting to make waves in the US. They toured relentlessly from 2000 to 2002, wearing their illuminated suits among pure white stage props, complete with monstrous lighting rig and crew. They embraced the clean *2001: A Space Odyssey* look with a clinical, almost hospital aesthetic to go with the tighter sound of the music. America was lapping it up too.

Steve recalls: 'EMI weren't great at handling The Beta Band, in the way that no major label is good at handling true artists. Businessmen will never understand artists and vice versa. But the one good thing EMI did was to pump shitloads of money into the band. We were able to take this incredible show all over the world, and in many ways that was the making of the band. EMI probably thought: "They don't want to do promotion, they don't want to put out singles, but they're brilliant live! The longer they're out there, the less they're in here whingeing." So we toured the show in all its glory. It was never diluted, whether it was in the Hollywood Bowl, the Shepherd's Bush Empire or Bumblefuck in the American wilderness. It blew people's minds – lives were changed.'

John remembers: 'Robbie Williams was on *The Letterman Show* and doing all the big publicity at the time, but our tour was shadowing his, and we were playing the same venues and selling the place out while he was selling fifty tickets! In America you have to earn your fans slowly over the years, and that's what we were doing.' Steve adds: 'I realised we had to be really good to cut it in America. Even their pop stars are seriously talented there. We had our own ideas, our own songs, and we were offering something that no one else was.'

Having seen their live act many times, I remember two stand-out shows at the Glasgow Barrowland. Not only is the Barrowland probably the perfect live venue – somewhere between an intimate club and a big hall, with a sprung dancefloor and easily accessible bars from which you can see the band – but the shows had the feeling of a happening or a gathering of the clans. Never before or since has a band united so many different fractious youth tribes. There would be mods, hippies, punks, indie kids, B-Boys and electronica fans listening to a mash-up of styles from the band and DJs. Steve says: 'We'd do a little bit, but we'd try to have friends of ours DJ'ing before, as it was nerve-wracking for us before the show. I remember two songs in particular, Busta Rhymes's "Woo-Ha!" and "Wichita Linesman" by Glen Campbell. Essentially they sum up the Beta Band.' Although the mash-up culture is huge now, and flirts with the mainstream continually, back then those genres would rarely sit together in a DJ set. Crowds listened and absorbed them without batting an eyelid.

In 2000 the band was extended an olive branch that would massively help their US campaign. They were offered two tours of the US, four weeks and two weeks, as support to Radiohead, who were on the same label, Parlophone. The Oxford miserablists were huge fans and personally asked them to support. It may seem an ill-matched partnership, but you have to remember Radiohead were moving into uncharted territories themselves with *Kid A* and *Amnesiac*. Gone was the stadium bombast of *The Bends* and the bleak prog-rock of *OK Computer* as they too embraced electronica. Radiohead invited them on tour, paid them decently, treated them well and were warm and welcoming. Not only that, but Radiohead watched them every night. The tours were a massive help to The Beta Band. They played to between 20,000 and 40,000 every night, cutting out two years of touring in six weeks. John and Robin both say: 'The best time we ever had was on tour with Radiohead.' Although appreciative of the support, and keeping his lips sealed otherwise, Steve says he was not a fan then and isn't now.

To add to the thrill, Radiohead had A-list parties which The Beta Band often attended. It wasn't unusual to go back to a hotel and meet Brad Pitt and other film stars. At one get-together John talked to Jack Black for hours on a sofa while Steve pinned Fred Durst against a wall and told him how shit Limp Bizkit's music was. John believes the rap-rocker was probably scared shitless of the little drunken Scotsman. The shenanigans continued outside the parties too. At a concert on Boston racecourse The Beta Band were in the jockey room, doubling as their dressing-room and chill-out space. They spied a wooden training horse on wheels, tied it to the back of a golf cart and sped around the queueing crowds. Causing a ruckus with security and breaking the horse as well, they were ordered offsite only to be rescued at the last minute by the Radiohead entourage.

The Beta Band had toured the US twice before the Radiohead gigs and would do it twice more after. Their hard work was paying off as they eclipsed acts such as Robbie Williams and The Manic Street Preachers in ticket sales. Robin says: 'It was tiring but it was brilliant,' John adding: 'It was hardly hard work though, playing to appreciative fans every night.' Richard missed his wife and being at home, but everyone had a great time doing something they said they never would: playing the support band. To keep tensions to a minimum, there was a huge entourage of their own to interact with, so the bandmates could hang around with the crew as well as each other. Nevertheless, although spirits were high and the future looked bright, there were controversies. 'We were banned from MTV because I told 30,000 Americans to shoot President Bush in the head,' Steve recalls. 'We were also banned from *Top of the Pops*. Dunno why, but it may have been for the same reason.'

The next step in their stateside success was the inclusion of 'Dry The Rain' in the film of Nick Hornby's best-selling novel, *High Fidelity*. In one of the record-shop scenes, John Cusack's character boasts that he 'will now sell five copies of The Beta Band,' brandishing 'Champion

Versions' and playing the lead track loudly on the store's stereo. The song blasts out and he succeeds in his task. Not only was this a great moment in the film, but the Fifers were immediately introduced to the film-loving public across the world. Music fans who might not have chanced upon the band were handed the opportunity on a plate. Perhaps the most important moment in the band's promotional history, the film was a big success and doubled their US fan base. John Cusack also became a fan and a friend. Typically, the band got drunk at the premiere in London and left after their bit, missing the end.

Now the door had opened to support slots and promotional opportunities, you'd think their label, their publishers and the band would have leaped in at the deep end. You couldn't be more wrong. U2 wanted them as support – no! Budweiser wanted to use their music in an ad – no! Gap wanted to give them £10,000 each for a photo-shoot – no! Perhaps most cussedly of all, The Beta Band turned down $1 million for an Oldsmobile ad. 'We thought adverts were the devil. We grew up on Bill Hicks,' says John. Steve says: 'Back then, adverts were seen as being dirty money. It would be a difficult decision to make now. Having said that, when Iggy Pop and John Lydon do adverts, a part of me dies.' They did, however accept 20,000 euros for a milk ad in France. 'I think we did it just to annoy the publishing company,' Steve adds. They were also offered Radiohead's European tour and their massive Oxford homecoming show, declining both.

Despite their refusenik attitude, the Betas were starting to look like a conventional group. They had LA management and were on the treadmill of single/album/tour/promotion. To criticism that The Beta Band were less like the art-project they'd started out as and more of a standard rock band, John says: 'We wanted to do everything. We wanted the album covers to look like paintings. We wanted the albums to be like your favourite albums and the videos like your favourite films. We weren't a pretentious art band who want to release an album of forty minutes of farting.'

But an air of change was sweeping over them, and the time seemed right to go home. Although they loved the buzz of London, reality came calling. Robin says: 'We were shelling out all this money in London to live with no space and massive noise restrictions, and by moving back to Scotland we'd be able to live like kings. Or so we thought. We never made any money. We were on a record company wage and that just slowly went down over the years.' John adds: 'I had this romantic notion of returning to Edinburgh, but it wasn't the same as it had been. Everyone kept telling us we'd made it, but we felt like underdogs. MTV wouldn't play our videos, radio wouldn't play our songs and the internet didn't exist. We just got on with our lives. It wasn't like we got recognised everywhere.'

Outsiders, critics and ambitious musicians assume that a group on a major label march into a world of luxury and excess, with huge pay-packets and expense accounts. Unless you consistently sell hundreds of thousands of records, the truth is harsher. Each member of the band had started on a personal £1,500 a month when they'd first signed, and was now on a more spartan £1,000. Although promotion, touring and distribution budgets were taken care of, living allowances were frugal. Any money they'd made had been pumped back into paying off their advances and bankrolling their monumental stage show. Worse, it wasn't long before they found the books were being cooked and the taxman wasn't receiving what he was due.

The decision was made. Steve put down roots in Fife again and the others holed up in Edinburgh. With a slower pace of life, cheaper living and a selection of well-known faces to kick around with, the band set to work on album number three. They hired a huge room in a new arts and music centre called the Lighthouse in down-at-heel Granton in Edinburgh. An interesting and ambitious operation, the Lighthouse was an attempt to motivate the factions of the city's art and music scenes and create a space in which to create, write, rehearse and record. However, it didn't yet have proper heating, so the rooms were freezing. When the boys set to work on their ProTools set-ups, they wore gloves. A change is as good as a rest, but when money is tight, outside interest parties waning and you're working in the cold, spirits can be dampened.

It was on the minds of all four members that the next album would probably make or break the band. It had to be different and it had to propel their career further upwards. Again determined not to repeat themselves, a certain fatigue, however, began to set in. Discussing the origins of the album, Robin maintains: 'We wanted to make the record more live-sounding and the songs to have a bit more soul.' John says: 'With previous albums, we'd record the songs, then play them live and they'd get better and better. With this record, we played them over and over until they were good, then recorded them.' Robin recalls: 'Setting the microphones up was quite often enough though! We did a lot of thinking.'

Unfortunately, Steve was still suffering from manic depression. In the documentary about the rehearsals on the Beta Band DVD, shot by close friend and Old Jock Radio supremo Pete Rankin, you see his unpredictable sides. The band would often wonder when the door opened which Steve they were going to get. It wasn't a particularly creative environment for them, and Mason was still flagellating himself under unbelievable pressure. He claims: 'By the time we got to rehearsing the songs for *Heroes to Zeroes*, it felt like a job. It wasn't what I wanted. When you start feeling like art is a job, it's time to stop. I felt tired. I felt like it was dying and there was nothing I could do about it.' The (as usual) self-deprecating title was almost prophetic in its honesty. It was as if they were resigned to their fate. One camp had wanted *Zeroes to Heroes*, but the other triumphed. John won't say which camp each member was in, but he thinks it was the right way around. 'The band split up soon after, and we'd photographed the clothes and smashed instruments on the beach for the back cover. Looking back, it just seemed like a last album.'

Recording began in Rockfield again with engineer Nick Brine, but tensions grew to new heights. One night Steve and Richard started a pointless argument when out for a pint. This was dragged back to the studio. In Steve's opinion Richard was prone to getting drunk and into trouble, then calling on his mates to help him out. Mason this time wasn't prepared to do that and Richard was offended, feeling betrayed. As a result, a huge divide between the two appeared, and this felt like another tipping point. With Steve's self-imposed pressure as frontman and songwriter, he also looked on the others with disdain at times. 'My abiding memory of mixing that album was that John spent the entire time learning to play chess,' he says, 'and in a way that summed things up.'

Fans now love that final record as much as anything else the Betas produced as it shows another facet of what they could do. A more muscular, dynamic and 'rock' album than previous efforts, it displayed their growing skills as a forceful live band in the way Robin had wanted. The electronic edge was still there, as was their ear for a good sample.

The band produced the album themselves and then had Radiohead producer Nigel Godrich mix the results. He was impressed, by all accounts. To me, it was head and shoulders above most releases at the time and further cemented their reputation. John is a little less sanguine. 'There weren't many singles off it, and people didn't seem to like it that much. I think it was underappreciated, though. "Rhododendron" and "Troubles" are great.' Steve says: 'There's some great stuff on that record. "Liquid Bird", with the Siouxsie and the Banshees "Painted Bird" sample, and "Assessment".' Less well received by fans or not, the media were certainly cooler. The love affair with The Beta Band was over and only the hardcore supporters were still flying the flag.

Steve points out: 'By the time we got to *Heroes to Zeroes*, things had changed. We were done and dusted in terms of the mainstream. *Hotshots* should have been the album to propel us there, but it didn't. All I wanted was the mainstream to be full of interesting art, not just music to get drunk to. I wanted to be successful, but on our own terms. I felt we should have achieved more by that point.'

It wasn't over quite yet, though. The album was promoted, to positive reviews. A handful of singles were released, with 'Assessment' being a minor radio hit, and more tour dates were booked. In one last attempt to breathe life and energy into the group, they went on the search for a new manager. Frank Gironda, the great white shark, hadn't cut the mustard. A nice if somewhat weird guy and a real 'vibes' man, he had done almost nothing to raise the band's profile or bolster their coffers. He had to be cut loose. When the Betas bumped into Primal Scream in a rehearsal studio, they discussed managers and the Scream suggested . . . Alan McGee. As has been well documented, he had set up the iconic Creation label and released some of the most incendiary rock, indie and dance music of the past fifteen years. From The Jesus and Mary Chain to Teenage Fanclub, Super Furry Animals, Oasis and beyond, he was an impresario, a loudmouth, an iconoclast and most importantly a huge music fan. He had recently started a new label, Poptones, distancing himself from the Sony/Creation merger and going indie again. What's more, he had experience, money and fire in his belly.

The Beta Band got in touch with him and he unhesitatingly agreed to take them on.

Their first official meeting was in Paris, where the group were performing for French TV. He enthused: 'It's gonnae be amazing, man! McGee and Mason, ma Goad!' He didn't know that Steve had conducted another meeting with the band on the same trip, announcing: 'I have had enough of this. I don't want to do it any more.' Today Steve says: 'In all honesty, I thought they'd agree with me. I certainly wasn't expecting the huge falling-out that happened.' Robin sees it slightly differently: 'There wasn't a lot of resistance at the start. It wasn't much fun any more. It was a bit stale.'

However, no one thought to tell McGee until their appearance at T in the Park a couple of weeks later. At only their second meeting with the new manager, he proclaimed: 'Oh ma Goad, I cannae believe it! I managed The Beta Band for a week!' Steve says: 'I have total respect for Alan McGee and I don't have a bad word to say about him. He saved my life. He paid me a wage for a year after The Beta Band and didn't ask for it back. If you're a friend of his, he will go out of his way to help you.' McGee helped Mason set up a fictitious label called No Style and financed it all the way. Then, with no money coming in, he and his lawyers had to deal with The Beta Band splitting up. They had to sift through contracts, meet other lawyers, argue with accountants and go through the entire trauma. He managed the existing band for a week, but had to carry the baggage for years to come.

The rest of the band were annoyed with Steve for leaving. *High Fidelity* was out to huge acclaim, *Heroes to Zeroes* was doing the rounds and the group were well on their way to breaking through in the US. But when Steve ordered the cancellation of a final US tour, which was booked and ready to go, there was an almighty row. By all accounts it was going to cost the best part of $1 million, and the group already owed a fortune to accountants, lawyers and the taxman. 'That's why I wanted to split the band up,' says Steve. 'They wanted a two-week holiday in the US. Where's the art, where's the passion, where's the music?' John says: 'Steve wasn't that happy in the band, and you don't want to drag someone around. I was kind of relieved the band was splitting up. But I was glad I wasn't the one splitting it up, because Rich had a wife, child and mortgage.'

Although they're still friends, John bristles slightly when reminded of the split. 'Steve was probably engineering his own solo career by then. He'd gotten in with Creation Management and was probably discussing his first proper solo record. It wasn't some Machiavellian plot, it just overlapped.' Robin adds: 'When it happened, it all hit in different ways. It was all very depressing. I need to be busy and part of something. I'll just sit around and feel depressed when there's nothing going on. Suddenly everything stopped and you don't have a trade or anything. There'll be no more touring, no more giggling into a microphone at the radio station. Afterwards I did quite a bit of drinking.' John says: 'I just got ill with sore stomachs and migraines.' Robin and John had split up with long-term girlfriends around the same time, adding to the weight of disappointment.

By way of a final farewell, a last UK tour was booked. It was the first tour to make any of them any money. Having never personally been paid for a single Beta Band gig before, they hit the road with a skeleton crew and no visuals or lighting rig. They used what was available at each venue. I was at the last show of all, on 4 December 2004 at the Liquid Room, Edinburgh. It was a triumph: it showed how strong the songs were and how good a live band they'd become, with no distractions or gimmicks. They played everything you could have wanted, from the 'Three EPs' to the most recent album, with grace, charm and a distinct lack of saccharine sentimentality.

However, there was no group-hug backstage or afterwards, simply because the other three didn't want it to end. I attended the after-show party in Cabaret Voltaire and enjoyed the boozy hospitality and teary-eyed nostalgia. There I met Mani from The Stone Roses for the first time. Although blind drunk and incomprehensible, he came across as a genuine fan and supporter of the band. Knowing that Gordon Anderson, Steve Mason and John Maclean had been so inspired by his former group, it rang true to me how important a moment this was. Steve remains stoical: 'If we hadn't ended then, I suspect we wouldn't have this untouchable legacy that we have now – this beautiful little piece of history. It means everything to me.' John says: 'It was a relief in a way to know it was coming to an end, and the crowds at those last gigs were really emotional.'

From here on in it was a matter of number-crunching. There was an enormous debt to be sorted out. They'd been ripped off by their accountant, and their former manager hadn't helped. Why didn't they take it up with him? John explains: 'Our manager was a fruitcake. You can't really blame someone who's not all there.' Tax bills were unpaid and the band were left, according to John, 'holding a shitty stick'. It was more than enough to bankrupt them all personally. The accountants paid them off with a bit of money, threatening them along the way. John says: 'The accountants showed us the really horrible side of a huge company. They threatened us, saying: "If you try to sue us, we'll ruin you." They even got private investigators to go through our press, finding quotes like "We're having a great time and we don't care about money" from years ago in some *NME* interview.'

Each member of the band settled with the Inland Revenue, paying off their own bills in instalments. 'Going bankrupt was a great thing,' John maintains. 'I can't go into debt now. I can't have an overdraft or use a credit card. I'm no worse off either. I'm now with the Co-operative Bank, which helpfully takes on bankruptcy cases.' As so often happens, something that had existed in a beautiful artistic bubble had crumbled in a sea of litigation and bankruptcy.

Steve has the last word. 'Who wants to be famous? Only the vacuous want to be famous. I still don't want to be famous. I want to be appreciated for what I do. Only cunts want to be famous, and we spotted that back then. Now I'm more prepared to bend and be accommodating. Back then, everyone outside the band and the manager was the enemy. I don't regret any of it, but we could have achieved more if we'd been a little more relaxed. We were very militant and very punk about the whole thing.'

So The Beta Band was over, but not forgotten. A certain sadness was felt by fans the world over. Although they'd delivered a worthy back catalogue and left the world of pop a more interesting place, in many ways they hadn't realised their own potential. They had, however, inspired a new generation of musicians and songwriters to do things in a different way. Just ask the Fence Collective and most of the people in this book. The Beta Band, much like The Velvet Underground, The Stooges and My Bloody Valentine, hadn't sold millions but they had changed lives. And it wouldn't be long until Steve, John, Robin and the estranged Gordon would reappear with more music.

8

KC Rules OK

Onwards and Upwards for King Creosote

Sometimes a window of opportunity opens at the right time, in the right place to a person capable of taking advantage. Only a fool or a coward doesn't jump through. An opportunity doesn't guarantee success, but it does occasionally mean a change of fortune. In 2004, such a prospect was about to befall Kenny Anderson. Having slowly built a name for his DIY Fence label and collective, and worked almost continually at music for over fifteen years, his time had come. Playing at the Green Man festival, he bumped into Billy Campbell, who worked at the Rough Trade shop in London and had been a huge supporter and advocate of Fence.

Laurence Bell of Domino Records says: 'Billy from 679/Warners came along and wanted to release a record by Kenny. I was tempted, and I did want to put out the King Creosote albums on Domino, but I didn't want to take over this thing. Billy was excited and phoned me up asking if he could put it out on his Names imprint through 679. I said it was fine and totally up to Kenny. I thought it would be good for him and good for everyone.' Kenny recalls: 'Billy asked what Domino was doing with my next album. I said: "I'm not signed to Domino. There's some informal licensing agreement with Fence, and Johnny Bradshaw's helping me put out my next album, but I'm not signed to them."' Billy was amazed and suggested recording a batch of King Creosote songs in the same way that *Kenny And Beth's Musikal Boat Rides* had been put together, but with superior production and playing. He had a small imprint called Names and was working with The Earlies. They were great players, but were angling at production jobs and backing singer-songwriters. Kenny was reticent, saying he didn't know them. As luck would have it, The Earlies were playing Green Man that weekend.

Although he didn't watch their entire set, because there were wasps in the tent (a phobia of Kenny's), the connection was mooted to the band and various recordings passed their way. Their initial reaction was: 'Why do you want to change this? These songs and recordings are fine the way they are.' But Billy was still very keen. Names had released a selection of 7-inch singles, but with King Creosote and The Earlies he wanted to do a 12-inch EP with financial backing from 679 Records, a subsidiary of Warners. Finally meeting The Earlies and liking their down-to-earth Lancashire humour and charm, Kenny agreed to the project with a few reservations about recording techniques. Having met Rob Cotter and Julie McLarnon from the Analogue Catalogue studio in Manchester via mutual friends at the Twisted Nerve label, Kenny booked time and set to work. Initially recording in March 2005 with friends of the Analogue Catalogue crew, he recorded versions of 'Vice Like Gist Of It' and 'Rain Weekend'. These were fine, but not outstanding. On this visit he also went to the Air Tight studio in Chorlton, where in one day he nailed 'Not One Bit Ashamed' and 'Fly By The Seat Of My Pants' backed by The Earlies. The chemistry was immediate and undeniable, and those first recordings would make it on to the next King Creosote release. Kenny loved the 'Try it, and if it don't work then fuck it!' attitude of the band, and got on like a house on fire with them. He now says: 'It was effortless. I was walking into a ready-made band. I said to Billy: "I'm going to do it."'

So the day after Fence's Homegame Two festival in the East Neuk, Kenny drove down to Manchester in May 2005 to begin his real breakthrough album. A few months earlier, the only songs of Kenny's that Billy Campbell had heard were those written in 2000 to 2002. Now he had a whole new batch, including 'Not One Bit Ashamed', 'Spystick' and 'Fly By The Seat Of My Pants'. These were fresh, Kenny was excited, The Earlies were primed and Billy was totally in the dark. Although they were some of Kenny's best songs to date, Billy still wanted the cream of the back catalogue recorded, with only minimal new songs added. He wanted to know what he was spending his money on. On arrival in Chorlton, The Earlies encouraged Kenny to do what he liked and ignore Billy's wishes.

Other new songs crept into the recording schedule, including 'You Are, Could I', 'Casino Clubbing' and 'Bootprints'. When phoning to ask which songs they'd recorded, Billy heard a list of new titles and sped from London to Manchester to find out what was going on. As soon as he heard the music his fears were allayed, and he knew something special was being created. 679 Records were expecting an EP of music, but in only twelve days King Creosote and The Earlies had recorded, produced and mixed sixteen tracks, enough for a full album and B-sides. Kenny even bagged the skills of old St Andrews friend and collaborator Kate Tunstall, who happened to be in Manchester, to add some backing vocals as well. Some kind of magic was in the air.

Kenny returned to Fife a happy man, and 679 were gobsmacked to have an album's worth of material for the price of a single EP. It just shows what is possible with good songs, a tight band and a decent work ethic. Most major-label artists wouldn't have got out of bed for the £5,000 or whatever that 679 initially spent. Johnny Bradshaw hit the phone and asked Kenny what he was doing. Why wasn't he doing the next record with Domino? Kenny said: 'Well, all you have to do is offer me the deal.' Domino hadn't and didn't. Laurence Bell felt he had enough Fence material, with James Yorkston and UNPOC signing to his books. They didn't know how good the album was, and had no idea The Earlies were involved, but simply weren't prepared to make the move, so 679 took the plunge. By all accounts Johnny Bradshaw was gutted not to have released *KC Rules OK*.

The year 2005 would be the most successful so far for King Creosote. Not only had *Rocket DIY* been released in April, but only six months later his most high-profile album yet, *KC Rules OK*, was released, preceded by the 'Favourite Girl' EP. Kenny says: 'Each one helped the other. It was like bang . . . then *Bang!* I thought it was quite good for me too. One album was on Fence/Domino and the next had nothing to do with Fence.' It helped Kenny connect with a new audience as BBC6 Music and Radio Scotland put songs on constant rotation. The press loved it, with four- and five-star reviews across the board. Although the project was conceived as short-lived, due to the costs and commitments of The Earlies, it was expected that they would showcase the new material to fans and the media.

Though specialist press and radio had championed King Creosote from *Kenny And Beth's Musikal Boat Rides* onwards, their support had hit a ceiling. How long could you write about this outsider songwriter without any success? Suddenly it was possible to dedicate swathes of pages and airtime to this new collection of hi-fi recordings on a major label, with the critically acclaimed Earlies underpinning his songs. It was obvious they meant business, as did the company promoting the album. Now London-based media and those who had previously been too cautious were involved, and wanted a piece of the action. This is how the media works. Goodwill was now being manifested in concrete terms. Talking about that exhilarating time now, Kenny says: 'Warners realised they were on to something. Suddenly I was fast-tracked! It went from Billy and me talking about an EP to Billy and me having conversations with Warners about singles.' He was now entering a world where money and marketplaces mattered, and where a company would try to squeeze a six-minute song into a three-minute, radio-friendly record. Things were changing for good and bad.

So much has been said about *KC Rules OK*, with reactionary Fence fanatics rejecting the album as a sell-out. But Kenny has never shied away from success: he just wants it on his terms. Like any good artist, he enjoys experimenting. Why shouldn't he make an album for a major? Though the playing was more proficient and the production values higher, there was no dilution. It was a pleasant surprise to hear his voice, lyrics, melodies and arrangements in widescreen. Adding brass, keys and backing vocals seemed like a fun and acceptable kind of progression. What's more, many songs had appeared on Kenny's more lo-fi albums already. Wasn't it nice to hear newer, crisper versions? Even the artwork paid homage to his shop, label and collective, with KC RULES OK painted on . . . a fence. Ach well, you can't please everyone. In many ways this was his finest album to date, with the best running order, song selections and production. It still had humour, heartfelt vocals and highly original lyrics. It was no wonder it crossed over.

When an artist starts to break through, all the parts of the industry machine fall into place. In an age when album sales are dwindling and the live show is an all-important source of revenue, the importance of a decent booking agent becomes apparent. Approached by the Coda agency, Kenny suggested he tour with his own Fence band, including

Gav 'Onthefly' Brown on drums, Johnny 'Pictish Trail' Lynch on lead guitar and Manchester-based Nathan 'The Whip' Sudders, a friend of The Earlies, on bass. Warners were afraid this band couldn't replicate The Earlies' musicianship and virtuosity, but they were soon put at ease when the band showed fans old and new how professional and emotive they could be. Having seen King Creosote live more than any other act, whether solo or with other musicians, I have never seen Kenny with a better band. When Christian Madden from The Earlies guested on certain gigs it was even more spectacular. Some purists prefer Kenny when he plays alone in a room to twenty people, but I like both. These band shows were proof that his songs and delivery were up there with any singer-songwriter's, past, present or future.

Occasionally there would be trouble back at the ranch, however. Offered a Folk Britannica gig at the Barbican to coincide with Vashti Bunyan's comeback, it was considered whether Kenny should do it or not. Astonishingly, the label wanted to distance Kenny from the 'folk' tag. When an email came around, Johnny Lynch at Fence was cc'd into it and voiced his opinion: 'I think this is perfect for Kenny. It's his perfect audience. Most of them won't have the record yet, but they'll love him.' Billy Campbell phoned Johnny and let rip at him for voicing his opinion, but Johnny defended his position, pointing out that Kenny was not only a gifted songwriter but a forty-year-old man perhaps not suited to the pop trajectory. Kenny did the show, people went wild, the press loved it, and they sold a wad of extra tickets for Kenny's next London headline show at the Scala off the back of the event.

Noting the potential in *KC Rules OK*, the record company wanted more. Kenny and his new band were sent into Rak Studios in London towards the end of 2005. The plan was to record new, beefier and more focused versions of album tracks '678' and 'Margarita Red', an older song 'So Forlorn' and a new song, 'You've No Clue, Do You'. These were to be released as four singles at 679's insistence. Label exec Nick Worthington was convinced that '678' was the song to launch the album into the stratosphere. The idea was then to repackage *KC Rules OK* with the extra singles on it for a huge re-release in summer 2006. But Kenny maintains: 'I signed a Mickey Mouse EP deal with Names, remember, so that I'd have complete control. There was a lot of trying to rejig the deal to get me to hand over control.' It was clear he needed some guidance, with Billy Campbell saying: 'I can't manage you and run a label . . . you don't even have a phone!' With help from a new manager, Derek McKillop, who had looked after Elton John, Lloyd Cole, Jamiroquai, James Blunt, Sophie Ellis-Bextor and many more, the compromise was a double album. The original would be smartened up with a second album containing the new songs, a Jon Hopkins remix and extra tracks from the Chorlton sessions, titled *Chorlton And The Wh'Earlies* in tribute to the 1970s children's TV show *Chorlton and the Wheelies*. Kenny was happy: 'At least people buying the album again would get a complete extra disc.'

Things didn't go to plan, however, as release dates were missed and there were pressing-plant problems, ensuring a damp squib of a re-release. On top of that, Warners took this fairly raw, indie-sounding album and remixed and remastered it, making it sound more polished and less quirky, more typically major-label. Soon Kenny was to feel the controlling hand of Warners. They'd say things like 'You choose the photos. You have control over which ones get used,' and then press shots would be released without consent. With the money, might and publicity that come from being signed to a major also comes loss of control. There was always a feeling of 'must do better, could do better', leaving the band disappointed when they should have been elated. *Kenny and Beth's* had sold roughly 1,000 copies, *Rocket DIY* an initial 3,000, and now *KC Rules OK* had done 10,000 and rising. But that was 'only' 10,000 to Warners. They rarely told Kenny: 'You're doing great!'

What's more, Kenny and the band were seen as bedraggled beardy-weirdies and asked to clean up their image. They made a video to accompany the single '678', which, somehow inevitably, bombed. The grand relaunch of *KC Rules OK* in summer 2006 had fizzled. On the never-ending promotional tour of the time, Kenny remembers almost every radio DJ saying 'I did you a real injustice not playing "678" at the time. I absolutely love it now!' Although I gave it a good few spins, when I saw them play it at the ABC Glasgow it sounded so magnificent I wept. Here was my old pal and bandmate playing a big venue to a capacity audience, singing his songs on his terms with an extraordinary band behind him. It was like stadium rock without the cliché, cheesiness and bombast. Quizzed about the career trajectories of Travis and Snow Patrol, Kenny is appalled that people criticised their 'big songs'. He says: 'Anyone who says they don't want a big song is lying. We all want that. We all want the crowd to sing our songs back at us. The first time it happened to me was probably at the Belladrum festival with "Not One Bit Ashamed", and we all went *Fuuuuuuck!*' He then balances his statement, admitting: 'I still get as much pleasure playing to thirty people in a hall in Cellardyke as I do playing a big venue with a band, though. Just as long as I'm singing well.'

Not everything went according to the rulebook, however: Kenny liked to do his own thing. The band played a Highlands and Islands tour, with Beth Allan and Blair Young from Forest of Black following them around, before making a bizarre tour documentary. They played the Green Man again in 2006 and performed virtually nothing from *KC Rules OK*, instead opting for new songs from start to end. These would appear on the next album. Even new manager Derek agreed it was a brave move. Like many others, he was coming round to Kenny's way of doing things. If every time he toured he had a different band and different songs, the audience would keep coming back – sometimes on the same tour. The diehards knew it could, and probably would, be different every night.

After the mess of the re-release and the flop of '678', the record company announced it was time to make a new album. Suddenly 'You've No Clue, Do You' was the priority. It was time for new material and Kenny should get cracking. This suited him as a prolific writer, and off he went. Looking back on 2005 and 2006, Kenny had been thrust above the parapet for the first time and flirted with the mainstream. Although the new label had backed all the touring and always insisted on the full-band show, Kenny wasn't necessarily seeing any real increase in fees. Yes, audiences were bigger, but Kenny was just concerned that it wouldn't end up losing him a lot of money and holding him in debt to the company, as had happened to The Beta Band. With a major label, you take the rough with the smooth.

As the KC bandwagon trundled towards the end of 2006, Kenny's stock was rising. Respect was growing among his contemporaries. He was invited to take part in a songwriting workshop called Burnsong, where a group of distinguished writers would stay in a country house and create new material. He was unsure at first, but when he shared a bill with Edinburgh popsters Aberfeldy, their lead singer Riley Briggs said: 'Do it. You'll love it!' So he did, and became entangled with a disparate group involving Sushil 'Future Pilot AKA' Dade, Karine Polwart, Chris Difford of Squeeze, MC Soom T, Kim Edgar, Emma Pollock and Canadian musician Michael Johnson. From this came a band, The Burns Unit, and an album, *Side Show*, released in 2010 to serious acclaim and a slot on *Later . . . with Jools Holland*. Where does he find the time for all these projects?

Although Burnsong took up a little time, as 2007 began it was time to start work on his next collection, *Bombshell*. 'I don't ever actually demo songs,' Kenny admits. 'I just record them.' In between recording sessions and tours, Kenny had been working with an electronica artist and producer called Jon Hopkins. Everything they'd worked on had ended up on a B-side, and Jon was keen to get to work on something more substantial. Kenny had begun working on the *Bombshell* songs at Air Tight, and Warners' producers of choice couldn't do the album in spring 2007 as planned, so delaying the release until 2008, which would kill momentum. 'Why don't I do it?' Jon asked, and Kenny thought: 'Yeah, why not?' He told Warners that Jon had worked with Brian Eno and Imogen Heap, among others, and they became more interested. Kenny and Jon recorded versions of 'The Racket They Made', 'Leslie' and 'Admiral', polished them up and played them to the label, who gave Jon the job.

With a working title of *Israeli Handspan*, the album was worked on in several studios. Eight tracks were started at Air Tight in Chorlton with Onthefly on drums, Uncle Beesly or Nathan Sudders on bass and Kenny doing the rest. He already had three tracks with Jon Hopkins too. Some of the eight weren't working, so Kenny reworked bits at Chem 19 studio with the Scottish-based musicians and in Jon's London studio using friends of Jon's. The first few months of 2007 were focused on getting the album together for a September release. After a spate of festival appearances over the summer, the lead single, 'You've No Clue, Do You', came out and did fairly well. Blair and Beth were on video duties again and spirits were high. Warners were banking on the next single, 'Home And A Sentence', being playlisted by Radio 2 and Kenny gaining a spot on *Later . . . with Jools Holland*. That was plan A. There didn't seem to be a plan B.

Kenny remembers a lot of arguing about the sequencing of *Bombshell*. Opinions like 'It's commercial suicide to open an album with a song like "Leslie"' and so on began to rankle with Kenny, who says: 'Jon and I made the record that we wanted, given that it had to be a big-sounding record and a full-band record.' He wasn't used to all this strategy and manipulation in the lead-up to a release. Surely it was best to just get the thing out there with the strongest songs as singles. The artwork was markedly different, however. Gone were the home-made collages and outsider paintings, in came black-and-white photos of Kenny looking dapper in a suit and trimmed beard. Did he enjoy that? 'No! I'm never comfortable in a suit. But you have to try things. You have to try.' Kenny chose the photo and was adamant he didn't want a shot of himself looking directly at the camera. He did all the inner sleeve artwork and is happy with that.

However, a worst-case scenario was about to unfold as 'Home And A Sentence' stiffed. Radio 2 said it was too indie and all the stations that had backed him so far said it was too mainstream. The record company blamed Kenny and Jon. Suddenly the campaign ground to a halt. The KC band did two support tours at the end of 2007 with KT Tunstall and Squeeze, losing money on both, and that was it. Sales weren't increasing, and even after a performance on *Later . . . with Jools Holland* there was no dramatic upward shift in sales.

Almost prophetic in title, *Bombshell* dropped off the radar and sank without much trace. Not only that, 679's deal with Warners came to an end and wasn't renewed. Other than The Streets and Plan B, everyone was binned – Mystery Jets, Futureheads, The Earlies, Death from Above 1979 and so on. 'It felt like three strikes and I was out,' Kenny mourns today. The music industry was haemorrhaging money and blaming the artists rather than its own wastefulness and stupidity. Even the stronghold reacted badly too. 'From the Fence camp there was a real resentment of that record. It was always: "Why's it not you up there?", but when it came out there was a backlash. Funnily enough, people tell me now they like it, but at the time it was treated unfairly. Onthefly is on it, Uncle Beesly is on it, Lone Pigeon is on it, Pictish Trail is on it, Barbarossa is on it, and I'm all over it! It's as much a Fence album as any of the others, so fuck you!'

Much of the criticism was that the record sounded too smooth and shiny, to which Kenny responds: 'Where's this "big production"? Jon

Hopkins did it the same way he did *Diamond Mine*, which everyone adores. It was mostly the same team on *KC Rules OK* and *Flick the V's* as well.' Discussing *Bombshell* now, Johnny Lynch admits the label pushed Kenny away from the Fence style as far as possible. 'Kenny probably wanted to see how far it could go without the Fence thing behind him. None of us were bitter about it. We were all "Go for it!" The label then collapsed. I think if they'd given it the proper push, it would have done really well.'

Nevertheless, the album did well with the press and opened him up to the broadsheet newspapers, earning five stars almost everywhere. Even the notoriously harsh punters' reviews on Amazon were complimentary. 'Why was it a failure? I don't know,' Kenny says. 'I think the wrong songs were chosen to lead it. "Home And A Sentence" was squeezed into a single format and shouldn't have been. It was not fair! Maybe Warners were trying to push me as their James Morrison, James Blunt or KT Tunstall, but they got it very wrong. They wanted me to distance myself from the Fence thing. The album was for a whole new group of people who were going to love it. No one gets a King Creosote album on a first listen. It's "What's this accent?" or "It sounds like two songs running at the same time!" Then a few weeks later, "God, I can't stop listening to this!"'

Billy Campbell, Kenny's point man, had been fired from 679, and Derek McKillop realised this label was not the right home for an artist like Kenny. Looking back on the success of *Diamond Mine* years later, it's clear that Warners got the whole thing wrong with *Bombshell*. They pushed it in everyone's faces when they should have let it creep up on people. Kenny insists: 'The people who worked that record loved it, and some say it's a lost classic. One day people will find that record.' It also coincided with the downturn in record sales in the UK. File-sharing and illegal downloading had taken hold. The single was dead. A label like Warners put lots of money into something and expected a big return: that's how the music industry worked. But now that return was not coming back on any of their acts, and King Creosote was one of them. It was time for Kenny to get independent again.

♪

At the end of 2007, though times seemed darker, Kenny's status in the music world had gone up along with his publishing value. Critics had loved both major-label albums and his profile had soared. Fellow musicians were full of praise, despite some snobbery from his own backyard. Domino, who had been happy to see him sign to 679 and were a tad derisive towards *KC Rules OK* and *Bombshell*, were now interested too.

By 2008 Kenny had started recording the follow-up to *Bombshell*, the more visceral and uncompromising *Flick the V's*. His feelings were: 'I'm going to record an album myself. I'm going to pay for it myself. It's going to be exactly what I want to do. It's going to tie a thread through those last four records. The Earlies have to be a part of it. Jon Hopkins has to be a part of it. It's going to be lo-fi. It's going to have Uncle Beesly. It's going to have Captain Geeko. I wanted this to seal that whole time off.' He set to work on a tight schedule and budget, just the way he liked it. It was compiled from home recordings, material recorded in London with Jon Hopkins and various rhythm sections, one track with Steve Mason at the controls and four tracks with The Earlies, and it was finished off and produced with Paul Savage at Chem 19. 'Making the album was a laugh,' Kenny recalls.

Paul and Kenny became good friends and musical allies. In many ways the album is as much Paul's as Kenny's. Unlike a lot of acts today, Kenny looks at an album as an album. Every track has to be in the right place. They discussed every detail. Kenny asked himself: 'What's going to make the biggest impact?', and they opened with 'No One Had It Better'. It was a statement of intent that sounding brittle and jarring compared to anything on *Bombshell*. The idea of the record was to incorporate lots of weird song connections and reference the past four King Creosote albums: for example, the last song, 'Saw Circular Prowess', has three tunes from *KC Rules OK* in it. With no major-label backing, no confusion over artwork or promotion, and no one shouting orders at him, Kenny had the album finished by December 2008 and released in time for Homegame in April 2009.

Knowing there was a new album in the offing, Domino started sniffing about. A mastering session was booked in London, and Kenny was adamant he wasn't going to change a single thing. He invited the team at Domino down to listen, saying: 'I'd love to do a record with you, but if it's not this one, then no hard cheese.' The Domino team listened and said: 'Yes, we're having it!' Manager Derek McKillop summed it up: 'Domino is the right label for you. It's where you should have been all along. You are not major-label fodder.' Laurence Bell adds: 'Warner's had worked hard, put out some good records, and Kenny made a bunch more fans. When the relationship ended, he was maybe a little bruised. I'm not sure he's cut out for major-label machinations. After it finished it was time for us to look after him for a bit. He needed a home with people he trusted. He was really close with Johnny in particular, and he had a lot of pals here. He just wanted some control back and to restate his independence, which is what we let him do. It just made sense.'

Kenny knew he wanted to call it *Flick the V's*. He says the title is not aimed at Warners specifically, but at himself and those who had sniped at the last two albums, saying: 'Why did I let that whole thing get to me? The whole thing was made by me and my friends in Scotland – fuck off!'

Now Kenny was signed to a team that understood how the underground and specialist music world worked. They weren't afraid of success, and had had their fair share with Franz Ferdinand and Arctic Monkeys, but they could make connections between an artist and the people who might like him. 'Coast On By', produced by Steve Mason (who says he only did it for the money), became the first single, which was seen as a return to form. The lyrics were spat out over a brutal electronic backbeat that swept aside the naysayers. His supporters in the media were back onside too, and the single got plenty of airplay. This was followed by a Bullion remix of 'No One Had It Better', which even ticked the Zane Lowe box on Radio 1.

The album entranced those who wanted something a little darker and weirder from King Creosote. It wasn't an easy listen, and Kenny says: 'It got a lukewarm reaction from some Fence fans. They were catching up on *Bombshell*, ha-ha!' Those who got the album really got it. His close friend and critic The Pictish Trail loved it, and Jon Hopkins was gutted he didn't get to produce it. If anyone thought Kenny was going soft, *Flick the V's* laid those suspicions to rest.

It's safe to say *Flick the V's* didn't change the world. It didn't sell millions or shoot Kenny to the top of the charts. There wasn't a huge amount of promotional or touring support, but Kenny didn't mind. He was glad to put it out there and let it do the work. It cemented his reputation as a no-compromise artist who did things on his own terms. The marriage with his new label seemed to work too. It was as if he was growing into his own skin. He had danced with the major-label devil and come out the other side alive. But yet again, Kenny was already moving on.

He started thinking about his live-album concept. At a time when sales were flat-lining he decided he wanted to make a stand against illegal downloading and file-sharing. 'My inner voice was saying: "It's wrong! It's wrong you can spend that amount on making an album and not even get the recording costs back." I make albums in ten days.' Consequently he and Johnny Lynch would think up increasingly bizarre ways of making music valuable again.

But as 2010 took hold, Kenny returned to his concept of 'My Nth Bit Of Strange'. Here was a selection of songs that would be performed seven times at the Homegame that year to an exclusive audience who would be encouraged to record the performance for their own pleasure on whatever gadgets they had. It would be a 'celebration of community, intimacy, exclusivity, rarity and physical artefact'. These songs would in principle never be commercially released or made physically available. I was at one of those performances, and it was spellbinding. After a brief introduction from Kenny, the first side was played in its entirety, with no applause permitted between songs. After an interval, side two was played and final applause allowed. With a specially made whisky handed out at the event and a reverent crowd, it was one of the best concerts I'd been to in years. I have a lo-fi recording of it from a dodgy phone I had . . . ah, the memories!

King Creosote never sits still for long. Like his brothers and talented friends, he constantly creates. 'All the time I was signed to Warners, I was also doing my own thing on Fence. I've got another version of the songs on *Bombshell*, called *Waltzer*.' With a little investigation you can find a list of every recording Kenny has released in his life as King Creosote, Skuobhie Dubh Orchestra and Khartoum Heroes. There are over fifty albums and counting. Some are fully distributed CDs or vinyl that you'll find in shops and online, some are small runs of CDs, cassettes or home-made box sets. He has songs all over various compilations and has collaborated with all sorts of people. Around this time he released the excellent *Love Hate Hate* album with his then girlfriend, Jenny 'HMS Ginafore' Gordon. He had only recently unleashed the awe-inspiring *They Flock Like Vulcans To See Old Jupiter Eyes On His Home Craters* and taken part in the *Cold Seeds* album project with Neil Pennycook. These countless releases are solely for Kenny's 'peace of mind'. Whether on one-off Secret Seven singles, remixes or guest spots on friends' records, Kenny always needed the ability to be experimental while his more mainstream material was coming out.

Another ingenious idea was Kenny's World Tour of Fife, when he played seven shows across St Andrews, Anstruther, Crail, Pittenweem, Colinsburgh, St Monans and Cupar with a skeleton band and his own car as transport. 'I had as much fun doing that as touring the UK or anywhere else,' he says. It might not seem like the most adventurous jaunt, but it earned the 'dedicated homeboy' a little money and saved him from the tougher sides of touring. Approaching his mid-forties, he doesn't necessarily want to be going on long hauls around the UK or Europe. 'It's not playing every night. I love that. It's the waiting, the sitting about, the parking etc. I find travelling so tedious.' He goes on: 'I would like to get to a point where for one or two years King Creosote only plays Fence events. If you want to see KC play songs from certain albums, you have to be at a Fence event.' This may sound uncompromising and even self-indulgent, but also rooted in reality. Without investment from Domino, he doesn't think he'll ever be able to tour extensively with a big band again.

To augment his live shows and unleash another fine set of songs on the world, Kenny pressed up the self-recorded *That Might Be It Darling* vinyl-only album and made it available only at gigs. Telling friends and fans in private that these songs might be his last, it was another way of making something exclusive, earning a crust and diverting attention from the free-downloading and file-sharing world. The album was another masterstroke. These songs would, however, reappear in a different form in the not too distant future, as would another long-awaited and highly anticipated collaboration with Jon Hopkins. At a time when some might have written King Creosote off as a cult concern who'd had his fifteen minutes, another creative and critical rebirth was just around the corner. The best was yet to come.

9

Astronomy for Dogs

Gordon Anderson and The Aliens

A lot has been said about Gordon Anderson, the Lone Pigeon. Most is little more than gossip and conjecture. It's a testament to his talent and reputation that these myths surround him. He is a wonderful artist and figurative painter who has exhibited his work far and wide in national and outsider galleries and embarked on various weird and wonderful installations. He once decorated a bathroom entirely in glow-in-the-dark Plasticine. He's an enigmatic, eccentric character, and the wayward-genius label allotted to the likes of Brian Wilson, Syd Barrett, Roky Erickson and Daniel Johnston is also applied to him. As his brother Kenny says, in the liner notes to the *Time Capsule: 001-010* CD box set: 'He is the most infuriating, funny, depressed, charming, vain, childish, puzzling genius I have the honour to call my wee brother. His music could not be anything other than it is – gloriously flawed and a wee bit alien.'

Often labelled as mad, Gordon says: 'I don't like the tag. I can see why, as I've done lots of crazy things, but I'm the one sitting here with this very troubled and cluttered-up mind. My life is very real to me.' Very real to anyone who has the chance to spend time with him, too. He is all the things Kenny says, and extremely confused, but he is never anything other than exciting to be around; ideas, jokes, songs and philosophies flow from him constantly. He explains: 'Before I was ill I knew what I wanted. I wanted to make music, write songs and get a band together. After I became ill I lost all my determination and ambition.' While avoiding sensationalism, it would be churlish not to talk of Gordon's illness, as it informs his music and art and has affected everyone around him.

Unfortunately, Gordon became very ill indeed. Initially, as things were taking off for The Beta Band, he tried to overcome his problems and continued to be involved in their progress. 'I went down to London, thinking there was a possibility I was okay, but I was too ill. I came back up after a day or two.' He continues stoically: 'They'd just been signed. They had to carry on. Steve had to step up and get on with the mission.' Asked what he thought of The Beta Band without him, he pauses, then says: 'I thought the "Three EPs" were good. But at that time I wasn't really that into music. The whole industry just seemed like commercial claptrap. All the other albums weren't maybe quite as good.' Of his state of mind at the time, Gordon elaborates: 'Imagine this cold, evil thing slowly invading your soul and gradually getting a bit more of you, eating away at you. I was so well: I'd been signed to EMI, I had a possible wife and a new band. I was planning out my future, then something came up and said "Gotcha!", and after that that was it. I've probably never been the same since.'

The years 1994 and 1995 plunged Gordon into a living hell. After his notorious French trip and subsequent satanic visions in London, his demons were beginning to manifest themselves in his actions and his day-to-day living. His behaviour became more and more erratic. With increasing frequency he would have frightening episodes, and it was clear he needed serious help. Returning from London to live full-time in Fife, he spent most of his time at his parents' house and eventually in hospital. Looking at a few of the countless scrapbooks he began to fill, you see both works of art and upsetting documents of a man's descent into madness. They are crammed full of childish doodles, elaborate drawings, unhinged rants, pseudo-science, comedy sketches, Egyptology, star maps and conspiracy theories. He managed to destroy a number of these hard-bound sketchbooks, but a few remain with Kenny and Gordon today, and they are astonishing and terrifying artefacts.

One tragic story goes that he decided to run up to his friend Toby Malcolm's cottage at Denhead Hill, near Craigtoun Park above St Andrews, where Een and a young Kate Tunstall were staying at the time. He set off with the top bar of a cross attached to his shoulders, walking barefoot through waterlogged fields, stinging nettles and broken branches, dressed in boxer shorts and a T-shirt. Apparently he'd seen a vision of St Andrew's cross above Drumcarrow Hill. 'A voice told me to get to the top of that hill. I got to the top of the hill and then started walking home. I saw a shadow of myself with the bar across my shoulders and it looked like Jesus on the cross. I suddenly had a feeling of peace.' In his desperate state he couldn't walk home, and ended up at Toby, Een and Kate's cottage, where he went into a full-body spasm. 'I can't remember anything after that,' he says.

Kate Tunstall recounts the event: 'He had a real psychotic episode. He had been talking about building a twelve-foot cross and we were getting quite worried. He built something and dragged it through a field in his underpants and bare feet in mid-March. He walked through a barbed-wire fence and up a hill. The others went out to find him, and he was half-naked and slashed up. He was babbling and talking in tongues. We managed to get him inside and he kept screaming: "I'm burning, I'm burning in hell!" Een wanted to call an ambulance, his dad arrived and was shouting at him, and our friend Toby just couldn't handle it. I tried to role-play with him and pretend to be an angel, saying: "I'm immune to the fire, give me your hand." In a flash he snapped out of it and went "Fuckin' hell, that was mental!", and he was back, laughing about it.'

After that episode Gordon was admitted to hospital and stayed there for most of the next year. The hospital diagnosed him with 'religious delusions, schizophrenia and possible epilepsy'. His family and friends were shocked, but there was nothing they could do. He was a loose cannon and liable to cause himself serious damage if unsupervised. Kate continues: 'At one time he said he was Jesus but his left hand was the devil. He had an evil left hand. It got to the point when we thought he was really going to hurt himself.' When Kate talks about these times today, you can see how traumatised she was. Later she would write a song about Gordon called 'Funny Man'.

Like many former psychiatric patients, Gordon is scathing about the care he received in Stratheden Hospital. 'They prescribe you all the medicines under the sun until they've got you where they want you. I remember seeing people come into the hospital with depression and within twenty-four hours they'd be walking around like zombies.' The stories sound almost fictional, as if describing a scene from Ken Kesey's *One Flew Over the Cuckoo's Nest*. 'I'd have medication that made me rock back and forward, do repetitive movements and grind my teeth. I wouldn't be able to talk properly. I remember once my dad visited me when I was like that. That's when I stopped taking the medication. I'd put it in a plant pot or hide it under my tongue.'

He was prescribed a hundred and forty-four electric shock treatments over twelve weeks. Entering an oppressive room full of ancient 1940s equipment, he'd be hooked up to a drip, given a hot water bottle and administered this inhumane treatment. He'd wake up hours later with soft, spiky hair and a glazed look on his face. 'I remember going to a Christian convention years later, and this guy said: "You've had ECT, haven't you?", and I said: "Yeah!" I felt like I had two concrete blocks at the front of my head for years. It was like I'd been slightly lobotomised.' He's still extremely angry with the hospital, as is Kenny, who says: 'He went through hell on earth. Electric shock therapy, the works . . .' Gordon adds: 'It would be good if someone exposed what happens in these hospitals. You see, once you've got the rats in a cage you don't have to show people what you do to them.'

It's difficult to prove one's sanity to the relevant authorities after you've been sectioned once. Gordon couldn't leave hospital until he received permission. He would go home and try to live a normal life until he did something 'wrong' again. He would walk around St Andrews barefoot, praying openly. Soon his father would call the nurses, soon he'd be sectioned again by force. The longest continuous period he spent in hospital was nine months. Imagine what that was like for a creative, energetic man in his twenties. He remembers that everyone he knew came to visit at first but they all stopped eventually or came less and less, except for his parents. He is sanguine about it. 'It's tough. You understand you're in there and you might be for life. You're not going to get visits for the rest of your life. No one's going to do that. They've got their own lives to lead.'

He made some close friends on Lomond Ward, including David Crow. 'David is a great songwriter. I christened him Lomond's answer to Lennon. We talked about two albums we were going to write, *Too Disturbed To Hae A Bird* and then the follow-up, *Too Many Birds To Be Disturbed*, with us surrounded by bottles of champagne in a swimming pool.' There was a piano in the hospital, and when Kate Tunstall and Gordon's dad visited one day, he and Kate wrote a song, 'Sweet Carolina'. It's never been recorded, but I have heard a solo rendition from Gordon and it's a wee classic.

Kenny thinks Gordon may have been playing a continuous game of trying to escape. Gordon counters: 'There's a strange urge you have when you're locked up twenty-four/seven that makes you want to escape! It's as simple as that: if you're locked up, you want to escape. It's not a game.' Playing cat and mouse or not, his spiritual calling was getting louder and louder. Soon he decided to travel to the Holy Land, on foot. 'I tried to walk to Jerusalem from Fife five, six or seven times and would sometimes get as far as Edinburgh, Newcastle or wherever, and that was the kind of thing that would take me back into the hospital again. But God was telling me to go there. And I eventually got there too! In 1997 I went to London, then walked from London to Canterbury, then got the bus to Dover, took the train to Nice, then flew to Israel and arrived there with £40. When I spoke to a girl at the tourist desk in the airport, I asked where I should go. She said "Go to the Gordon Hostel, Gordon Street at Gordon Beach," which is where I stayed for the first week.'

He enjoyed Israel and spent a happy time there, staying two and a half months and meeting girls before, unbelievably, ending up in prison. Looking for money to travel to Mount Sinai, he took a volunteer job on a boat. It's illegal to work in Israel without proper papers and visa, so when police inspected the boat they found a ranting Scotsman working there without the correct documents. He was slammed into prison. For six weeks he spent twenty-four hours a day in a small cell with seven other inmates. To pass the time and make friends he drew all the prisoners he met. In tune with his religious beliefs he grew a beard, wore white robes and took to fasting. His recollection of prison is that he felt fine and actually enjoyed the experience.

Another disturbing event was to unfurl behind bars. Gordon explains: 'I heard God say "Go, circumcise." I went into the toilet and held the connecting tissue underneath the tip. I looked up and said "Father . . ." I just snapped it with my fingers. There was no blade involved, no pain and only a few drops of blood. When I walked back into the cell the others started shouting, and the guards took me away to a locked ward and eventually the prison hospital, where I ended up drawing everyone.' With the help of the British Embassy he was released and taken to the airport to be returned home under guard. As soon as he got back to Fife, he was seen walking around in bare feet and praying, and was brusquely shoved back into hospital and pumped full of drugs.

Gordon maintains: 'How I got better was by *not* taking my medication, and fasting quite a bit and getting help from Christian friends Tom and Donna Jennings.' Tom would visit the patients at Stratheden to give some comfort to the suffering. 'Tom and Donna loved the fact that I did music. Tom loves my art and always wants to come and learn to sculpt and become more creative.' Another helping hand and shoulder to cry on was an elderly lady named Morag. Gordon remembers: 'She was a lovely old Christian friend of mine who sadly died of cancer in 2011. She was sixty-seven. She'd visit me in hospital and invited me in to live when I had nowhere to stay. She'd always let people share her house. But she was too nice. Some people stayed, took advantage and cleaned out her drinks cabinet. She had an open house and never locked her doors. She painted stones with Jesus on them and gave the money to charity. She sold loads of them. I'd get away to Morag's for some spiritual help and healing. At the time I kind of called her my second mother. Now Morag's gone, I'm a lot closer to my real mother. But there was a time when I wasn't well enough to be around my real mum. Morag was quite tolerant. And she always encouraged me with my music. Always!'

Gordon maintains these Christian helpers were his salvation. 'A lot of my Christian friends are trustworthy and were always there to help. When I needed them, they were there more than anyone else.' Asked if he still feels religious, he says: 'Of course, I believe in Christ. I don't go to church often, as I don't find the environment easy to be in unless I'm with my Christian friends. I'm not the greatest Christian ever, and I may have fallen quite a few times, but I hold on to Christ. I sternly believe that Christ did bring me through my illness. I never went back.'

In the second half of the 1990s Gordon lived an unpredictable life, in and out of hospital. He furthered his religious obsession and tried to commune with his idea of Christ, searching for an enlightenment that forever seemed unattainable. As mentioned previously, one summer he shared a cottage with Kenny ('Let's put the crying one together with the holy one!'), in which they had lots of parties and bonded as brothers and friends. They played a lot of music together and even thought about forming a group. Gordon says: 'That's when I thought Kenny's songs got better and better, and when I heard his true voice. I felt I was the vehicle Kenny needed to hear his true voice.' Despite his own anguish, he was thinking about music again and would record whenever he was feeling well enough. Kenny remembers him sometimes strumming a single chord for hours. In most people's hands this would have been torture, but somehow with Gordon it sounded almost transcendental. Kate Tunstall remembers those monochord solo jams from when she briefly shared a cottage in Fife with him, and concurs about how musical those experiences were.

It was around this time that I met him properly, at T in the Park in 1996. It was the weekend when he and Kenny discovered that bag of pills. I had heard a few stories about Gordon but had yet to meet him. I recall him gazing at my girlfriend and using the opening line: 'I can see oceans in your eyes. I could swim within your eyes.' She was indeed a pretty girl, with saucer-like blue eyes and a rosebud mouth, but she had never met Gordon before and was extremely embarrassed. I thought it was quite funny. Gordon now puts this kind of behaviour down to his medication. It's hard to tell whether it was that, or his natural state of mind, or extracurricular drink and drug use on top of the medication. Whatever the case, he was impish, mischievous and incredibly intense, but also charming and full of life. That encounter will always stay with me.

Towards the end of the 1990s it seemed most of his worst trauma was behind him, and he was discharged from hospital for the last time in January 2000, moving in with Tom and Donna Jennings, who helped 'heal him with prayer'. Kenny had taken on the Fence shop in St Andrews and remembers Gordon turning up at the counter one day in flowing white robes, white prayer hat and a massive beard. Gordon says: 'I felt like I was trying to follow Jesus to the full. If you walk around Jerusalem, a lot of the Christians are wearing white robes, sandals and beards. I'd been there and I knew I wanted to live a spiritual life.' It was obvious that, though the doctors deemed him able to live within society's boundaries, he was still out on a limb and walking his own path.

Soon he was able to move out of Tom and Donna's and find his own flat in St Andrews. It was from this point on that his music began to re-enter the public consciousness for the first time since the early stages of The Beta Band. This is down to Kenny's diligence, foresight and goodwill. As Kenny was setting up his own micro-label and shop to sell his own material on limited-edition CDs, he wanted to do the same for Een and Gordon. He rifled through boxes of cassettes and Minidiscs to find music to include on *Moses* and *28 Secret Tracks*. Gordon says: 'I was never aware of what was being released on Fence. I didn't know and I didn't mind. It was all Kenny's doing. I still don't know which of my songs have appeared on Fence! There are people who've covered my songs on Fence and I haven't heard them. I wouldn't dream of listening to them. I think Kenny's done a good job of releasing my music, though. I probably don't appreciate what he's done to help me get where I am.'

Two pieces of vinyl would really prick up the ears of the music industry and fans from further afield. As the fickle London spotlight was turning towards this strange little outpost, thanks to James Yorkston's success, the desire to hear more outsider musicians had to be sated. James was quick and forthcoming about turning on interested parties to UNPOC, King Creosote, Pip Dylan and Lone Pigeon. First the 'Touched By Tomoko' EP, and then a split 7-inch single, 'St Patrick'/'Rocks', with Yorkston, appeared on the Bad Jazz label, on which James was releasing his own material. These tracks had been recorded in brief spells when Gordon was out of hospital, then compiled and edited by Kenny.

Gordon recalls: 'I asked Kenny: "What did you call me?", and he said: "Lone Pigeon, because you were in The Pigeons," and I thought, "That's all right."' Kenny had also given Gordon his name. His parents were about to name him Stuart when the five-year-old Kenny intervened. It may have been after the footballer Gordon Strachan. Gordon adds: 'The thing is, I hate pigeons. I absolutely detest that bird. I mean, would you like to be called "Daft Budgie"? I've got another name, "Snow Boy Cosmos", but it's not very good. I don't even like the name Gordon.'

The reaction to these releases was delight in an understated, underground kind of way. These were the early days of the internet, and the relevant chat rooms and message boards lit up. As Radio 1's new music DJ in Scotland, I was always searching for new sounds. When I heard the Lone Pigeon releases, I was stunned and booked Gordon to play a live session on my show. Backed by Fence collaborators including Kenny, they played 'Rocks', 'T.R.U.T.H.S' and 'Harper's Dough/Don't You Stop Trusting In The Lord', with limited chat from Gordon. Those who heard it were captivated, and Gav 'Onthefly' Brown first became aware of Fence through that show. It was an exclusive too – no one managed to coax Lone Pigeon into a radio studio again, as far as I know.

Joff Gladwell at Bad Jazz had a new label project called Sketchbook and soon wanted to release a full-length Lone Pigeon album. Again, Kenny sourced the material and pulled together the music that would find its way on to the seminal *Concubine Rice*. Gordon is untypically upbeat about this album, saying: 'It was nice to have a record out and get a few reviews. I did all those songs by hand, lo-fi, and I like the fact that Kenny put it together. People seemed to quite like it. It was an honest piece of sketching.' Those first releases were written, recorded and produced in the 'mad years', little outlines of infinite possibility from a genuinely gifted individual. To a hardened, cynical ear they may sound half-finished, but for those who want something pure, untouched and naive in the twenty-first century they are special. Much like demos for The Beach Boys' *Smile* or some of Daniel Johnston's output, these were simple melodies and lyrics aimed straight at the heart.

But all was not well. For others it would have been plain sailing and the first step towards success, but almost immediately he shunned any fame and prosperity that could spring from these new beginnings. 'I thought lots of fake "isms" started to creep in,' Gordon says. 'People would come up to me and say: "Hey it's the Lone Pigeon – I bought your album," and so on.' He started behaving irregularly again. 'I was on the road to getting well again, I'd feel brilliant and then go and get drunk like everyone else. And the slightest bit of drinking would make me go crazy.' Once when students insulted him on the streets of St Andrews, he answered them back and was thrown through a shop window. Unbelievably, he came out almost unscathed. Police didn't even charge him. Another time, trying to impress a girl, he karate-chopped a window and fell through it. He paid for that, but got away without charges as he was deemed 'unwell'. 'Being unwell sometimes helped,' he admits.

Although these timelines are not absolutely clear, you can roughly say that before 2000 Gordon was unwell and spent long stretches of time in hospital, whereas after 2000 things got slightly if unsteadily better. Laurence Bell's account of his guitar-burning incident on the beach after the Fence Cosmos Centre gig is mentioned in Chapter 6, and that seems typical of his behaviour at that time. It was for the most-part alcohol-fuelled. He explains: 'I missed out on a lot of my twenties, so I did party a wee bit.' He would, in his own words, 'go on a bender', which would result in him destroying his room or smashing random windows around town. He got to know the police quite well, and they'd look after him when arresting him and charging him with breach of the peace.

They say you always hurt the ones you love. Once, after drinking a mug of vodka, Gordon hit John Maclean over the head with a penny-whistle before punching Kenny in the face and giving him a black eye. He saw him the next day at a festival and asked: 'Did I do that?' These aren't stand-alone incidents. The patience of friends and family was frequently tried. His brothers and other Fence acolytes were forgiving, but only up to a point. He says: 'I think I've burnt a lot of bridges. There's something inside me that is always trying to destroy me . . . that isn't me.'

Despite these episodes, it was clear that Gordon was starting to feel better, rehabilitate and recover. If not back to his old self, he wasn't as troubled as before. He bought himself a Boss BR8 digital eight-track recorder in 2000 and set to work building up an extensive catalogue. 'I loved that thing and I was great at using it,' he says. He spent weeks recording a never-ending flow of musical ideas. Until 2000 his recordings had been analogue, mainly on a basic four-track recorder. From here on it would be easier on digital. He continues: 'I had a period when life was a lot better than it had been. Because I was a lot better, I could record quite easily, and that's pretty much all I did! I don't know why I have the inkling to record so much. It was great though. I loved it, and when I recorded and finished a good track, I felt it was part of me.'

The next step was to play live. He hadn't done anything like that for years, but began to attend Kenny's Fence Nights in Aikman's. He describes those nights as 'the golden Fence years. I remember looking around the pub to see if there was anyone I *didn't* know! I'd turn up late and Kenny would say: "Oh, it's Gords", and Een and I would just go into this big harmony thing. It was great!' A myth was building around the brothers and their effortless songwriting and singing. Locals and visiting devotees would hope for those rare occasions when King

Creosote, Pip Dylan and Lone Pigeon would play together. In the early days it happened quite a bit, though Gordon is a little dismissive now. 'I'd just end up doing "Rocks", "Waterfall" and "Summertime Beeswing", and people think that's my only repertoire. It's always good fun and sounds fresh, but I do have other songs!' Asked about his brothers' music, Gordon is noncommittal. 'I don't go out of my way to listen to their music, but some songs filter through, and I like them. But then, I don't listen to my own music either.'

Aside from local Fence gigs with brothers and friends, Gordon's reputation was reaching across the country. Old friend and mischief-maker Andy Guest coaxed Gordon into doing solo Lone Pigeon shows and started to organise short tours and attempt to manage him. 'It was just me sitting on a stage, playing – not very well, probably,' Gordon says. 'Andy encouraged me to play in front of people, which wasn't very easy. I didn't play the piano at the time, and I wasn't that great on the guitar either, just a strummer. Mental guy starts strumming onstage, ha-ha!' These shows are legendary among those who saw them. Whether transcendental, heartbreaking affairs when the audience was spellbound by the ethereal songs, or complete disasters with Gordon tuning a guitar for hours, half-finishing tunes, getting bored and walking off in a strop, they were always memorable and uncompromising.

In a further show of support, Lone Pigeon's second solo album, *Schoozzzmii*, was bankrolled and released by Andy, containing some semi-coherent songs as well as great artwork depicting King Creosote, Pip Dylan, Uncle Beesly, Captain Geeko the Dead Aviator and friends in effigy. Asked about his compositions on *Moses*, *28 Secret Tracks*, *Concubine Rice* and *Schoozzzmii*, Gordon says he simply sat down until the music and words came out. Rarely does he write a song to order or plan it in advance. 'They're not always about someone specific. Usually my songs are about, you know, a girlfriend or a feeling. I did write some songs about Morag when she died, but they're not the kind of songs you want to listen to.'

He does, however, take on different personas and voices. 'Maybe because of my slight schizophrenia, I've amalgamated so many different characters into my brain,' Gordon says. You'll hear The Beatles, Neil Young, The Beach Boys, Bobby Gillespie, The Stone Roses, Elvis Presley, Leonard Cohen and Monty Python in there, percolated through the

Lone Pigeon filtration system. I never think he sounds exactly like any of these, and keeps his own character throughout, but Gordon is harsher. 'The key is to take all these influences and push them out as something new. I don't think I've ever done that. I think my music is copycat. Steve sounds like Steve, Kenny sounds like Kenny. Een's in the same vein as me – he's used his influences to the point when he sounds like them.'

Perhaps because of the nostalgia his music evokes, or the Beta Band connection, in the early days of Fence Gordon was acclaimed beyond anyone else. Once James Yorkston signed to Domino they were desperate to get their hands on Lone Pigeon too. Laurence Bell remembers: 'There were two sides for me. There was this whimsical, British, psychedelic pop side with very playful lyricism and almost nursery-rhyme tunes, mixed with these plaintive, heartbreaking ballads and laments. And he has such a staggering voice as well.' James had helped spread the word, Kenny had recorded and compiled his material, and Andy Guest had encouraged him to tour. Labels were now courting him, and offers were on the table. Says Laurence: 'Joff Gladwell was the only other London person who was on to that scene when I first visited. He was planning to put out *Concubine Rice*, and I'd have loved to have put it out, but we got to do it in America. We were trying to get involved.' Still Gordon resisted. Sometimes he wouldn't even preserve his best music. 'There are some songs I never want to record. Sometimes recordings don't do a song justice. It's like taking a photo of a beautiful scene and not quite capturing it, or bringing a pebble back from a beach. It doesn't feel right.'

Why do the songs rarely resolve or sound complete, more like snippets and snapshots of songs? He is lucid, analytical and more than capable, so why? 'Firstly, I can't be bothered, and secondly, I just have to get all the ideas down as quickly as possible. I write songs all the time. I always try to make these little pictures with music. My phone is full of songs. I wrote one yesterday in the Co-op.' Candidly, he continues: 'I've got the bricks, the pipes, the windows and the good floors, but I can't build a house. If only I could find the strength to do it. I'd need help.' When you first hear the Lone Pigeon recordings, it's an epiphany of sorts. You feel like you've met a long-lost friend and you're looking into the inner workings of his fragile, mixed-up mind. They sound like the recordings of a disturbed individual at times, and there is little quality control. If he has an idea, he records it. It's an assault on the senses by someone whose senses have been assaulted, but among the incoherence and gobbledegook there are moments of true beauty and genius.

$$\oint$$

As Gordon embarked on his solo journey, John Maclean had been thinking about working with him again. He was his close friend, and with Robin had tried getting him back into The Beta Band. They broached the subject with Steve Mason, but were rebuffed. It probably wouldn't have worked. The Beta Band were fractured and fragmented enough without having Gordon to deal with. However, they were to join forces again soon enough. John explains: 'Before The Beta Band split up, Gordon and I had had a go at making music. I tried to sort out his song "Rocks". So when we did split up, I had something started already.' So, in 2005, after a depressing few months post-Beta Band, John made contact with Gordon again. 'I was close friends with him and would go to see him in hospital whenever possible. He'd send me everything he did, but always said he needed the right producer. I loved the lo-fi sound, but I don't think he's lo-fi; I think he's capable of being Brian Wilson with an orchestra. But people love that straight-from-the-horse's-mouth stuff – "I've got this and no one else has, he's speaking to me person-ally." So I guess with The Aliens I wanted to try to realise his bigger stuff. He's a musician and he heard symphonies in his head, not little lo-fi recordings.'

They roped in Robin and visited Gordon in Fife and began to make music. John says: 'It was fun! It was like the start of The Beta Band again. At the end that had got more oppressive, with people saying "You can't do that" all the time. It was back to being totally free and doing whatever the hell you want.' There was also excitement among the music community and fans that three of the original Beta Band had a new project that might even eclipse their previous efforts. A lot of Beta Band fans had heard Lone Pigeon material and realised Gordon's poten-tial. They knew the history of 'Dry The Rain' and wanted more. The combination of these untapped musical ideas with John and Robin's skills and experience was a mouth-watering prospect.

Ensconced in West Newhall Farm cottage, Gordon recalls: 'They came to my house and said: "Gordon, let's start doing music together," and we started recording pretty much there and then.' This was how The Aliens came together. 'It was good to have some help with the music,' says Gordon. 'John and Robin were very caring and encouraging. It was good to be busy.' Een says: 'He'd been fine well before The Aliens got together, but everyone needs to be part of something.' They needed a name, and John recalls that this was down to Gordon. 'I wasn't sure about it. Gordon's obsessed with aliens even now and insisted on it, and I was fine with it. He missed out on The Beta Band, and we were trying to help him get his stuff done, go on tour and show him a good time. Creatively I wanted to do the videos and musically I was happier to let him take control. We had a few Roky Erickson fans saying "You're not The Aliens", but we weren't aware of that band.'

I visited West Newhall Farm cottage when making a BBC radio documentary, *Songs from the Kingdom*, about some of the characters in this book. With fluorescent coloured walls, alien sculpture installations, huge paintings, electronic equipment and band gear strewn everywhere, it was total madness but hugely inspiring.

Gordon, John and Robin set to work on what became the 'Alienoid Starmonica' EP, comprising 'Intro', 'Robot Man', 'Only Waiting' and 'Ionas: Look For Space', a song that goes back to the start of The Beta Band. They wanted to record these older songs properly and make the definitive versions. John explains: 'We went to a cottage in Edinburgh with a friend, John Williamson, who helped produce the first EP. We recorded half of it in his bedroom and half of it in the Forest Café. It was a mixture of us giggling and being creative and Gordon being absolutely mental.' Gordon adds: 'The most fun was doing that first EP. We'd experiment by recording a song, then put the song on a tape and record the tape playing in a car going past. You could almost see the music.'

The recording process was less than conventional. For example, Gordon was given the task of recording the vocals and stayed up all night to do it. When the others found him the next morning he was sitting with a towel around him, sweating, and there were *three hundred* vocal tracks. The end of 'Only Waiting', for example, had roughly as many tracks to be sorted out. He'd record vocals on all the music tracks too, so they had to salvage vocal takes from random drum and guitar channels. They had to cut, trim and edit a total mess. Eventually it was mixed in London. Gordon was unwell, so couldn't attend, and John says frankly: 'It was a beast! But Gordon had it all in his head. If you took out one of the three hundred, he'd probably notice.'

'Gordon wanted a bigger band with two guitarists,' John recalls, 'but I was adamant that it was just the three of us. I wanted it to be like at the start, just lots of fun. But it changed. Gordon wanted it to get bigger and bigger. I went along with it for a while, but I had to keep control of it. Gordon's great at inviting people in and changing his mind. Then someone has to get rid of them. Gordon lives for the moment. At that moment he'll sign away everything – "I don't care about the money or the percentages. You can all own my songs." Then three weeks later, "Why am I not making any money?" I keep using the words mad, mental and crazy, but to me Gordon wasn't any of those. However, when you're following someone who changes all the time, it *is* kind of crazy.'

With impeccable timing, John received a call from an old ally, Keith Wosencroft, who was head of A & R at Parlophone. He was keen to hear this new post-Beta Band project, and when he heard 'Alienoid Star-monica' he wanted to sign the band there and then for a five-album deal, but John, cautious due to past experience, settled for one. They set up their own label, Pet Rock Records (Gordon's choice), run by John and their management. They had hooked up with Troika Talent, a formidable team of Michelle Curry, who had been a club promoter and had looked after Goldie, and Connor McGaughan, an actor's agent and still John's film agent today. Troika immediately saw through all the crazy deals being made. Companies were offering artists nine per cent and managers were saying 'Oh yeah, that's fine!' This meant Troika would end up crossing swords with EMI. John enthuses about Connor and Michelle: 'They were the best management we'd ever had. Much better than anyone who looked after the Beta Band.'

Sadly for the band, Wosencroft left EMI almost immediately after signing them, with management claiming their deal with EMI had been a mistake. John says: 'Slowly we realised that the imprint didn't mean anything, and they're still the same deals that massively favour the record companies. You start to realise why they have big houses, big cars and eat in all the best restaurants while the band leave with nothing.'

Regardless, it was thrilling to have The Aliens land on the pop landscape at that time. Rock 'n' roll needs outlandish characters to add colour and be subversive, and it seemed like The Aliens were here to do just that. The first EP was just the right mix of electronics and traditional band set-up. It was slightly off-kilter and quirky, yet emotional and heartfelt. Beta Band and Fence fans took to it quickly. It was also well received in the press and won airplay on Radio 1, 6Music and elsewhere. They had Single of the Week in *NME*. John says: 'Even getting back into the *NME* when you're a bit older is a struggle, so that felt like quite a compliment. You want to feel like you're making something a bit relevant.' Radio 1 wanted them in for a session, and they made the front cover of the *Guardian Guide*. This EP is the only Aliens release that wins Gordon's approval today. '"Robot Man" sounded good on the radio. I'd never heard a song of mine on the radio before. John and I were in a car in Crail and we heard it. It was probably your show!' The future looked bright.

Now, however, Gordon looks back with disappointment. 'The Aliens was meant to be just three laptops. It was supposed to be computerised, alien sounds . . . then the guitars crept in and the drums and so on. John did all this interesting electronic stuff and I ended up masking it with all this derivative 1960s stuff, the crappy Beach Boys harmonies and guitar solos. It wasn't meant to be like that.' John Maclean, on the other hand, says: 'Gordon's problem is that he always wants perfection, and halfway through recording a song he thinks of a new way to make it better and scraps the older version . . . again and again and again.' Gordon declares: 'It was no one's fault it didn't turn out as electronic. One of the keys, though, was that we had to play live. Robin's a drummer, John's on keyboards and I play guitar, so the band thing just happened naturally.' But John counteracts the laptop/electronic argument. 'Gordon changes his mind all the time. You'd be playing a song, having spent two weeks learning the parts, then Gordon would say: "Stop! Stop! This should all be done on laptops." But we'd get to the same point on laptops and he'd probably say "This is all soulless!"'

Whatever anyone says today, the album, released as *Astronomy For Dogs*, was keenly awaited. The artwork is a photo of Gordon looking up at the trees from his cottage, with Een's dog and a telescope Photoshopped on to the picture. The telescope is pointing towards

Left. Pre-teen punks in matching T-shirts, James 'Yorkston' Wright and Michael 'Vic' Galloway in front of 1970s curtains. Oh dear . . .

Middle. A fresh-faced Skuobhie Dubh Orchestra with Kate Tunstall, Een Anderson, Andy Robinson and Kenny Anderson.

Bottom left. Streetwise. Busking in Stirling, a slightly later incarnation of the Dubhs with Jason Brass on fiddle and Atholl Fraser on guitar – note the T-shirts and CDs for sale.

Bottom right. Your 'blond bombshell' author as a Khartoum Hero on Teases Estate in Fife, with a rabid fox under-arm. OK, it was stuffed and mounted on a plaque.

Right. Accordion King, a youthful Kenny Anderson looks for his cues. And looks a lot like his daughter Beth.

Middle left. Kenny Anderson playing with his hairy banjo. I mean, bouzouki.

Middle right. A right slapper: Een gies it laldy on the double-bass with a cheeky smile, while Andy accompanies on snare.

Courtesy of Kenny Anderson

Courtesy of Toby Malcolm

Right. Khartoum Heroes in a shadowy room. L–R: Vic Galloway, Kenny Anderson, Stu Bastiman, Een Anderson and Pete MacLeod. A nice array of hats too.

Above. Jamming *au naturel*, Gordon and Kenny Anderson trade licks in the countryside.

Left. Aaaaw. The twins, Een and Gordon Anderson, in matching tops and *de rigeur* helmet haircuts. We all had them.

Bottom left. Art student Gordon Anderson dreams and strums away – a guitar was never too far from reach.

Bottom right. Gordon in Edinburgh, strumming a guitar again . . .

Cross-eyed and painless: Kenny Anderson, Bruce Bell and Gordon Anderson. Love those blond highlights and tie-dye. It must be the early 1990s.

The vinyl countdown . . . King Creosote puts the needle onto his beloved 1980s records.

The reigning monarch of the Fence Collective, King Creosote today.

Left. Los Amigos de Beta Bandidos. L–R: Richard Greentree, Robin Jones and Steve Mason.

Middle. The Beta Band and friends hang out in the pool during a video shoot.

Bottom left. Original gangsta! John MacLean will almost certainly pop a cap in yo' ass.

Bottom right. The name's Mason . . . Steve Mason.

The Beta Band: they could only occur right now

Above left. Robin Jones gets carried away.

Above right. Tucked in, The Beta Band get deadly serious about press-shots and rock-star chic.

Right. Causing chaos on tour with Radiohead in the USA, Steve and Robin are sweethearts of the rodeo.

Bottom. Robin on set at *Top of the Pops*. Sadly, the performance was never aired.

Left. Too much, too young: James Yorkston (with school cap) and Steve Mason (with Adam & the Ants patches and calendar) with assorted friends and family.

Middle left. Orchid Segura: Teenage goth James Yorkston and pals in his first serious school band.

Below. A gothy, punky, baggy, tie-dye nightmare: James Yorkston and Vic Galloway in Edinburgh.

Above. Huckleberry pose at the bar in the Venue in Edinburgh. L–R: Stu Bastiman, Vic Galloway, Reuben Taylor and James Yorkston.

A Fence Hallowe'en. L–R: King Creosote, James Yorkston, Sean Dooley and The Pictish Trail. Scary!

James Yorkston and the Athletes all fit in a boat, circa *Moving Up Country*. L–R: Reuben Taylor, Faisal Rahman, Doogie Paul, Wendy Chan and James Yorkston.

Jon Thorne and James Yorkston play it by the book, in the St James Library, St Andrews at Eye o' the Dug, 2012.

Courtesy of KT Tunstall

Kate (not yet KT) Tunstall's first ever press shot as a teenager.

Courtesy of KT Tunstall

Simply wonderful, darling. Kenny Anderson, Kate Tunstall and Steven Phillips in St Andrews in the early 1990s.

Courtesy of KT Tunstall

Cheeese! KT, Beth and Kenny Anderson, and a wee bit of pizza.

Boho chic from a
bona fide pop star,
KT Tunstall.

KT Tunstall lets her hair
hang down at Eye o' the
Dug' in St Andrews.

Desert rose. KT Tunstall in Arizona for her *Invisible Empire/Crescent Moon* album.

Left. Up close and personal with the Lone Pigeon, Gordon Anderson.

Right. The pilgrim and his donkey. Gordon in full religious robes and sandals in Israel.

Right. The Aliens have landed! L–R: Robin Jones, John MacLean and Gordon Anderson.

Below. Heading into space, the Aliens' launch their official press shot.

Courtesy of Toby Malcolm

Courtesy of Toby Malcolm

Een Anderson using a trusty road sign as a wobble-board in the Skuobhie Dubh Orchestra.

Een stares out the camera as a Khartoum Hero – lovely beret!

Courtesy of Stephanie Gibson

Playing his first Pip Dylan live show in ages at the Fence Gnomegame, Een puts his heart and soul into it.

Courtesy of Stephanie Gibson

Gold, always believe in your soul! Johnny 'Pictish Trail' Lynch pimps it up and shows us his heart.

The Pictish Trail sheepishly records backing vocals on the Isle of Eigg.

Courtesy of Stephanie Gibson

Johnny is given his lines at Homegame 3.

Ladies and gentlemen, please welcome onstage . . . The Pictish Trail.

Steve Mason, renaissance mod and boy outside.

Monkey mind in the devil's time, Steve Mason comes of age.

Anstruther, rock city! A Fence line-up in the Wade Academy gym hall.

Diamond geezers: King Creosote and Jon Hopkins.

As the show comes to an end, Johnny 'Pictish Trail' Lynch and Kenny 'King Creosote' Anderson embrace.

Sirius, the Dog Star. It's a dog looking from the Eye of the Dog, a name for St Andrews that Gordon and Steve Mason had coined years before, towards the Dog Star. Gordon adds: 'Sirius is a double star, where the pyramids point to, and it's supposedly where life originates from.'

The album was recorded in a proper studio (Olympic), which was a first for Gordon, but old hat for John and Robin. John remembers: 'The producer, Tom Stanley, was a really nice guy and understood Gordon. Gordon wants to do everything, so it's hard finding someone who can work with him.' Gordon moans: 'It was done in a rush one summer. I wasn't pleased with it; it was flat, shiny and overworked. But I think something happens when you put music on a record to sell. It makes you regret it and judge it. It doesn't belong to you any more.' John adds: 'It was fun doing the demos, but not so much when we came to recording the album. Partly I lost interest in making music. And also, we'd have to start from scratch again, touring little venues and so on.'

The album contains some outstanding songs and a few silly ones. In 'Robot Man', 'Setting Sun' and 'The Happy Song' there were natural pop songs and singles for newcomers as well as the initiated to explore. Naturally, Gordon disagrees: 'I killed "The Happy Song" by recording it. I hate The Aliens' version. It was one take. If you had a piece of cheese stuck between your arse cheeks, it would probably sound like that.' John agrees: 'We shouldn't have done that. But again, at that moment Gordon said: "It needs to be faster", but I would have made it slower and darker. Every band has a different dynamic. Should we follow Gordon? Well, it was his song, and he's more musical, so you want to follow him. But you want him to be right! There's a whole side of the record, with "Honest Again" and so on, that's very Gordonesque, and I didn't really feel part of it. There were a few tracks that I was involved in, like "Rocks", but others that are completely Gordon. In The Beta Band I kind of did my own thing. It was a bit boring playing some-one else's melodies, but annoyingly I couldn't come out with a better one, so I just did it.'

Gordon didn't enjoy the sessions either. In an airtight, professional underground studio he found it hard work doing take after take of vocals and guitar parts. It would be a lovely sunny day in London and he was stuck in a dark, sweaty studio. Almost immediately the cracks were beginning to show. Was Gordon cut out for the life of a professional musician? To make things worse for him there were problems with artwork, hence the confused lyrics on the sleeve. Then the album's marketing went awry, with copies not making it to the shops on release day. What had started as an explosive concept primed for success was slowly turning into something else.

It was no one's fault in particular, and despite Gordon's gloom-laden view today, all was not lost. They'd made an accessible, albeit eccentric, album and stepped out of the shadow of The Beta Band. It was obviously not the same group, and that was clear. The songs did have a more traditional 1960s rock feel, but were augmented with John's burbling, bleeping electronics, indebted to his much loved *Screamadelica*. The Aliens had arrived.

$$\oint$$

As they took to the road to play live, with a friend, Jamie Dargie, on bass, expectation was high. Much like Lone Pigeon shows, these were unpredictable affairs. When firing on all cylinders, the band and their songs could transport you to that celestial place where only good psychedelic pop can take you. When Gordon was discontented, however, things could be ramshackle and volatile. He would berate the audience or pick on someone in the front row. He took to pouring bottles of water over his head onstage, practising karate kicks and acting out comedy routines he was interested in at the time. It could be awe-inspiring one moment and cringeworthy the next. Gordon recalls: 'As a frontman, you're on your own. I know I had the other guys around me, but when you say the wrong thing or you fight with the crowd or whatever, they're not always going to jump in.' I saw them in Edinburgh at the Liquid Room and Cabaret Voltaire and in London at Koko, and had the pleasure of introducing them onstage at the Rock Ness festival. They were eye-opening every time.

John reminisces: 'Live, it was always chaos. I had a stick with a pad on the end and I'd nudge Gordon if he went on too long between songs. When he did his solo stuff, I think Andy Guest had a bell and he'd ring it when it was time to stop talking and play the next song. Sometimes it was funny, but sometimes it was too much and he'd break the thing you'd just built up. To get to the juicy stuff, you had to go through the cringe-making stuff. But I didn't mind the comedy – it was like Andy Kaufman or something. It was when it got angry that I didn't like it. He'd go into the audience and pick fights if people were talking or whatever. When we did a relatively normal gig, with song after song after song, then an encore and leave, Gordon enjoyed it. I'd say it was a great gig and that he didn't have to do the crazy things. I'd want to leave them wanting more, but often Gordon would want to go back on. I'd say no, but he'd go on and do a half-hour version of a slow song and people would start leaving. Then again, other times we'd go back on and it would be the best bit of the gig.'

And the stories continue. 'Sometimes Gordon just wouldn't stop playing, he'd go on and on. We had promoters screaming at us and even turning us off. Once at a festival in Stockton, Beth Jeans Houghton threw a painting wrapped in brown paper on stage. Gordon was rolling around on the stage and took ages to unwrap it while singing the refrain from "Bobby's Song". Eventually he unrolled the painting and the audience cheered! But it was like *Spinal Tap*. He wouldn't leave the stage. So I left, then Robin and Jamie, and we stood in the audience and watched him singing the song on his own.'

Gordon enthuses about the live experience. 'There were some great gigs with The Aliens. My first stage-dive was amazing. I used to pray before going on to ask Jesus to make it special. One night in London I felt this finger pushing me from behind, so I went with it and ended up being passed around the crowd. I made this cross shape and couldn't even feel the hands holding me up! It was such a weird experience. I started doing it tons after that, even if there was only a handful of folk there. Another gig in London I felt I was tripping, I was so nervous, then I felt the whole audience were tripping. Your audience can be a total reflection of the way you are on stage.' Another night they went on as zoo animals. Gordon was a zebra in a black-and-white striped, tasselled jumpsuit. 'I look back on that and think I looked like someone out of Kiss – horrible!'

They all enjoyed touring the US, which sadly they did only once, to promote the first album. Although the venues were the same three-hundred or four-hundred capacity as in the UK, they had stand-out gigs in LA and Chicago among others. What made the difference? Gordon says: 'Appreciative audiences, a big bus, an open road, swimming pools, deserts, beaches, cities, futuristic visions, girls, glass hotels, food, juice, "You're welcome, sir!" and so on.' Put like that, it does sound enticing. But John says: 'He's a total revisionist. He found it tough too. He didn't always want to go on stage every night. He'd get too drunk on the bus. Obviously there was some great stuff, and you forget the bad.'

Gordon did eventually tire of UK touring: 'It's like driving around a cold, wet, soggy, minky farm in a tiny wee minibus. You stay on the farm, then you drive around the farm the next day and maybe see a cow. That's touring around Britain.' He has always been a hard man to please. John recalls: 'He and I almost had a fight on stage once when I started a sample at the wrong time. But we were close enough that we could talk to each other like that. It was different in The Beta Band – if anyone did anything to upset anyone, it would take weeks of reconciliation. But I think Robin got a bit bored with Gordon and me constantly falling out.'

It was never plain sailing. John says: 'The best gig we ever did was in London at the Hoxton Square Bar and Grill. It was sold out months before and there were people crying, pleading to get in. It was the last time we played London. The last ever gig was terrible. It was in Paris, for a radio station, and the head of French radio was there and it was a big deal. Someone was being a jerk in the crowd, so Gordon waded in. The atmosphere turned weird and a lot of people left, but Gordon didn't give a shit: "Fuck it, it's rock 'n' roll!" Some people just didn't get us – it was too out there.'

What would they do next? In 2006 Damon Albarn was setting up the Africa Express project, bringing western and African musicians together to collaborate and exchange ideas. In its inaugural year The Aliens were invited to take part alongside De La Soul, Massive Attack, Magic Numbers, Get Cape Wear Cape Fly and others. Quite an honour, you might think, but Gordon just remembers everyone drinking beer for five days solid in the Democratic Republic of Congo. John remembers the atmosphere being slightly fraught amongst the gathered stars. 'I wanted to talk to De La Soul about hip-hop, but they were too cool for school. I mean, I toured and DJ'd with Maceo from De La Soul and he totally got The Beta Band. He'd come and see us when we played America. But the other guys were a bit more standoffish. Musicians are weird . . . especially successful ones.'

Gordon wasn't impressed by his own behaviour either. 'I did terribly among that bunch. My performances were awful. I just jumped off stage all the time. They all thought I was a nutcase. I'm not one for jamming either, and there was quite a bit of that. I didn't end up making music with anyone out there. I wasn't in the right place, and I always felt I was doing the wrong thing.' He got on well with Robert del Naja (3D) from Massive Attack, but of the Blur frontman he says: 'Damon Albarn's got enough friends.' John says: 'I thought Damon was really cool, and he was nice to me. But Gordon was being particularly difficult. It was a strange dynamic between all the people there. Gordon picked a few fights, and a few of the other musicians didn't understand him at all. They thought he was an ass. We weren't invited back. People say you go to Africa and you go a bit loco. Things are heightened. Take Gordon there and things get extremely heightened.'

$$\oint$$

If The Aliens hadn't taken off quite as they had hoped, their stock was still fairly high after their debut album. They'd caught people's attention and everything pointed towards an exciting next chapter. One good thing out of Africa was a photograph that would make the cover of their next album. Taken at the edge of the jungle, this bright and juicy portrayal of some fruity vegetation looked both dreamlike and psychedelic, perfect for its purpose. Titled *Luna*, their second album would be recorded and produced by themselves on their ProTools set-up in Fife and Cornwall. This would be exciting but daunting, especially when dealing with Gordon the perfectionist pigeon.

The harsh news soon came that EMI were to drop them. Times were tight for the industry and labels were laying off staff and artists. Keith Wosencroft had jumped ship and the skeleton staff at the company saw these weirdoes as surplus to requirements. John says: 'When EMI dropped us, it was a relief. It was almost like: "This place is going to shit, we'll let you go." But I'm glad those companies are being punished now. You work in a label like EMI because you want to make money. If you didn't want to make money, you'd probably be a musician! All those guys know when to jump ship, though – all those smooch cocaine people. Just like bankers, they know when to move on.'

As we know now, the industry was in a state of flux. Fewer and fewer consumers were buying albums, and the way music was consumed was changing, all down to the internet. So The Aliens decided that if they couldn't beat them, they could join them. They had their own label, they had a following, they had the technology and skills to do the job themselves, so they did.

They moved into a house in Pittenweem in the East Neuk that had until very recently been occupied by Steve Mason. They set to work recording the album with an overriding sense of cabin fever, using each room in the house to record different instruments – vocals in the conservatory, piano in the kitchen, drums in the sitting-room etc. John missed Edinburgh and London and went a bit stir-crazy, but they worked hard and finally travelled down south to mix it at Sawmills studio, the old Beta Band haunt, which John calls 'the best studio in the world, as far as I'm concerned'.

Once more, Gordon is doubtful in retrospect. 'It started off as good fun. There was a lot of lost direction on it from me. It was sounding great on my KRK speakers. But it was the same story: once we got it to the mixing desk and finished, it was nothing like I'd imagined.' He continues: 'I didn't get my say. John wanted "Bobby's Song" at the start, and I didn't. I wanted it towards the end, so people could listen if they wanted to, but not start the album. But John lived in London and was good friends with the management. There's so much of that second album on various hard-drives that we should have put on there, beautiful long pieces of music. I wanted this piece of music I'd written to start the album – this piece that's twenty-one-and-a-half minutes long. It got chopped to half a minute. Then Robin did a piece that was ten minutes long, and that got chopped to half a minute and joined on to my one.' John adds: 'At the mixing, John Cornfield and I caught Gordon at the right time and said we should cut back all this extra stuff and edit it. He agreed, but regretted it later. Maybe one day we should make a redux three-hour version for fans only, but at the time I thought it was better edited the way it was. It needed it.'

You can see the problems John was facing in trying to rein Gordon in. Gordon adds: 'The album was hard work, especially "Bobby's Song". There was a lot of me sitting there for endless nights with John saying whether it was right or wrong. Again, all the music was there, but there was never anyone to make it sound good, to strip it down or to beef it up. There was no production.'

Although far less 'pop' or commercial than its predecessor, *Luna* is a better album. The delicate and tender passages are more intimate, the full-throttle rock element is more unashamed, and the untamed psychedelia is allowed to roam free within its grooves. John says: 'I was more pleased with the second album. It was more the three of us, whereas the first album was more Gordon. It's probably better for it in a way. It was the best album we could possibly make of Gordon's vision.' Gordon remains scathing. 'It was like "Let's put the more melodic one here, then the Stone Roses-y one next and then something faster after" – it was all that kind of thinking. I'd rather have done it the way it should have been done. There are three people's ideas mismatched together and only sometimes do they blend. I think we needed someone to step in and go "Guys, this is crap!" But the management company were not music managers. They operated in the film and TV world.'

John says: 'I thought *Luna* was a better album, but it wasn't as well received. There's definitely something fishy going on – if your record comes out on EMI, you immediately get better reviews or bigger reviews. When the first album came out, *NME* and the *Guardian* were positive and other good reviews followed on from there. When *Luna* came out, *Music Week* and *Pitchfork* wrote bad reviews and everyone quoted those. No one stuck their neck out for it. We were trying to be free and not concerned with being cool, but the press are so obsessed with trying to be cool.'

The main criticism was that the songs were too long and self-indulgent. John laughs. 'We got *Luna* down from three hours to eighty minutes. People call it indulgent now, but they should have seen it before we mixed it!' He continues: '"You do what you do" is my motto. Robin and I would say albums are just recording the periods of time you make them in. But Gordon couldn't really see that. He always wants it to be a classic. He calls me up about my films and says: "John, this has to be a masterpiece", and I'll think: "No, it doesn't!" It can just be what I make. When you look back at 'Alienoid Starmonica', 'Champion Versions' or 'Inner Meet Me', they were done without much thought. But then overthinking comes in. You've just got to do things and keep doing them.'

The band came to the BBC in Glasgow around release time to do a live session for my Radio Scotland show. They performed 'Sunlamp

Show', 'Theremin' and a version of 'Billy Jack' that ran almost nine minutes, the longest session track *ever* performed on my show. My producer and I thought it was going to crash into the News and I'd have to fade them out. With about forty-five seconds to go, the track ended, I thanked the band and we went to the newsroom bang on time! It was almost as if we planned it, and, it being radio, no one saw the beads of sweat on my brow.

$$\text{\clef{treble}}$$

Not long after *Luna* was released, Gordon wasn't feeling well, so the tours booked to promote the album were cancelled. Gordon then went travelling in India for months. That was a real setback. They lost all momentum and their profile waned. Instead of moving up to larger venues, they were back on the toilet circuit. John blamed Gordon, but says: 'He just follows his whim. He works harder than anyone I've ever met, but it's always on his schedule. He'll only do it if he wants to do it. He's great at recording, but when it comes to the band stuff like writing press releases, sorting out lyrics or getting the artwork together, it's difficult. When he went off, I realised I needed something else to do – i.e. my film stuff. I couldn't rely on him.'

This is when John's film career really began to gather momentum. He'd always wanted The Beta Band to be an art collective, and from the start insisted they made their own videos. Along the way he wrestled with record companies that wanted flashier promos, but usually got his way. He was a natural film-maker, developing without major budgets or outside control. For The Aliens, he made short films to accompany 'Robot Man', 'Setting Sun', 'Magic Man' and others. They were made on little or no money, in a DIY spirit. The backwards 'Magic Man' shoot took a day, cost £500 and was filmed in a studio outside Edinburgh at Nine Mile Burn, referencing Spike Jonze's video for The Pharcyde. 'Setting Sun' was shot on John's own camera and cost nothing except for travelling to the south of France, where it was filmed at a friend's house. John recalls: 'I made that for Gordon. I wouldn't have made something quite so soppy, but I knew Gordon would like it. He loved it.'

Then there was the hilarious *Maintenance* short that cuts in *Star Trek* footage with John's own. It was filmed in Robin's living-room, and

John recalls: 'When we were recording "Alienoid Starmonica" in John Williamson's place in Edinburgh, we were always tripping over cables and wires, laughing all the time. I started imagining there was a spaceship above us and we were the drunken Scottish crew below.' As well as the Beta Band videos, there are daft little vignettes including *Chalk and Cheese*, a trailer for an imaginary cop show featuring Steve Mason and Andy Guest as the policemen and Mani from The Stone Roses as the bad guy. There's also a spoof of the film *High Fidelity*, with Pete Rankin from Old Jock Radio working in a charity shop. Most of these are on the Beta Band DVD or on YouTube. Others featuring Gordon are still in a half-edited state, but John may complete them one day.

Increasingly John knew what he wanted to do. 'Making videos for the bands was probably a better school than film school. Learning at every stage, from holding the camera to editing, filming, telling a story, making use of no budget.' He adds: 'Gordon was the hardest worker in the band. He would have rehearsed from 9 a.m. until 2 a.m. every day. But I just hate rehearsing, and was always the first one to stop during a jam. I was probably getting a bit sick of music in general. I like DJ'ing and I like making videos. They're the things where I'm in control and the things I'm good at.'

The Aliens might have had greater success, and felt somehow defeated. There were further mishaps too. John remembers: 'We were booked to play a live session on Zane Lowe's Radio 1 show, and the night before Gordon slipped on a log and broke his collarbone. We had to cancel the session and any gigs around it. It took months to heal properly too. After that he wasn't as lively onstage. He used to crowd-surf, and I loved it when he did, but after that he was more careful.'

So far the public hadn't taken them to their hearts, the media hadn't championed them very much, and the band themselves didn't seem happy. It was time for a break: maybe just a hiatus, but more likely an end. Gordon now looks back with a fairly scathing eye. 'I don't like the majority of The Aliens' stuff. It sounds like three guys in a room with ProTools. Everything had gone a little bit tinselly. It was generally okay, but we made mistakes about which programs we used, what we left on and off the records, how over-busy it was.' It's sad that Gordon looks back at The Aliens like that. In my eyes they were an explosive flash of light in an increasingly dull mainstream pop world. They made two joyous albums and an EP with little or no plan, pretension or artifice. Those who listened or saw them live had a knees-up too. But if the band had been a massive success, I think Gordon might have had another opinion altogether.

Gordon has plenty to say about it all, and most of it is brutally honest and negative. 'I saw a poster for The Aliens in the US and it had a photo of me on there with my belly sticking out. A fat guy on stage doing "Robot Man"? Nah! Music is a young man's game – it's not for the over-forties, is it? Put it this way, I've seen old guys with guitars on stage and it doesn't look good. To grow old gracefully in music is a difficult thing.' On touring, he adds: 'It's not a spiritual life being in a band, you can't pretend it is. You spend your life in a tent at a festival with a pint in your hand, or standing on a stage with people gawping at you, or in a minky wee hotel on the outside of Manchester.'

These are words tainted by a sense of failure – his own perception, one not shared by those who enjoy his music. John talks of his and Robin's despondency: 'I think Robin thought being in a band with Gordon would be the best band in the world and the songs would shine. I think he was a little disappointed. He maybe didn't realise how damaging it could be. I would get depressed when Gordon would put us down and say we were shit. The negativity was really the last straw.'

They were a gang of misfits who made uproarious music, art and film. In a scared and conservative music industry, it would be almost impossible to sell them to the masses. John now says: 'It was still more fun in The Aliens than The Beta Band. We were freer and we could say what we liked. Steve's illness, depression and attitude were different. There was always a black cloud hanging over the band, whereas The Aliens didn't have that cloud – it was just thunder and lightning!'

Like many who feel burned by the industry, Gordon treats the whole business with suspicion and contempt. 'I still like bands like The KLF, where there was no "voice" or message in there. There are so many points of view in the world. I don't want to be famous any more. I'd like some money to buy a house, but I don't want to be famous. After my small taste of it . . . nah! Someone said to me: "Fame is just a room full of men wanking." And it is. If people saw that, they wouldn't aspire to it.'

John talks frankly about Gordon. 'The time I saw him happiest was when we took him snowboarding after we'd toured Switzerland, and he was out every day. He was too tired to be crazy! It was amazing, he was so much better. That was probably the time I decided not to do The Aliens any more. He was miserable at the gigs, then as soon as they finished he was really happy. It was too much responsibility and pressure for him.

'We tried to make another record after *Luna*, and went to Robin's cottage in the countryside. But we just pissed about and made stupid films. Every time we went near the computer to record something, it just felt wrong. Everyone wanted a different thing.' Is there any frustration at not making it bigger? 'We were an older bunch and all in our thirties, and if we'd been a bit younger and good-looking, things might have been different. I remember when we were trying to get played on Radio 1, and we heard that the playlist team said: "We only playlist bands who look like our listeners." It didn't come to an end. We're still together, in a way; we've just stopped and we may start again. I definitely think that after the feature film I'd like to do something musical again.'

10

Travelling Country Crops

Een Anderson and Pip Dylan

The most technically gifted of the twin brothers, Een is a supreme musician and a complicated character. Unlike Gordon in many ways, Een is slightly taller, with boyish good looks. A little calmer and more self-assured on the surface, he is less flighty and more inclined to focus deeply on a particular task. He is also more defensive and probably less naive than his twin. Perhaps watching Gordon tripping up and making constant mistakes taught him lessons. More grounded, practical and dependable, he may be harder to get to know, but as he lets you in you're able to forge a bond. Een is always practising, rehearsing and edging closer to becoming the master musician he aspires to be.

Growing up with a twin, he is frank about their relationship as children. 'I've always been the passive one. I would always be the one pushing the go-kart or the sledge, or giving him a backie on a bike. Gordon would be "Een, go and get me that!" and that kind of thing. Very early on, you get into a role. He was always "I'm first!" But that sometimes has its advantages: he'd fall off the wall first, or go down the deep, dark cave first.' He adds: 'Gordon and I were left a lot of the time. We'd run riot, I suppose. We'd be allowed to stay out until ten or eleven at night unless my dad was back off tour, and then he'd say: "Get to bed!" and expect order in the house.'

'I used to be deaf,' Een says unexpectedly. 'It's called glue ear, when the tracts of your ears close up. No one noticed for ages, probably until primary six at school. There was a teacher, "Buggy" Baxter, who'd turn around and write on the blackboard. That was me screwed because I couldn't hear what he was saying. I learned to lip-read from a young age. I can still do it to this day.' Gordon adds: 'Een had to have an operation to open up the grommets in his ears. After the operation I remember him complaining about how loud everything was. He could partially hear before, but once the passages were opened up he could hear properly. People thought he was a bit daft before the operation. Years after the operation he started to pick up the guitar and other instruments, and now he plays pretty much everything.'

Een was quiet and withdrawn as a result of his hearing problems, but didn't want to cause any fuss. 'As a kid you don't want to draw attention to yourself, and you imagine everyone's like that. You don't know you have a problem. But I had an operation, and after that I could hear everything – I could hear the moon moving around the atmosphere!' Before that, he'd retire into his own world. 'I just used to make things out of cardboard boxes.' Creative from an early age, he and his twin had different skills but complemented each other. 'When I created something, it was like building or making something in 3-D. Gordon would draw and paint all the details like the windows, doors and books. I was making the stuff and he was colouring it in.'

Een took a great interest in nature, bird-watching in particular. 'If half your world is shut off, you just go into your own world. What better than to look at little birds? Like the birdman of Alcatraz, I was in the solitary confinement of my own head. The vision of a bird flying is like freedom.' He'd sit in the garden and feed the birds, setting basket traps to catch them and have a closer look before letting them go again.

Growing up in St Andrews, with access to the beaches, coastline, rolling hills and forests, Een became more and more fixated on nature, befriending others who were similarly interested. He began to keep small birds in an aviary he'd built and was instinctive when tracking animals in the countryside. When Een and I were in Khartoum Heroes together, in our early twenties, I remember him lying down next to a rabbit warren, utterly silent, and suddenly grabbing a baby rabbit to cup in his hands to show me and drummer Stu Bastiman. The animal wasn't scared, and Een treated the tiny, shivering furball with delicacy and respect. To me he was Nature Boy!

As a young lad, keeping small birds wasn't enough for Een, and he began to breed them in his parents' garden. He started with cockatiels; the first one was called George and the next one was Susan. He bred more and expanded his aviaries. He says today: 'It was just an extension of making things with cardboard boxes, except with wood and wire netting.' He also built nest-boxes and put them in trees within neighbouring forests and parks. He'd make show cages, and even entered the occasional competition. Proudly producing photos, he adds: 'I showed my Latino cockatiels and I'd get £40 each for them – that was a lot of money when you're ten. They'd have eight babies, and I was "ka-ching!" It all got a bit ridiculous; I was getting into genetics! I was mixing the chromosomes to get different colours of cockatiels. I remember writing down Xs and Ys and working out how to get the dominant genes. I'd cross a cinnamon with an albino or greys. I liked the pure colours, though.'

Despite this back-garden biology, Een did not shine in the class-room. He did just enough to get through and admits: 'I wasn't great at school, because I'd missed the fundamentals at the beginning. I couldn't hear what was going on. I bet there are people who don't even remember me being there, I was so nondescript. I went in, did what I had to do, then headed home and went bird-watching or worked on my aviaries.' Een left in fifth year, not completing his Higher exams. He shrugs his shoulders: 'I didn't have any interest. I wasn't going to university. Later in life I started working everything out for myself. Everything started to make sense.' Strangely enough, Een has a very quizzical, engaged and somewhat mathematical brain today. School just didn't suit him at the time.

Judging by both their accounts, Gordon and he didn't see each other that much at school. They were in different classes and had different friends from beginning to end. For his entire time at primary school Een hung out with Keith Douglas, another super-talented guitarist (now with his own band, The Corps of Discovery) and lover of Django Rein-hardt and jazz via rock 'n' roll and rockabilly. At secondary school he made friends with David 'Wearie' Waters, Gordon Hastie and Sandy Duncan, all of whom took an interest in nature, farming and outdoor pursuits such as birdwatching.

During his childhood and teenage years, music played almost no role in Een's life whatsoever. He recalls: 'The only time was when I got a Louis Armstrong tape. That was the very first music that I liked on my own. I even thought about playing saxophone. I tried one and thought:

"What am I doing? I can't even blow up a balloon!"' Although his father was a gigging musician and owned two record shops, he says: 'The only thing I remember was when someone was sleeping over – there'd be some hairy guy stinking of booze on the sofa, or sneaking in the window late. Dad had lots of great musicians in his band, though, and people who went on to bigger things. But he never encouraged us to do music professionally, because he knew how hard it is and all the downfalls that go with it. You had a job in the day and played music at night for fun, so you had financial security. It was always "Get up and get a real job!" He worked in insurance before and only became professional later on.'

As Kenny and Gordon attest, the Anderson household wasn't as all-singing, all-dancing as you might expect. Een recalls: 'I don't remember any music in the house, really. There wasn't anything to listen to music on until Kenny and Lynne got into their teenage pop stuff in the 1980s. I suppose I was aware of Michael Jackson's 'Thriller' and Frankie Goes to Hollywood etc. I quite liked it and would tape the chart show off the radio. I heard a lot of punk thanks to Wearie Waters, but I didn't get into it. At that point when you're becoming influenced by music, I wasn't listening to very much at all.'

He remembers one key influence, though. 'The only thing I remember that I think is a big influence on my songwriting is Simon and Garfunkel. They did the *Live from Central Park* concert on TV when I was a kid. I watched it with my dad and friends and thought it was great. Since then I've listened to them a lot and taken a lot from them. That's how I got into that kind of 1960s Americana sound. When it came to singing and playing, that's what I would go for.' He wasn't really aware of his older brother's accordion lessons and hard work either, mainly due to a five-year age gap. 'I never remember Kenny going out to play shows as a teenager with his accordion. We would have been sent to bed or whatever. We had very little to do with each other at that age.' As school drew to a close and the big, bad world beckoned, that would all change. For the next few incredibly formative years, the twins didn't have much contact with each other at all. But soon Kenny and Een's lives would become entangled, with music the glue that bound them together.

Applying for a course in Countryside, Conservation and Wildlife Management, it looked as if Een had discovered something he could throw himself into. It covered animal husbandry, gamekeeping, gun management, building traps for vermin, dykeing, fencing and hedging. Based in Perthshire, he would occasionally study at college and lived on the farm estates where he was learning his skills. 'It was a good course. I've used pretty much all of it since. I've not shot anything, right enough.' Lasting the full three-year course, he earned his diploma.

A huge life-change was just around the corner. When he was staying on a Perthshire estate in a caravan, the first incarnation of The Skuobhie Dubh Orchestra, featuring Kenny, Bruce, Etienne, Martha and Eric, turned up unannounced. Een clarifies: 'I hadn't seen Kenny for about five years. He'd been away at university for four years, then went busking around Europe. Even before that I hadn't seen him, because while he was out and listening to music we were still playing with Action Men. When we started playing music together, I thought to myself: "I don't know you!"'

Regardless of how well he knew his brother, he was impressed by the motley crew that had arrived out of the blue. Their colourful clothes, *laissez-faire* attitude and wandering lifestyle appealed, but also the music they were playing. Een says: 'When I first saw the banjo, I thought: "I have to get myself one of those!" I'd hardly ever heard one and I'd certainly never seen one. I went out and bought a cheap Hondo, which was like a frying pan. I learned how to play clawhammer stuff, then got a better one, a Washburn, and taught myself out of a crappy book. I had no interest whatsoever in music until I was nineteen or twenty, when I first started playing an instrument. I think one of the reasons I didn't have any interest in music was because it didn't seem like an enjoyable thing to do. You'd been taught in the classroom.'

After this life-changing visit, the band went back to Europe and busking while Een applied for countryside ranger jobs in Fife. Realising these jobs entailed mountains of paperwork and public speaking at schools and colleges, he took on a hedging job and then a deer-fencing project on Mull. Soon enough Kenny and Eric returned to Scotland, this time without Etienne and Martha, who had eloped together. They immediately suggested Een take up the double bass to make a busking trio. He recounts: 'At first I got a guitar, took two strings off it and accompanied them at a wee pub gig on Mull. I found it quite easy. So I sold my car, a lime-green Vauxhall Chevette, and bought a half-sized double bass off Ged Grimes from Danny Wilson. When I started playing the real thing, I took to it immediately. I had a good sense of pitch and time.'

The lure of the travelling, music-making life was a huge pull on the young Een. Floundering after college and working half-heartedly on Mull, the decision was easy. He chucked in his job, moved briefly back to Fife, sold his birds, and headed off to join Kenny and Eric in the Dordogne. From there the trio went busking around the country while Een began to master his instrument. He first learned how to slap the bass with a single beat between notes, then in double time and finally triple time, playing what was basically light-speed bluegrass and giving the trio its rhythmic click and harmonic bottom-end. It was his musical initiation, and he lapped it up while Kenny and Eric looked on in awe.

Een and Kenny returned to Scotland, for a while playing gigs as an accordion and bass duo, briefly teaming up with singer-songwriter Andy Laing from Little Green Monkeys to gig as a trio. Een branched out from double bass to mouth-organ and clawhammer banjo. While performing at a craft fair in Tayport, the two brothers bumped into Andy Robinson, alias Captain Geeko the Dead Aviator. He and Kenny had been at school together, and although he was into prog-rock and clueless about bluegrass, he offered to play drums with them. It wasn't long before the French banjo aficionado Eric made his way over to make up a quartet. Een recounts: 'That was the beginning of The Skuobhie Dubh Orchestra that I remember, playing proper bluegrass.' While twirling the double bass and slapping away, Een was also watching over Eric's shoulder and learning his tricks, and so improving on the banjo. 'With the bass I just took to it, but the banjo was something I actually had to learn.'

This was the first of two classic line-ups of The Skuobhie Dubh Orchestra. With the Anderson brothers out front harmonising, Eric's lightning dexterity on the five-string banjo and Andy's rock-solid back-beat, the live Scottish grassroots scene took them to their bosom. They were faster and tighter than any band on the circuit, and they had youth and good looks on their side. In today's music scene it's not uncommon to see acoustic, folk and traditional instruments on display, but back then there was a huge division between the indie/rock scene and the acoustic/folk world. The Dubhs had a foot in both camps and attracted large numbers of young people. Not only did the band look youthful and grungy, which was the prevalent alternative style of the time, but they played their hearts out and went really, really fast. It was the perfect soundtrack to a party.

Their following became a fan base that began to swell across Scotland, not least among young ladies. Een became the pin-up of the band and enjoyed himself immensely. 'When I first started playing the bass, it was all about the show and spinning the thing around. I didn't have to think about playing it, and I got this attention from girls and everything. It was great, but I got sick of it early on. They hang around with you and expect you to be "Mr Party" all the time.' With a long-term girlfriend, two children and a relaxed and settled life today, it may be hard for him to remember that as a handsome young man with an ass-kicking band, he was Mr Party quite a lot of the time.

As the music progressed and the bookings expanded, it was clear that Een had ambitions beyond the double bass. He often practised the banjo twelve or fourteen hours a day, especially when the band wasn't on tour. I remember touring in Europe with Khartoum Heroes a couple of years later and sleeping in the van after shows. I'd wake up first thing in the morning to hear Een twanging away on the roof. On Eric's frequent returns to France, Een would take over the lead instrument with no detriment to the band's sound or speed.

It was around this point that Kenny started introducing his songs to the group and things began to change. On top of the traditional Irish songs, country, rockabilly and bluegrass, Kenny wanted to move forward and have original material. The band adapted, on the whole, but key instrumentalist Eric finally decided to leave. Not only had he had enough of the Scottish weather, but he wanted to continue to play the faster, more traditional bluegrass that the band had made their trademark. Een stepped in. He says: 'As good as Eric was, he had to teach himself timing. He wasn't versatile enough to play something that would fit. Everything he played, he'd actually learned. But in order to step in, I had to be as good as he was in that style.'

The lives, ambitions and attitudes of Een and Kenny would slowly diverge on to separate paths that for many years ran side by side, and eventually veered away from each other. To talk of sibling rivalry is simplistic, but all would not always be well between them in the years to come.

$$\text{\textxi}$$

The Dubhs played relentlessly all over Scotland for the next few years, headlining Aberdeen's Hogmanay in front of thousands, selling out venues across the land to audiences of four hundred to six hundred people, and recording their traditional barnstormers and Kenny's originals on a couple of sterling albums, as discussed in Chapter 1. They sold cassettes, T-shirts and CDs and welcomed local press coverage and plaudits from peers and rivals. There was quite a bit of hyperbole around them, and egos were brandished as they hit their peak.

Around this time Een first became romantically involved with a young singer-songwriter and Dubhs fan, Kate Tunstall. The St Andrews girl had been befriended by Kenny and would occasionally sing backing vocals or provide percussion for the group. Youth, good looks and ability were on both their sides and the attraction was mutual. Een sees it as a fairly casual affair to start with, as Kate would commute between London and Fife for her university course over the three years. It wouldn't be until the later 1990s that the two would live together and collaborate musically.

Een claims it was at this point that Kenny started giving him a hard time on and off stage, calling his playing 'sclaffy' or 'noodly'. Een had only recently started playing music, and says he needed reassurance rather than criticism. Maybe he was overplaying, but where someone else might have been more diplomatic, Kenny seemed to come down heavy-handed on him. It's a feud between the brothers that continues to this day. Een is adamant that Kenny bullies him about his playing and appearance, and Kenny maintains that Een is belligerent and difficult. Even at a one-off Skuobhie Dubh Orchestra reunion show in Stirling in 2010, they apparently hardly spoke to each other. Een remembers the early 1990s and says mockingly: 'Maybe there was some jealousy because I was better-looking. Maybe it's because he's insecure onstage he felt he had to put me down to take the heat off him. It doesn't happen with anyone else. I've done gigs with Gordon and my dad, and you get gratification for what you've done and it's a good laugh.' There could be truth in that. Een was five years younger, he was becoming a fine musician, he was captivating onstage and he'd usually get the girls he wanted. However, to an outsider this looks like a simple case of older-brother syndrome and younger-brother paranoia. There was a lot of laughter too, but whatever the case, there is a massive bone of contention between them and Een is still bitter about it.

The band was incredibly tight and played brilliantly together despite family disputes. They never had rehearsals, using only soundchecks and gigs to perfect their songs. Each time they played they would get better and better. I saw them at the Vic Café in St Andrews, the Subway in Edinburgh and at the Cupar Festival, and they were always unbelievably fast and exhilarating, with Kenny's recognisable croon breaking through on the slower, self-penned numbers. In their armoury they had the mighty *The Van Album*, a great showcase of the band's bluegrass roots alongside a couple of full-throttle rockabilly tracks. Een says: 'The only album I really liked was *The Van Album*, because you could hear everything. The really early stuff – that was when it was good fun.' Then the official albums *The 39 Stephs* and *Spike's 23 Collection* were released on CD, now incorporating Kenny's songs. Een adds: 'I played lots of banjo on *The 39 Stephs* and sang on "Nelly Kane", but on *Spike's 23 Collection* I played a bit of bass, mouth-organ, wobbleboard and backing vocals. It was clear it was Kenny's band and his songs. I felt it was all about him – we just felt like players. We didn't have a say.'

Quizzed about the studio, Een is equally abrasive. 'It was a huge disappointment for me. I'd come up with a part and work on it for weeks. I'd take ages to put it down and make it sound really good, then I'd get the album and it would be taken off, or so low in the mix there wasn't any point in it. Maybe what I did wasn't any good or wasn't what he wanted. They were his songs and the style was predominantly 1980s. I remember saying he should get a keyboard player in and make it sound the way he wanted it to sound. It was the lack of guidance from him – he didn't suggest I play something or show me what to play, he'd just ask me to play a bit somewhere and that was it. I felt like it was a massive waste of my time, and that's why I left.'

It was clear that Een wanted his musicianship to shine on the recordings and Kenny preferred to arrange things for the songs themselves. To anyone else, his playing throughout The Skuobhie Dubh Orchestra and Khartoum Heroes is inspired. He is his own harshest critic. Een admits: 'Even now I wouldn't call myself a singer-songwriter. I'm an instrumentalist. I don't sit around the house singing songs. If I play something, I play intricate instrumentals, and I've been interested in that from since I started the banjo.' Een feels it was unfair that Kenny was running everything, but the truth is that Kenny was the only driving force. He was writing the songs, booking the gigs and organising every facet of being in a band. Een had nothing to do with the label, Lochshore/Klub, and says: 'I don't know if there was an advance or anything. We certainly didn't see any of it if there was. We were just picked up and taken to the studio or turned up to play at gigs.' It's a double-edged sword, having a hands-off attitude. Een on his own admission just wanted to be a musician, but then complained when events were out of his control. As a result he took more of a back seat, simply playing the gigs and going home afterwards. He says: 'Kenny's incredibly business-minded. I could imagine he's got a tidy wee penny. He's bought his two houses in Crail – that's a fair amount of property right there.'

In spite of the ill-will on display here, Een enjoyed playing with the band and they had some great success. Athol Fraser played double bass for a while, to be replaced by a guitarist turned bassist, Pete 'Uncle Beesly' Macleod, whose style was funkier and more melodic. Pete was an undeniable talent, and he and Kenny struck up a friendship and a musical partnership. These may have been the twilight years of the Dubhs, but the songs were great and the musicianship always spot-on. The next album, *Gordonov*, was recorded and a name change to Khartoum Heroes mooted, but the end was unavoidable and quick to happen. Kenny attempted to steer the ship onwards while Een became more and more unhappy. Arguments were more commonplace, and Een remembers Kenny saying 'I don't need a band! My songs are great without a band!' Andy and Een walked out, and that was the end of The Skuobhie Dubh Orchestra.

After the band broke up, Een went to France to play bluegrass with Eric and try some more busking. There he got the compliments he desired and deserved for his musicianship and skills. Kenny honoured various engagements and played a handful of gigs with Pete and a hastily reshuffled band, then called it quits and set about finding members for a new project.

As Chapter I explains, my band Miraclehead had bumped into the Dubhs at the Cupar Festival, and I'd met Kenny again at T in the Park. Khartoum Heroes was born and took to the road.

On his return from France after months away, Een came to watch us play in Edinburgh at the Stones rock bar. After his bust-ups with Kenny, it was unbelievable that he wanted in, but he did. Maybe it was the new sound, now with added punk/indie/ska, but Een joined the ranks and became a Hero. In our short life of just a year, we accomplished a lot, playing across the UK and Europe, recording some mad songs and learning a lot about music and each other. We've remained friends to this day. Een's bizarre role in the band was to play mouth-organ, wobble-board, backing vocals and banjo, albeit through crazy effects pedals. He would pad out the sound with sonic experimentation and use his blue-grass skills to run up and down the fretboard. My memories of that time are almost all fond as we toured, busked and laughed our way around. Een was a bit of an odd fish, and probably felt a little frustrated that we weren't a straightforward bluegrass band, and that his banjo wasn't right at the forefront, but we all got on and blazed a trail for what would become Fence.

Pretty much ignored by the media in the early and mid-1990s, Khartoum Heroes played a weird fusion of styles when electrified, and more straightforward bluegrass, country and rockabilly when unplugged. Een now fondly recalls: 'There was a point when we were busking under a tunnel in France and there was a natural reverb. I didn't have to work to get the runs in. I was playing it fast, but I was sitting back on it and there was space in it. Five or six years after starting to play the banjo, I'd finally cracked it.' At the end of it all, although two bands had folded and we were all penniless unknowns, there was some kind of silver lining for Een and his burgeoning talent.

From 1995/1996 until the end of the decade was a strange time for Een. He was moving forward in leaps and bounds as a musician, but jumping from one project to the next. Kenny was going into meltdown with crip-pling self-doubt and depression while trying to keep some projects on the go. Khartoum Heroes anagrammatised themselves into Shoe Market

Hour, which became The Skuobhie Dubh Orchestra again. If Kenny was clutching at straws creatively, Een wasn't exactly helping matters. Although they argued and made snide remarks, they seemed lost without each other. Kenny was the driving force of the band with his organisation and songwriting, while Een was the master musician.

Een and drummer Stu Bastiman became thick as thieves. They moved into a cottage in Kincaple, playing music by day and going out by night in St Andrews to chat up students and exotic visitors. They lived on big pots of pasta and bottles of cheap Bulgarian wine. By this time Een's banjo skills could hardly be improved upon, and his attention turned to the guitar. Listening to Django Reinhardt compilations, the joyous, free-wheeling but complicated style connected with him. Een hadn't really played guitar at all, so he sat down to learn bluegrass flat-picking. Django Reinhardt had been a banjo player until he had an accident and burned his hands, and when he was recovering he took up the guitar and pioneered a new style using only thumb and two fingers. Een says: 'I'd played the bass, then the banjo, and then got into this. It was like the banjo but faster. I thought: "I need to learn that now!"' Stu accompanied him on rhythm guitar, never having played that before either. 'He was good on the guitar,' says Een, 'he had a really good rhythm technique. He's the best and most creative drummer I've ever played with. He was always on it. He took that rhythm on to the guitar. We took quite simple Reinhardt songs and recorded them. Two of them are on my first album.'

This was an aside, of course, as the dying embers of the Dubhs recorded and released the album *A New Cat*. Revolving line-ups included the two brothers, Pete 'Uncle Beesly' Macleod and Stu Bastiman, with occasional fiddle from Steve 'Thievin' Steven' Mackie, and prodigal daughter Kate Tunstall, who had made the East Neuk her home again after a fairly unproductive time at university in London. Kate and Een rekindled their romance and moved into a Denhead cottage together. Een confides: 'It started properly in 1996, and we ended amicably but with musical differences in 1998. To be honest, it was all about the music, gigs, playing, recording. It wasn't a relationship in the normal sense – we were young and it was convenient.'

To make life stranger and more chaotic, Gordon was at the nadir of his mental illness and would spend months in and out of Stratheden

Hospital. Een says: 'When Gordon was ill, it was so horrific and unreal. Since then I've blanked it out and stored it away.' Een would see him at his worst, babbling nonsense and speaking in tongues. Een would visit and find Gordon completely sedated, little more than a zombie, occasionally foaming at the mouth. At other times he would be able to converse sensibly with his brother. Een says today: 'I first knew he was ill when he was admitted to hospital. He was like someone else's twin brother. I though he was going to die. My parents couldn't get a handle on it at all. It was pre-internet and there was no info to be had anywhere. Nobody really knew anything about it. We went to see him in hospital almost every day. He was only in for about six weeks initially, and then he got kicked out. These people don't care, it's just a job.'

Of all Gordon's family and close friends, Een was the most seriously affected. Een thought Gordon's life was over and he was distraught. It was a truly disturbing time for Gordon, but it was difficult for those around him too. Een says: 'I think boredom and time to think too much about things were his greatest enemies. We always, even to this day, live next door or really close. He listens to me. When situations started getting out of hand, I'm probably the only one that was able to reel him back in without falling out with him. Now we sit and have a good grumble about everything – such a laugh!' Musically, Een is full of praise for his twin. 'His music has always been the same. I can't hold a candle to his stuff; even his throwaway ditties surpass anything I could ever do. How is Gordon now? He's probably better than the rest of us.'

Around this time Kate and Een started playing together, with her songs as the focus. If Kenny had been band-leader before but was starting to lose the plot, here was another songwriter who knew what she wanted and how to get it. She had a fully formed group of musicians at her disposal in Een, Pete and Stu. As said before, Kenny felt betrayed and disappeared from view, allowing Een to focus on a new sound and new songs. Kate settled on a name, Elia Drew, and they forged a 1960s/1970s-influenced Americana-folk sound with Een moving on to guitar. He started to finger-pick and flat-pick on a gut-string guitar, augmenting Kate's songs with lead runs and vocal harmonies. Een explains: 'Elia Drew started in 1996. It was a duo – Kate played rhythm guitar and sang, I did lead guitar and falsetto harmonies. It was acoustic, with tight vocal play around catchy melodies. Everywhere we went, everyone loved it. We started playing in the West Port Bar in St Andrews about once a week and at the university. We got a following locally, meantime popping down to London to play the Twelve Bar Club.'

Success beckoned for a while and major labels were phoning them up at the house. They tried to document their sound as best they could. Een recalls: 'We first recorded a tape on four-track and sold it at gigs. Then we recorded a couple of tracks at a studio outside Crieff that I remember was crap. I recall watching London people trying to jump on the bandwagon, so we did a few tracks at Pink Floyd's boat studio on the Thames.' As the act progressed, the name changed to Tomoko, after a girlfriend of Gordon's, adding the bass skills of Pete 'Uncle Beesly' Macleod. 'Around this time, though,' Een says, 'the music was heading in a post-beat, ambient kind of direction, and I left.'

Een now says Kate was hugely ambitious. She would write constantly, improving her guitar playing and lyrical slant, but Een insists he helped her not only musically but in other aspects of her career too. He remembers a trip to London when they played and drove back to Fife the same night, with Een at the wheel all the way. He supported her quest to become a professional musician when others, including her parents, were trying to dissuade her. 'Her parents, like any others, wanted her to have a proper job. I continued to urge her to do music. After all, you could always get a job later on, but fame comes but once.' In many ways Een was her rock, emotionally and professionally.

Now Kate is KT Tunstall and a star, he hears the singles and the first album, *Eye To The Telescope*, and realises how many of her early songs she used on that record. 'It was only in about 2010 that I first heard it all the way through. I saw it in a charity shop. Yeah, I thought it was very good, but it was made up of a lot of songs that we did at the time. They had all been cleverly rearranged and well produced.' Some of the songs the public now know contain parts of different songs from the late 1990s. A verse from one song is glued to the chorus of another and the middle-eight of yet another. It seems that her writing partners and producers in London had ransacked her back catalogue for the juiciest and catchiest bits. 'But I was now heavily into playing Django Reinhardt, and I never did listen to mainstream pop,' says Een.

Een is generally cagey when Kate's name is mentioned. He is keen not to be overly associated with her or look like he's jumping on the back of her success. He concludes: 'Her songs were proper songs, but I suppose it's always good to have someone else's input. I don't think I can take any more credit for it than that.' When they split there was the usual awkwardness, but they both continued to revisit St Andrews. Een remembers: 'I spent a lot of time in Italy and Spain and decided to take up flamenco guitar in Madrid. I bumped into her a few times back in St Andrews, and she came to gigs in Edinburgh when I was doing Lone Pigeon/Pip Dylan tours around 2005.' Kate believes they had only music in common and their relationship was bound to end. Perhaps Een preferred the simpler life. Whatever his thoughts, it must have been strange to watch his ex-girlfriend rocket skyward with the music he had helped to form. It's hard to say, but perhaps without Een's support and tutelage Kate might not have had the tools to cope with success. Having said that, she helped deal with Gordon's highs and lows and supported Een throughout. They played a major part in each other's lives, whether they like it or not.

$$\text{\clef treble}$$

Towards the end of the 1990s Fence was taking shape. Kenny's confidence was building again and his King Creosote persona was emerging with a prolific run of songs and recordings on CD. Everything was home-made and local, with no pressure or stress, all for the fun of taking part. Reminiscing about the St Andrews Citizens outfit that Kenny had formed, with Een playing occasional cajon and sitar, Een laughs. 'It was a shambles! It was the beginnings of a collective and had lots of people playing lots of things. Kenny, Pete and I were probably the only ones who could actually play. It was mainly Jason Kavanagh and Kenny's project.' On learning the sitar, he says: 'I've always liked Ravi Shankar. I had a chance to get a proper Indian-made instrument and thought: "Wow! I get a chance to play it," and I did. The most peace-loving instrument in the world, and Gordon smashed it!'

Home recording was now affordable, and anyone could make something intimate and personal, with decent sound quality. This kind of recording presented the listener with something less polished than anything from a serious studio, but equally valuable. The US underground had been trotting out lo-fi heroes for a few years. Ween, King

Missile, The Flaming Lips, Daniel Johnston and Beck were all showing music fans that the idea was more important than the production.

Een says: 'The reason I did the Pip Dylan stuff was, it was the beginning of Fence and Kenny wanted two tracks for a sampler. I recorded a whole album.' The two brothers were now reconciled, so, armed with a four-track, a microphone or two and a roomful of stringed instruments, Een set to work. 'All I'd done before that was backing vocals, and I thought my singing voice was awful. What I was doing was nothing like the music that I played before. It was a virgin experience – writing a song and then playing and singing at the same time. Pip Dylan was my first proper musical project.'

This was the start of the Fence pseudonyms: everybody needed one. Kenny was King Creosote, Gordon was Lone Pigeon, Pete was Uncle Beesly and other characters such as Gummi Bako were appearing. Een needed a name. He chose Pip Dylan because PIP was finger-picking tablature for thumb (Pulgar) finger (Icho) and thumb (Pulgar), and Dylan because it sounded like an authentic, Americana styled name, complementing the kind of music he was playing. Having been engrossed in American bluegrass, country, blues, jazz and folk for a decade, it seemed like a natural step for him. He instinctively knew the chord changes, the swing, the arrangements, and even adopted an American singing voice. He explains: 'Americana and bluegrass don't work in a Fife accent. Everyone would say: "You should sing in your own voice", which is fair enough, but it is what it is. I wanted it to be a character and leave it on stage. It's not like I walk around in cowboy boots and go "Yeehaw!"'

The now legendary debut album, self-deprecatingly titled *Ain't A Classical Piece, Not By A Long Shot*, was recorded largely in 1999 while Een was living in a friend's spare room. It saw the light of day once Kenny had Fence up and running, attributed to Pip Dylan and His Travelling Country Crops. It was meant to be a bluegrass band, with Een playing almost everything on the record. Captain Geeko did some drums and Stu Bastiman is credited with a few rhythm guitar parts. There's some significance to the imaginary band's name too, as it referred to his father's legacy. Een explains: 'He's got an album, as the Billy Anderson Trio, called *Travelling Country Hops*.' So Een Anderson now had a solo project, and the Andersons all had alter egos that would be celebrated for years to come.

Although crucial to the early days of Fence, Een wasn't always in Fife. Now he'd moved on from the Django Reinhardt style of guitar playing and become fixated on flamenco, deciding to spend time in Spain learning his craft. He based himself in Madrid for eight months and later for another four months, earning some money playing at various Irish bars. He attended the La Solea club, where all the great flamenco players went to showcase their virtuosity. He'd get in for free, then drink from a carton of cheap wine he'd sneak in. Starting at 11 p.m. and finishing at 4 a.m., the guitarists were right there in front of him. He watched their fingers and took it all in.

He now admits: 'When Fence started I wasn't even here. I came back and everyone was into the stuff. You just end up doing some gigs. When people stopped me in the street and said: "Hey Pip!", it was a bit weird.' It was the glory days of the early Aikman's gigs, but, remembering them as little more than bi-monthly pub gigs with a sense of humour, he is slightly dismissive of those days and chooses not to embellish stories told by others from the early 2000s. But by others' accounts, Een was almost always the funniest onstage and the most inventive with his costumes. Johnny 'Pictish Trail' Lynch recalls: 'I missed the Four Davies, but I saw the Four Mavies! They came out in drag, having raided the charity shops for headscarves and so on. Een had pushed cushions up his blouse and skirt – he had a *massive* arse.'

If Een's attitude to Fence is more critical today, he was very much involved in the performing and play-acting at the time. He'd sing his Pip Dylan material and show off his prowess on the banjo, guitar, cajon and sitar, accompanying others and singing with his brothers. Those rare occasions when the Andersons sang three-piece harmonies are the stuff of legend. Although unrehearsed and impromptu, hearing the siblings sing together is always a joy. Een adds: 'It's not rehearsed and organised, like the Bee Gees where all the harmonies are perfect. It's off-the-cuff and has to be on stage – kind of like "two minutes and you're on."'

While staying close to its roots in St Andrews, the years 2001 to 2004 saw Een take to the road as Pip Dylan on a number of occasions, usually as part of a Fence Collective package. The rumours were spreading among Beta Band and DIY music fans turning on to underground acoustic music. Fence's name was growing, albeit slowly, and pockets of supporters and friends appeared all over the UK. Een went on tours with King Creosote and other collective members, calling in on Stockton, Leeds, London, Brighton and Bristol among other places. Once while on the road, Een broke his wrist vaulting over a wall. This cramped his style quite seriously, and he still has to play the guitar or banjo sitting down. Initially turned on via James Yorkston and his success on Domino Records, or the releases by Lone Pigeon on Bad Jazz and Sketchbook, the audience was catching on to the Anderson brothers and the growing Fence collective.

As well as the live forays, Een spent the next few years recording freely too. Soon a large and varied back catalogue developed. His next album proper was *Of All The Things That I Can Eat, I'm Always Pleased With A Piece Of Cheese* in 2002. Here he introduced bits of flamenco into the countrified sound as well as quite a bit of theremin. It was one instrument he could play with a broken wrist – check out 'Senorita'. Again the record featured Een on every instrument, and was his only album to have an official release via Domino/Fence. Laurence Bell says: 'It was part of the whole Fence thing. We wanted to put out the two best and most appropriate albums at the time. He's a fantastic singer and a great writer. I lost touch with him, sadly. He wasn't around on the Fence scene when I was going up and hanging out up there so much.' Een is scathing about the arrangement now. 'They only put out my stuff so they could get to Gordon. I don't think they could care less for my stuff. Not one of them has told me it's a good album, or asked to do anything else in the future.' Kenny dealt with the Domino deal, and Een says: 'I didn't get anything!', though he and Kenny both received a small advance of publishing money. Moreover, Een didn't like the sound, saying: 'They stripped out the entire bottom end in the mastering. It doesn't sound as good as the original.'

Another contentious issue is the tale of a double-header English tour offered to King Creosote and Pip Dylan to promote *Kenny And Beth's Musikal Boat Rides* and *Of All The Things That I Can Eat . . .* albums, which had just been released simultaneously. Kenny maintains that a week or so before the tour, Een pulled out. Kenny asked The Pictish Trail to join the tour and set out to play the shows. It was largely uneventful and unsuccessful except for a Fence bill at the Domino Records tenth-anniversary party. Headlined by man of the moment James Yorkston, it was one of the first steps in breaking the Fence name to the London media. Een says: 'I don't remember being offered the tour by Kenny.' Maybe he'd had enough at the time, or maybe his memory is selective today, but Een was tiring of the Fence gigs and his own lack of success. One theme that runs through our conversations for this book was that of cementing his own identity. 'If I'm going to have any success, I want it to be through my playing, where I stand up and get recognised as me, not because I'm Kenny's brother or Gordon's brother. I'm a person in my own right.' Gripes that had haunted him towards the end of The Skuobhie Dubh Orchestra were reappearing as Een and Kenny drifted apart again.

Setting off on his own singular path, yet not cutting ties with Fence, he set to work on his third LP, *Flamenco*, which was self-released on CDs in 2003/2004 to be sold at gigs. Once more he performed it in its entirety on his own. 'I recorded it to see how my technique was and how it sounded. When I heard it back, I thought it sounded pretty good.' It did indeed, and showed that the years of travelling to and from Europe and learning his craft had reaped huge benefits.

Having nailed the *Flamenco* album and astounded friends and fans, he had one more musical fish to fry. Ever since the early days of The Skuobhie Dubh Orchestra, with the possible exception of *The Van Album*, he'd yearned to make the ultimate bluegrass album. This he did with the 2005 album *Parsnips*, his fourth as Pip Dylan. He explains: 'I did this because I'd been playing bluegrass for over ten years and had nothing to show for it. I wanted to show what I could do. There's guitar, mandolin, banjos, and I even learned the violin.' Kenny, who had had an interest in that music ten years earlier, now reckons Een nailed it and the album is near-perfect in its style. Not only was the playing astonishing, but rather than churn out an album of traditional songs, he wrote his own, creating a brand-new, ancient-sounding world. If you're wondering about the title, the intros on traditional bluegrass tunes are called 'potatoes'; these being his own songs, they became 'parsnips'.

Searching for another challenge, Een bought a pedal steel guitar and recorded a country covers record called *Join The Herd*, which has eight songs that no one's ever heard, purely to teach himself how the instrument worked. Here's a basic list of what he plays: mouth-organ, double bass, banjo, bluegrass guitar, mandolin, flamenco guitar, ukulele, Django Reinhardt guitar, pedal steel, sitar, dobro, lap steel, fiddle, cajon, wobbleboard and theremin. If you're ever in search of a session player or someone to accompany you on tour, you could do a lot worse than look this man up.

His fifth album, *Orange Dirt County* (2006), heavily featured the newly mastered pedal steel guitar. It included some songs from his previous records, but with a real country twang added. He explains: 'I couldn't get the pedal steel not to sound country. I thought if it sounded like that, I should do a country album.' He loved Johnny Cash, Willie Nelson and other country greats, anyway, and thought it was good to get that out of his system. To those who queried why he was singing in an American accent again, he responds: 'Why not? It's a country album. I thought if I did a straight country album, people might take to it in the US.' Steve Mason plays drums on five tracks, and Gordon, living next door at the time, added backing vocals and keyboards. Beaming, Een says: 'The harmonies on that are amazing, thanks to Gordon. I think that's a really good album.'

Once Kenny heard this album and Een's new toy, he wanted a flavour of it in King Creosote, and Een toured in the KC band playing pedal steel around the UK. Never quick to compliment Kenny today, he is vague about which songs he performed on and where they played. He recalls that he was moved around the stage from gig to gig and could never quite get his sound right onstage. As he improved as a musician and songwriter, his relationships with Fence and Kenny were deteriorating.

As Fence's reputation grew, it was probably tough for Een to watch the acclaim being heaped upon Gordon as Lone Pigeon and Kenny as King Creosote. His Pip Dylan project attracted less attention, which is a travesty. He was losing confidence and craved reassurance. He says: 'From the whole Pip Dylan thing, there's not been one bit of positivity or encouragement for me. I don't understand.' His frustration mounted, saying he couldn't get played on the radio and wasn't offered support slots for more established artists. He continues: 'I was always told it wasn't marketable because of the style and the accent.' To make problems worse, in his own mind, other Fence acts such as UNPOC began appearing. 'Where did he come from?' MTV came to film the Fence Collective and Een feels hard done by here too. 'There's a bit of me playing an instrumental through a pint glass for a few seconds. That's all I got.'

Een was desperate for a break, yet unwilling to compromise his music, change his style, market himself or schmooze for it. It's understandable, of course, but he was missing opportunities left, right and centre. He owns up to not being career-minded. He pines: 'If it's any good, I shouldn't have to do that. There are people that do that for you.' Therein lies the problem.

Een was losing faith in Pip Dylan and losing touch with Fence and its ethos. Was this simply to do with lack of personal success? He admits: 'I don't know what Fence is today. It started off as the Fence Collective. Then it was Fence Records. It's only Kenny who's got any success out of it, but that's because he's the only one at the end of the phone. Kenny's wanted to be famous ever since he started. People say I've fallen out with Kenny. I haven't. I've just stopped playing music with him.'

He talks about a photo of him on the Fence website, taken when he was a little overweight. 'I could have given them some great photos, but they used that one and probably had a great laugh.' His irritation was compounded by the biographical snippet that read along the lines of: 'Brother of King Creosote, twin of the Lone Pigeon, builds a great stane dyke and loves his shed.' Furious that there were no details of his career achievements, he asked to be taken off the website and have nothing to do with the label. Perhaps these slights were just the silly, self-deprecating Fife humour prevalent in Fence. Perhaps he should have supplied a different shot and written a better description of himself. Perhaps he should have lightened up. Or maybe Een's view of his own music and how it should be presented was now the polar opposite of what Fence had become.

I know that Kenny and Johnny Lynch love Pip Dylan and Een's music. They always want him to play at Homegame and other Fence events. Een counters: 'Every one that they've asked me to play, I have.' I know they would also like Een to have more of a presence in the collective, on tour and online should he want to. He says: 'I admire them. I certainly couldn't do what they do – their motivation, their willingness to carry on the vision of what they want. If I was like that, I might have my own collective of jazz musicians or whatever. But it's just not me. All I'm happy doing is playing, and I'd be just as happy at the back or as a session player.'

Pip Dylan's last album to date is called *Probably*, short for *Probably The Last Pip Dylan Album*. It was due to be released in 2006, but was delayed. I bought it at the Homegame in 2010, which was Een's last gig as Pip Dylan. He completed the tracks just as a newspaper began to snoop around, asking him about Kate Tunstall. If his confidence was ebbing away, it would be completely sapped by what happened next.

𝄞

When KT Tunstall broke into the mainstream, the press inevitably wanted to investigate her past. They searched out Fence Records, which pointed them towards Een. They then asked Een questions. Admirably, he refused to answer and said he wouldn't dish the dirt on Kate. They tracked him down on his home phone, although his number was ex-directory. He fobbed them off as unresponsively as possible. A day or two later a huge spread appeared in a national newspaper, 'exposing' Een. He says: 'It was one of the trashies. They accused me of being a hippie cult leader with devotees living in tepees and wigwams, and I was some three-thumbed, inbred banjo player who wasn't very good. They said I was a broccoli rustler, roaming round Fife kidnapping vegetables and insulting potatoes. That was from a first interview Kate did, when she said she was so poor that we had to steal vegetables to survive. But I knew the farmer, and he told us exactly from what field to help ourselves! It was all because I didn't dish the dirt on her, which was what they wanted. They even used the photo from one of your BBC radio sessions. I felt so humiliated.'

Not only did he feel increasingly sidelined within Fence, he'd seen his ex-girlfriend become a bona-fide pop star. This must have been hard to take as he slaved away making albums and mastering instruments. He was skint and demoralised, and now falsely accused of being someone who'd had an adverse effect on Kate's life. In his own eyes, he'd been exactly the opposite. He'd had enough, and stopped performing or recording as Pip Dylan almost as soon as the paper hit the street. He wanted separation from everything. 'If you searched for "Pip Dylan" online, every association was with Fence or KT Tunstall, and I wanted rid of it.'

Far from hunkering down with his friends at Fence, Een is adamant that Fence were jumping on the KT Tunstall train. There were more press and online articles linking Kate to Fence, and Een was amazed. 'You'd see things like "KT Tunstall – honorary member of Fence", but at that time she hardly even spoke to them.' He wanted distance from her success, from Fence, from Pip Dylan and from the article that had knocked the wind out of his sails. He started afresh as Third Part, named after an area of land near Kingsbarns, where he was staying. Originally a trio with female singer-songwriter and Fence Collective member Jo Foster in the line-up, Third Part soon became a solo project, with Een playing guitar, cajon and bass drum. In this incarnation he played tour support to Steve Mason, then operating as King Biscuit Time with Pete Rankin on bass and Colin Emmanuel on keyboards. He also supported Gordon's new band, The Aliens. Een maintains: 'I got more out of that than the six years previous.'

He formed another combo, The Black Yaks, with Een on electric guitar, Steve Mason on drums, Richard 'Scruff' Francis Parkinson on second guitar and Pete 'Old Jock Radio' Rankin on bass. With a more low-slung, bluesy, rock 'n' roll swagger to them, they played two gigs before vanishing from sight. I saw them at one Homegame and enjoyed them thoroughly. Somehow, though, it didn't seem like Een playing to his strengths. He was an acoustic player, and he now freely confides: 'That's all I've ever played, really, so whether it's in or out of fashion I'm purely unaware.'

In 2006, downhearted after the newspaper debacle and stripped of self-confidence, he moved on to another project entirely, making musical instruments. 'I wanted to make music in a physical form,' he says. Handy from his early years with cardboard villages and wooden bird-boxes, it seemed like only one step to making guitars, violins, cajons and double basses. He threw himself into his new mission with gusto. He explains: 'I got car-boot guitars and charity-shop guitars and took them apart and made drawings of them. The first ones were plywood guitars, made from old wardrobes to get the templates. Then I'd spend two to three hundred pounds on proper wood and build the guitar.' I've seen some examples around Een's house today, and they're beautiful, but he confesses he couldn't make a profit on them. 'I'd spend a year making something and get absolutely no return,' he says. Eventually it dawned on him that his new plan was unsustainable, a hobby rather than a business.

Returning to playing, Een decided on yet another bizarre rubric under which to perform: LENDF, or La East Neuk de France, using a doctored map of France and Fife combined as artwork. He'd fallen back in love with Django Reinhardt, and between 2007 and 2010 he diligently practised as many pieces as he could. He recorded his favourites, showing off his mastery of the material and satisfying his ego. He proved he was good enough, but says: 'I couldn't get people to play. The whole point is to have bass and guitar doing the rhythm.' This is still a potentially ongoing project, should Een one day meet musicians interested and gifted enough.

Despite having retired his most famous alter ego, he performed a couple of solo Pip Dylan gigs between 2008 and 2010, but now insists it's all over. 'Instead of banging at it for another five or ten years, I'd rather stop, have a break and try something else. Pip Dylan is done.' With no more gigs or albums planned, there is a finished but unreleased seventh album, *Once Upon A Time*. As I write, Andy 'Captain Geeko' Robinson is working on new drum parts and a different mix and master. We shall watch that space. Throughout all this Een is painfully honest in his quest for perfection in writing, playing and recording his songs. 'I never listen back and enjoy stuff I've recorded. Obviously when you're recording you listen to every little detail, and when it's finished I might listen to the final product, but it's never the way I want it. I am my toughest critic and I always want it better.'

Een will always make music, professionally or otherwise. He's too brilliant not to. Sadly, brilliance doesn't always guarantee success. It's tragic that Een feels so alienated from Fence, as it is his natural home as a label and an umbrella. It's also a shame that he has retired Pip Dylan and withdrawn his presence from the collective. They love him, but he feels they don't. Just as interest in the whole movement is growing, he is nowhere to be seen. As a family man now, maybe he doesn't care. He has walked his own path and made his own way. I hope we'll hear from him again soon.

Drastic Fantastic

The Rise and Rise of KT Tunstall

A small-town singer-songwriter goes from playing local pubs and clubs to selling millions of albums and becoming a household name: it's the stuff of dreams. However, it does occasionally happen, and when it does . . . . Inspiration, perspiration, perseverance and persistence all had a major part to play, but Kate Tunstall looks back now and is humble. 'If it hadn't all kicked off, I'd still be playing and I think I would have managed to make a living out of music. It so easily might not have happened. There was a timing to it.' There was indeed. With that fated *Later . . . With Jools Holland* appearance, a door opened and a once in a lifetime opportunity presented itself. Thank God NAS pulled a sickie!

Until then she had put in the hard work and suffered plenty of knock-backs and indifference. A lesser mortal might have jacked it in, but Kate was utterly dedicated. It was payback time. To this day, though, she takes nothing for granted. 'I've always had this weird sensation that this golden hand has picked me out and put me in this idyllic situation, right back to when I was adopted as a baby. It's total luck of the draw who picks you up. You're the baby in an adoption clinic above a Chinese restaurant in Edinburgh, waiting for someone to come and get you. I ended up with this family and I couldn't have wished for a better one. Again, with this whole ride with my music, everything seemed to go so well. It was Midas-touch time. I approached everything with a positive attitude, worked my arse off and enjoyed every minute of playing. I made sure I had good people around me and kept an eye out, thanks to good advice from people like Bobby Heatlie in Edinburgh.'

Kate had built up a small but loyal team from musicians to manager. She'd learned lessons and was putting them to good use. Now the mainstream was beckoning and decisions had to be made. As neither disposable pop-starlet nor indie iconoclast, she had to define her role. Would she embrace her success or shirk away? I feel slightly guilty about my lack of support for her as a BBC DJ and champion of the underground. I'd known her for years and was aware of her talent and her years of hard slog, but my role was to uncover the alternative side of music from Scotland and beyond. I looked for the weird, the wonderful and the slightly off-piste. John Peel had been my jumping-off point and I was determined to discover the oddballs out there as he had. KT Tunstall was an artist who could connect with a more conventional audience and appeal to a wider demographic. I assured her that Radio 1 and Radio 2 would come knocking. She says: 'I remember badgering you to play me on the *Evening Session* and you said I had to get on daytime radio. I understand now, I didn't at the time. It was liberating when I realised I was making a more accessible kind of music. I wasn't trying to, it just came out that way. I was on my own path. I loved my time with the Fence guys, but it wasn't where I belonged. Funnily enough, I feel I belong there a lot more now.'

With an album ready to go, a well-received TV appearance under her belt and an artist champing at the bit, the record company now had its *zeitgeist* moment in which to release *Eye To The Telescope*. Although dissatisfied with the smooth mix and master that had rubbed the rougher edges off the songs, now she is more stoical. 'It's less polished than I thought it was at the time. Going back and listening to it, it always sounds better than I think it does.' It was released at the end of October 2004, with 'Black Horse And The Cherry Tree' added to the album later. The first 10,000 copies had the *Later . . . With Jools Holland* TV audio on them from earlier in the month. In fact, they hadn't even recorded the definitive version yet. In a studio owned by Chris Difford of Squeeze, Kate and Luke recorded everything themselves in time for the next pressing.

Surprisingly, the album didn't immediately take off either. Going into the charts at number seventy-three, it slowly climbed over the course of a year, eventually embedding itself in the Top Ten. Kate adds: 'That album wouldn't have gone so far without "Black Horse" as its platform. Suddenly I began to have more faith in my record company – they obviously knew what they were doing! It was a really maverick move, and all thanks to main man Shabs Jobanputra. I had a really difficult but exciting relationship with him.'

Whether you know Kate's music intimately or not, you can hardly not have heard 'Black Horse And The Cherry Tree'. It's a song that has connected with millions of people, a classic pop song, and every musician wants to write at least one of those. Whether she likes it or not, it has become a kind of signature tune for her. Is it an albatross around her neck? She admits: 'There's an innocence to that tune that I sometimes feel I've grown out of now, so there's a feeling occasionally that you're covering your own song. But that's the same with all your material.' She realises the importance of the track, but still finds it a challenge. 'I think fate has done me a favour by granting me a single that requires some thought to get it right every time. I always play it with that loop pedal and it's so easy to get it wrong. I'm on my toes every time I play it.' Asked where it came from, she divulges: '"Black Horse" was an exercise in automatic writing. I don't really know what it's about. It's lots of different things – a dream I had, a trip to Greece where I saw a massive stallion tethered in a field, and being at a crossroads in my life where I was about to sell my soul to a record company. I was also quite influenced by Bo Diddley and embracing my rhythm guitar style at the time. It's all those things.'

Released to follow her debut smash was another FM playlist pleaser, 'Suddenly I See'. A deeper, more complex song, it still has melodies to die for and has snared many a fan with its hooks. Kate says: '"Suddenly I See" is about the Robert Mapplethorpe photo on Patti Smith's *Horses*. I'm glad it has overtaken "Black Horse" in a way.' Thanks to countless appearances in soundtracks and heavy radio rotation in Britain and the US, the song is a staple of the modern pop canon and cemented her status as a real and rootsy songwriter, albeit with one foot in mainstream pop. 'It's affirming that people recognise a sound that I've got, and that came from "Black Horse" and "Suddenly I See".'

Units began to shift and diaries began to fill. She was beginning to live the dream, but that dream would entail a lot of hard work. After all the years of preparation and apprenticeship, she wasn't about to let it slip. If there was one negative at that time, it was the unfair perception of the alternative/DIY/underground scene that she was nothing but a vacuous MOR pop star. In her defence she says: 'I'm not a cynical person or a body full of angst, so I'm not going to communicate that in my music. I listen to a lot of it, but I realised early on that there was no point in shoehorning in elements that aren't there. If you're not in pain, don't try to be in pain. Sad songs are no better than happy ones. Songs that come from a place of pain are just more useful to the listener.' She was and is more than capable of writing sad songs, but now was the time to shine.

$\oint$

As 2004 turned to 2005, the KT Tunstall juggernaut was gathering speed and she was enjoying every minute of it. 'Part of me felt wide-eyed and high that this was working. All I wanted was to have a room full of people listen. When you're starting, it's trying to get people in the room that's the hard thing. I was cocksure that if I got enough people in, at least some of them would like me. I'd got good and could put on a show. I was fed a sense of confidence from my early gigs, where a hand-ful of people liked what I do. If no one had ever liked what I was doing, I might have packed it in.'

Now that the media were taken with her natural charm, the public and the sales would soon follow. The first figure she heard was that the album had sold 11,000 in the UK, but that was to increase dramatically in the coming months. She was running her own website at the time, and the emails from fans poured in. Messages as disparate as: 'I'm a 55-year-old Punk but I LOVE your album!' and 'Are you black?' appeared, while a diverse set of new fans engaged with her image, her technical ability and ultimately her music. From emo kids to their gran-nies, her inclusive pop had a wide appeal – edgier than the competition, but palatable to the masses. She says: 'The kids love the tech but the grannies love a sing-song. My fans range from six to sixty. It's pretty much anyone but hipsters.'

For the next year Kate and the band hit the road, playing venues and festival slots that grew stealthily in size. They concentrated heavily on the UK for the first year of the album's life, getting the campaign going. As capacities increased, so did the size of her band. 'I needed a lead guitarist to fill the bigger venues. When a friend, Sam Lewis, joined, it marked a change in what we were capable of playing. Suddenly we had a lead electric guitarist. That opened up a lot of opportunities.' The hard work was paying off. 'I never felt daunted by the increase in size of venues. I wasn't uncomfortably worried at any point, but I was flabbergasted. I remember the first Shepherd's Bush Empire gig. I thought "Holy shit!" It's a prestigious and special gig, and it can be pivotal to what happens next.

'By the end of the year the record company said: "You can go to the Europe to promote it or we can try the US." It was a no-brainer. If it happens in the US, it's more than likely you'll get Europe as well,' Kate says. 'My music is transatlantic, and my formative year in America had been a huge influence. It all made sense.' It's not hard to imagine why they took to her either, but they certainly did, both musically and personality-wise. She laughs. 'I'm Scottish. It's basically a green card!'

Touring the US for the best part of two years, she and the band played show after show on a punishing schedule. She was slowly exhausting herself, but enjoying it too. To deal with things, she acknowledges she was drinking quite a lot, albeit as a positive drunk. 'I'm like a Labrador puppy.' Mentally fried, she says: 'I finally understood the saying "The baby's too tired to sleep",' and drinking was a way of winding down. She would then be up at 7 a.m. for another batch of interviews. It's reckoned now that she sometimes did fifty ten-minute interviews in a day in Japan. Though shattered, she was enjoying even the promo as well at that stage. 'After ten years of no one giving a shit, suddenly a country or a continent does. And I can talk the arse off a horse!'

As you climb the ladder to success, it's hard work but also a heap of fun. Kate was doing what she'd always wanted. The concerts were fantastic and the travelling and interviews all added to the experience. Even today, a good eight years later, the smile never leaves her face as she casts her mind back, but at times it could be mind-boggling. 'After touring for over a year, it all gets a bit *Spinal Tap*. The amount of times I've been on stage and had to ask my tour manager "Where are we?" The bus pulls up and I'd get taken straight to a radio station, so you don't get a chance to see anything local. Now I won't do it to the same level. It's much better to know a little bit about where you are.'

As well as the extreme workload, a world of fame-related extracurricular activity was open to her, about which she knew very little. She was working like a dog, but she was . . . famous! Was this everything she ever wanted after all? She says: 'Fame for me is really helpful if I want to work with someone or make something happen. But above and beyond that, I don't really need the other stuff – there are probably loads of people who could make more of my fame than I have.

'It became obvious pretty quickly that there was the celebrity side to it that didn't interest me at all. It was really shocking how simple it is to avoid it. I've only been papped once, the morning after I won a Brit. I don't relish feeling different from everybody else. I prefer sitting at a table with friends as an equal. I've been really impressed at how my friends have dealt with it. They couldn't be happier for me.'

Like it or lump it, her star had risen and her face adorned billboards, websites, magazines and Sunday supplements. The Scottish tabloids talked about her all the time, in a supportive and non-sleazy way, whereas in London they didn't really care, perhaps sensing her lack of interest in that side of the job. 'I'm not drug-addicted and single. You need displays of lack of control to be interesting, and I've always enjoyed getting pissed in private. I prefer to be anonymous and do my thing.' Nor was she one for debauched, bad-girl rock 'n' roll shenanigans. 'I've always liked to leave goodwill behind me. To this day I cannot trash a dressing room. I've worked in cafés and bars, I've been a dishwasher. It's absolutely fine if people want to call me a Goody Two-Shoes, but somebody's got to clean it up.'

Despite her resistance, however, the inevitable showbiz parties ensued, with celebrity guests and fans in attendance. In the higher echelons of pop, it's a thrill to be part of it and hard to avoid. Even her once suspicious parents were in on it, she recalls. 'My mum and dad love the social side of it and the after-show parties. They're always the last to leave. I remember my mum saying: "Tonight I don't want to speak to anyone I've ever met before," so I'd introduce her to Kevin Spacey and Mags from A-ha and let her get on with it. I tell you what, it's a good photo!' To this day she counts Billy Bragg and Jools Holland as friends, but is not in awe of other musicians. She is, however, awestruck when she meets actors and actresses. 'It was really embarrassing when I met Miranda Richardson!'

$\oint$

Success breeds success. The more successful you are, the more in demand you become, the more work you do, and the more successful you become . . . It is also a matter of luck and serendipity. If someone is consistent in the hard work they do and the quality with which they do it, the plaudits will keep on coming. The fact is that an opportunity had presented itself to Kate Tunstall and she was more than able to cope with it. She was a natural songwriter, a consummate performer and an effervescent pop personality. Interviews were dispensed a cheeky grin, all in a no frills, down-to-earth manner. Being attractive to both men and women didn't harm her chances either. Soon she was the talk of the industry and of the more conservative crossover pop/rock-loving public. Here was an artist who mobilised a section of society who liked going to occasional gigs, buying records and having a dance, but felt left out by specialist scenes and indie cliques. Many of her fans were those who perhaps only bought ten CDs a year. But there are a lot of those people.

Soon it would be hard to escape her music. Songs were licensed to renowned TV shows such as *Grey's Anatomy*, *Ugly Betty* and *The OC*. The Hollywood hit *The Devil Wears Prada* prominently featured 'Suddenly I See', exposing it to an enormous amount of people who were new to her music. She says: 'It was a once-in-a-lifetime opportunity to have a three-minute track at the start of a film with Meryl Streep in it. Hello!' Catherine McFee sang 'Black Horse And The Cherry Tree' in the final of *American Idol*, and other songs were featured in contexts as varied as gridiron football, football in Scotland, and the soap opera *EastEnders*. It seemed that every facet of pop culture wanted a piece of KT Tunstall. She wasn't complaining, though.

Soon awards started to materialise, as they do when a new artist is welcomed to the bosom of the industry. A nomination for the Mercury Music Prize started it. 'It was the first,' Kate says. 'It's such a prestigious and music-centric prize. I was made up to be on the same nomination list as the others. There was no disappointment at all in losing to Antony and the Johnsons. I was asked to play at it. It wasn't my best-ever performance, but it was great! It just cemented who I was and what I was about.' Then music monthly Q nominated her in Best Song. The Q Awards take place at lunchtime in central London, so she took a couple of hours out of rehearsals, donned a pair of Vivienne Westwood shoes and headed along, expecting little. She was up against Oasis, Coldplay and James Blunt. 'And I fucking won it! But I couldn't walk because of those shoes! It was the first time I met famous people. In an hour, pissed, I met Nick Cave, Björk, the Gallagher brothers and Coldplay.'

Perhaps most importantly, she was nominated for two Brit Awards. Though ridiculed by musicians and critics, the Brits are the most visible, lucrative and high-profile of all the pop ceremonies. More concerned with sales and celebrity than artistic integrity, they can still be game-changing moments in an artist's career. Kate had been nominated as Best British Female alongside heroes such as Kate Bush and PJ Harvey. 'It was one of my favourite nights of my career. People say the Brits are bullshit – whatever, maybe they are. I had the best night ever. I played at it, and told the record company I wanted it to look like black-and-white television. I wanted stairs going up behind me, twenty tap dancers with canes, black-and-white visuals, black-and-white trousers and a Gretsch White Falcon guitar, which they hired especially for me. There I was playing "Suddenly I See", with the tap dancers on stage with me. It was crazy! My mum and dad were there with me, and it was the first time they really understood what was going on.' As well as Best Female, she had a nomination in another category. 'I was up for Best Live Act, and that meant a huge amount.'

The sheer magnitude of this level of glitz could make the mind boggle, especially if you happen to be a budding singer-songwriter just starting out. But Kate dealt with it all graciously. 'I didn't know I was going to win. I said in my acceptance speech: "Ladies, disregard your limits", as a play on the *Fast Show* sketch, because I didn't understand why there weren't more girls in this male-dominated music scene.' But the high jinks would continue further into the night, with a poignant moment for her to treasure. 'Afterwards the record company threw a massive party, the best party ever. In the middle of it, Shabs, whom I had this love/hate relationship with, said: "Get up on that table, we've got something to give you," and they handed me the Gretsch White Falcon as a present. A £10,000 guitar! I was speechless. I don't know if they realise how meaningful it is to me. Since then I've written songs on it. If there was a house fire, that's the first thing I would grab.'

KT Tunstall had definitely arrived. With another award under her arm, an Ivor Novello for 'Suddenly I See' as best song, it was back to the grindstone and the touring treadmill. She was a workhorse, and as a result the album sold over a million copies in the US alone. However, not everything was perfect behind the scenes. 'Things were really kicking off in America at the time when I needed a second record. So, in between recording, I was flying off to do the Golden Globes after-show party. I was totally exhausted and my health started to suffer. I've got kidney problems and have had since I was a kid. I was getting sick a lot, and I had proper rock-doctor prescriptions in the US. It's just drugs to get you through. I was never really getting better, and I was burning out.'

$$\text{♪}$$

At a perfect time to take stock and step away from the maelstrom for a few moments, Kate was determined to keep moving forward. She dealt with her immediate health issues and quickly set about organising the follow-up album, *Drastic Fantastic*. Beginning the recording process, she was persuaded to go to Rockfield Studios. 'It's an amazing studio, but I hated it. It's fucking Led Zeppelin and Queen – no pressure, then! We got "Beauty And Uncertainty" out of that session, which was great, but it was very expensive and stressful. So I demanded we go back to Eastcote and then Eden Studios in London. I needed to go home and sleep in my own bed at night.'

Kate was determined to branch out and expand her signature sound. She recalls: 'It was me experimenting in a more polished, band-orientated sound, and I wanted to make a big album. I loved the live shows and wanted to get it on record. It was more of a rock record.' In terms of songwriting she never lacked material, but she admits: 'I had to grave-dig a little bit. There was stuff that didn't make the first record. Not because it wasn't good, but because it didn't fit. I was happy with everything except "I Don't Want You Now", which needed extra work. But aside from that, I was really happy. The album could have benefited from a little more time, perhaps.' Again, she wanted a rawer sound. The record company had a different view. They didn't want their new pop prodigy ruining this enormous success with some scrappy punk record or a heavy-duty rock assault. 'It was frustrating, because I really wanted to record it live, but the label and the producer, Steve Osbourne, were against it. There were questions about whether we were tight enough to record in such a short space of time. I suppose I'll never know. I wanted that live energy, and it didn't have it. It needed it and it should have been rougher around the edges, rather than polished and technically better. I was disappointed by that.'

Released in September 2007, *Drastic Fantastic* had Kate on the cover again, this time with a more glam-rock aesthetic in high heels, a short skirt and a glittering Gibson Explorer guitar complementing her brilliant white dress. It was a contrast to the homely-looking girl fronting *Eye To The Telescope*, with her rainbow braces and tangled hair. The guitars were louder in the mix and the move towards a more muscular rock sound was evident, if not exactly visceral or searing. This was not an album that was going to alienate existing fans or turn away newcomers. It was bold, brassy, bubbly FM rock with hooks aplenty and stadium-sized choruses. She now says: 'I'm really proud of the songs on that album. It had some good radio hits on there, and a few that have become stalwart tunes in our live set.' If anyone thought KT was a pop puppet or a one-trick pony, this album proved them wrong. It was hardly a reinvention, but she wasn't claiming to be subversive or revolutionary. It was another batch of well-crafted pop-rock music from a gifted professional and her band. Singles such as 'Hold On' and 'Saving My Face' were hits, and in the global marketplace it earned acclaim and decent sales, if less impressive than the first album's. Laughing, she says: 'My proudest chart position was ahead of 50 Cent and Kanye West in the Scottish album chart when I was number one.'

Kate and the band hit the road for another year or so. Up to 2008 they ploughed across most of Europe (other than Scandinavia), Singapore, China, Korea, Canada, Australia, New Zealand and Japan. In the UK she sold out gigs of up to 6,000 people a night, playing at the legendary Hammersmith Apollo, three nights at the Roundhouse, the Eden Project, a forest tour, Glastonbury, T in the Park . . . the list goes on. In the US the band opened Live Earth at the New York Giants' stadium in front of 60,000 people. 'That's the biggest gig I've ever played,' Kate says. 'It wasn't daunting. It was "Come on then, let's 'ave you!" A great gig and an amazing experience.' She managed to get the crowd to carry out a Mexican wave. Alongside Roger Waters of Pink Floyd, the event was headlined by Bon Jovi, whose introduction, 'Please be upstanding for the national anthem' before playing 'Wanted Dead or Alive' in dedication to George Bush, was a highlight. 'My big brother came out for it, and it was very emotional for the two of us singing along,' Kate recalls.

The monumental experiences continued. She set off on a sculpture park and botanical garden tour in the US, and performed at the Nobel Peace Prize in 2007 with Annie Lennox and Earth Wind and Fire, in front of Al Gore and the Intergovernmental Panel on Climate Change, sparking her continuing interest in environmental matters. As the year ended she headlined Edinburgh's Hogmanay celebrations. 'It was like a homecoming. It was such an amazing reaction. I had my friend make me a sequined dress in the colours of the saltire. I mean, you have to do something.'

The touring was 'dreamtime, absolutely brilliant! The only thing that was difficult was the promo. We went to New Zealand for a day and I had to sit and do promo. Same in Tokyo. You don't get to see anything. That gets frustrating. That why I took four months off in 2008/09 to go back and see these places.' Concluding the tour in South America, she says, was 'a great way to end it. It was joy on a stick! It was mind-blowing playing in Rio and São Paulo to 4,000-capacity venues in a place we'd never been. It was crazy love, everyone singing along to every word. I probably won't ever have that again, because you need a massive hit for that to happen.'

It was 2008 and Kate Tunstall had worked herself into the ground. As well as a rest from the roadhog lifestyle, it was time to evaluate her personal and financial situation. Unknown to her, an enormous bank balance had built up while she had been living on the bus. She was now a rich woman, and it would be only right to do something useful with all this cash. She explains how she was feeling at the time: 'I don't really want anything and I don't really need anything, but I'd be a fool not to do something with it. Because I'd earned all these American dollars but didn't want to exchange them, as you'll lose half your money, I ended up buying a flat in New York that I never stayed in.'

Back in the UK she hired an eco-housing adviser, eventually going into business with him. He has since developed Radiohead's recording studio and Colin Firth's house, but started on KT's north London flat. As she realised her incredible good fortune, she also bought a country retreat in Berkshire. It was an old, rambling, stone gamekeeper's house with an outhouse, perfect for a studio. The years of slog and indifference, and then the hard touring, publicity and releasing records had paid off in ways she could only have dreamed of. 'I remember writing in my journal at the cottage in Denhead about what it would be like not to have to worry about money, not have to go to work, and just be a musician. That's what I can do now.'

$$\oint$$

Kate's relationship with Scotland and the East Neuk is complicated. Much as she loves the place and took inspiration from it, her big break had come from London. 'In London I have a network of friends, musicians, producers, writers and people whom I find very stimulating. They're good relationships, and I love London and I love Berkshire. I'd like to spend more time in Scotland, but I don't think I could move back.' She continues: 'I've always felt nervous playing in Scotland. I've always been slightly paranoid about people saying I've got too big for my boots, but it's never been like that. But nothing would have happened if I'd stayed in Scotland. I couldn't get arrested.'

Consciously or subconsciously, she was reaching out to her roots. Let's back-pedal slightly. Between *Eye To The Telescope* and *Drastic Fantastic*, Kate embarked on a project she called Acoustic Extravaganza, which appeared on CD, DVD and very briefly on tour in 2006. It was originally available only via her website. She explains: 'It was an attempt to reconnect with Fife. It was really a fan release to say thanks. I needed some respite from touring, studios and the promo world. It was important to get back to basics. It was my band and Donna Maciocia of Amplifico. She's got a great voice and she did backing vocals. It was a very Scottish thing. I missed home and the simplicity.'

Although she had moved to London, signed with a major label, and succeeded as a pop star, part of her yearned for a less commercial, uncomplicated life in which the music, lyrics, artwork and ideas were more important than business strategies and marketing plans. With her fortune, she could afford it. She wanted to reconnect with her old friends from The Skuobhie Dubh Orchestra, but, she says: 'I'd unknowingly severed myself from Fife a little bit, in case I wasn't going to get welcomed back again. Kenny was utterly against the industry and there was I in bed with it, naked!' Her fears proved groundless. 'Kenny kept in touch, even sporadically, and I kept an eye on the King Creosote stuff and saw that Fence was getting a good reputation. It was great to see him have some commercial success. He was fighting with the ideals of a major and it wasn't easy. Eventually he got in touch with me, and asked if I'd come and sing on *KC Rules OK*. I couldn't have been more touched.'

As her mainstream success had mushroomed, she thought that the two sides of her musical personality could never be reconciled. On one hand she was an FM radio-conquering pop persona, and on the other she was a rootsy singer-songwriter from Fife. She now says: 'It's so nice that the Fence thing is where I grew up. It's a reason to go home. When I went to my first Homegame, I knew the area and the people, but it felt like a new place. I felt proud of being part of it and having a history with Kenny. I was scared I wouldn't be welcomed by Fence because I'd been such a commercial success, that it would take away from the kudos it had and the fact it was an outlet for hidden treasure. I was no longer hidden treasure. But I had a great time playing Homegame. I just went up and did new material, in front of people who probably weren't that interested, and it was great. I was perhaps embarrassed about what I'd done career-wise, but Kenny and Johnny just went: "For God's sake, will you just get up there and sing!" It was massively encouraging.'

She'd known almost from the start that she wasn't making the same kind of music as the Fence Collective and that her music was a lot more accessible. She maintains: 'I've never worried or felt a sense of competition. It's apples and oranges. The thing that concerned me was their attitude to my success, but that was underestimating Kenny. He was just "Well done, you!"' This sense of relief helped formulate, in her mind and the minds of King Creosote and Pictish Trail, as well as the less purist members of the Fence Collective, the idea that it was possible to unite the two sides. 'I sang a Christmas song with the London Community Gospel Choir on Terry Wogan's Radio 2 breakfast show, and was doing an electronica side-project with Jim Abbiss. I've always enjoyed having a foot in different camps.' It was dawning on her that she could have hit records and tours while also stepping into the psychedelic DIY world of Fence. She says: 'I got to know Jon Hopkins's music and loved it, and I heard his album with Kenny and thought it was beautiful. Kenny asked me to sing with them at Celtic Connections and the Shepherd's Bush Empire. So I finally got to play there with Kenny!'

The circle was complete. She was a big star, yet still able to sing backing vocals with her old pal Kenny Anderson. 'It was so satisfying sitting in my pyjamas watching *Later . . . with Jools Holland* with Kenny on it. After that, *Flick the V's* was a really important record for me. It was great to hear Kenny using electronics in the way I think The Beta Band used it. It's used as an instrument and doesn't have to be the be-all and end-all.' She also helped instigate a more collaborative project in her and Luke's studio in Berkshire. The first thing they recorded was with Kenny and Johnny. 'It felt like being seventeen again. But I realised that Kenny's lyrics are fucking weird! My favourite lyric of his on the *Diamond Mine* album is "The white flour in my diet will be the death of me."'

The feeling was mutual. When Kate toured in autumn 2011, Kenny and Johnny went to see her play. 'It was so emotional afterwards. Kenny said: "That's the best gig I've seen all year. I've always been a fan, but you've just won me back." We exchanged these pissed text messages until 4 a.m., saying how great it was to connect properly again and to know that I'm still on the right track. He ended the texts with "Please come back into the fold!" and I felt like crying.'

&

It looked like KT Tunstall had it all, and maybe she did. Millions of albums had been sold, countless awards won, old friendships reunited and a sense of artistic contentment established. But her work ethic had been herculean and the rewards had come at a price. She needed a break. She says: 'I've always lived with the thought that it might just stop at any point, and I don't want to piss it away. It's too precious. Up until 2008 I just couldn't turn things down.' However, as 2008 drifted into 2009, she was ready to take some time off. She and Luke were married in a private ceremony with selected friends and family, away from the tabloid glare. Normal life and love took precedence for a while.

Away from the treadmill, she could take on other projects. She was invited to Greenland on the *Cape Farewell* boat, along with artists such as Jarvis Cocker, Laurie Anderson, Martha Wainwright, Feist, Robyn Hitchcock and others to investigate the effects of climate change, collaborate and swap ideas. Far from being a mutual love-in for Kate, she found it intimidating, 'It fucked my confidence. Being with them made me feel like I was this total jingle-writer and that there was no weight to what I was doing. It was just "lite!"' She felt that those artists were somehow more significant and important than she was, and that they embraced pop far less than her. 'I felt I had a massive hill to climb with the next album.'

While one side of life was relaxed and homely, pressure was mounting on her to follow up her two pop albums with something more substantial. She began to take steps towards what would become *Tiger Suit*. She explains: 'There was a big process to get there. I'd taken a year off to write and wrote seventy-five songs in a year. I picked the best twelve that all went together. It was a really positive experience, and the first time I fell in love with working in a studio. I enjoyed recording with Steve Osborne before, but I wasn't ready to start properly recording at that point.' Until this break she hadn't written a lot on tour. 'I was not in the right headspace to write on the road. I find being a performer and a writer totally different things. One of the French band Phoenix said to me: "You can smell a tour bus in a song." That's why I took a year out to write *Tiger Suit*.'

Kate was also getting involved with her old passion for dance music. She'd loved the Ninja Tune label in her early twenties and the Chemical Brothers, Leftfield and Orbital as a teenager. 'I always loved it, but didn't think it was my music. Meeting Jim Abbiss opened me up to this world of synthesisers. I'd always been wary of them, as I thought they would take away from the intimacy of my songs. But it was completely the other way – they added so much.' This was very much the direction the new recordings were to take, albeit with Tunstall's anthemic touchstones. Soon the synth was her new obsession. 'I'd always loved Vangelis from the *Chariots of Fire* and *Blade Runner* soundtracks, so we got hold of a CS8 keyboard, which is the size of a sofa! That's all over the record. We were choosing between three studios in Belgium, London and Berlin and it was a no-brainer. I'd always wanted to go to Berlin, and it all felt very progressive and artistic. It's an amazing studio.'

The studio she talks of is Hansa, the birthplace of era-defining masterpieces by some of rock's pioneers. She enjoyed standing in the studio hallway, gazing at photographs of David Bowie, Iggy Pop and U2, Hansa's most famous visitors. With Luke, Noisettes drummer

Jamie Morrison and Seye Adelekan, she set to work. Seye was a big influence on the record, an unbelievably talented Nigerian guitarist and bassist of only twenty-one. He signed his own deal soon after, so was replaced on the tour by Charlotte Hathaway, formerly of Ash. As far as the recording itself was concerned, Kate says: 'The whole process was total joy!' To immerse themselves in the atmosphere they'd go clubbing together and soak up the sights and sounds of Berlin nightlife.

Released in September 2010 with singles including '(Still A) Weirdo' and 'Fade Like A Shadow', *Tiger Suit* had less fanfare than her previous efforts. Kate was now a household name, so perhaps the first blast of public excitement had worn off. There wasn't a particular buzz around its release other than within the fan base, but it went top five in the UK and was reviewed generously. Kate says: 'I totally love the record. Unfortunately, my label boss didn't get it, didn't understand the influences and the dance thing. Then it didn't get Radio 1 interest, so they pushed it to Radio 2 with the least electronic song on the record, and it died! Some bad decisions were made for that album. They wouldn't even press vinyl. It sold a couple of hundred thousand, so it wasn't exactly a flop.'

Set up for life, sales were no longer Kate's primary reason for making records. 'One of my goals is not to repeat myself. I might go over similar ground, but I'm not going to *not* experiment to keep people happy.' Still, *Tiger Suit* was critically acclaimed and earned a healthy amount of respect from peers and fans, though it didn't tie up any notable TV or film sync deals, unlike the other two. And the record company weren't completely behind it. *Eye To The Telescope* sold over four million copies, *Drastic Fantastic* between one and two million, and *Tiger Suit* less than half a million. It might look like a downward spiral, but those collections will continue selling far into the future. If any of the other artists in this book came anywhere near selling these amounts, lives would be changed immeasurably.

Kate is practical and no-nonsense about it all. 'I thought every gig sold out and every TV show was a success. I've been incredibly lucky with the press and so on. But when it came to the third record, it became apparent that the momentum was all because of the first album and because I was new. It dawned on me that that was not normal, all that happened on that first curve.' She was also struggling with her label again. 'The record company have always had a real stranglehold on artwork and imagery, and still have. It's really frustrating. On all three albums I've wanted artwork instead of my face on the front, and every time I've lost the battle.' But, she continues: 'Artists and labels are not meant to be friends. They have such different agendas. I'd be a little worried if I was getting on really well with my label.'

Kate had jumped on a rollercoaster and held on for dear life. Given the chance, she stepped up to the mark and stood her ground. She'd touched the hearts of millions with some timeless pop songs. The peaks and troughs of stardom and success were par for the course, and she knew it. As friendly, modest and straightforward now as when she was a teenager in St Andrews, she is still a joy to be around. Looking back, she says: 'In some ways, I feel as naive and as untouched as I did at sixteen. I feel totally uncorrupted by the whole thing. But I do feel very cynical about record labels, and as a businesswoman I won't put up with any shit. But in terms of my worldview, I'm the same.'

12

Secret Sounds

Johnny Lynch – The Pictish Trail

It might have been established, extolled and advocated by its reigning monarch, King Creosote, but it's a fact that Fence would not be what it is today if not for Johnny Lynch. Though not an indigenous Fifer, Johnny has invested his time, energy and love in the music it has produced for over a decade. He loves the East Neuk and may be singly responsible for putting the legendary Fence events on the map, raising the profile of the label and reaching out as a collective to embrace different styles and genres. He has been Kenny Anderson's right-hand man for years.

Johnny is an irrepressible character and a big bag of contradictions, utterly embodying the collective spirit. Balancing the absurd and comedic with trustworthiness and honour, he is an underground music nerd with a leftfield DIY approach and a keen pop sensibility. He's a mischief-maker with a serious heart, a comedian whose singing voice can make you weep, a talented artist and a budding businessman. Realising that to take on the big boys you have to be hard-working, alert and aware, he can also be very silly indeed. Usually sporting a beard, a bobble hat and hoodies in various dashing, clashing colours, Johnny is a one-off – a team player and a true gentleman.

Born in Edinburgh on 28 September 1981, he grew up in Colinton before moving to Harpenden, London aged three. Staying there for three years, his family moved back to Edinburgh until he reached the age of eleven, attending St Augustine's High School in Oxgangs for a year. Briefly touching down in Harrogate, North Yorkshire, the Lynch family settled in Connecticut, New England, when Johnny was thirteen. The reason for all this moving about was his father's job at General Electric.

Unlike many described earlier, Johnny grew up in a musical family. There was always singing around the house, and his father had been in a light-hearted folk band called The Cobblers, among other groups, as part of Edinburgh's folk scene in the 1960s and 1970s. His mother also played large old wooden recorders, and the couple actually met through the local music scene. As family life took hold, his father would only play his guitar occasionally, when tipsy and at special occasions. Music was always encouraged, however. Dad liked The McCalmans and The Corries, while Mum liked Joni Mitchell and owned a David Bowie hits compilation, which impressed Johnny. Slightly rebellious sister Suzy, seven years older, was a big music fan, favouring 1980s electro-popsters such as Erasure and The Pet Shop Boys. See a picture of Johnny's musical mind building here?

With hungry ears and an open mind, Johnny started his musical pilgrimage in Harrogate, spending his pocket money on compilations such as *Now That's What I Call Rave '92* or releases by The Prodigy or Utah Saints. As his teens erupted, Oasis featured heavily as his focus turned away from happy hardcore and chart rave. 'My dad noticed I liked Oasis and Radiohead, then Blur and The Smiths. He gave me an acoustic guitar for Christmas when I was fifteen, alongside a Beatles chord book . . . I hadn't actually heard the Beatles, but in America they're obsessed with classic rock, so bizarrely I heard them there for the first time.' In some kind of FM-radio rock initiation, Led Zeppelin, Rolling Stones and The Who were on constant rotation as he and friends drove around the American suburbs to that worthy, denim-clad soundtrack.

Johnny wasn't simply a music fan. His mother enrolled him in an acting and improvisation class in their Connecticut town. For years he'd mucked about at home and in class, and this seemed like the natural next move for his talents. Brought up a Catholic, he'd attended mass every Sunday until making his feelings known at the age of fourteen. Fortunately his was a liberal-minded family, and soon he and his sisters were able to be as irreverent as they liked; before long his parents joined in too. It's liberating to be allowed to express oneself amongst one's closest family and not be shot down. This was perhaps his inaugural step into the world of performance he revels in today.

Sadly, his school wasn't so quick on the uptake. It had neither an arts department nor a music school and, strangely enough, no sports either. 'They had religion class every day, though. And this was the sophisticated east!' Slowly his view of America was changing, but he kept his head down and got on with school, finding the work easy. He admits: 'I would tutor my classmates in maths and chemistry after school, and their mums would pay me for it. I spent all my money in the record shop.' Yes, there was a record shop – and it specialised in imports. His life was about to change irrevocably.

As his fascination with music grew, his relationship with the US was cooling by the minute. 'By the end of school I'd fallen out of love with America. I hated the mentality. At the same time I was getting into lots of different music. This record shop I'd go to was one of the few things I liked about being in America, an import store called Secret Sounds. I'm still in touch with Chris Razz, who ran it. He's moved it further south.'

Those of you familiar with Johnny's music will recognise the words Secret Sounds as the name of his albums under his alias The Pictish Trail, so it's obvious how important this shop and its treasures were to him. As an antidote to chart fodder and classic rock, Secret Sounds opened a door to new music, mainstream and underground. And lots of it seemed to come from Scotland. 'I realised there was an incredible music scene developing in Scotland. Belle and Sebastian and The Delgados were really big bands for me. Then I discovered The Beta Band. The hype was huge in the UK for them, and it began to trickle through in the US, so I'd get promo cassettes and releases.'

Most people's favourite record of all time is something from when they were seventeen or eighteen, so this Caledonian-indie awakening was an epiphany for Johnny. He explains: 'I was still buying mainly mainstream indie records, and then I heard The Beta Band. They had a voice that was definitely Scottish, but with touches of The Beatles and The Beach Boys in there. I found them quite haunting and very odd. Steve Mason's vocals on "Dr Baker" and "The House Song" were incredible – this kind of Scottish monotone thing. I was like, *what?* I was singing along to it and I thought: "I could do this." It was kind of my punk moment, I suppose. I assume it was the same when people heard the Sex Pistols – let's start a band! I heard the "Three EPs" by The Beta Band on one CD in the US. Within six months the self-titled album came out. This sounded like the kind of music I wanted to make.

'Hearing The Beta Band made me want to do Fence. Beck and the Beastie Boys are huge for me, and I hear a lot of them in The Beta Band.' Talking about cut 'n' paste aesthetics and DIY attitude, Johnny says: 'They've inspired people around the world. You'll feel their effect all over the UK when you're touring. People would come to see Kenny and they'd be massive Beta Band fans. There were Stone Roses and Primal Scream fans that needed a band to turn to, and fans who only really liked hip-hop before.' He concludes: 'I think the humour of it is definitely something that Fence drew on. John Maclean was a little wary of us to begin with, but he's become a mainstay DJ for us at the Homegame. I remember him saying: "I love you Fence guys – you've made it all fun again!"

'It was a similar thing with Stuart Murdoch from Belle and Sebastian and his way of singing. It was a Scottish voice. It was effortless and it wasn't over-singing. The songs were quite funny too. Hearing *If You're Feeling Sinister*, the "Three EPs" and Mogwai was important.' Travelling to New York in the late 1990s, he saw Mogwai posters everywhere. As someone who didn't particularly identify himself as Scottish, he realised he was getting to know the place through music. Maybe it was time to return.

After school, university beckoned. But where should a music obsessive go? Johnny recalls: 'The guy from Secret Sounds said he'd gone to study in Athens, Georgia, because he was a massive REM fan, and he suggested I find out where in Scotland The Beta Band were from. That was the only reason I applied to St Andrews University – that, and they did the English Literature degree I wanted. I didn't know anything about Fife at all. Growing up in Edinburgh, it was seen as some kind of joke.'

Although St Andrews has the reputation of housing Oxbridge dropouts and the children of privileged backgrounds, it is also a very fine academic institution. As Scotland's oldest university, it is hugely respected for all the right reasons. However, it is definitely not a rock 'n' roll university. It is the polar opposite of some anarchic art school, and probably wasn't the perfect breeding ground for creative thinking. Or was it? Johnny says: 'All my friends who did something creative at St Andrews have ended up doing it afterwards too. It's such a microcosm. You could do something and get noticed. People would go and see something because there was nothing else to do.'

Yet the clichés have some truth. There were massive class divides, with posh Brits, rich Americans and working-class and middle-class Scots mingling together. Johnny says: 'I was the only Scottish person doing English Literature who wasn't a girl or a toff.' Having spent some time in America, Johnny was a little exotic. He found it easy to make friends and wasn't bothered by class. 'The people who were most unpopular were the social climbers. People who'd arrive as greasy, down-to-earth teenagers and by year two were wearing pashminas and clothes from Abercrombie and Fitch.'

As curious about comedy as music, Johnny began doing stand-up with a friend, Andrew Laurence, who is now a successful comedian. It wasn't long, however, before he formed his first group, The Prince William Golf Band, with his friend Adam, who still performs in a Brighton band called Foxes. 'I was doing bits of stand-up, the occasional gig, putting on DJ nights and performing in the odd play. I had so much free time doing the English degree. Every year we'd do something at the Edinburgh Festival. I'd act in things, or help out with the production. I didn't take any of it seriously until my last year, when Andrew and I did this last attempt at a sketch show and it went really well. But we had a really fraught relationship, and I thought it would be much more relaxing to do music. I thought I was probably a lot better at it too.'

It wasn't long before Johnny stumbled across something that would soon envelop him completely. As he now declares: 'The Fence thing was incredibly inspiring. Within the first two weeks of arriving in St Andrews, I saw Kenny play in Aikman's, and over the course of a couple of years my life totally changed.'

$$\text{\clef treble}$$

Aikman's has been mentioned in almost every chapter of this book, but it's unlikely that anyone who played those fortnightly shows at the time thought very much about it. But these happenings were to have a deep impact on Johnny Lynch. 'I'd never seen gigs on this scale before. In the US, I'd only seen bands play in 2,000-capacity venues or bigger. I'd seen a friend's hardcore band play supporting Atom and His Package in a small venue, but I'd never seen music in a pub before. To me in the

States, pub culture didn't exist at all.' Kenny and his brothers were simply entertaining themselves and their local friends, so imposed no rules on themselves or the audience. Johnny says: 'He did this thing every second Wednesday for ages. They would be three-hour gigs with Kenny and a bunch of other players – Pip Dylan, Captain Geeko, Super Shitbox, The Jose, Billy Pilgrim, Gummi Bako and so on. But every time the set would be completely different.' The sheer work involved and the ingenuity of the improvisation impressed Johnny. 'You'd go to gigs and they'd be making toast onstage, or playing with Scalextric or whatever. There was something really joyful about it.'

But where would Johnny, 3,000 miles from Secret Sounds, buy his records in Fife? When I was growing up near St Andrews, there was only John Menzies, a musical-instrument shop and Tracks that sold a few new releases. Soon after Johnny arrived, Kenny and Jason Cavanagh opened the Fence shop. Johnny, by all accounts, was their best customer. 'The Fence shop was phenomenal,' he says.' It reminded me of Secret Sounds. I was discovering tons of new stuff. I wasn't good friends with them, but I would say hi and ask what they recommended.'

Jason was friendly and knew his music, Johnny recalls. 'He was a typical record shop-owner. I remember him lambasting this young guy who was buying Kings of Convenience's *Quiet Is The New Loud*. He stared at him and shouted: "What is this? Loud is the new loud. LOUD IS THE NEW LOUD!" It was a *High Fidelity* moment.' Johnny put two and two together and realised who Kenny was as well: '"Wow, that's the same guy who does those mad nights in Aikman's." You couldn't avoid it. They were always putting on nights and doing stuff.' Johnny was simultaneously investigating Lone Pigeon, who was getting some press attention via the Beta Band connection. The 'Touched By Tomoko' EP was available on 7-inch vinyl and Gordon would be featured in the *NME*. Johnny would often see him in the Fence shop, dressed in white robes as a messianic Jew.

Johnny started listening to John Peel on Radio 1 and took over the alternative music society in the student union, claiming to live there most of the time. He put on a club night called Bulletproof and promoted two events at the Sea Life centre with out-of-town guests Seedling and Ballboy playing. But he was increasingly drawn to the Fence Collective and their mob of unlikely pranksters. Their next outings took shape as the

Sunday Socials, again in Aikman's. Spawning what would become the Homegame, they'd start at lunchtime and go on to 1 a.m. It was non-stop music from King Creosote, James Yorkston, Lone Pigeon, Pip Dylan and Uncle Beesly. They would all do sets and Falkirk DJ Onthefly would play records. Johnny recalls: 'They made a song and dance about their own thing. I can see why people might feel intimidated by the Fence thing, as it may come across as a clique. But everyone was doing their own tunes; that was the most amazing thing about it. People prized having their own songs. It was really inspiring and I got the bug. I started demoing my own songs and handing them to Kenny.'

The Prince William Golf Band were invited by Kenny to play, as a duo of Johnny and Adam, at a Sunday Social. Kenny would say: 'Just use the guitars that are there.' They didn't have a drummer, so 'Chee-hee will do it.' They didn't have a bass player, so 'Oh, Uncle Beesly will join in.' It was an amazing environment, not intimidating at all. Johnny adds: 'The collective was probably at its strongest at this point. You wouldn't know when one act finished and another one started. Everyone would swap instruments and sing on each other's songs. Local music tends to be covers bands, but if you did a cover at a Fence event, it would have to be a comedy cover.'

Johnny offers some insights into Fence people of the time. Of James Yorkston he says: 'He always seemed a little bit apart. He kept a little bit of distance, though in the last few years he's really embraced the ethos. Initially you'd see him at Fence events and wonder who he was. Then he'd play a song, and you'd think: "Wow, that was pretty amazing!" He was quite mysterious. His singing and lyrical style were different from everyone else's. His music seemed quite folky and authentic, but also had that Krautrock thing and that don't-give-a-fuck attitude.'

Of Gordon and Een, Johnny says: 'Gordon wasn't just a character at gigs, he was a character in town. You'd bump into him and he'd say: "Listen to this" and make you listen to his new Lone Pigeon opus. He was a bit of a legend. Een is one of the most talented musicians I have ever seen. He can play so well and pick anything up so quickly. His singing voice was American, and that put some people off, but I was like, why not? Why can't he do it? He always had a good band with really slick songs and fast playing. When everyone else was just playing chords, you'd think: "That guy is amazing!"'

Unfortunately, the Fence shop hit dire straits and finally closed. All its customers, especially Johnny, were shocked and saddened. After that Kenny did less and less in St Andrews and the town really missed him. Johnny stresses: 'The Milne family played a large role in Fence. When the shop went bankrupt, Eric Milne helped Kenny out, so he could do the label more seriously.' Johnny was friends with Eric's son Ben, of whom he says: 'Ben Milne is probably the world's biggest King Creosote fan. I think he's one of the few who have everything he's ever recorded.'

In the summer before Johnny's finals year the Prince William Golf Band was winding down, and Johnny decided to record his first solo album. As his association with Fence grew, he was told: 'You can't use your own name. You have to have something to hide behind. This has got to be your mask.' Everyone in Fence had a pseudonym. 'My flatmate Harry constantly referred to me as 'the Pict' because I was short, fat and hairy! One year he went on a holiday up north and sent me a photo of him pointing at a sign saying "The Pictish Trail". I was writing these songs and I needed a name, so I just used that. I thought I should change it, but all my friends went "No!"'

Johnny's student life ran from 1999 to 2003. He achieved a 2:1, and his girlfriend of three years tempted him with a move to Manchester. She thought Fence were a bunch of under-achieving hippie stoners and even enrolled him on a music course in Manchester as a birthday present. That was the final straw in a dwindling relationship, and it ended unceremoniously there and then.

Having escaped marital bliss and further student life in Manchester, Johnny's preferred options seemed to be closer to St Andrews. He was enjoying the Fence ideology of DIY music, recording and events. Kenny asked him if he wanted to start booking live Fence shows on a more permanent basis, starting with something at the Ship Tavern in Cellardyke. Johnny says: 'It wasn't until my third year that I realised there was life outside St Andrews. Everybody just lives in a little bubble in the centre of town.' After a fleeting visit back to the US to see his parents and collect his belongings, he moved back to Fife and into a house with Alan 'Gummi Bako' Stewart in Cellardyke. 'That's when I really got to know Kenny, Jenny [HMS Ginafore] and Alan. Staying in Fife was a no-brainer.'

He signed on the dole and took part in a government scheme of the day, New Deal for Musicians. Though scorned by some as a way for the workshy to avoid reality, Johnny says: 'I was allowed to work on the Fence stuff and accumulate money in a bank account that I wasn't able to touch. After a year or so I signed off and was able to live off the money that was there. It worked for me. Without that, I wouldn't have been able to do Fence. The Fence thing is the only job I've ever had. I'm not entirely proud of that!'

Johnny says: 'I came into Kenny's life when things were on the up for him after his depression in 1995 and 1996. He was doing everything in very small numbers, but by 2003 a lot of people were very interested in him and Fence. I came in at the right time for him and me. As soon as I was involved in Fence, I said: "There are so many possibilities with this." Out of that came the Homegame idea, plus it was a busy time for the label. I've never seen a label release as much music as that in such a short time, 2003 to 2005.' Domino Records were also beginning to pay attention, and Johnny saw a massive creative playing-field opening up.

Promoting *Kenny And Beth's Musikal Boat Rides* in 2003, Kenny had fallen out with Een and asked Johnny to go on tour with him. 'I said yes. It was my first Pictish Trail tour, and it was proper venues. They weren't all that well attended, but it was my first experience of life on the road. It was just the two of us with guitars and an accordion.' They spent endless car journeys together putting the world to rights, usually with Kenny's beloved A-ha on the stereo. Of this special relationship, Johnny says: 'It's quite odd. Kenny is one of the most flirtatious men I've ever met . . . with everyone. And not in a sexual way. With guys, he's got this thing that will just hook you in. He's great in conversation and will always find your slant on things and compliment you. It's really endearing and really funny. Kenny has informed me on everything I know and think about music. Completely. He's ruined me.'

If there was a *modus operandi* for Fence, it was to start off small and make it successful on its own terms first. It was important not to be too ambitious. Kenny had learned from previous bands and the Fence shop. Johnny agreed. 'I don't want to be a big rock star. I want to do music for a living and I'm lucky to be doing that. I also get to work with other people's music that I love.

'I don't understand why there aren't more collectives. I think it's because there's no one else like Kenny! I think he managed to get everyone in the collective together by flirting with every one of them!' But what about him inspiring Kenny? Johnny confides: 'I hope that I helped him realise he had something really special and that he was very much loved by the people around him. He's been integral to the success of Fence and I hope I spurred him on to carry on with it.'

Johnny set to work booking strange, intimate gigs at the Ship Tavern in Anstruther and in St Andrews and Dundee. However, it was almost impossible to book Fence shows outside their local area and cover costs. Manchester, London and Edinburgh, for example, were all bad at paying the acts decent money, unless you promoted the shows yourself. He therefore set up his own company, Trailer Park, to do that. But it was another event, far from Fife and indeed from Scotland, that made a special impression. Johnny and Kenny attended the Green Man festival in Wales in an old, run-down stately home in the summer of 2003. Johnny says: 'It was a really cosy vibe with all these amazing acts playing.' James Yorkston headlined, Four Tet DJ'ed, King Creosote performed and everyone from the Fence Collective went away thinking it was brilliant, haphazard and not unlike a classic Sunday Social.

The timing was perfect. Kenny and Johnny had been thinking about doing a big one-day event and this was the inspiration they were looking for. After checking out a hostel near Inverness, Johnny thought: 'Why don't we just do something in Anstruther, on a small scale, and maybe do something up north in the future?' It seemed more in keeping with their home-grown mindset.

Anstruther's Erskine Hall had a maximum capacity of one hundred and fifteen persons, so Fence hired a PA, a local publican said he'd do the bar, a poster was made and it was announced on the Fence website. To complement the Fence stalwarts, they asked friends from labels 679, Twisted Nerve and Analogue Catalogue to play. James Yorkston headlined on Friday evening and they put on an all-day Fence session on Saturday. The hundred and fifteen tickets sold out on the day at £15 each. 'We thought it would be like a Sunday Social but on a slightly bigger scale,' says Johnny. 'But when it happened, it was completely different. There were people up from London! We were thinking: "Who are these people? How have they heard about this?" That amount of people was a big deal for us at the time. It was like a proper gig.'

So began the Homegame. Fence were now capable of booking their own festival. People stayed in the East Neuk and rented cottages, Johnny recalls. 'We realised Anstruther was a great place to visit, and it could have a real identity among our audience.' It was out of season, but they noticed the town coming to life. Another tradition started that year, however: Black Monday. Jenny 'HMS Ginafore' Gordon called Johnny to describe Kenny's post-Homegame hangover and warn that he was threatening to finish Fence. Thankfully, there were more good times to come.

If Fence was gaining recognition, Domino Records' involvement has to be credited for some of this. Johnny says: 'They've been really important. They signed James Yorkston on their own, then James did the collective thing of handing Laurence Bell a CD with songs by Kenny, Gordon, Een and UNPOC on it. That's how he became aware of Fence.' After that Domino took an active interest in the roster, especially the Anderson brothers and Lone Pigeon in particular. To this day Domino wants to release a full-scale Fence Collective album in a Greatest Hits style. Hopefully this will happen before long.

Fence took the encouragement, the praise and the investment and ploughed on. Three samplers were released: *Let's Get This Ship On The Road*, *Fence Sampler #3* and *Fence Reunited*, the latter getting some help from Domino, distribution via Cargo and a company called Hermana doing press. The people involved all came to Homegame No. 1 in 2004. Domino soon released Pip Dylan's *Of All The Things That I Can Eat . . .* and *Kenny And Beth's Musikal Boat Rides* in the UK, and licensed the latter and Lone Pigeon's *Concubine Rice* in the US. The London-based label was helping things along without putting too much money or effort in. It was a see-how-it-goes philosophy, but they took to selling some Fence titles through their website, including home-made albums by Pictish Trail, King Creosote, HMS Ginafore and others. They bought CDs in batches of fifty from Fence and sold them to Domino fans online.

When King Creosote's next album proper, *Rocket DIY*, was ready, Johnny, Kenny and Johnny Bradshaw from Domino met with Pinnacle distribution. This would be the first Fence album that went through all the official Domino channels. Even when King Creosote signed with Warners and Domino temporarily took a back seat, Bart McDonaugh and Johnny Bradshaw came to Homegame and kept in touch. Johnny reckons the London gang were fascinated with Fence, saying: 'They've always admired our thing from afar.' He has one disappointment: Domino offered him publishing money for his first album proper, *Secret Sounds Vol. 1*, but he turned them down on the advice of a friend. He regrets it now, but felt he didn't need the money at the time.

While Kenny's music was increasing in popularity and his schedule was filling up, Johnny was positioning himself at the helm of the ship. He was the mainstay of the Fence office and organised their events and releases with Kenny's approval and supervision. He says of the time Kenny was signed to Warners: 'I was the point of contact for a lot of stuff, because Kenny didn't have a regular email address or mobile phone.' Johnny was also the first to realise that the King Creosote story wasn't that of The Earlies, the Names label, or even the songs: it was that King Creosote was leader of the Fence Collective. Johnny admits: 'I think that irked Billy Campbell quite a bit! He wanted to make Kenny a pop star like David Gray or something.' The Scottish press and radio loved it, magazines like *MOJO* wrote about it and the *Observer Music Monthly* featured them. Fence was the story, and all the photos were of Kenny in Anstruther by the harbour, wearing odd clothes and a beard.

On top of his label duties and solo material, Johnny was lead guitarist and noisemonger in the King Creosote touring band with Kenny, who had now signed to Warners. Watching the major-label machinations from within, Johnny saw how the label ignored the band, and wouldn't allow the *KC Rules OK* and *Bombshell* albums into the online Fence shop. It was Kenny's new manager, Derek McKillop, who brought it all together. He knew the industry better than anyone they'd ever met, and was used to big egos and bolshy labels. He went into Warners and made sure Kenny got the best deal he possibly could. Kenny was treated like a proper star at times. 'I can say I played guitar at RAK studios and performed on *Later . . . with Jools Holland* because of that time,' says Johnny. 'It was different. We were a proper band, but Kenny wasn't massive, and we were all still doing Fence stuff. There was no point at which I thought he'd sold out or compromised, and I still don't think he has.'

Immediately after university Johnny had been catapulted into the life of a working musician and label boss. It was quite an achievement, especially based in the East Neuk with patchy mobile phone reception. Within a few years he was playing to big audiences, recording in top studios and appearing on TV. Touring with the King Creosote band, he would occasionally take centre stage and unleash waves of distorted, discordant noise from his guitar and effects pedals. It gave the band more drama and the music more edge. Soon his own music, as The Pictish Trail, would shine too. 'Even in Kenny's band, I was always introduced as The Pictish Trail onstage. You become your own persona. I'd sell my own records at the shows and play my own stuff whenever possible.'

Having played in the King Creosote band for four years, Johnny slowly pulled back and began to concentrate on his own material. It was time to put a solo album together, but the friends and allies fell out. In 2008 Kenny and Johnny had a massive bust-up concerning their friend and Fence member Joe 'MC Quake' Collier. Joe had been tour manager for King Creosote, and to Johnny's mind had been doing an increasingly bad job. Johnny had taken the flak for others exploiting Fence's hospitality backstage, was always on the receiving end of any complaints on tour, and infuriatingly had a guitar stolen at a Hogmanay gig in Edinburgh, which he assumed was Joe's fault. He and Kenny argued until he thought they'd got to a point of no return, so they had to distance themselves a little from each other. It was a major problem, mainly due to Kenny's loyalty to both parties. Astonishingly, Kenny tried to put an end to Fence itself, writing a letter to Johnny and Jenny 'HMS Ginafore' Gordon. Johnny fumes: 'I was livid. I couldn't believe it had come to this. We had some time apart and I carried on doing stuff for Fence. It all calmed down in the end. I wasn't going to let something stupid like this finish everything. It was bullshit!'

Fence survived, but Johnny wasn't invited on the next tour. It was time for Johnny to get back to his own music. He says: 'Having been kicked off a KC tour after that big debacle, I decided to finish off these songs that I had. A year previously I'd recorded some stuff with The Earlies, at Billy Campbell's request. He thought they sounded home-recorded and said "You can have them." Suddenly I had these full-band recordings for free! Kenny wanted to put them out as an EP on Fence, but I held on to them. Being out of the band and having time to myself, I had all these other songs that I wanted proper versions of, so I spent a bit of time at home recording them. My friend Christian sent me some artwork he'd done, a portrait of me.' And so *Secret Sounds Vol. 1* came together.

Secret Sounds Vol. 1 contains three tracks with The Earlies, with the other seven recorded at home in Cellardyke on a Zoom eight-track. On these he played everything himself, hence the reliance on keyboards and guitars and the lo-fi production techniques. He says: 'I've never been one for computers that much. I like to mix by ear.' The album was mastered by Reuben Taylor of The Athletes (and my own bands Huckleberry, Hail Caesar! and Deaf Mutes). Johnny enthuses: 'When it came back it sounded like a really cohesive album. I was really proud of it.'

The project was inspired by Kenny, who has recorded almost everything at home on a Fostex digital eight-track since 1996. Before *Secret Sounds*, though, there had been about three albums' worth of music dating back to 2003, including *The Pictish Trail*, *Pick At Pictish* and *Hot Trail*, all of which had been released on Fence CDs, EPs and compilations. Johnny's earlier tracks are heavily featured on Fence samplers including *Fence Reunited*, *Welcome The Hummingbeans* and *Don't Fudge With The Fence Made*, and he now admits: 'For me, *Secret Sounds Vol. 1* didn't feel like a first album, but it was the first proper release.'

By June 2008 he had manufactured the album himself, released it on Fence and was touring with Kenny again, this time as his support act as well as part of his band. He covered all of the album's costs within two gigs. He beams, saying: 'I realised I could make a living out of pushing my own thing more, so I set off on all those tours. I knew all of the promoters because of playing with Kenny. They were happy to put me on. Even with small fees I could make money because of merchandise, but by the end of the year I was getting £1,000 a show.' The critics warmed to him as well. Paul Mardles in the *Observer Music Monthly* said: 'Johnny Lynch's debut as The Pictish Trail should be compulsory listening for anyone under the impression that Fence is solely devoted to lo-fi folk. Indebted to Hot Chip, The Beta Band and Paul McCartney, this is charming, fresh and quietly *outré*.' *MOJO*'s Will Hodgkinson wrote: 'Johnny Lynch has spent much of the last few years helping friends and fellow Fence members like Kenny Anderson and James Yorkston get their careers off the ground. Finally recording an album in his basement, he reveals himself as a powerful songwriter in his own right.'

Putting together a band and playing solo from the beginning of 2008 to the start of 2011, Johnny toured relentlessly, taking in a DIY US tour and an appearance at the South by South West (SXSW) festival in Austin, Texas. He appeared on BBC2's *The Culture Show*, playing 'Words Fail Me Now' and a song with James Yorkston. Life was getting very busy indeed. *Secret Sounds Vol. 1* was selling by the bucketload at gigs, online and through indie shops, 'by the bucketload' meaning enough to get re-pressed a few times and earn the man a decent living. Isn't that enough?

Johnny's next project was a chance to combine his two loves, music and comedy. As a regular at theatres and stand-up clubs, he'd been a fan of Josie Long for a while. Keen on independent new music, she'd attended a James Yorkston show in London. Johnny says: 'I approached her and said hello, then we kept in touch. She wanted to do a tour. She was going to do something for a hundred days in a row, and did I want to be involved? I thought it was inspiring. I started having ideas for songs right away.' Johnny's project turned into an album of fifty thirty-second songs called *In Rooms*. 'It's just an album of ideas. There are a few shit ones, but that's what happens when you make fifty songs!'

He sold the album at gigs, shifting the entire initial run of five hundred. 'It's something I'm really proud of. I hope people discover it down the line.' With an official track listing on the vinyl, people were encouraged to make their own shuffled mix. The CD came with every album, but each one had a different running order. Johnny says: 'When you're listening to an iPod and one of those thirty-second blips comes on, it's like a palate-cleanser. I wanted to do a whole album of palate-cleansers.'

He toured with Josie as the two became firm friends and collabora-tors. He explains: 'At that time, any opportunity that came up I did it, unless I really hated the situation. I wanted to make sure I could play to any kind of crowd. The Josie tour was interesting because the *In Rooms* songs were a big part of the set. I was the musical act between two comedians. I had to be a wee bit funny, but there's no way you can be as funny as people who do it for a living. Josie Long is just inherently funny.' Opening up his music and onstage charisma to a whole new audience, he managed to sell about 1,000 copies of *Secret Sounds Vol. 1* and several hundred copies of *In Rooms*.

The ante was upped further when Johnny was asked to support KT Tunstall on tour. He says: 'That was totally different! That was six weeks long. I'd supported her as part of Kenny's band before in front of 3,000 people a night, and we hadn't sold any albums. After the first week in Ireland I had to rethink the set. I was trying thirty-second songs and bits of comedy and it was working a bit, but I'd lose momentum in parts. So, I started trying to involve the audience and have them sing along. It's the cheesiest thing in the world, but it worked. The UK dates got better and better and I started selling loads of albums. By the time we got to Europe, it was insane! I thought my banter-heavy set would be lost on them, but they got it more than anyone else. Paris was the best gig of my life.'

Not only did Johnny benefit from the tour, but his DIY approach rubbed off on the previously corporate Tunstall machine. Kate was charmed by his talent and humour, and she took to the idea of a self-made, low-key, tour-only release. Johnny advised Kate to make the 'Scarlet Tulip' EP and simply do it herself – composition, production, artwork and packaging. Unbelievably, ten days after the tour she had recorded and manufactured thousands of CDs and had a vinyl run pressed. She sold them at gigs, taking to the road on a solo tour a few months later. Johnny and Kate's friendship was blossoming, and it looks as though there might be future collaborations in the air.

With a final solo tour alongside Lone Pigeon immediately afterwards, Johnny brought this marathon live run to an end. He had established himself as an artist and proved to himself he could take on pretty much any audience on the planet. He says: 'I've managed to make my own name for my own music. Not on the same scale as Kenny's, obviously, but I make a living out of my music, not Kenny's.' He was exhausted after gigging for almost three years solid, and he took some time out to be with his family.

Johnny had always taken an interest in electronica, accommodating its influence into his Pictish Trail songs with drum machines and synthesiser bleeps. It had always been in the back of his mind to do a more electronic record, especially as Hot Chip were making waves with modern, heartfelt pop over 1980s-influenced synth backing while retaining a DIY attitude and approach. Soon his dream was to be realised in the form of Silver Columns, with his friend Adem Ilhan.

Having known Adem for years from appearing on various bills together, collaborating onstage and performing at his own Homefires festival in London, Johnny booked him to play at Homegame a few times and says: 'He is one of the most generous people I've ever worked with. It's just lovely being in his company. Some people might see him as little bit posh or privileged, but he's not at all. He's a proper London boy.' Adem has a chameleon-like approach to music. In the band Fridge he played post-rock, and as 'Adem' he went for a fragile singer-songwriter stance, but he was also writing TV scores under a different name. Adem heard *Secret Sounds Vol. 1*, which he liked, and probably saw Silver Columns simply as a project with someone he really enjoyed working with. Johnny continues: 'He knew I was a massive Hot Chip fan, and asked me if I wanted to do a real pop record and spend a day or two writing. So I went down to his warehouse in London, and within three days we'd written and recorded three songs: "Cavalier", "Yes, And Dance" and "Warm Welcome". It just felt so effortless.'

The results were quick, but the quality was high. It was playful, joyous and catchy. With no deadlines or egos to deal with, they'd started a new project about which they could both get excited. It was noticeably influenced and inspired by Hot Chip, but the BPMs were higher and Johnny's inner disco diva was surfacing. He was initially thinking about a De:Fence release on Gav 'Onthefly' Brown's offshoot electronic label, but Adem said: 'Yeah, I know a few people as well.' They knocked out another three songs in four days, then finished another three when Adem travelled up to Anstruther. As new songs emerged they continuously tweaked the older numbers, and soon they had more than enough material for an album.

They sent some recordings to Radio 1's Rob Da Bank, who instantly wanted his own label, Sunday Best, to put it out. Adem then handed the material to Stephen Bass of Moshi Moshi records, who had released the likes of Hot Chip, Florence and the Machine, Kate Nash, Bloc Party, Slow Club and many more. He loved it too and signed them, unleashing an anonymous, white-label 12-inch vinyl of the song 'Brow Beaten'. 'I was a little worried about that,' Johnny says. 'I didn't want it to become a big deal.' Ultimately it worked in their favour, as blogs, radio DJs, the specialist press and dance fans wanted to know who it was. People loved the record, comparing Johnny's high-pitched vocal acrobatics with Jimmy Somerville. The reaction was markedly different from the Fence scene and supporters. The blogosphere went wild with London taste-makers getting in on the anonymous hype. When I played it on Radio 1, listeners lapped it up and tried to guess who it was. The white-label mystery added to the excitement and the joyous nature of these skewed disco-pop tunes.

After a couple of singles the duo revealed themselves to the world before releasing the album *Yes, And Dance*. Johnny, touring as The Pictish Trail with Malcolm Middleton when it came out, says: 'I kept getting these emails saying: "You're at number five in the Dance Buzz chart", and I was like "What is the Dance Buzz chart?"' Response sheets returned by international DJs showed that the likes of Erol Alkan, Richard Norris and First Blood were all loving it. Taking to the stage for their debut gig at Homegame in 2010, everything seemed just right. I remember the sweaty heat of Legends nightclub in Anstruther as the drunken Homegamers tried to crowbar their way in to see the performance. Johnny recalls: 'It wasn't actually the best show we ever played. I had a terrible throat and massive tonsils. We weren't that good, but the atmosphere in the room was incredible.'

After the album's release in May 2010 on Moshi Moshi, the duo toured like crazy, taking in festivals, venues and clubs across the UK and Europe and playing support to dance crew Underworld across the UK. 'We played to a packed Brixton Academy and people went nuts,' Johnny recalls. Two guys best known for underground, indie-folk and post-rock were strutting their stuff, clad in silver body-stockings, even performing on the debauched party-island of Ibiza. Johnny recalls: 'One show we did in Barcelona was out of this world. We were making up lyrics on the spot and making live dance music – it was so liberating.' I have seen Silver Columns live on a few occasions, and while their hook-laden songs always grabbed me, the over-riding sense I took from them was one of joy.

Less than a decade after leaving university, Johnny Lynch had helped grow a record label, played lead guitar with King Creosote, made a solo career and formed a synth-pop duo, not to mention touring the UK, Europe and the US. From modest beginnings as a teenage music fan and import aficionado to full-blown underground troubadour, he'd accomplished a ton, and all with a smile on his face and usually a bottle of beer in his hand. Ladies and gentlemen, I give you . . . The Pictish Trail.

13

Just beyond the River

The Continuing Life and Times of James Yorkston

As the first member of the Fence Collective to break through to the wider world, James Yorkston had exceeded all expectations with his debut album *Moving Up Country*. An unlikely success story in an age of quick-fix pop, he'd been true to himself and recorded a deeply personal, largely acoustic album full of timeless songs at the age of thirty-one in 2002. The album had been incredibly well received, and after an extensive touring campaign in the UK, Europe and US it was time for a second helping. Yet with it came the burden of categorisation. He'd been branded a folk singer. This was largely his own doing, as it seemed easier to tell people that, but it rankled. He says: 'The word "folk" means something different to everyone. To some people it means absolutely everything, and to others it means only unaccompanied singers. For me, it's the traditional music of the country. I don't consider myself a folk singer. I'm a pop-song writer, but they're not very popular songs.'

He continues: 'When we got labelled folk, I asked the fiddle player I had at the time, Jon Bews, if it was folk, because he's a traditional player. He said: "I don't think it is at all. I think you're a folk singer, but not a traditional folk singer."' He recounts a tale of jousting with journalists. 'I remember two interviews I did on the same day. The first guy, from France, asked: "Would you consider yourself a folk singer?" I said no, I wouldn't, and I said why. He argued and said: "But you're taking traditional songs and keeping them going. You are part of the tradition." I said okay. Then five minutes later an Italian journalist asked the same question. So I said yes, I am a folk singer, and he said: "No, of course you're not a folk singer. You're a pop singer." And I agreed with him. I came to the realisation that it doesn't matter.'

It certainly wasn't standard folk music, and he sets the record straight on genres and music-business terminology. 'For me there's a big connection between Krautrock and traditional music. Krautrock was as much an influence as traditional music, if not more so. That first record was called alt-country, probably because it had "Country" in the title. It had nothing to do with that. It got called new-folk. The only label I liked was Kraut-folk, which was fun! I remember one guy describing Four Tet as Nick Drake with a laptop. I mean, you just want to get a shotgun out!'

Whatever he was playing, he would further entrench himself in acoustic instrumentation as he began work on the follow-up. It was perhaps more folk or less pop than its predecessor, and would be more difficult to make. He admits: 'The stress of that second album was extraordinary. I've never written that many songs, unlike someone like Kenny. If I'm lucky I'll write five songs in a year good enough to consider releasing. I'd had two years of no pressure to write the first album, and then it was "Follow that up, then!" If you've got no songs, that's pressure.'

Knowing James and his innate confidence, it's strange to think he was having problems at the time. He seemed to take it all in his stride. Talking of being relaunched into the public consciousness after the release of the first album, he says: 'It was exciting, but it was worrying. I enjoy it a lot more now, because I'm more confident and comfortable as a musician. I have some kind of status now, even though it's not huge status, and I can enjoy it because I have what I feel is a strong back catalogue. At the time, though, it was full of stress. I didn't have management and I was dealing with everything.'

Almost naively, he thought the songs would simply appear. That didn't happen exactly, but some of his favourites are on the second album – 'Heron', 'Shipwreckers', 'Surf Song', 'Banjo #1' – and remain staples of his live set. He says: 'I think there are some really strong songs on that record, but it was a struggle.' Still using his original band of Athletes – Dougie, Reuben, Faisal, Wendy, Holly and new fiddle-player Jon Bews – he set off to the Welsh studio Bryn Derwen, which would become his studio of choice. Although James had produced *Moving Up Country* with keyboardist Reuben Taylor, Domino Records thought the next step should be to connect with a like-minded producer. The choice of Kieran Hebden, alias Four Tet, was made. James explains: 'People said: "Get a producer on board and it'll make the record so much better." Kieran was so gracious, and incredibly inexpensive. He said he'd do it for next to nothing because he loved the music.' The band loved Kieran's *Pause* album, and it helped that he was signed to Domino. James played him Link Wray's 'Fire And Brimstone' and Lightning Hopkins's small-band records as touchstones, insisting he wanted the record to sound live, rough and raw. 'Kieran was brilliant,' James says. But did he actually need a producer? 'Maybe I did. Maybe I needed someone to help steer things. I probably wasn't seeing that straight.'

A few strange decisions were made. James left off some songs that he thought wouldn't fit, including 'Someplace Simple', which would come out as a single. But at the time he was going for purity, choosing solely from what had been recorded at the Bryn Derwen sessions. Although he still loves the album, he admits: 'It was a very dark album, and it didn't have any pop singles on it.' He'd been depressed before his first album, yet it had come out uplifting and tuneful. With the second album he was happier than he'd been for years, but it was far darker. 'I did feel I'd backed myself into a corner on that album. It was so challenging to people other than music fans. It wasn't a wallpaper album.'

Released in October 2004, *Just Beyond The River* won glowing reviews, though slightly muted ones in Scotland. The album proved that even at his more uncompromising, his music could be appreciated high and low. Pete Paphides of *The Times* wrote: 'Yorkston has reached a state of grace that writers can spend forever trying to attain: songs that sound not so much written as carefully retrieved from your own subconscious, played with an intuition bordering on telepathy.' *Just Beyond The River* was declared a masterpiece by, among others, *Time Out*, the *Telegraph*, *Record Collector* and the *Fly*.

Downbeat and drone-laden, the second album was a significant work by an artist unflustered by his success and unwilling to bow to commercial pressures. It might not have won him a new army of fans, but it didn't harm his reputation one bit. Laurence Bell says: 'He's just followed a very singular path. He's not one for compromise. He's made some brilliant records. They're not all sweet and accessible, but he's built a career by following his instincts.' Touring the UK with The Athletes, 2004 to 2005 saw James cement his standing as a thriving home-grown talent.

All was not rosy behind the scenes, however. He was appointed a different product manager at Domino and didn't get on as well with the new man. Bart McDonough had been his point of contact and they had built up a good relationship. Bart told the truth, good or bad, with no sugar-coating, which suited James down to the ground. The reason for the change was that Franz Ferdinand were taking off globally and Domino had had to grow massively to keep up with demand. Bart had been relocated and James was suffering as a result. But, standing by the label, he says: 'Domino have been an amazing record company. After *Just Beyond The River* I had an offer from a major and I told Domino about it. They offered me another contract and I re-signed. I wouldn't look elsewhere, and I'd be very upset if I was booted off the label. They're creative, and I get on very well with the small core of people I deal with at the label. They came to my wedding as friends.'

$\oint$

Although James may have felt a little sidelined by Franz Ferdinand's stratospheric rise, there were some advantages. Budgets went through the roof at the label and his next album, *Year Of The Leopard*, would cost roughly £50,000, an exorbitant amount for an independent label to spend on a rootsy singer-songwriter whose overheads were small and manageable. In retrospect, James isn't that happy about it. '"Summer Song" and "Orgiva Song" were demos I did in Insch House, "Woozy With Cider" was a demo with help from Reporter, and "Year Of The Leopard" was just me and a guitar, so it cost £50,000 for something like six songs.' The producer was Paul 'Rustin Man' Webb, former Talk Talk bass player and collaborator with Beth Gibbons of Portishead. His fee was high, but James is full of praise. 'He was great to work with and we got on almost immediately. He was so open and pleasant.'

Inspired in part by the Giuseppe di Lampedusa novel *The Leopard*, which James adored, the album was a slight change in direction. James's plaintive speaking-singing delivery was still there, but there was a lighter, airier touch, with more emphasis on melody and arrangement. Rhythms and textures were employed with a playfulness and looseness that hadn't been heard in the more morose *Just Beyond The River*. He discloses: 'The whole folk thing was getting me down. I felt like I was being hemmed in to a folk-music bracket, so I was trying to do something different. "Summer Song" has me singing in falsetto, there's a spoken-word piece, some Fender Rhodes and more drums. I wanted to do an album that had no barriers. I wanted it to sound absolutely fresh.'

He was backed by most of the same musicians as before, but this was his first album not to credit The Athletes on the sleeve. He was staking his claim and going it alone. Although they weren't upfront about it, it's safe to say the band weren't entirely happy. But what were they going to do? They needed him as much as he needed them, perhaps more.

Year Of The Leopard came out in September 2006 to another spate of amazing reviews. 'I've been lucky,' James says. Containing one of his finest pop songs in the hummable 'Steady As She Goes', the album also showcased the unplanned radio and TV sync hit 'Woozy With Cider', his first official foray into electronica since his experimental side project HeeHaw Hairhead, this time with Fence comrade Reporter manning the machines. Having prided himself on rootsiness and authenticity, it was a pleasant surprise to hear James branching out. *Year Of The Leopard* spoke to fans and critics again, endorsing his reputation as a weighty songwriter. 'The Fife man's quivering, faint delivery sounds both primeval and perfectly attuned to the twenty-first century,' said *Uncut*. 'Yorkston's subtle, ruminative songs and Webb's weightless, spare production are a perfect match,' enthused *Time Out*. 'Yorkston is the natural successor to Nick Drake,' said *The Times*.

With acoustic music being co-opted further into indie and mainstream culture, James was more established than ever, but beginning to see a lot more young pretenders. Artists such as Laura Marling and Mumford & Sons were arriving, using the acoustic template. Fence weren't bothered and neither was James. 'Every year there seems to be another "new-wave of folk music"', he notes. He had nothing to fear. Not only were his records selling reasonably well and being highly praised, but the Waterson/Carthy English folk elite began to accept him too. As an exceptional honour, he was asked to help with the tribute concert to Lal Waterson, and as musical director alongside Lal's son Oliver Knight he met Martin Carthy, Norma and Mike Waterson and Marry, whom he still occasionally plays with. 'I said yes immediately, but then I was a bit scared of meeting Oliver. I thought he would be a diehard traddie, but we both ended up not caring about that. His sister was a little more standoffish, because it was her mum we were paying tribute to. She found it all very distressing.'

Still gobsmacked by the experience, he says: 'When we went to Norma and Martin's house in Robin Hood's Bay, we sang "Midnight Feast" – it was extraordinary. I'd learned two versions of it. One was very faithful to the original and another was my Krautrock version. Ollie said: "We'll do your version" straight away. Then Mike Waterson came in and I asked if he'd like to sing on it, and he didn't bat an eyelid that it had been Krautrockified. Then Norma joined in as well.'

It was like a dream come true. He'd be playing onstage and then Norma, Marry and Mike's voices would come in with harmonies in layers. For any folk-inspired songwriter, this was a chance in a lifetime. James was now being seen in the same light as the legends of the folk world. Soon he would also play another show with Bert Jansch in Paris, reminding him how far he'd come.

James now having the cachet for a 'B-sides, demos and rarities' compilation, Domino soon released the *Roaring The Gospel* album. Although lo-fi in places, the songs are strong and, aside from the reissued *Moving Up Country* tenth-anniversary double album, this is a great way to explore James's formative years. The lazy shuffle of 'Blue Madonnas' is a personal favourite.

James also unleashed the unholy racket of *Lang Cat, Crooked Cat, Spider Cat* in 2007. This mini-album is full of noisy, atonal Krautrock jams, albeit on acoustic instruments, and was set loose via Fence Records. It was probably a shock to a lot of people who love his lilting, pastoral acoustic songs. 'It was recorded over two days in Insch House,' he recalls. 'Faisal, Reuben, Dougie and I were swapping instruments and improvising. I absolutely love that album! If people start buying albums again, I'm going to ask Domino to release it properly.' Then there was *30*, one thirty-minute track, of which he says: 'That's the great thing about Domino. They allow me to do these crazy little releases that are totally under the radar. That's where "Summer Song" and "Woozy With Cider" came from. I took them from the Fence releases and put them on the Domino releases. That's a great example of how those labels work well together.'

♪

He may not describe himself as prolific, but compared to many James now had quite a catalogue of material. With four albums including a B-sides collection, two experimental works, live recordings and various limited-edition EPs and singles to his name, it was time to start work on a new record. Hooking up with the core Athletes plus violinist Emma Smith and Sarah Scutt on clarinet and vocals, he worked on songs and arrangements for what would become *When The Haar Rolls In*. This time he would produce the work himself, allowing him more control and keeping big budgets at bay.

Natural musicianship and orchestration flow from the speakers on this album. With a warm, lush aura to it, it sounded more unrestrained and had a sense of freedom. James says: 'I produced it myself. I made it at my leisure. There was no pressure' – and it cost a mere £25,000. He'd call upon his new friends Norma, Marry and Mike Waterson to sing on one of the songs, and asked another singer, Nancy Elizabeth, to augment his vocals too. He says: 'I still consider this my finest album. Sonically it's gorgeous and I think the songs are really strong.' Sadly, his good friend and drummer Faisal was too ill for the sessions, suffering from Graves' disease. Faisal is still not fully recovered, but keeps in touch and hopes to play with James again soon.

When The Haar Rolls In was released in September 2008, sumptuously packaged in 10-inch double-album vinyl and beautiful artwork. Songs such as 'Tortoise Regrets Hare', 'Queen Of Spain' and 'Would You Have Me Born With Wooden Eyes?' became Yorkston classics and fan favourites. That said, he's now realistic about its impact. 'It had amazing reviews, but nothing really happened. It was just another album by James Yorkston.' The album was sold in various formats, including a box set which included a disc of cover versions of his songs, performed by Fence Collective alumni Rozi Plain, Pictish Trail, HMS Ginafore, Adrian Crowley, King Creosote, Jon Hopkins, Dougie Paul and UNPOC. King Biscuit Time, Onthefly, King Creosote, Four Tet and Reuben Taylor contributed to a remix disc.

For James's supporters this was an extravagant and satisfying release that sat perfectly next to his previous work. Radiohead's drummer Philip Selway, who had become a supporter and played alongside James, said: 'For me, listening to James Yorkston's music is like coming across the interesting-looking person on the fringes of a party. Before you know it, you've spent the evening listening to their compelling tale.' With new admirers and old, the album was a success.

However, due to spiralling costs and dwindling sales, as well as Faisal's illness, most of the touring around this album was solo, apart from key gigs. Touring is hard work as one gets older, and expensive with a large band to pay. But James says: 'I've made a lot of really tight, close friends on the road, and I love seeing them when I go and play in different places. Before I did music professionally, I didn't have that many good friends. You devote your life to music and nobody understands that you're not making a living out of it.'

Not an original album as such, but a labour of love, his *Folk Songs* album with the Big Eyes Family Players came out in August 2009. He explains: 'It was something I'd been working on for a while. When Kenny was selling my *J Wright Presents* CD in the Fence shop, he had twelve CDs of his material on sale and one of mine. I don't write many songs, and I thought it would be good to have an album of traditional songs as a companion to my first album, but one thing led to another and I hadn't the time to do it. I suddenly had the time, so I thought I'd finish *Folk Songs*. I'd met the Big Eyes Family Players on the road and they'd given me a CD, and it was amazing! Unfortunately it didn't quite work out, because rather than following the more extravagant musical ideas, they followed their simpler ideas. It ended up not being as different as I was hoping.'

With a lower-key release and disappointing sales, James may be a little too harsh on the album. It's a fine collection of British, Irish and Galician traditional songs, and it has his signature sound – maybe that's the problem. For those joining the dots in the revival of modern folk, it's a welcome if not earth-shattering addition to the canon. The single 'Martinmas Time' picked up a fair amount of radio play, and *Uncut* called James 'Britain's finest contemporary folk singer.' The *Observer* said: 'This is an inspired homage to timeless British song', while *The Times* commented: 'Too many folk albums should come with their own hairshirt. This is one you'll actually enjoy!' Warming to the record today, James says: 'It was a great thing to do, and people like it, but it's not as strong as I'd hoped. But I like a lot of the songs on it, and if I was compiling a "Best of" I'd definitely put some of those on there.'

$$\text{\large ♪}$$

By the end of 2009 James was happily married to Linda, with a daughter, Esme, and this life change warranted a move back to his beloved Fife. He says: 'I was beginning to find the city quite oppressive, even though Edinburgh is a wonderful city. I missed the silence and the quiet. When I moved out, it was like a massive weight off my shoulders.' As a recognised artist with a solid catalogue of material, a supportive record company behind him and a family home, life seemed sweet, if only for eighteen months or so. His life was about to be turned upside down. James's baby daughter had fallen seriously ill. The news was utterly shocking. She hadn't yet reached her second birthday.

I wanted to reach out and help James, my oldest friend in the world, but felt completely powerless. Others including Fence neighbours and friends felt the same way. He and Linda shut themselves off, spending the ensuing months shuttling between their Fife home and the Sick Children's Hospital in Edinburgh. As any father would, James took a year off to look after Esme and help Linda. Understandably reluctant to talk about it now, he simply says: 'Going through the ordeal was as close to hell as I've experienced on this earth, and by far the most horrific thing I've ever had to deal with.' Their second child, Theo, arrived while they were going through this traumatic time. James says: 'I'd thought about calling it a day just before Esme got ill. I was thinking: "Can I keep on doing this at this level?" But taking that year off revitalised me. There's nothing like spending months and months in hospital to make you realise how lucky you are to be spending months and months in recording studios and doing shows. Now I love almost every minute of every gig.'

James put himself to work in a different way. Unable to write songs as often, due to tiredness or to avoid disturbing the family, he began to write a book. He'd started the project before his daughter's illness, and soon the results would materialise as *It's Lovely to Be Here: The Tour Diaries of a Scottish Gent*. He says: 'When you have your first child, it's utterly exhausting, and I never had the energy to do much music, but always had the energy to write. I found it was something I could do at the end of the day.'

Laurence Bell of Domino continues: 'We bumped into the people at Faber & Faber, and we all had this idea with Richard King to do this magazine called *Loops*, a bi-annual literary almanac of some kind, writing mainly about music in a more extended way beyond the confines of modern media. James had written an article for one of the two *Loops* magazines, and the people at Faber really liked his style. They asked if there was any more, and James showed them his tour diaries. They said they liked it, but who would buy it? I thought: "Isn't this what we do? We like to do things we've never done before. How hard can it be to make a book?" We got it printed and asked Faber to distribute it. They said "Yeah, sure," because they didn't have to put in any money. It was well received and the first print run sold out. We're really proud that we made a book, and I think it's been good for James. It's tied his audience to him in a deeper way.'

Now James was a published author as well as an acclaimed song-writer. For a man approaching forty and a father of two, this was a good fit for him. Fans could imagine him sipping whisky by the fire, muddy boots on, telling stories and occasionally picking at his guitar. Yet the book divided his audience, due to its frank and earthy sideways glances at life. Concentrating on the more mundane side of touring, with the protagonist on a constant hunt for decent vegan food, it's a grumpy, self-deprecating and often hilarious take on life on the road. But to a fan base who'd come to him for his gentle and romantic songcraft, it was a bit of a shock. It earned excellent reviews from book and music critics alike, and people enjoyed this poignant insight into his character. He counters: 'It had some funny reviews, because my music is quite poetic and the book isn't poetic, it's played for laughs. It's supposed to be a light and amusing read. Some people would have preferred a book writ-ten with the same poetic mindset as the music, but that would have been pretentious.'

As a co-release with Faber & Faber, it outsold everything else they put out that week, soon warranting another print run. 'It hasn't done amazingly well,' James says, 'but it's covered all its costs and more. It was a bit of a punt from Domino, but it made everyone a little bit of money.' James is keen to get published again soon, and this time a book of short stories is mooted. Knowing James's wicked turn of phrase and over-active imagination, I'm sure it will be quirky and very readable.

With time off to tend to Esme and a well-received book behind him, in 2011 James returned tentatively to the live circuit. The audiences were still there, for the most part, and promoters were willing to double his fee due to his status as a songwriter. 'I did half as many shows for twice as much money, which was brilliant,' he says. His audience had changed a little, with his book opening him up to a different demographic. He was no reckless rock 'n' roller, but a mature songwriter whom people could cosy up to and enjoy at their leisure. He could play solo or with a band, with readings between the music. Humour had always been a part of his stagecraft, but now his spoken-word pieces and improvised songs were as important as his old standards. 'Whether it was having a year off, or people suddenly getting me, or the back catalogue, or the book, people are now warm and affectionate to me and my music. Maybe it's like a nice whisky – it takes time to appreciate it. My audience are almost always nice people, and I'm almost always happy to meet them. They're like friends.'

As Esme recovers, James has a new album, *I Was A Cat From A Book*, inspired by his daughter's imaginative conversation. He says: 'I'm hoping this record is the best one yet. The songs are strong enough, and I'm confident of going into album number seven with this genuine feeling, rather than "Oh fuck!"' He can look back at a long career in music with a steadfast, stoical view. 'None of my music screams at you. There are no hit singles or one-hit wonders there. The music business is all bullshit and hype. I didn't take any of it on board back in 2002 with *Moving Up Country*; I didn't think I was the best thing since sliced bread then. If I had to do it all again but had a hit single, I'd regard it all with a huge amount of scepticism. I'd go along with it though and get some more money for my kids.'

Having spent years in underachieving beat-combos with James since our teenage years, I know James can write catchy pop songs too. I often wonder why he doesn't allow them to sneak on to his albums. Surely they'd be good for business? He counters: 'I've written loads, but I tend to feel sick after I've heard them a few times. They just make me feel ill. When I constantly go over and over a song, I tend to erase those poppy hooks. I try and put in something with a bit of feeling.' I suppose James knows his audience and his musical niche in the world. He has hollowed out a place and he's happy with that. He explains: 'I approach an album and I think about nothing but the music. When the music's done, you think about promotion, treat it with respect and do the best you can. But the music isn't shaped by the marketplace. If you're doing the kind of music that I am, you're absolutely daft to chase an audience.'

The impetus to create may have changed since his teenage years, but a decade of people buying his music and telling him he's touched them emotionally has had a profound effect on him. 'Now I write songs and put as much honesty in the lyrics as possible, because that's where the truth is and that's what means something to me when I'm singing them live. And I think that's what other people get from it as well.' Of the continual adoration in the highbrow media, he says: 'The press have always been very kind to me. I rarely read a negative or nasty review. It does happen, but not very often.'

He has also inspired younger generations, with songwriters and acoustic singers taking influence and confidence from what he's achieved. Like his own punk forebears, they probably think: 'If he can do it, then maybe I can too.' Still he gets mentioned in interviews, press releases and books, with Ian Rankin an outspoken aficionado, and he is paid the ultimate compliment of people covering his songs. Contemplating the concept of quitting the whole business, he says: 'That's what I did when I was twenty-eight. I jacked in music to do music again. If I was to jack in my career now, I'd do music for fun again.'

14

Boys Outside

Steve Mason and Life after The Beta Band

Musical shape-shifter, belligerent artist and individual thinker, Steve Mason was the one to pull the plug on The Beta Band, one of the most important and influential UK bands of the 1990s and 2000s. Would they have scaled further heights? We'll never know. The pressure he felt as frontman was immense, and the will to create with his old friends had been snuffed out. By the start of 2005 the band was no more, having just completed their farewell tour. His bandmates weren't happy either. He says: 'They were angry. They didn't want it to end. I didn't realise that they didn't get it . . . the band was over!' As they walked away with roughly £12,000 each, Steve realised he had only a month's wages in the bank. He worked on a building site for a month alongside Een Anderson. After eight years of rock-star life, this was reality. Discussing his move to Fife, he says: 'I'd lived in London for around ten years and I'd had enough of it. I came back here because this is where I'm from. My mum's here, my dad's here, I know people here and I know what I'm getting. It makes sense.'

If he was unsettled creatively after the break-up, financially he was about to suffer far worse. He explains: 'As far as I can gather, the managers that we had in The Beta Band, apart from Alan McGee, decided in cahoots with our accountants that no tax would be paid, and it was something we were totally unaware of.' Weeks after the band's split, Alan McGee called Steve and laid out the situation. A deal had been struck and the taxman would accept a conservative £120,000. None of the members of the group could pay. Steve's share was tens of thousands, and it was arranged that he would pay a monthly sum from 2006 onwards. 'Something to leave to the kids, you know!' he quips.

To stay strong and keep his mind off his debts, he carried on with his solo material. It was important to be creative and busy, but also to bring money through the door. His King Biscuit Time alias was already established, and the 'Sings Nelly Foggit's Blues' in "Me And The Pharaohs'" EP was loved by fans yet floated under the radar, but the 'No Style' EP had been a potential breakthrough. Lead track 'I Walk The Earth' was heralded as up there with The Beta Band's best work and showed Mason could go it alone. Perhaps this had laid the foundations for the Beta Band's decline back in 2000. Steve says: '"I Walk The Earth" is as big as "Dry The Rain", it really is! People talk about that record all the time.' Gordon Anderson says: 'I loved the beat. I think that's the best thing he's done. I'm not so keen on some of his other stuff. I think when he does something good, you hear about it.' But it was 2005 now, and circumstances had changed dramatically. More emotional turmoil was on the way.

When The Beta Band was launched, Steve had embarked on a relationship with Nina Chakrabarti that lasted the group's whole life. As the band finished and lives began to change, they drifted apart and split up. He had no money, he had no band, and now he had no girlfriend. One thing he needed was a debut album, so he threw himself into the making of *Black Gold*. Recorded at his Pittenweem home in his Metal Biscuit studio and released through Poptones, the album combined his love of dancehall and hip-hop with his mournful vocals and acoustic guitar. Ragga MC Topcat guested on the lead single, 'C I Am 15'. Aside from a female backing vocal and some guitar from Pete Rankin, Steve played and programmed everything. He sought solace in the recording process and made an excellent ten-track album. With a collection of photos and doodled drawings on the inner sleeve, the cover was a kitsch Lou Shabner print bought at a Crail car boot sale. From the music to the aesthetics, it was bound to appeal to fans and followers of his earlier group.

Taking to the road with Rankin on bass and *Hotshots II* producer Colin Emmanuelle, alias C-Swing, on keyboards, they toured the UK to small but appreciative crowds. Steve says: 'It was one of the best tours I've ever done, it was so much fun.' This was before the album came out, however, and Steve noticed that the label wasn't doing much to promote it. 'I realised what was happening and there was nothing I could do to stop it. It was too late to get the label to pull their fingers out.'

Released in 2006, *Black Gold* came out to absolutely no fanfare. It wasn't sent to me to play on air, and I ended up buying a copy four months later when I chanced upon it in Avalanche Records in Edinburgh, languishing in the bargain bin. Steve explains: 'I realised that despite everything I love Alan McGee for, having a multi-millionaire and a man who's not driven by money as a manager was an absolute waste of time. You need a manager to want to make money for you. If you're making money, then your manager's making money. You want someone who's as hungry as you are.' Looking back, Poptones and those offshoot projects were little more than a hobby for Alan. His heart was in the right place, even if his marketing department wasn't. In many ways you can't blame McGee, who was a true believer and paid Mason a full wage for a year to help get him on his feet.

Everything came crashing down. Waiting to go on tour to promote a record that was already a failure, Steve slipped back into full-blown depression. He candidly admits: 'My plan was to kill myself. It wasn't quitting music, it was quitting life. It was a pretty scary time.' Finding it hard to cope, he turned to an old ally. 'Pete Rankin is my best friend, but he's also the person I go to when I've got a lot of problems. I wanted to be sectioned and I went to my doctor to ask to be sectioned. I was worried that I was going to kill myself. So my doctor took a bit of a gamble and told me to go and live with Pete for two weeks, so he could keep an eye on me. That was great, because getting into the loony bin is easy, but getting out is difficult. I was really lucky.'

On another road to recovery, Steve was sitting in his house in Pittenweem in 2006. His solo album had sunk without trace. He needed distraction and he needed worthy, interesting projects. Since the building-site job he'd been hanging out with Een Anderson, building on old friendship. Een had supported King Biscuit Time on tour, and he had songs that needed a band. Working on Een's Pip Dylan country album, *Orange Dirt County*, Steve helped him form his first rock band, The Black Yaks, with Steve on drums, Richard 'Scruff' Francis Parkinson on guitar and Pete Rankin on bass. Steve now looks back on what could have been. 'It was the classic case of Een not bothering. I don't get Een. He's waiting for someone to knock on his door and say, "I love what you're doing, here's £100,000, and soon we'll have loads of meetings and you're going to be set up for life." Some people don't realise that the people who become successful work really hard.' A little harsh, perhaps, but it was true that Een didn't know how to play the industry game and wasn't interested. He thought the music should do the talking. Steve counters: 'I've got both those things. I can talk passionately about what I do and make people excited. You have to have an element of that. I'm more confident, because music's the only thing that I feel confident about.'

After two gigs it was clear The Black Yaks weren't going anywhere. Simultaneously, Steve could see his former bandmates and school friends making inroads with their ventures. The Aliens, featuring Gordon Anderson and his ex-Beta Band friends, were making waves. Steve was well aware of Gordon's Lone Pigeon material and says now: 'I know a lot of it, because we used to do bits and bobs. The problem with the stuff he has put out is that none of it is really finished. People who love the Lone Pigeon can see the potential in it, but that potential has never been realised. I thought he'd do it with The Aliens.' On John and Robin working with Gordon, Steve says: 'Gordon was a good friend of theirs, and he was a lot better by then. He had been messing around with the Lone Pigeon stuff, and they had the contacts at Parlophone and so on, so it kind of made sense for them to do it.'

What were his thoughts on the new band? Admitting he didn't listen thoroughly to the first album, he says: 'I heard "I Am The Unknown" and I thought it was maybe a tenth of what it could be. But that's only because I knew the song from before.' To his credit, Steve says that it was unlikely that his former colleagues were listening closely to his solo work either. Both camps were gracious and more than civil towards each other, remaining friends throughout, albeit at a cautious distance.

Also close to home, the Fence Collective were forging ahead. King Creosote, James Yorkston, Pictish Trail and others were flying the Fife flag while pushing their own music in various different directions. Steve could see his former band's influence on what they were doing. 'I think The Beta Band has become different things to different people. I think the Fence Collective took their version and the elements they wanted to take and turned it into their business.' Having relocated to Fife, Steve was invited to perform at Fence events and even played a Homegame. Although reluctant to commit himself, he's matter-of-fact about his involvement. 'I was absolutely skint, they offered me money, and it was six miles away. I went down and played for half an hour. I've been down to a few others as well. I enjoyed meeting people, smoking cigarettes and chatting outside the halls.'

As regards Steve's music, his old friend James Yorkston says: 'I'd only really heard "Dry The Rain", "Dog's Got A Bone" and "She's The One". An Italian TV crew interviewed me about The Beta Band with Steven in his house once, and they asked me what I thought when The Beta Band split up. I said I thought Steve would be okay. Then they asked if I'd miss all that great music. I said I'd not heard a single Beta Band record, and Steve went "*What!*" I saw them live two or three times, but I don't know their records, other than the ones people have put on tapes or sing at Fence events.'

Steve keeps a distance from Fence even today, and is reluctant to be part of their umbrella collective. He casts his mind back to The Beta Band: 'John and I would come up every year from London for Christmas. We'd always go out on Christmas Eve and go to Aikman's. There'd be a gig on and Kenny would be playing. I remember feeling they ignored us; at the time, I thought it was because they thought we were the big London rock stars looking in. But now I realise they were quite happy doing their thing in St Andrews. That was the vibe, and if I'm wrong then I humbly apologise. I have no interest in being more important or famous than anyone else. But it felt odd at the time.' He's defensive about his decision to keep his ties with London. 'Let's just say that there was an aura around town that I shouldn't have moved to London and I should have stayed pure to Fife. I always thought that was absolutely pathetic.'

Although an olive branch was extended, he maintained his distance. He was feeling vulnerable and needed to establish himself artistically and financially. He was still ill and wasn't doing much of anything at all. He certainly wasn't making his own music, and that was the worst thing of all. Thankfully, he was about to get a jolt and slowly come out of the fog.

Meeting a girl in Edinburgh, Steve started down the path to quelling his inner demons and began having a good time with her. The tall, dark and glamorous Lucy Ross had worked behind the scenes in the London music industry but had relocated to her home town to make her own music as Dollskabeat. Steve recalls: 'She was into electro and electronic music. I felt reinvigorated because I knew a lot about that stuff from when it came out originally. There was a lot of new stuff happening too, like Jimmy Edgar and Kelley Polar.' First he helped on some production for her, forging the track 'My Dancer'. I played it on Radio 1 at the time, not knowing of Mason's involvement. Sadly the relationship would soon deteriorate. 'It didn't end very well,' Steve admits, 'but that's life, I suppose.' However, it led him back to making music under a new alias, Black Affair. Steve says: 'That album is like a snapshot of that time and that relationship.'

The album was almost an about-turn for Steve as he laid down his guitar and embraced an electronic soundscape. The result was a thirteen-track collection of 1980s-influenced electro-pop with synths set to stun and über-libidinous lyrics, titled *Pleasure Pressure Point*. It was almost a concept album about sex, domination and primal urges within the locked bedroom. Although it was undeniably a Steve Mason record, melodically and vocally, the backing tracks had a whipcracking clarity and ice-cold precision that suited the mood perfectly. Steve elaborates: 'I never felt that King Biscuit Time was as far away from The Beta Band as I wanted. I wanted to do something completely different for myself. I never like to stand still.' It was recorded in his home studio, and he headed to New York for the mixing with Jimmy Edgar at the controls. He continues: 'Some of the melodies are amazing. "Japanese Happening" is a fantastic track. "Just Keep Walking" is really, really good. I'm sure my fan base would have liked them if they'd been played on acoustic guitar.'

Pleasure Pressure Point polarised people. Like many others, I applauded him for the change in direction and the brave move he was making. It was full of ideas and the songs were razor-sharp. I played the singles and featured the album, as did other BBC DJs such as Rob Da Bank. However, Steve received a lot of flak for it, as he remembers. '"When's he going to do another King Biscuit Time record? When's he going to get The Beta Band back together? What the fuck is he doing anyway?"' The spectre of the 1980s hung heavily around the songs and it rankled with a number of people, especially those who considered themselves big fans. To add insult to injury, once again industry machinations were about to stop the record in its tracks. It was released in July 2008 via the V2/Co-op label, and Steve now complains: 'The problem with the Black Affair album was that it was ready to go two years before it came out. It took ages to come out. When it did, the whole electro thing had gone a bit mainstream. Its time had passed.'

Biting his lip, he tried to tour the record across the UK. The gigs weren't joyful, though. 'They were mainly me driving around in a Transit van, picking up band members on the way, doing the show and driving all the way back home again. Playing all those gigs to very few people in clubs was demoralising. It was frightening and humbling.' If there was a consolation, it was that Steve was back on top mentally. 'I must have been, to be able to cope with the crapness of what was happening. I think I was too old to be doing what I was doing. I wanted to be ten years younger and a cutting-edge electro artist, but I was too old for the music I was making. I think I just wished I was a young, good-looking guy who was able to make that music sexy, which is what it should have been. It should have probably been a bit darker too.'

Floundering slightly, he was probably having a crisis of confidence and dwelling too heavily on creating pseudonyms to escape his past. Maybe he simply wanted to lay the ghost of The Beta Band. He admits: 'There was a time when I was doing Black Affair when I had five or six different MySpace pages, all with different genres and different names.' He was also producing others when he could. This afforded him some cash and allowed him to flex his production skills. It would soon be time to do what his friends and fans and followers expected of him. 'I think age only plays on your mind if you've lost track of your position in music. Now I'm very happy with where I am.'

As 2009 came into sight, Steve's fortieth birthday was looming and he still hadn't delivered on the promise of The Beta Band as a solo artist. He confides: 'I thought it was about time I made the album that everyone's always wanted me to make because I owe it to myself. An album that's clear and concise, not rambling or in some weird genre. So that's what I did. It wasn't really that planned; I sort of stumbled across it. I wanted it to be uninhibited by style or fashion. I was fiddling around on the guitar and I wrote "Boys Outside", just like that! I thought: "I really fuckin' enjoyed that." I could sit and play it and it sounded like it was going to sound on the record.'

'All Come Down' was written in a similar way, but 'Hound On My Heel' was sculpted using a more hip-hop template. "It was supposed to be like a modern Robert Johnson-style track,' says Steve, 'but not blues.' He adds: 'Essentially I was trying to make a timeless album, and I think I achieved it. *Boys Outside* is an album that will keep selling and will spread by word of mouth. I wanted to make something that was a bit more pure and a bit more me, letting the human emotion come out.'

One good thing that had emerged from Black Affair was the patronage of Richard X, head of the Xenomania pop stable and producer of Girls Aloud, Sugababes, MIA and Rachel Stevens. It seemed like an odd fit, but the friendship bore fruit. 'Richard wanted to do another Black Affair album. He loved that record and thought he could do something with it. I invented this new genre called R 'n' G, which was goth R 'n' B – super-dark, vampiric R 'n' B. I had this four-track EP that was ready to go, but I don't think I ever played him it.' Steve was wary of such a move, but Richard X said: 'When you've got something finished, send it to me anyway.'

Steve wasn't expecting much, but sent him the new tracks. X loved them right away. His confidence boosted, Mason started going to London for a week here and there, laying down tracks during Richard's downtime in his own studio. The ensuing album took a year to record in this way. Steve had managed to produce the songs to a certain standard in his home studio, but reworked things like the vocals, acoustic guitar and live drums with Richard, admitting: 'Richard turned it from an album that would have been lost in the mists of time into an album that should have won the Mercury Prize that year.'

With the finished album in tow and optimism brimming, Steve and Richard decided to put it out themselves. They formed a label and looked into distribution and marketing. In a last-gasp attempt they sent a copy to Domino Records, but label boss Laurence Bell took ages to get back to them. Laurence elaborates: 'I started to hear he was making a really good record. I always loved Steve's songs, but I'd lost track of his career and he seemed a little wayward. He was flitting between different pseudonyms and you got the sense that all wasn't as good as it could be. I think it was James Yorkston who said: "Laurence, you should listen to this Steve Mason record properly." I thought it was pretty incredible. It was quite intense and moving, but also catchy and brilliant. I just reached out to his manager, Chris Butler, aiming to publish it at first. But we were so hooked, and they didn't have anyone else to put it out, so we thought we'd try to get it the audience it deserved. We were developing different avenues and imprints, so we put it out through Double Six.'

Laurence took a brief trip to the US, and on his return phoned and said he wanted to go ahead with the release. The feeling of relief was tangible. Richard got paid, Steve had a record deal and the album went on to have a proper release. *Boys Outside*, under the thirty-eight-year-old Steve Mason's own name, came out in May 2010. It is seen as his true renaissance as an artist, and Steve says: 'I feel incredibly lucky. After Black Affair I could have just disappeared. I managed to pull it out at a critical time and get that deal with Domino. Everyone wants a deal with Domino, but they won't sign anything unless they think they can give it a good chance. They're the best label I've ever worked with. They're tight with money, but that's what I want in a label now.' Laurence beams and says: 'It was brilliantly received and rightly so. It rehabilitated his career, and people who got that record loved it. I think his audience came back and connected with it in a huge way.'

With broadsheet press, 6Music radio play and people like myself behind the record, it sold well and proved to be his reinvention, critically and commercially. With a tight band in place Mason toured *Boys Outside* relentlessly. Previously audiences were baffled by his obstinacy, but now they could welcome their former hero into their hearts again. The shows had an ecstatic response and the album appeared on many an end-of-year poll. Steve could breathe a sigh of relief.

$$\oint$$

Steve Mason the artist had finally been vindicated, six years after the end of The Beta Band. *Boys Outside* was a pure, unsullied, fragile record that didn't shout from the rooftops, rather it whispered to you and drew you in. The songs were anthemic but understated; they were catchy and concise, but didn't bear the sprawling hallmarks of his previous band. You could hear that voice and those chords, but the frivolous humour was left at the door for a more heart-on-sleeve approach.

His next move would again connect with fans of a certain persuasion, as Steve explains: 'I've been a reggae fan for a long time, and I always wanted to make a reggae record or better still a dub record. But you've got to be careful how you do it. There's a lot of scope for embarrassment. I know a few people in the London reggae community.' Throughout his career reggae had always been an influence, from ska at mod rallies he'd attended to the graphics on the 'Champion Versions' EP and the ragga records in his DJ box. Rather than the obvious option of a remix of *Boys Outside* from the hippest electronic producers on the block, Steve set about planning *Ghosts Outside*.

Bumping into Daddy G of Massive Attack, Steve ran an idea past the reggae aficionado. He wanted to instigate a dub version of his album, mentioning Adrian Sherwood of On-U Sound-System as the man for the job. Daddy G shook his head and suggested Dennis Bovell, bassist and band-leader in British reggae pioneers Matumbi and a noted producer for over thirty years. The two were related, and with Dennis's experience in producing punk, post-punk and indie as well as reggae, he seemed like the perfect choice. Mason sent him the album right away and Bovell loved it. They hooked up in London and hit it off immediately.

Dennis constructed a full reggae backing track for every song, playing guitar, keyboards, occasional drums and that all-important bassline. A horn section was added to occasional tracks, and then he went through every track and dubbed it right up with copious amounts of reverb, echo and delay. The result is reminiscent of *LKJ In DUB*, which Bovell had scored and dubbed, and *Garvey's Ghost* by Burning Spear. Steve says: 'I wanted to find some middle ground between frontline Brixton in the 1980s and *Garvey's Ghost*. That's why I called it *Ghosts Outside*.' The collaboration really hit the spot, the album picking up many favourable and respectful reviews. I love how Steve's plaintive vocals float over the top of the deep bass and echo-laden horns. It's one of the few white reggae records that actually works.

With a little thinking outside the box, Steve had struck gold. It showed that Domino and their new signing could work well together. With a three-album deal for the label, Steve stresses that he will tour again when necessary, and even as I type I know there's a lot more to come from him very soon indeed.

There are often unforeseen problems around Steve's corners, but with his first two Domino albums behind him he seems as established as he's ever been. With the Beta Band's legacy as its bedrock, his catalogue of songs and reputation is building up nicely as he heads into his forties. Like all of the musicians in this book, he has taken a gamble in life, but so far that gamble has paid off. Approaching his art in the simplest and purest of ways, he maintains: 'It wasn't an easy option. I'd say it was a brave move that few people take, but more people should. We're locked into this society now that is entirely governed by material possessions. So, to give up a job, to be prepared to live a life of relative poverty, is a decision you don't take lightly. You have to keep that single-minded goal.'

Although he owns a modest house in Fife and has a functioning career in music, Steve is by no means a wealthy man, possibly as a result of his own belligerence. Laurence Bell says: 'I was rooting for The Beta Band. They needed the help of their audience, I think. You'd read interviews with them, and you'd think: "Oh no, you're not doing yourself any favours here." It was like being a fan of a football team and watching them struggle. They kept missing open goals. They were outsiders in a very success-orientated culture. There was a perversity to it that was appealing.' Steve simply says: 'I'll do it as long as I want to do it . . . then I'll do something else.' Amen to that!

15

Shouting at Wildlife

The Fence Collective and Beyond

Ah yes, the Fence Collective! Most of them don't even live in Fife these days, but it had to start somewhere, with a small core of key people. If King Creosote was the spark, Pip Dylan lit the touchpaper and Lone Pigeon started the fire, there had to be others to keep it burning. On his doorstep in St Andrews and the East Neuk, Kenny Anderson found his partners in music in the late 1990s and into the 2000s. Some were old friends and some new arrivals, but they all wanted to join in the fun. At the start, on those freeform nights at Aikman's, there needed to be willing players who weren't scared of giving their own songs a shot, mucking in and wearing ridiculous costumes, and potentially making arses of themselves. Here are a few words about some of those people.

CAPTAIN GEEKO THE DEAD AVIATOR

Andy Robinson, alias Captain Geeko, the Dead Aviator, was a Forces child, born in Malta, who travelled with his family until settling in Fife in 1977. Born in 1967, he shared a class with Kenny at Madras College but didn't know him well at the time. He took piano lessons as a boy and then gravitated towards an extremely loud steel snare drum and eventually a full drum kit, much to his parents' delight. By the time he was a teenager he was playing in bands and had a formidable array of noisy records. 'I was into the Sex Pistols, Blondie, Sham 69 and XTC, then I got into heavy rock bands like Iron Maiden, AC/DC, Deep Purple, Led Zeppelin, Rush and Black Sabbath, ending up in the ambient world of Robert Fripp, Brian Eno, Harold Budd, Penguin Café Orchestra, Talking Heads and The Police.' From the list alone, you'll detect that Andy became a musician's musician. Of all the players in the Fence

Collective then and now, Andy is one of the most skilled, and one of the few who enjoys prog-rock.

As Andy turned eighteen it was clear he could hold his own in a gigging unit, and he followed his love of heavy-rock and blues into an established act. 'My first working band was Bedlam, from Dundee, in 1985. Before I joined they were a really neat blues-rock band, playing Clapton, Hendrix, and all the classics. With a new guitarist, Lou Lewis from The Headboys, a bass player with Spandex trousers and a French-Canadian bear, Alain Breitenbach, on vocals, we played something like four hundred shows in two years. Hard-rocking blues was popular in Scottish pubs in the late 1980s. Bedlam folded in 1988 or 1989, but they were eye-opening times for me!'

Within a couple of years Andy's life would take a massive swerve in a different direction when he helped out at a friend's craft fair in Newport one weekend. 'I just sat on the door and took the £2.50 entrance fee. I had no idea any musical entertainment had been booked, so I was surprised to see two guys in dungarees carrying an accordion box and a double bass. Once we'd got over that "I think I know him, but not enough to say anything" moment, we started chatting. As it happened, Kenny (box) and Een (bass) had just moved to a cottage about three miles away from where I was living. Kenny was looking for a drummer and asked if I'd be interested. I was a rock drummer, what could I bring to folk music? I started cycling up to the cottage with my snare drum – I think I borrowed Kenny's brushes. There was no electricity and we used to just hang out and play music with the idea of busking to earn some money. I agreed to go busking through Europe in the summer with Kenny, Een, Eric on banjo, and for some of the trip Joe Collier (MC Quake) on washboard and harmonies. That was me in the famously unspellable Skuobhie Dubh Orchestra.'

Andy's rock style soon mutated into lightning-quick punk/bluegrass as the Dubhs became an astounding live band. Of the album *The 39 Stephs*, Andy says: 'It was really just a first go for Kenny to see what his songs would sound like with the band. We had our own style, and the album was an attempt to capture that vibe but with original songs.

'Kenny is a prolific songwriter, so we never had any shortage of material. Live we were pretty experimental. My kit had evolved from one snare to a Heath Robinson affair that allowed me to stand up with a kick drum. Een was flourishing as a musician. Everything he put his hands on, he'd do something interesting with it – he used a road traffic sign as a wobbleboard on "The Seminar". There was a spirit of adventure, but the songs were more pop-oriented in their structures.'

However, the good times were not to last. By the third album, *Gordonov*, credited to Khartoum Heroes, Andy admits: 'For me this was a hard album to do. We'd been doing the Dubh thing for a few years and my relationship with Kenny was at a low point. The band was pulling itself apart. There wasn't a single day the entire band was in the studio together. It was a struggle for me to be motivated.' By 1993 the original Skuobhie Dubh Orchestra was over. Andy quit the band, moved to Aberdeen and married. He would not have much to do with Kenny and his brothers for a long while.

Almost eight years later, however, after really giving a new city and a new life a go, Andy returned to St Andrews, sadly without his wife and family. He took a job at the university and reconnected with his old pal. 'Upon my return to Fife in 2000, Kenny presented me with a picture he'd made for me. It was entitled "The Return of Captain Geeko" . . . *et voila!*' He was welcomed back into the fold and threw himself into the Aikman's insanity, performing whenever possible under his Fence pseudonym. Looking back to those early days, he now says: 'I was there when the shop opened – in fact, I spent most of my day there when I should have been at work. I liked the fact that local musicians and artists got together a couple of times a week and had fun doing crazy but always interesting stuff. It was brilliant while it lasted but as with all good things, they come to an end. '

Over the past decade Captain Geeko has made music a priority again. Still working at the university, he spends the rest of his time recording himself and others in his semi-pro home studio. He also plays percussion and djembe with King Creosote. 'Gav "Onthefly" Brown plays drums now, but when he can't make it, I do it.' He has joined the reformed Khartoum Heroes, with myself on electric guitar and harmonies. And can he hit those drums! Andy never seems happier than when he's playing music. 'I strive for that moment live when everyone is in sync with everyone else. My highlights are moments like that from Skuobhie Dubh Orchestra days to the present.'

UNCLE BEESLY

Dealing with the low end throughout Fence's unsteady trajectory has been a bass-Buddha by the name of Pete Macleod, alias Uncle Beesly. He has cropped up quite a bit in this book, connected as he is to so many phases of the Fence story and Kenny Anderson's musical life. A gifted player, a natural musician, and an extremely funny mimic, he is also incredibly self-deprecating and says: 'I think of jacking it in every year that I get older.' Nonsense! Some of his tight, melodic basslines have lifted many a recording and live performance to sublime heights. He's also a nice chap.

Pete was born in Aberdeen in 1968, then moved to Glenrothes, finally settling in Cupar, and there was a fair amount of music in the Macleod household with his parents and brothers Derek and Gilmour. He remembers the brothers dancing around the house to Beatles compilations, and Pete himself delving into Abba, Queen, Simon and Garfunkel and even Ravel's 'Bolero', which he played endlessly. As school approached and allegiances were forged, he admits: 'I pretended to like some terrible heavy metal like Iron Maiden, basically because my peers did. A lot of schoolmates were into the whole 2-Tone thing. I can remember liking some pop stuff like Adam and the Ants, but the guys I spent time with all liked metal.' He continues: 'I'm loath to admit this even now, but from the age of sixteen I secretly got into U2 and The Smiths. It should be pointed out that listening to stuff like Simple Minds, U2 and Morrissey definitely wasn't okay! It had to be done in secrecy.'

With one brother enjoying the post-punk sounds of The Fall and Joy Division and another listening to 1980s poodle-metal, then The Stone Roses and so on, Pete was exposed to a lot of different sounds. Gilmour became a concert pianist and now teaches music. Pete soon nailed his colours to the prog-rock mast. 'Having left my teens, and living with an older cousin, I was given access to stuff like Jimi Hendrix, King Crimson and Pink Floyd. I think I started to enjoy 1960s and 1970s rock from about this age.' Later in life he began to write his own music. 'I started to write songs in my early twenties. They were all pretty awful, influenced by Ian Curtis lyrically and Roger Waters musically. I never played any of them to anyone; I never thought about a career in music. I still don't!'

Dabbling in music lessons at school, he packed them in to rediscover various techniques years later at college. 'I took lessons at college and learned to read music to an extent, and play classical pieces adapted for bass. I almost missed the birth of my son by going into college for a music exam.' But first, in the early 1990s, there was an encounter that would change his life. 'I met Kenny and Een at a pub in Cupar, the Imperial,' he recalls. 'A guy used to play really bad but entertaining acoustic sets on a Monday night. He used to drink his beer with one hand while the other hand just kept strumming away! I think I saw The Skuobhie Dubh Orchestra a couple of times around this time too, at the Younger Hall in St Andrews and at Glastonbury in 1992. My friend Swith liked them so much he auditioned for a guitar slot. He failed to impress, but was immortalized in the song "St Swithin". I also lived with a girl who knew their banjo player, Eric. I must have vaguely known Kenny and Een for at least a year before being drafted into the band in 1994.'

As described in Chapter 1, Pete joined The Skuobhie Dubh Orchestra around the time when the wheels were falling off. However, they were still a going concern, and Pete remembers his first experiences. 'Around about April of 1993 I started to hang about at Een's cottage. We practised a lot in that cottage. If you consider my lack of knowledge of the bass guitar, you can imagine the amount of work I had to put in. I remember being blown away by their musicianship and energy. I've never been a fan of Scottish folk music, so it was probably good that their music was still rooted in bluegrass. I liked Kenny's songs and admired his way with lyrics. Een seemed like some sort of child genius. It was like he would take up an instrument, go away for a week and return a master. I think he did it just to spite us.' This line-up wasn't to last very long, however, and soon the band would re-emerge with Stu Bastiman and me in the ranks after they recorded the *Gordonov* album with Pete on bass. Whether he admits it or not, Pete was a supremely talented and versatile musician.

In that next incarnation as Khartoum Heroes, Pete remembers various highlights and his original qualms. 'I'd never been in a band with electric guitars and proper drum kits. It was a little bit daunting. I remember enjoying the practice sessions at Kenny's cottage later on. We supported the Bhundu Boys after several months of honing the songs, and I remember being very happy that they shared our backline. Khartoum Heroes had improved enough that we received positive feedback from festival staff. I benefited from being in a band that was not afraid to try out different styles. We got tremendously tight after busking and gigging in Europe, though that was also perhaps the straw that broke the camel's back.' Yes, and yet another band would bite the dust before Pete would go on to divide his skills between Kenny's revived Dubhs and a young Kate Tunstall.

Talking about his role in Kate's early bands, Tomoko and Red Light Stylus, Pete is open and candid. 'I learned a lot from Kate, she would encourage my abilities. She would see something good in those high, melodic bass lines and coax me into refining them. Kate is very funny in company. Although not musically, I think she was insecure regarding how the lads in the band were around her. I think we kind of excluded her in some ways. She didn't like other girls in the band getting attention either.'

Pete continues: 'I think, if I'm honest, she was fairly ruthless in sacking us off one by one. She had a lot of people paying her way, and as a band we got free rental of practice rooms, and often free transport and accommodation to music industry events. I don't care to mention any names here, but I do hope the benefactors were recompensed. I think it's fair to say also that she went through a great many mentors and would-be managers. I don't think any of the A & R lot who came to see the band rehearse were ever all that impressed by us, her backing band. I retain a distrust of industry types.'

As an unemployed musician living on occasional gigs and the dole, Pete decided to improve his already accomplished musicianship at college. 'Circa 2000, I went to do music in Edinburgh and ended up with an HND in modern music. I was playing with Kate Tunstall at the time and we were all looking for ways to legitimise what we were doing. I applied to do the course at Jewel and Esk Valley college.' Pete's job with Kate came to an end, as did his playing with the Dubhs, as the 2000s rolled on, but his alliance with Kenny and brothers would soon be reborn under a new banner: Fence!

The early Aikman's gigs have taken on huge significance in the Fence story, and Pete was one of those early, crucial performers. Retrospective stories often exaggerate what actually happened, but Pete can shed some light on those nights. 'I think the whole Fence thing came about largely by accident and not by design,' he says. 'Pre-medicated, rather than premeditated. It started with Een and Kenny playing under some daft names. At some point Jason Kavanagh must have got involved, as he became a joint creative force with Kenny, despite having little in the way of musical ability. He would turn up with random things like a Vietnamese glockenspiel and bluff his way through several sets and solos.

'You could liken it to a bizarre cult cabaret club, a sort of Bonzo Dog Dubh-Dah Band if you will. The emphasis must have been on comedy. I can't imagine anybody took it too seriously. We had Scalextric sets and lava lamps, for God's sake! I think James Yorkston turned up a few times and would do odd things like Motorhead covers on the mandolin. I can remember being riveted by Gordon's stuff, which was influenced by his Christian leanings. A couple of times I saw Chicken & Chips, Gordon backed by Steve Mason on drums. It was shambolic, but made for some hysterical interludes. They'd argue over who was Chicken and who was Chips. I remember Gordon smashed up the keyboard of a harmonium, and Mason chipped in with: "It's okay, we don't need *all* those notes!"'

While backing whoever was brave enough to creep onstage at these events, Pete reinvented himself with a new persona. 'I became Uncle Beesly in 2002. Kenny and I were arriving back in Rosyth after playing at a wedding in France, and Kenny came out with this on-the-spot demand that I invent a new name. I had been calling myself the Fat Messiah, which was a song title cribbed from a King Creosote album and written about Gordon, so not very appropriate. I opted for Uncle Beesly, from a character in Chris Morris's *Brass Eye*, a reformed paedophile uncle. The character may have been called Beezy or something else; the fact that I may have got it slightly wrong means that few people have picked up on the reference. I remember a guy shouting out: "Beesly! Beesly!" all through a gig in Cardiff. When I told him it wasn't my real name he looked at me, practically in tears, and said: "Well, it's *my* real name!"' From here he began to write material as a solo artist, releasing a Picket Fence CD in 2002. Apparently Kenny described it as 'prog-tainted'. Although little else has surfaced since then, he has continued to write and record, confessing the material is still 'prog-tainted'.

Over the past ten years Pete has been one of the cornerstones of the Fence Collective, playing bass in the King Creosote band and lead guitar in the Gummi Bako band, among other things. He has attended almost every Fence event since its inception and has played at most of them too. His relationship with Kenny has been tempestuous, and he says: 'Now I think I get on well enough with him. I think we understand each other a bit better, which helps. I don't think he's ever been changed by success. I could tell you a hundred stories about how Kenny has been bad to me . . . but basically he's helped me out as many times, and besides it goes against my ninja code.'

On future projects, Pete says: 'We've been doing an exciting thing called the Alter Ego Trading Co. It's a natural progression from what some of the King Creosote band do down the pub, which is our own stuff and sometimes covers of ridiculous prog bands. I now enjoy the local scene far more than touring, because I am part of the local scene.'

Living in Pittenweem, Pete is now a father and enjoys a fairly quiet life when he's not playing live or recording. Asked why people hold the East Neuk in such high esteem for Fence's sake, he laughs and says: 'I think it's because of all the wonderful festivals that sometimes people get carried away and actually move up here to Scotland, abandoning their lives, jobs and families. Perhaps they share some notion that this is some sunshine Shangri-La or creative utopia. They must think it's all sun and music here; they should really move to Jamaica or Cuba. Every week I'm regaled with tales of woe by these recently uprooted thrill-seekers. We had a party on the beach the other night in Cellardyke to celebrate the end of summer. It was 24 November! It was dark, there was no music, and it was possibly five below zero. There was booze, though, and good nosh. I'm not complaining.'

GUMMI BAKO

If you've attended a live Fence event, from their beginnings in Aikman's to the bigger festivals, you may have stumbled across the unhinged yodel and knowing smile of a bald, bearded bard by the name of Alan 'Mr Alan Stewart' Stewart, or Gummi Bako as he is also known. Fusing dishevelled, shonky elements of country, folk, rhythm and blues and rock 'n' roll with daft wordplay and deft rhyming couplets, Gummi performs both solo and in a band with the help of Eleisha Fahy on bass, Uncle Beesly on lead guitar and Alan 'Chee-hee' Reid on drums.

Imagine Vivian Stanshall meets The Smurfs fronting Creedence Clearwater Revival: Gummi Bako's uproarious concoction is guaranteed to get the Fence fanatics moving their feet and grinning. Alan's been part of Fence since its inception. On that all-important Fence pseudonym, he says: 'I've always liked alter egos and aliases. Although there was never a royal mandate, back in the day every Fence collectivist had a stage name, and that suited me fine. Anyone who knows me knows I enjoy word play and *double-entendres*. I never set out to use a stage name that had multiple meanings, but because I don't discuss its origin people have developed their own theories.' Apparently, Gummi Bako roughly means 'rubber wastepaper basket' in Japanese. What a guy! What a beard!

Born in 1975 and brought up in Ayr, Alan's first exposure to music was at church. 'Sombre hymns of remembrance, upbeat Sunday school choruses and stirring songs of salvation. That's the three major food groups right there. We didn't have a lot of secular music in the house, so apart from the churchy stuff, my early years were soundtracked by *Father Abraham in Smurfland*, *The Muppet Movie Original Soundtrack*, *James Bond's Greatest Hits* and a smattering of musicals.' As a teenager he was duly turned on to the rock and indie pantheon of the day. 'In chronological order, I liked early Whitesnake, Bon Jovi, The Mission, The Cure, The Byrds, The Jesus and Mary Chain, My Bloody Valentine and the Pixies. Save the best for last!'

With a piano and a broken ukulele in the house, his first musical instrument was actually a glittering blue zither, which he still owns. 'It could do with some new strings on it. I've been putting it off since the late twentieth century.' Eventually asking Santa for an electric guitar, he actually got one. 'I picked up a copy of *Fifty Easy Hits for Guitar*, but I just couldn't make other people's songs sound like they ought to, so I ended up making up my own.' As the class clown and comedy buff, he made skits and sketches with friends on cassette. Soon it was time to leave home, and he claims his options were limited. 'After my dream of becoming a model spaceship designer was shot down in flames by my guidance teacher, I applied to do a random selection of courses in different cities across Scotland. As luck would have it, St Andrews was the only place that would take me. I moved there in 1992, and for some reason or another I never got around to leaving.'

Although he stumbled into an early Skuobhie Dubh Orchestra show at the student union in 1992, it wasn't until around 2000 that Alan got to know the Anderson brothers properly. 'I probably met Kenny for the first time in Aikman's. I remember Kenny seemed like a regular fixture there, but it was never the same show twice. Kenny and Een did a stint as a duo at Aikman's under the name Bobbydazzler for a while. I really liked seeing the brothers play together. Een brought more than his share of the daftness to the part – his "tongue stuck in the moothie" skit was priceless. It was some time before I met Gordon. He materialised in the Fence shop one day with a headdress and full-on biblical beard, babbling about pyramids and prophecies. He knew how to make an entrance.'

Drawn into a circle of like-minded lunatics, it wasn't long before Alan had to join in the fun and perform some of his own songs. 'I played my first solo set as Gummi Bako supporting Kenny on his *Twelve o'Clock on the Dot* record launch at the Links Hotel on 11 October 2000. I don't recall much about it, but I think it went down okay.'

Alan was the natural accomplice for the Andersons, and for Kenny in particular. He needed no encouragement to behave like a fool in public. 'We never needed an excuse for fancy dress. so we were in our element at Hallowe'en. I once played an entire gig with a giant *papier-mâché* Godzilla head on. Never again!' As the label grew and releases came thick and fast, Gummi Bako would feature heavily on Fence samplers and Fencezine compilations. Alongside the mainstays of King Creosote, Pip Dylan and Lone Pigeon, Alan's surrealist ditties and squawking comedy rock-outs established him as an essential part of the collective.

Having graduated years before, Alan was now working in IT and began helping out with design and artwork on Fence's website. 'I was working as a design monkey in Cupar at the time, and I'd always stop by the Fence shop after work, and I found myself redesigning the website and preparing the artwork for the next proper release, *Fence Sampler 3*, which was going to be a real CD and everything. Exciting times!' As the website's main technician and the man in charge of designing the artwork, he set up his own company, Midget Squid, in Anstruther to deal with these vocations. He explains: 'It was thanks to Fence that I took the plunge and started my own business, making artwork for print and the web with the things that the everyday folks leave behind.' Alan adds: 'The Fence office was unlike any other. It was essentially a box-bedsit room in an old dilapidated building with a pigeon-infested attic. There was no heating, no water and no power when we moved in, but we eventually got one of the three. I'm not sure how many winters I spent there, but eventually I retreated to a series of attic and basement offices around the town.'

As a musician, Alan's tunes and rip-roaring live shows are often the highlight of any Fence festival today. Describing his unique vocal range, he says: 'I couldn't rightly say where my vocal style comes from. Maybe that's what listening to a lot of novelty records does to a developing mind.' On his particular take on songwriting, he elaborates: 'I love writing lyrics. I usually get my best ideas when I'm daydreaming my way along the street, so I'm often caught jotting things down. I never leave home without a notebook.

'I have dreamed songs before, and I was once lucky enough to scribble one out when I awoke. Lyrics always come first, but the melody is very close behind; so close, in fact, that they may appear to arrive simultaneously.' Search among the piles of Fence compilations, Picket Fence releases and samplers, and you'll hear a smattering of classics like 'Lament of the Eternal Virgin', 'Dope on a Rope' and 'Your Wicked Ways'. Sit back and prepare to giggle.

As Fence has gradually reached a wider audience, so the collective has grown and Alan has thrived. He's watched it grow from a muck-about in the pub to Kenny Anderson being nominated for the Mercury Music Prize. He has appeared on around fifteen albums, released a 7-inch vinyl single, and more recently contributed to King Creosote's run of 'Three EPs'. He has also joined the King Creosote touring band. He says of the collective: 'They're a good bunch. I like the feeling of brotherhood and sisterhood that comes with it. When everyone mucks in and has a laugh along the way, then it's a great thing to be involved in. As long as folks are having a good time I'm happy. Dicks and divas need not apply.'

A resident Fifer now, Alan lives a quiet but happy life. 'I like the fact that the East Neuk is off the beaten track. Unless you've made a point of visiting, you're unlikely to end up here. As a result, it just gets on and does its own thing, safe in the knowledge that the outside world doesn't really exist.' Whether as a songwriter, web-designer, comedian or plain troublemaker, Alan Stewart is a one-off. I'll leave the final wort to John Maclean: 'The best Fence thing I've ever seen was Gummi Bako at a Hallowe'en show in Glasgow. I thought they were absolutely brilliant! Why aren't they huge?'

HMS GINAFORE

One of the best-loved songwriters in the collective is the shy, elusive HMS Ginafore. Known to many as Jenny Casino (and by her real name, Jennifer Gordon), she and her brother Calum and parents Mama Casino (Elizabeth Gordon) and Papa 'The Rootsman' Casino (Alan Gordon) have been integral to the development of the label and the running of the Fife-based Fence events. Whether making out-of-towners cups of tea or bowls of soup, offering musicians floors to crash on, or silencing audiences with her plaintive vocals and stunningly intimate songs, Jenny is a special person.

I count her as a friend, and have benefited from her kindness many times. Unfortunately, she declined to be interviewed for this book. I should have liked to tell you her story and recount some of her anecdotes. She is extremely funny, an adept storyteller and mimic, and one of the most warm-hearted and friendly people I've ever met. However, she doesn't rate herself as an artist and songwriter, and now wants to remain completely out of vision in terms of her involvement with Fence. The fact that her decade-long relationship with Kenny Anderson has come to an end has obviously played a large part in this.

I will, however, let a few other people tell you their thoughts. Johnny Lynch says: 'Jenny is an incredible lyricist, with a distinctive voice that sounds like the world in slow motion. Her onstage banter is hysterical and her delivery is engaging. I'm hoping her recordings won't become buried treasure.' James Yorkston enthuses too: 'Jenny encapsulates one aspect of the Fence spirit – she has no desire to use her music to make a living, or even release records, but her work is as valued in the collective as anyone's. We all sing her songs. I've had her singing on one of my albums.

James continues: 'For a long time the music industry was spurting out a stream of pretty but anodyne white girls who sounded a bit like Billie Holiday. Jenny could sing them all under the table. But her songs are the main attraction for me. They're poetic, fresh, vivid and amusing.' He adds: 'I think she's been offered deals by Mute, Domino and 4AD, but hasn't followed them up. She said to me once: "Imagine if someone suggested that you became a TV chef, or someone that does ghost tours or plans weddings – that's how I feel about doing music!"' Laurence Bell of Domino Records confirms that. 'I've offered HMS Ginafore a deal, but she's not interested; she'd rather go swimming or something. I'd like to do an HMS Ginafore record with Jon Hopkins. I think that would be extraordinary.'

I'll let Kenny Anderson conclude: 'Jen's elegant songwriting has set an unattainable benchmark for my own efforts, and although I've got close on a few occasions I haven't quite lit a celebratory cigar. Her lyrics reflect the inventive, quirky imagery of everyday speech, and while her wordplay may have rubbed off on me a wee bit, her old-world decency and humble values have not. I'm working on it. She's a hugely talented cook, too, and I love her.'

UNPOC

One of the first non-St Andrews-based musicians in Fence was singer-songwriter Tom Beauchop, alias UNPOC. From Crook of Devon on the border of Fife and Perthshire, Tom was a late developer when it came to songwriting, and he may be the most unlikely of the collective to have forged some kind of name for himself. He's a shy, reserved character with a sharp wit, an observant eye and a quirky sense of humour. You could probably call him eccentric, but he might not agree. All these things, however, have helped make Tom the astute pop songsmith he has become. His manner may be understated, but his songs chime with bold, bright melodies and a sense of unashamed naivety.

In the early 1990s I shared a flat with him in Edinburgh for a few years alongside the drummer in my bands at the time, Stu Bastiman. As we all worked in low-paid jobs, drew the dole or went to college, our main interests were listening to music, drinking tea and discussing things late into the night. We were all trying to write songs. My bandmates and I were dead-set on trying to make it while Tom idled away his time in his boxroom, writing songs he'd occasionally let us hear. They were rough, recording-wise, but they were always beguiling. Tom liked Manchester bands such as The Stone Roses, Oasis and The Charlatans, but was open to other sounds and styles. As time went on he seemed to return to the orchestration and experimentation of the Beach Boys' *Pet Sounds* album and the garage-thump of the Velvet Underground, as well as the Beastie Boys and whatever Britpop had to offer. Genres and styles were less important than the tunes. Tom was constantly searching for the ultimate hook in a song, whether a chart hit or an underground non-starter. We'd pass the time with guitars on our laps, trying our new bits or listening to the radio for catchy riffs, harmonies and rhythms. He was always analysing structures and tunes. When he wrote a song he wanted every section of it to be catchy. The songs he was whittling away at in his room would become the *Fifth Column* album, released almost ten years later. He explains: 'It was recorded on a Yamaha cassette four-track. I had done four collections of songs before. I'd started recording on cassette players, then on four-track machines, each batch an improvement on the one before as I learned to do choruses, or add a bass guitar or more vocals, or proper words. But they were all bad in one way or another until the fifth lot, which were much better for some reason. It being my fifth set of songs, I called it *Fifth Column*. The phrase had lots of other resonances for me too. It speaks of outsiders inside and that sort of thing, and *The Fifth Column* is the name of Ernest Hemingway's only full-length play.'

These songs have now had a proper release via Domino Records, but twenty years ago Tom, like us all, was trying to get to grips with basic recording techniques. The music was lo-fi because that's all he had access to. The compression, tape hiss and tuning problems all added to the charm and didn't take away from the great music. He continues: 'I recorded in a little boxroom, where it was easy to concentrate, and in a small, triangular room I lived in later, and we recorded Stu Bastiman's drums last – not easy for a drummer, but it gave them a terrific, top-heavy energy. What a great drummer!'

Tom hadn't gone through the usual hopeless school bands or made fledgling attempts at cracking the Edinburgh scene while at college or signing on. He was happy just writing songs. 'Around the time I was doing

Fifth Column, lots of my friends were busy trying to get record deals, sending demos off to London and trying to get on the radio. But my thing felt more home-made than that, and with a sound as unmusical as mine, I preferred to focus on improving my songs and recordings. I had a theory that if I could write a song good enough, it wouldn't have to be played to more than one or two people and the rest would take care of itself. I had read about Bob Dylan's *Basement Tapes* and liked the idea of good songs badly recorded, ripe for others to cover and polish up.'

Whether he was expecting it or not, that was pretty much what happened . . . eventually. Made between 1993 and 1996, *Fifth Column* didn't reach the public until the early 2000s. It was his old flatmate and guest drummer Stu Bastiman who finally introduced Tom's home-made recordings to Fence. Tom recalls: 'Stu played my songs to James Yorkston, who liked them and played them to Kenny at Fence, who invited me to be on one of his early compilations, *Fence Sampler 3*. My song was on the CD with Lone Pigeon, James Yorkston, King Creosote, HMS Ginafore, Gummi Bako – terrific!'

Around the same time, James Yorkston had sent Laurence Bell a compilation of his own songs and those of various Fence alumni. UNPOC's songs were on it, they struck a chord with the label boss, and eventually the phone rang. Tom says: 'A rough version of *Fifth Column* had worked its way into the pile of CDs they'd play in the Domino office, which is quite an accolade. For a long time they weren't sure about releasing it as a Domino album, given how rough the recordings were. People might not get it. In the end, after a year or so of playing the thing in the office, they decided to release it anyway.'

Laurence is full of praise, saying: 'After that compilation James handed me, I wanted to hear more from everyone. The UNPOC songs were becoming anthems when we played them – we were singing along. The songs were unreal! I thought, could we make this a little more hi-fi to take it to the mass market? It wasn't possible, because it had been made on a four-track that had long been lost. But it was still brilliant. There's a symphonic quality to it. The words were great, the melodies were great and it was so catchy.' James Yorkston adds: 'Tom pulled out of his pocket, or so it seemed, a cassette full of amazing tunes. *Fifth Column* is extraordinary.'

While so many other musicians had tried every trick in the book to attract the industry's attention, Tom had somehow stumbled into it. It was almost as if he didn't particularly want the potential career he was being offered. He says: 'When Laurence got in touch, I told him he could put the record out, but I couldn't do any live shows to support it because of the difficulty and technical complexity of my songs. He seemed to be okay with that.'

Here was a reluctant, reclusive artist who didn't even want to play live. However, Kenny Anderson, James Yorkston and Johnny Lynch had other ideas. They loved the songs and were determined to see Tom perform. He says: 'They'd been inviting me along to the Fence Nights, and each time they'd ask if I'd like a go and I'd say no, thanks. But one time I said "I'm okay", meaning no, and Kenny misread it as "okay", and in a flash had me up there, singing badly while chopping away at a guitar, with Kenny, James and Pictish filling it out. They built me up quickly, and within two months they'd cranked me up to doing a proper support slot, almost a full half-hour at King Tut's in Glasgow. Good work all round!' The King Tut's show was recorded and a limited-edition live album made available.

With the release of *Fifth Column* and the single 'Amsterdam/Here On My Own' in October 2003, the world had a chance to hear Tom's strange but captivating mini-masterpieces. Winning good reviews and limited radio play, the album connected with a sector of Domino and Fence followers, but it was Scandinavia, and Sweden in particular, that took it to their hearts. Tom recalls: 'A few months after King Tut's I got an email inviting UNPOC to play at a big festival over in Sweden. I didn't have a booking agent and had never been to a festival. I was still quite apprehensive about singing live. Including King Tut's and the Fence Nights, I'd done four gigs. So when the festival offer came through, I tried to politely decline for a bit, citing concerns over university dead-lines and that sort of thing. After a bit I figured the festival audience would surely be quite far away, so I said yes. The festival was up and running when we arrived, thousands of people milling about between three stages. Backstage there were big plastic boxes full of cigarettes and sports socks and things like that. Those are the other bands' riders, I was told. I didn't realise we could ask for stuff. Free socks!'

His touring band consisted of James, Kenny and Johnny. James remembers Tom being uptight about the gigs, saying: 'I wondered why he would get so upset about stuff. It was just a gig! What I didn't realise was that when we walked onstage in Sweden, in front of hundreds or thousands of people each time, from the moment he started "Amsterdam" they would go crazy, singing along with lighters in the air.'

Tom has an uncanny knack of writing songs that have this innocent magic to them, though he may not know it himself. Soon more recognised musicians would take an interest, as Laurence Bell recalls. '*Fifth Column* is still one of those records I give to anyone I can. I gave it to the guys in Franz Ferdinand and they all loved it. Nick McCarthy asked them to play at his wedding in Bavaria.' Tom adds: 'Nick was getting married near Munich and asked us to go over to play at the reception. Franz Ferdinand were very big and I'd never met Nick, so it was quite an honour.

'We flew over and did the full thirty-minute set. The next day they let Kenny and me borrow their van to tour the area. There was a sat nav in case we got lost. We drove off towards the Bavarian Alps. After a couple of hours the scenery had changed quite a bit, and we thought we'd turn back. We'd got a bit lost, so we flipped the sat nav on. Suddenly it hit us that we were in Austria. We'd crossed the border. A phone rang and it was Franz Ferdinand's manager, asking: "Is there a laptop in the back of the van?" I had a look. There was a bag with a laptop and some recording equipment and a CD with a handwritten title, "Franz Album 2". We'd left the country with their new, unreleased album.' This jaunt led to the stage-shy Tom, backed by Kenny, James and Johnny, supporting Franz Ferdinand at a huge Alexandra Palace show.

'I've not done many UNPOC shows, twenty-five or so,' says Tom. 'But I feel very lucky with my twenty-five. They've been a nice, varied bunch of shows, what with the overseas stuff and the tiniest of the Fence things and some big festivals, and a birthday and a wedding too. But I remember being in the middle of a small slot at a Fence Night in Anstruther, just three songs, and it was sounding terrific. James was pushing the beat, Johnny cranking the pace with his tambourine, Kenny leading the counter-vocals, and Steve Mason on drums, unrehearsed. It's the best we've ever sounded, I'm pretty sure.'

Fifth Column is an effortless outsider pop album, though ten years later there is sadly no sign of a follow-up. It has become a cult classic. Perhaps that suits Tom. Director David Mackenzie featured 'Here On My Own' prominently in his film *Hallam Foe*, and no doubt others would follow if they got the chance to hear that collection of simple, direct and hugely emotive songs. Beauchop is still writing and has ventured into the studios, but doesn't seem to like the results so far. Maybe he needs a boxroom and a four-track once more. Laurence Bell says: 'If he came up with another record, I'd be pretty damn tempted to put it out. He probably feels like he's made a masterpiece and doesn't know how to follow it up. It's a classic case. I know he can do it. I've heard songs and they're fantastic, but he's obviously not happy enough to deliver something.'

If you're wondering what UNPOC stands for, you'd probably have to ask Tom Beauchop. It was initially United Nations Peacekeepers of Cool, but then it was Unable to Navigate Properly on Course, then Usually Not Proven or Corroborated, then Until November Perhaps or Christmas, then Unusually Nervous Performers of Course . . .

ROZI PLAIN AND FRANÇOIS

As Fence spread its DIY love across the UK, playing festivals and touring the pub, club and toilet circuit, its impact was felt at the most important of levels, the grassroots. If musicians can impress audiences and other musicians, they create friendships and connections that last. Two such musicians touched by the Fence ethos and music were based in Bristol and have become regulars at Fence gatherings across the land. They are now fully fledged collective members with releases for the label. Not only do they bring their own music to the party, they help extend the collective's reach to new audiences.

Rosalind 'Rozi Plain' Leyden was born in Winchester and now lives in London. Like so many in this book, she says The Beta Band changed her life. With a musical brother, Sam, who ran an open-mic night in Winchester, she had space to begin making her own music as a teenager. 'We would all play there every week and coax each other into playing. I don't think I would have ever started playing live if it hadn't been for friends encouraging each other.'

In its early days, Fence was one of the few small labels to have a website, which brought a lot of people to the collective. Although hundreds of miles away, Rozi and her brother (now known as Romanhead) felt they could be kindred spirits and soon met the Fife-based songwriters, as Rozi explains. 'My brother first discovered Fence by getting a Pip Dylan album, *Of All The Things I Can Eat* . . . for £1 in a second-hand record shop in London, because he liked the cover, and it turned out to be amazing, and from that we got to hear all the other stuff. We went to the first Green Man festival, and there was a thing on their website saying: "Please make us a tape so we can listen to it on tour." So we made one, each choosing one song after another to put on it. We each put a song of our own on it too, and on the train on the way to the festival we were making the cover and writing the track listing. Sam said: "What do you want to be called?", and I thought, probably not my own name, and went "Hmm . . . Rozi Plain?" I need to come up with a better story, because people always ask me: "Why plain?" We went to a James Yorkston and King Creosote show in Bristol and gave them some more of our own recordings, and then they invited us to play at the Homegame and we put them on again in Bristol. Then they said they'd like to release some stuff.'

Around the same time, Rozi had become aware of a kindred spirit in Bristol in the shape of a French musician who called himself simply François. 'He had been in Bristol a year or so and played quite a lot of shows, with lots of toys and friends on stage, having a great time. I started to play in his band sometimes. We made a couple of animated films and we'd play live soundtracks to them. It helped with my nerves, playing my own things to get used to performing with someone else. Same with Rachael Dadd, too. Everyone would put on shows and organise tours. My brother started a thing called Cleaner Records as a way for us all to release our stuff.'

François Marry, from Saintes in south-west France, moved to Bristol in 2003. Proclaiming an eclectic list of musicians including Fela Kuti, Mahmoud Ahmed, Kurt Cobain, John Maus, Jimi Hendrix, Nina Simone and Aphex Twin as influences, his main inspiration is his own band The Atlas Mountains. Although he'd begun writing songs at the age of twelve, he says: 'I didn't consider becoming a proper musician until I moved to Bristol at twenty and played my first solo shows. Until then I considered it an unreachable dream.'

Bristol had a serious impact on him, as did his developing interest in DIY music and improvisation. François says: 'I had started recording songs and releasing CDs under my name back when I was a student in France. I moved to Bristol in 2003 and made friends with local musicians Rachael Dadd, Tom Bugs and people from Movietone. I did some open-mic nights, played in the bands of some local musicians and invited them to my house to play on my song'. The idea was to have a free line-up that would change according to where I was, whom I was friends with, and who was available. Two years ago we started getting into a more professional routine, and started keeping a steady line-up.

'The early days of François and the Atlas Mountains featured a lot of cheap Casio keyboards and shambolic horn sections floating into a haze of exiting friendships and lo-fi touring. We played a lot of volunteer-run cafés, house shows, and little independent galleries. We did go as far as doing some US and Scandinavian tours. I don't think we ever got paid more than £150.'

His route to Fife was through Rozi Plain, and it changed his life dramatically. 'In 2005, thanks to Rachael Dadd, I was introduced to a bunch of musicians from Winchester. I gave my phone number to Rozi at a King Creosote show at the Cube Cinema, a volunteer-run venue I was tending bar at. This was the first Fence event I went to, because I knew that she was going to be there. I'm not sure I paid much attention to the music that night.' Soon, however, his mind would focus again. Fence heard his music, invited him to their next Homegame and soon added his music to their roster. 'I wasn't trying to make an album for Fence when I recorded *Plaine Inondable*,' says François. 'I wasn't even trying to make an album. I didn't think the album was very Fence-sounding, but Johnny Lynch seemed really enthusiastic about it.'

Fence, and Johnny in particular, took to both Rozi and François's music from the start, inviting them to their live events and eventually committing to releasing their albums. Rozi specialises in quirky folk-pop with strange rhythmic elements atop her clipped, cute delivery. François's Afrobeat-inspired indie-pop is bashful and gauche in its delivery, with a freewheeling spirit. Although unlike anyone else on the roster, they suited Fence fine. In autumn 2008 Rozi's debut album, *Inside Over Here*, and in December 2009 François and the Atlas Mountains' *Plaine Inondable*, were released. Both records appealed to Fence fans immediately, as did their live performances.

Critical plaudits came along too, as did praise from indie-folk sweet-heart Devendra Banhart, who asked Rozi to support him on tour. Rozi says: 'Fence have been absolute pals and a great help to me over the years, especially Johnny. He invited me to tour with him a lot of times, which was so great.' François concurs: 'I have a lot of admiration for The Pictish Trail. I'm inspired by the way he pushes Fence forward and invests himself completely. He's always been very generous with me, inviting me to stay in Anstruther and of course inviting me to play at Homegame. He passed on my music to Domino.'

From DIY gigs to the present day, Fence helped these artists along the way, and François has since signed to Domino Records, of which he says: 'You can't refuse signing to a label which has the best roster in indie music, that will help you make a living from your music.' He continues to tour to promote his latest album, *E Volo Love*, and make people dance. He now calls Bordeaux home, but spends most of his time on the road. Rozi is following a similar path and has recently released another excellent record, *Joined Sometimes Unjoined*, through Fence and the Neednowater label, picking up more BBC6 radio play than ever and positive reviews across the board.

François has the last word on Fence and their live shows: 'It's the best thing when people bring music they like to the places they love. It's like they're showing the locals the music they're proud of, and they're showing musicians the landscapes they're proud of. They're bringing two worlds together. Homegame was impressive, and Away Game puts the bar higher. I'm looking forward to Outer Space Game in 2017.'

ONTHEFLY AND JON HOPKINS

Electronics, production, beats, beeps and bleeps have been part of the Fence story from fairly early on, and the collective involves more than sensitive beardies with acoustic guitars. Producers such as Clock and Reporter have paved the way initially, but almost everyone has benefited from the remix treatment from another member of the collective at some point. Stalwarts such as King Creosote and The Pictish Trail actively encourage electronic influences, and the non-organic sound of machines permeates many of the label's releases over the past decade. But two electronic artists have been particularly involved in recent times, and Fence might not be Fence without them.

An outside advocate for Fence since around 2001 was Gavin Brown, alias Onthefly. Born and based in Falkirk, he would like to move to Fife in time but says: 'That's close enough for now!' He took piano lessons at school but soon realised that playing drums in a thrash metal band was more to his liking, so his parents bought him a drum kit. His formative musical years were split in half, as he explains: 'My influences and inspiration back in the day were bands like AC/DC, Metallica, Anthrax and Acid Reign, but switched in 1991 to The Orb, Aphex Twin, Happy Mondays, Dave Clarke (DJ), The Beta Band and The Fall.' After short stints in local bands Belt and Citrus Soul, he attended a life-changing concert by The Orb at Glasgow Barrowland in 1992. A set of record decks and a pile of vinyl were bought with the aim of DJ'ing and eventually making electronic music.

He kept in touch with his old bandmates, however, as Belt morphed into Fence acolytes Viva Stereo. Gav now says: 'I started producing my own tracks when I got an Akai sampler and a Tascam four-track. I got my first PC at the age of twenty-one, primarily for audio production. Using the PC with the sampler opened things up, and I started producing sounds I was more satisfied with, though the tracks still weren't very good. I was learning to get my head around music production, as I still am. I now use mostly hardware to produce music as I'm fed up with computers. It's more fun, albeit more expensive.'

As a drummer, DJ, producer and remixer, Gav's skills were abundant, but they needed an outlet. He describes how he first became aware of the Fence Collective: 'I put on the radio while I was driving to a rehearsal with an East Kilbride band called Sixth Member, and a DJ by the name of Vic Galloway had The Lone Pigeon in for a session! I only caught a bit of it, but it was enough. I remembered the name Fence Records, went online and ordered *Moses*, *Touched By Tomoko*, *Fence Sampler 1* and *Fence Sampler 3*. The samplers were great and introduced me to King Creosote, James Yorkston, Pip Dylan and all the others. I bought everything I could get my hands on.'

After that, he and his Falkirk comrades Viva Stereo would invite the Fence Collective to the Martel, their local venue, to play and have a knees-up. They were invited to Fence's Sunday Socials in St Andrews, where Gav soon became resident DJ. He says of his relationship with them: 'Kenny was really the first friendship I established within the collective. He's a very approachable guy, and he was interested in what I was doing production-wise, so I posted him some tracks. Kenny asked to use one of the tracks I wrote with Paul Hughes, as Aerodynamico, on the *Big Avalanche Small Fence* sampler, and he started posting me CDs with snippets from his eight-tracks to remix.'

Like all Fence members, he needed a pseudonym to join the gang properly. 'I got the name Onthefly from a CD burning application on my first PC. I preferred the look of it with no spaces. I hate it when people write it as On the Fly. That's a different band altogether. It's even a men's clothing store.' He immersed himself in Fence events as DJ and a player, and is full of admiration for the label and those who have helped out along the way. 'I've been to most Fence events, and I like to be involved as much as possible. Kenny, Johnny, Gummi, The Canaverals, The Casinos and all the other volunteers have all worked hard with gigs, artwork, web stuff and releases. I'd say the majority of ideas came from Kenny, who likes to do things differently, always good at coming up with whacky ways of doing things like gigs and releases.'

When King Creosote needed a new drummer as the *KC Rules OK* album began to take off in 2005, Gav got the call. 'Kenny just asked, and I said "Absolutely!" right away. I was pretty honoured that he asked, still am.' As the drummer for a rising star and part of a collective that was growing by the minute, the world opened up for him. 'Because of Fence I've had quite a few WTF! moments – TV appearances, video shoots, gigs and releases. Standouts would include playing on Jools Holland's show, touring the UK, playing in Europe, India and China, and supporting KT Tunstall on one of her UK tours. Our Green Man shows are always fun. Getting to perform as Onthefly at Homegame is always great, and performing for your show on Radio 1 was a proud moment too.'

Not everything went smoothly, though. 'My first performance as Onthefly at Homegame was a disaster. My laptop refused to play ball and the sound guy didn't give me any monitors when I tried to play drums. I got a shit write-up in the press because of that. Kenny and Geeko thought it was hilarious, rolling about laughing at the side of the stage. I've since ditched the laptop for live shows.'

As if Gav's schedule wasn't packed enough, he volunteered to run the electronic offshoot label De-Fence. Since then he's kept himself busy pressing the '10x10' 10-inch vinyl EPs, which are hugely collectable and can be bought in a box set, and the occasional CD album for the label. Soon his debut album proper will be released, and he's about to take the drum stool with fellow collective members FOUND. Simply, if you took Onthefly out of the Fence equation, things might just fall apart.

From the opposite end of the country, a producer who has helped raise the Fence profile enormously is Jon Hopkins. A Londoner by birth, he still lives there and is signed as a solo artist to Domino Records. Starting on a diet of pirate-radio drum 'n' bass, he had a short dalliance with prog-rock and ended up listening to artists on Warp Records. 'Brian Eno has been a constant influence, then I've had a random selection of musical obsessions over the years including Deerhunter, Border Community, Sigur Rós, Seefeel, Four Tet, Smog, Jim O'Rourke and John Martyn.'

Like most producers, he learned his trade by trial and error. 'My first experiments started when I was about nine, when my parents bought me a second hand four-track cassette Portastudio for Christmas. I plugged a home keyboard into it, and the results were simply unlistenable. By the time I was about fifteen and we had our first home computer, I started experimenting with sampling and sequencing and put together a few questionable pieces of drum and bass. I got lucky three weeks after leaving school and happened upon an audition for Imogen Heap's band. I spent a year or two as her keyboard player and after that started making my own music.'

What really adds firepower to Jon's musical arsenal is his classical training. He studied piano at the junior department of the Royal College of Music, and though he didn't pursue classical piano as a career, this training has infiltrated his own composition and playing, giving him an acute melodic sensibility. He now has his own studio. 'It's in east London, about twenty minutes' walk from my house. I make music all the time with computers, old synthesisers, a piano and months and months of time.'

Soon Jon extended his reach and produced other artists, leading eventually to King Creosote. 'It was kind of by accident. I released two solo albums, and while the first did okay, the second did shit, so I had to work out something else to do. I started thinking about production. A friend had some Pip Dylan playing at a party and I loved it. I made some enquiries and through that discovered James Yorkston and King Creosote. I went to a KC gig and introduced myself, asking him to send me a vocal so I could try a remix. He was into what I did, and so we started working together, first with a couple of remixes, then on *Bombshell* and *Diamond Mine*.'

Asked what makes Kenny Anderson and his music so special, Jon says: 'For me it's the voice. I've never heard a voice like that, it's a total one-off. I was immediately filled with ideas about new ways of presenting that vocal.' But how did the much loved *Diamond Mine* come about? Jon explains: 'It was totally organic. After the original remix I did for Kenny, "Vice Like Gist Of It", he came to my house the next time he was in London and we recorded a new version of "Your Own Spell". This would have been 2005, and pretty much that exact version appears on *Diamond Mine*. We kept up that method of recording bits and pieces whenever we were in the same place, and by 2009 there was the basis of an album. I got Kenny down to my studio to record the final vocals, and two years later we found time to finish it. It probably took about seven or eight weeks in total, but spread out over seven years.'

Jon's CV looks mighty impressive. As well as his own work and King Creosote, since leaving school in the late 1990s he's played with, written for or produced David Holmes, Coldplay, Purity Ring, Brian Eno, Wild Beasts and fellow Fencer James Yorkston. He's also supported The XX, Royksopp and Four Tet and has been tour DJ for Coldplay. But probably his most high-profile and most lucrative appointment so far was to create the score and original soundtrack for the science-fiction film *Monsters*, which was a big success. Despite all the work that continually comes his way, he feels a real affinity with Fence and regularly performs or DJ's at events in Fife. Jon says fondly: 'All Fence events are things far apart from any other music events I've been to – particularly the Away Game, both of which I was lucky enough to play at. They feel like family affairs, focused on having a laugh and listening to some of the best music in unusual places.' Their approach seems to have rubbed off on him too. 'I found their whole DIY ethos very inspiring. It made me approach my own music differently and focus more on feel and energy rather than precision and pointless details.'

FOUND

The Fence back catalogue has grown substantially over the years, from the early days of handmade CDs to its status as fully fledged label today. Other than Kenny Anderson, and possibly Johnny Lynch, there can be very few people, perhaps none, who have everything Fence has put out into the world. Branding itself as a micro-indie label, Fence now has official mastering, manufacture and distribution networks in place and has developed beyond belief since the small runs of Picket Fence releases in numbered cardboard wallets in the early 2000s. Johnny Lynch has taken a more active role in the artistic direction of the label, and his influence can be felt in some of its key releases of recent years. Although no one is officially signed to Fence, as they don't want to own anyone's recordings, it requires Johnny and Kenny's commitment to the artist to warrant a full vinyl or CD release today.

Edinburgh band FOUND – yes, all in capital letters – are an enigmatic bunch. Ambitious and industrious, they leap from art project to art project and label to label, leaving a trail of unique, inspired albums and live shows behind them. Any FOUND release is different from the one before. They pull together disparate elements of electronica, hip-hop, collage, conceptual art and traditional rock 'n' roll songwriting to make something new. Although no longer releasing their music on Fence, they're still part of the community.

Meeting at Gray's School of Art in Aberdeen, the three original members – Ziggy Campbell, Tommy Perman and Kevin Sim – were almost destined to work together. Tommy explains: 'We formed the band by accident. All three of us were making music independently – Kev on an Akai MPC 2000, Ziggy on a four-track and me on a bright orange iMac that seemed so cutting-edge at the time. We were all trying to shoehorn music or at least sound into our Visual Art degrees. Some of the tutors suggested we work together, as we were experimenting with similar things, and we've been working together ever since.

'We put together a touring exhibition of our artwork, called *Stop Look Listen,* and decided to play live, improvised electronic music at the openings. We only did this to avoid having to talk to people about our work. A promoter saw us and booked us into the Sub Club in Glasgow for a techno night that Luke Vibert was DJ'ing at, so our first real gig was to about three hundred clubbers.'

FOUND are as diverse a group as you're ever likely to meet when it comes to influence and inspiration. Led Zeppelin, DJ Shadow, The Pastels, Miles Davis, Peanut Butter Wolf, Arab Strap, The Temptations, The Who and old-skool hip-hop and reggae: it's all in the FOUND blender. Ziggy also recalls how important The Beta Band were to him. 'In 1997 a friend played me "Champion Versions" and I couldn't believe the sound. It had none of the bravado and strut of Britpop. I bought a Fostex four- track tape recorder and tried to make everything I recorded on it sound like "Dry The Rain".'

Tommy also felt some kinship with the Betas. 'We listened to the "Three EPs" intensively. I could hear that they were into a lot of the same records as we were. I really liked their experimental approach, combined with catchy songs. I loved the detail on the sleeve artwork. There was a lot to look at and listen to. John Maclean came up to do a guest lecture at Gray's and chatted to me, Kev and Ziggy separately about our work. He gave a great talk about his own work, showing lots of the weird videos he made for The Beta Band.'

At college, Ziggy found himself helping out at a local venue and booked an early show by Gordon Anderson. 'I put Lone Pigeon on in Dr Drake's. When it came to showtime, though, nerves got the better of Gordon and he struggled with his songs. He ended up mostly ranting and doing flying karate kicks. I and a drummer called Big Jimmy Stax joined him on stage to try to get him back on track, but the flying kicks were coming dangerously close to my head, so I had to let him get on with it. Although it was a bit of a disaster, I still think that show was one of the best in all my time in Aberdeen.'

Relocated to Edinburgh after Gray's, the trio wanted to continue their project and turn it into a group of sorts, recruiting a drummer and keyboard player. Ziggy recalls the band's first album: 'I'd written this song called "Mullokian", a real slow-burner that had no chorus and no hook to speak of. We had that one song and a few sketches, plus some Krautrockesque live recordings from our improvised sets at art openings. We stitched it together into forty minutes of nonsense called *FOUND Can Move* and Tommy released it on his own label, Surface

Pressure. We released "Mullokian" as the single, which was probably a bit naive, but strangely enough it got loads of radio play. I think if "Mullokian" hadn't been championed we probably wouldn't have taken things any further.'

Tommy also remembers the time fondly. 'My wee brother and I started Surface Pressure and released a handful of records by friends from Aberdeen and Edinburgh. I loved being able to design the whole look of the label and the artwork. It was an incredibly optimistic and exciting time for me. When things started to pick up for FOUND as a band, it seemed like the obvious thing for Surface Pressure to release our first album. I released a 7-inch first and then the album on CD.'

As a DIY enterprise FOUND had common ground with Fence, and it wasn't long before they both hooked up. Ziggy remembers an early Fence Collective gig at Aberdeen's Lemon Tree. 'It was pretty empty, but there was a really enjoyable vibe. Gummi Bako, Pictish Trail, Uncle Beesly, Onthefly and Pip Dylan were all heckling each other and capering on stage. Then this guy came on with an accordion. It was King Creosote, and he played this bonnie tune where he pumped an old metal spinning top with one hand to keep the rhythm and played the melody on his accordion with the other.'

Years later, Tommy bumped into Kenny and Johnny on separate occasions. 'I first met Johnny Lynch and a certain Vic Galloway at Born to Be Wide, a musicians' networking night run by Edinburgh legend and raconteur Olaf Furniss. Olaf was good at getting people to speak to each other. He thought I should meet Johnny because Surface Pressure and Fence Records had common interests. I remember giving Johnny a bunch of CDs and a copy of the *Stop Look Listen* tour publication. He seemed to be really impressed with the packaging, and we resolved to stay in touch. I met Kenny at the end of an Earlies gig at the Venue, you introduced me. I gave him a FOUND demo CD and he made a bunch of impromptu puns on the name by using his fingers to cover up letters on the CD cover, spelling FUN and FUD. I remember thinking: "Who is this strange small man, and why is he taking the piss out of me and my band when I've only just met him?"'

These meetings soon led to a fruitful relationship, and FOUND and the label ended up working together. Invited to play at Homegame in 2005 and 2006, Tommy recalls: 'I chatted to Gavin "Onthefly" Brown about releasing a De-Fence 10x10 with FOUND. He seemed receptive to the idea, so not long after we released a split 10-inch, "10x10:04", with Weasel Squeezer on the flip. I reckon this helped pave the way for our album. We didn't properly approach Fence about our second album until I was in Brazil in 2007 at the same time as the King Creosote band. We all got along really well, and I felt confident about handing Johnny a demo version of *This Mess We Keep Reshaping*. The next day Kenny came up to me in the lobby of the hotel and said that he was glad to hear we were interested in releasing our album with Fence. When we returned to the UK, I spoke to Johnny on the phone and he genuinely seemed to want to put the album out on Fence. I was over the moon.'

Ziggy recalls: 'FOUND were Johnny's first signing to Fence. He's a funny lad and we clicked instantly. We used to go for these daft label meetings with him, which were usually just an excuse to have a few drinks. He'd start by putting on a mock Alan Partridge voice and sacking us from the label. Kenny didn't really deal with that side of things with us, but I've always respected his advice. When we finished *Factorycraft* I sent him a copy to get some initial feedback. It's always a good time hanging out with them. At the risk of sounding sentimental, it's like being in a family, albeit some kind of slightly dysfunctional cartoon family.'

This Mess We Keep Reshaping was released and enjoyed by Fence fans and many others. Picking up good reviews and radio play, it showed the band were capable of writing more succinct songs while still retaining their experimental edge. It fitted Fence perfectly – musically, lyrically and in its DIY ethos. Their live shows as a five-piece saw them play prime slots at Fence events and gigs across the UK in their own right. Soon, however, they ditched the drums and keys, employing more electronics, and moved labels to another Scottish indie institution, Chemikal Underground.

Tommy explains: 'Fence has always encouraged people to move on to other labels if it's a good opportunity. Kenny has released lots of records with Domino, and Johnny released his Silver Columns collaboration on Moshi Moshi, so when the Chemikal opportunity came up they were very supportive. At the time we were putting our third album together, Johnny and Kenny were busy touring and I felt that they didn't have enough time and resources to spend on another FOUND album. Also, *Factorycraft* was so different from what we'd done before that it made more sense to go with Chemikal. It was a better fit for that particular record.'

Whether talking at global interactive conferences, designing sound installations with their friend Simon Kirby, backing King Creosote, or being an electronic indie-rock group in their own right, the three members of FOUND are prolific and visionary. But are they comfortable with the 'art collective' tag as opposed to just being a band? Ziggy answers: 'I really like the way things have turned out. I still consider FOUND to be a largely unknown band, but if we'd been more successful we wouldn't have had time to develop the art side of the collective. I also like the way each project, whether it's a record or an art piece, feeds in to the others. For example, when we were building the installation *Cybraphon* I started looking at early technology and bought a set of books called *Hawkins' Electrical Guide*, which is full of stunning illustrations. I suggested we use them for the artwork on *Factorycraft*, which ended up working really well. These little spillovers happen all the time.'

With a fourth album planned and a stripped-back, two-piece line-up without Tommy, Ziggy says: 'Even though we're now signed to Chemikal Underground, we're still very much part of Fence and play at a lot of their events. I've just finished a record with Kenny, Johnny, James Yorkston and Slow Club. It's a collaborative record for Dewar's Whisky called *Experimental Batch # 36* where we all play on each other's songs, and it has a real Fence Collective vibe to it. In all these years it's the first time I've recorded with them. I'm hoping we can do some more in the future.'

'I love the Fence Collective,' Tommy enthuses. 'They are inspiring in their own unique way. Johnny has been a close friend and I've really enjoyed working with him over the years. His hard work and drive is inspiring. These days I feel well and truly part of the Fence family, and that's a real honour. They can be a fickle rabble of dour Scots, but ultimately they are a fantastic bunch of people and I've had some of my best times hanging out with them. They're doing their own thing and that's brilliant. They stand up for their beliefs and go their own way.'

KID CANAVERAL

Kid Canaveral have long been have been vaguely associated with Fence for a number of reasons. They formed in St Andrews and soon became close friends with Johnny Lynch, who encouraged them ceaselessly in their early years. Lead singer and songwriter David MacGregor says:

'I've known Johnny since we were involved in the Indie Club night at St Andrews student union. He's been a good friend and support to the band since its incarnation.' Guitarist Kate Lazda continues: 'Johnny's been one of Kid C's top supporters. I think he gave us the confidence to think that we could do it on our own. We didn't need to hang around waiting for that non-existent big-money record deal.'

Citing The Clash, The Cure, early REM, Kirsty MacColl, Grandaddy, The Smiths and the Chemikal Underground label as influences, their music started out rough but eventually grew into the soaring, buzzsaw indie-pop sound it is today. In their format of guitar, bass, drums and vocals they may be Fence's most conventional band, but their emotive songs and high-octane guitars have settled firmly in the heart of most Fence fans.

Talking of their roots in St Andrews, Kate says: 'There are loads of well-documented things to dislike about St Andrews, archaic sexist/ elitist societies and privileged toffs being the most talked-about, but it wasn't difficult to make it what you wanted it to be. It was a great place to start something without getting completely lost like you would in a big city. When we arrived, the university-affiliated live music society was focused on jam sessions and covers bands. This was definitely not our thing – for one thing, I couldn't play guitar well enough for that. It bored all of us to tears, and that common ground brought us together and pushed us to be pro-active. At St Andrews, if you want to play a gig, you organise it yourself. If there's something not going on, you make it happen.'

'It was bizarre, quite a culture shock at first,' David adds. 'To be suddenly surrounded by such privilege was strange. There were plenty of normal folk, but you had to endure a fair amount of braying cousin-fanciers with senses of entitlement the size of Balmoral. The onus was on you to make your own fun if you weren't into social climbing, endless binge drinking or the Christian Union. There's no way I'd be so ambitious with some of the things we do now, were it not for the fact that we had to do an unofficial degree in events management back then.'

Kate admits that their early days were unpromising. 'We murdered our fair share of covers, and original material too, but that's why it took us a good few years to release our first album. I think we knew we were a work in progress, learning how to write proper songs and do proper performances. Waiting until we had an entire album's worth of songs that we were proud of was the best decision we ever made.'

Being among the few who warmed to original, new, independent music in the St Andrews area at the time, it wouldn't be long before they formed a bond with their neighbourhood chums. Kate remembers her initial encounters with Fence from university. 'I think the first show I saw King Creosote play was upstairs in the student union. Johnny, Gummi Bako and Pip Dylan played too, and I can remember being really impressed not just by the music, but also the amount of merchandise they had for sale, mostly CD albums with intriguing covers.' David continues: 'I think I saw the Fence Collective play at freshers' week in my second year, upstairs in the union. It certainly looked like Kenny. Aikman's or a Sunday Social would definitely be my first less-fuzzy encounter, though.'

With Fence's inspiration and influence they would soon learn to play better and write some worthy songs, releasing a selection of singles on their own Straight to Video label. David says: 'They inspired us to set up our own label. I'd always been fascinated by the whole punk/DIY ethic and had grown up buying the records of Chemikal Underground, but I never thought I could do something like that myself. Then there was Kenny and Johnny, releasing records right in front of us. Out came the CDs, glue and scissors and we were away. From our poorly recorded beginnings we've released 7-inch singles, cassettes and an album, all under the Straight to Video Records banner, since 2007.'

As Fence grew in stature Kid Canaveral ploughed on regardless, helping out at Fence gigs with door duties and at merchandise stands – anything to be connected with a pro-active independent scene. Johnny Lynch would take time out of his Fence and Pictish Trail schedules to advise and promote the band whenever they had a new release, tour or festival appearance. As the group progressed as songwriters and players, they grew closer as friends to Fence.

The band would soon release an outstanding debut album, *Shouting At Wildlife*. David confesses: 'I'd had terrible writer's block and I was pretty dissatisfied with the last single we'd released. I wrote a song for the first time in about a year that turned into "And Another Thing!!" I started to feel more confident about songwriting. We went in for our first session for the album and things really started to look up. I started writing more than I ever had before, taking it less seriously, and, when I didn't have my tongue in my cheek, being much more honest in it. We recorded it all with a brilliant engineer called Gal in a studio in the youth centre in Castlemilk. I've never been so proud in my life as when we released that album!'

'We released our album in July 2010 on our own label,' says Kate. 'I guess some people were surprised, given our close affiliation, that it didn't come out on Fence from the beginning, but I think the timing wasn't right and the label had other things going on at the time. We were shocked and thrilled at how well it was received and how many copies we sold. By the beginning of 2011 we'd pretty much sold out of the first CD run, and when Johnny suggested a vinyl re-release on Fence we jumped at the chance.'

The band applied and were accepted to play at the huge South by South West (SXSW) festival in Austin, Texas, and King Creosote was so enamoured of them that he had them back him on a Fence-released single, a Scottish tour and some gigs in America. 'Our joint tour and split single "Home Run And A Vow" in October 2011 were definitely career highlights, and joining Kenny at SXSW for a few shows was totally surreal,' says Kate. 'Johnny and Kenny have been very generous to us, and hopefully we've repaid that with a couple of albums they can be proud to release.'

Reinforcing their position in the inner Fence circle, Blair Young of Forest of Black made a video montage of the first Away Game on Eigg in 2010 and used a Kid Canaveral song, 'Her Hair Hangs Down', as its soundtrack. Tears were shed and the Canaverals' place was cemented. They were bringing a new audience to Fence and Fence was bringing a new audience to them.

With a new album, *Now That You Are A Dancer*, out on Fence in 2013, with singles and more touring as appropriate, the future looks bright. Kate helps run the Fence online shop and is part of the label and collective's operations on a daily basis. Of Fence's growth, she says: 'People are so inspired by what is going on, and that's a difficult balance when the number of fans keeps on increasing but they all want to feel that personal belonging. When people say a Fence event was the best weekend of their lives, and that does happen frequently, it makes you pretty proud!' David adds: 'I'd like Fence to get as big as it can, because

I'd love to see all the hard work that Johnny, Kenny and Kate put in be as far-reaching and rewarding as possible. It has a wonderful personal touch, and it should never lose that, but I'd love to see it reach as many people as possible.'

WITHERED HAND

Dan Wilson, alias Withered Hand, has taken his slacker, indie-pop, folk-punk vignettes and connected directly with hearts and minds. With his wobbly falsetto, thrashy acoustic guitar and singalong choruses, he has brought a witty and brutally honest collection of songs about despair and self-loathing to an audience ready to lap them up. Growing up in Bishop's Stortford in Hertfordshire, Dan grew up in a household governed by the heavy hand of religion. This would resurface as a major theme in his songs.

As a teenager obsessing over his father's T-Rex and Kinks records and his uncle Derek's Bowie and Hendrix collection, he discovered his own generation of guitar-slinging ne'er-do-wells in the form of Mudhoney, Sonic Youth and the Pixies. He remembers: 'As a kid I used to go and see whatever was on in the Square Club in Harlow. It was a real toilet of a place, but it had heart. I saw a lot of stuff that opened my eyes and ears to alternative music and more, from Gallon Drunk to Mega City Four to Carter USM to Snuff. It was heady stuff for young ears. It felt like a way out of a small town without actually being able to leave.'

Dan lived a relatively happy life until his parents' divorce, when he was eighteen. 'I stayed in Bishop's Stortford longer than I would have, to support my father after the divorce,' he says. 'Then I gave up my job in the chip shop and moved to London, where I started studying Fine Art Practice at Middlesex University.' A few years later he graduated with a first and moved to Edinburgh for love. 'It was a rollercoaster, but we married in the end and are bringing up our kids here. I hope they will thank us some day; it's a great place.'

On the genesis of his own music, he recalls: 'I messed about with electric guitars from about age sixteen, playing blues scales badly with a wah-wah pedal and a cheap fuzzbox. I would play that, and I found another friend who could play chords. That kept me occupied for years. I wrote a couple of terrible songs for a band I was in when I was eighteen. They weren't any good, and I certainly wasn't able to sing them. It was more of a social thing for misfit kids to do, being in a band. It was all for that feeling of belonging and trying to do something, anything.'

Once established in Edinburgh years later, after playing briefly in an outfit called Barrichello, he formed a noise outfit called Peanut that helped him connect with people who are part of his life to this day. He says: 'When I formed Peanut with long-term artistic collaborator and friend Neil Sylvester, I started to feel like making music was akin to making art. We wanted to be a mess, uneasy listening, to clear rooms. Peanut was the first time I really shouted into a microphone. It made me realise I could do some kind of vocals. I started to write a few songs/ rants, but it was a battle, and singing usually involved getting very drunk first, so we had a lot of instrumentals. We played a few shambolic, drunken gigs in Glasgow and Edinburgh and disbanded. Surprisingly, I sometimes meet people who have fond memories of that band.' It should be noted that 'My Struggle' on the 'Heart Heart' EP by Withered Hand is a reworking of an old Peanut song.

Losing faith in his ability to make music, Dan reached the point where he wanted to sell his guitars and forget music altogether at around the age of thirty. He says: 'My wife and I had just had our first kid, and it felt like it was time to stop making music and art and start trying to be more serious. I was working in the ladies' shoe department of a store in town when my wife got my friends and family to club together and buy me an acoustic guitar, so that I could play around the home without waking our daughter up. We disbanded Peanut, but I started playing the acoustic at home a lot. Once I thought music was behind me, I began writing songs I thought nobody would hear.' Many of those songs would appear on his acclaimed debut album, *Good News*.

Bart (Gordon Bartholomew), a friend and bandmate from the Peanut days, and member of new Fence signings Eagleowl, encouraged him to continue his songwriting and try a public performance. 'Bart was putting on a day event called Foodstock in the Clock Café in Leith, and he invited me to play a few of those fledgling acoustic songs. Luckily for me I decided to do it, and I met several people that day who became very important in my story. A few people there saw something in it and stuck by me while I got my shit together. Through my friendship with Cammy "L'Enfant Bastard" Watt, which started that day, I met Neil "Meursault" Pennycook, and he said: "Let's record this stuff you're doing." Emily Roff of Tracer Trails was there and started giving me support slots at her early gigs. This was all amazing to me. It still is.'

Developing their own loose collective, Dan joined forces with Meursault, Eagleowl, Rob St John and L'Enfant Bastard and played shows promoted by Emily and Tracer Trails, including their own Retreat festival. Informed by New York's 'anti-folk' movement, Edinburgh's indie roster on SL Records and the developing Fence Collective, they took the anti-authoritarian DIY stance of punk and indie-pop and began to form their own scene, infiltrating Edinburgh's venues, church halls, libraries and community centres. Fence took notice and began to invite some of these acts to perform at Homegame.

Dan was cajoled into recording a full album, *Good News*. 'Neil Pennycook was a massive part of that album being made, he really kicked my ass. Also Ed Pybus of SL Records, who initially distributed it, gave me a lot of his knowledge and help.' Since its release in September 2009 (it has been re-released since) this almost accidental album has had some enthusiastic reviews, helping him establish a fan base and shift a fair number of units, warranting various re-pressings and a US release on San Francisco label Absolutely Kosher. 'It's been fun headlining a packed Queen's Hall two years running. Strange, also,' he says of his adopted-hometown success.

Dan has since become a full member of the Fence Collective and released a 7-inch vinyl EP on the label. 'I was thinking about self-releasing it, but Fence had been planning a limited-edition 7-inch vinyl series and Johnny and Kenny were interested in the 'Heart Heart' EP to launch it. I had never seriously approached another label, and I had no chance of getting it out myself any time soon. And Johnny Lynch is easy to deal with, works damn hard and knows how to get things done to a deadline.'

His first meeting with King Creosote, however, was complete chance. 'I was reluctantly playing an early show in Prestonpans and had a chat with a lovely guy outside the venue as we admired each other's decrepit old vans. Something just totally clicked with this beardy, smiley guy as we talked rust spots and bodywork filler. I realised much later, when we met to work on an EP, that the guy with the other rusty van had been Kenny Anderson. Later that week, at work at a press cuttings agency, I read an interview with King Creosote, not realising I had just met him!'

Soon the two songwriters would end up working together. 'Ed Pybus suggested I should make an EP to precede the album I had just recorded. He suggested doing it with King Creosote and I laughed it off. Then I think he contacted Kenny or Fence, which resulted in a meeting in the National Museum of Scotland café, where I realised I had met Kenny in Prestonpans. It felt right, and we arranged I would go over to Anstruther on my own and do an EP.' Looking back fondly at the recording, he continues: 'In the AIA Hall at 3 a.m., when the road outside and the whole town were completely silent, I recorded "No Cigarettes", a much better-realised version than the one I had just recorded for the album, in one take. It remains one of my favourite recordings of any of my songs.' As a compliment to the blossoming songwriter, Kenny recorded his own version. 'He covered "No Cigarettes",' Dan says, beaming. 'It's very sweet of him. I can't separate him from his music now.'

Having toured with King Creosote on various occasions, performed at Fence festivals and released his music on the label, a strong link has been forged as Withered Hand moves on to his next album, which may come out on Fence or his own label. Whatever happens, he's a key part of the collective. He remarks: 'I think the Fence Collective is inspirational. Broadly speaking, I like the music and the people involved. I like the music of James Yorkston, Rozi Plain and so on. King Creosote is my main reason for being involved. At its best Fence has seemed about much more than music – it has often felt more about the people, especially the lovely people who attend the events.'

For the future, Dan says: 'I hope to collaborate with Kenny again soon. I have my own label, called Brother & Dad, which handles my debut album and my last EP, "In-betweens", but it's just a vehicle to get my own music physically out there on my own terms. Darren Hayman (of Hefner, and a hero of Dan's) once asked me what I wanted to achieve, and when I told him: "A minor cult success," he replied: "Dan, you're already there". So I guess I am!'

DJANGO DJANGO

Although they're not strictly part of the Fence Collective and are now based in London, it would seem a little odd not to include a band who in many ways are pushing forward what The Beta Band and Fence have started. Django Django have also appeared at two Fence events, the Homegame and Eye o' the Dug, and feature Dave Maclean, brother of John, as the group's drummer and producer. Born and raised in Fife, Dave and his friends could potentially make a global success out of what they're doing. On the strength of their debut album and live show, their psychedelic-electro-surf-pop is addictive to critics and fans.

Born in 1980, Dave, a Madras College FP like most of the people in this book, grew up with his brother, sister and artist parents in Tayport. Like the rest of his family he was drawn to art, to comic books in particular, dreaming at one point of becoming an illustrator. He was also surrounded by music. 'The first music I remember listening to is the Beatles. I'd lie in bed and listen to a tape over and over again on a Walkman with big spongy earphones. I was pretty young; it's one of my first memories of anything.' Soon he'd be learning the trumpet, reading music and performing in school concerts.

'The first album I bought was *Yellow Submarine*, but the first album I bought that was modern was Public Enemy's *Fear Of A Black Planet* when I was ten. That album blew my mind and I never looked back. From there I got into Nirvana and The Stone Roses, but the next album to change it all for me was The Prodigy's debut. That opened up a whole world of rave music for me that I had previously shunned. It was glow-sticks at dawn for the next three years. I got an old set of decks and began to teach myself to DJ.'

Dave continues: 'I guess I was into what you'd call rave music, but it was broken down into a lot of scenes. I liked everything from acid house and techno to hardcore and jungle. Through those records I went backwards down the line and got into hip-hop and funk when I was fourteen or fifteen. That's what got me into drumming, because I wanted to learn the hip-hop breaks I was DJ'ing with. I had a few drum lessons at Stage 2000 studios in Dundee. Every Saturday I'd go over and play for an hour, then up to Groucho's to dig old hip-hop and jungle records out the bargain bin.'

But didn't he find it isolating and alienating living in Fife as a teenager? 'It was the best of both worlds,' he says. 'Tayport is rural, fields and forest all around with an amazing sandy beach, so most of my time as a youngster was spent outdoors playing and camping out. When I grew up Dundee was just a stone's throw from my house on the bus.' By the time he was fifteen he was DJ'ing illegally in a Dundee bar. 'I was far too young to be there! The barman was none other than Colin Martin, alias The Lonely Piper, who now does artwork and writes for Django Django. The night was called Beat Quest, and I was under the experienced wing of a guy called Mark Wallace, who ran the night. He made me realise all music was connected, and from there I just got into everything.'

Of course, having an older brother who was a member of The Beta Band was going to have an impact on the younger Maclean, but it could have gone either way. Thankfully, as Dave explains, 'I was a huge fan. They put together all the stuff that John and I grew up with, from folk to dub and hip-hop. We have the same approach to music-making that comes from the collages and painting methods that our parents have, so it all made a lot of sense to me. I'd see the inner workings, hear demos and watch them record. I used to DJ at their gigs, too.'

His career was almost predestined. Like his parents and his brother, he knew what he wanted to do after school. 'I was into art from a very young age. I spent a lot of time in my dad's studio making stuff. I knew from the start I wanted to go to art college. I spent hours and hours drawing. It was all I wanted to do when I was a kid.' Soon he'd follow John to Edinburgh College of Art. 'I went there with my friend Craig Coulthard [an award-winning artist who makes music as Randan Discotheque, and with whom Dave runs the Bonjour Branch record label alongside fellow Fifer Andy Wake of The Phantom Band], and we shared a flat. I had a hard time at first. My head wasn't in a good place; I wasted a lot of time and was nearly kicked out.

'But I got through it, and by third year I was living in a flat with people who were into music but didn't really want to make it. I didn't know what music I wanted to make, either. So I put my energy into DJ'ing. I never wrote songs. I always wanted to be a producer. I liked drums, structure, rhythm, and I wasn't fussed about lyrics at all. Craig lent me his four-track recorder and I'd sample loops by sticking Sellotape to a record, making it skip on the beat. Then I'd dub over that with drumming, or acoustic guitar tuned to a chord. These experiments went on and on through college, but it wasn't until much later, when I got a PC, that I could really explore the possibilities of production.'

Around this time Dave would send me demos of his rhythmic experiments, calling himself Hugo Paris and dealing in rudimentary electro-house soundscapes. He was looking for feedback and ultimately radio play. I aired a track or two and saw the potential in what he was up to. It wasn't long before he sent me a more song-orientated project he was working on, called Django Django. Teaming up with an art-school friend, Vincent Neff, it brought together Dave's house and hip-hop thump with delicate, harmonised vocal lines and twanging guitar riffs. Sounding like something beamed in from space in the 1960s but utterly contemporary at the same time, it was the bare bones of what we know and love as Django Django today.

I remember demo versions of songs such as 'Firewater' and 'Storm' many years before they surfaced on the debut album, and they bear up as songs. I played them and waited for more. More would arrive randomly, but there didn't seem to be a group as such; it was more a studio, songwriting and production project. But it sounded fresh and harked back to the more immediate side of The Beta Band. Eventually, Dave and Vinnie would move to London. 'I moved to London,' Dave says, 'because I'd been visiting John there for years and was always in love with the city. I still am, but one day I'd like to move back to Fife and settle. North-east Fife has everything for me, but London had an edge that keeps me on my toes right now.'

In London Dave and Vinnie set about putting a band together. Dave says: 'We met up for a drink in London in about 2007 to take up a conversation we'd had in an Edinburgh pub years before. We'd always wanted to record some songs, but it was never the right time. Being in London made us get our act together, literally, and we started to record songs in my bedroom. Art school friend Tommy Grace and Duncan Marquis from The Phantom Band were asked to make up the band for a live show. When Duncan went back to the Phantoms, James Dixon, a friend from Glasgow School of Art, stepped in.'

By 2009, Django Django was officially a band and could play more frequent live shows and start releasing records. I remember seeing them perform to a packed Hot Club night in Glasgow's Nice 'n' Sleazy. They were a little chaotic and under-rehearsed, but the magic was there. A few months later I saw them play the legendary Transmusicales festival, in a dilapidated old church in Rennes, to around 1,000 people. They couldn't have played more than a dozen or so gigs by that point, but their performance had been tightened up and their promise was huge. It was clear that with the right team behind them they could take it a lot further.

Dave paints a tranquil, stress-free picture when discussing the band's early days before signing to hip French label Because Music. It seems they weren't in any rush. 'We were happy just ambling away, making a song every so often. We didn't ramp things up until we got signed to Because Music and they expected an album. They never said how or when – just "Call us when it's finished." It was pretty relaxed! They said they would let us do what we wanted with the music and artwork, and they've stuck to their word, so it's the perfect home for us.'

The debut album was released in January 2012 and went Top Forty in the UK, also making inroads into Europe, the US and Australia. In many ways it's a classic album, with a clutch of catchy singles, instrumental sections, a retro tinge and electronic production that makes it sound familiar and cutting-edge. There isn't a dull moment. With the sweet vocal lines and psychedelic squiggles atop tribal drums and electronic beats, inevitable comparisons were made with The Beta Band. Dave shrugs and happily acknowledges this connection, but his brother John says: 'I see the differences between Django Django and The Beta Band more than the similarities. They have more of a dance element, that 1960s influence, and are computer-made, whereas we were tape-made. Our loops were always a bit lop-sided. I'm a big fan.'

Since the release of the album, their success has rocketed as they keep up with demand for their increasingly powerful live shows. Awards and plaudits flood in, airplay is constant and their lives have been changed forever. They may end up being the most successful of all the artists in this book.

HONOURABLE MENTIONS

It has been impossible to write comprehensively about everyone from the ever-expanding collective, so my apologies to those who get only a brief mention or a solitary shout-out here. For all those who have released something on Fence or De: Fence, been part of the collective, played a Homegame, done a remix, or just showed up and partied – we salute you:

Adrian Crowley, Amino People, Angels Fight The City, Animal Magic Tricks, Art Pedro, Ballboy, Barbarossa, Candythief, Chicken Feed, Clock, Come In Tokyo, Con Brio, Deaf Mutes (that's Reuben Taylor and me, by the way!), Delifinger, Down The Tiny Steps, Eagleowl, English Bore, Eyechildz, Gangplank, Good Morning Captain, Gorlkeepers, Hand, Hardsparrow, Ichi, Immigrant, Jonnie Common, Little Pebble, Love.Stop.Repeat, MC Quake, Monoganon, Mystery Juice, Northern Alliance, OLO Worms, Player Piano, Pumajaw, Rachael Dadd, Randolph's Leap, Reporter, Reuben Taylor, Rich Amino, Romanhead, Seamus Fogarty, Shinya Mizuno, Super Shitbox, The Diamond Family Archive, The José, The Soft Eyes, The Son(s), The Süpergun, The Red Well, The Shivers, Things In Herds, Trilemma, Viking Moses, Viva Stereo, Volg4, WeaselSqueezer, Wilmacakebread and wiQwar.

Apologies to anyone who isn't mentioned here . . . I did my best!

16

Home and Away

The Fence Ethos

If the original idea was dreamed up by King Creosote as the simplest way to release his and his brothers' music in Fife, it has blossomed now for well over a decade. With hundreds of releases under Fence's belt, it started with small runs of handmade CDs and progressed through manufactured CD albums to vinyl singles and albums in various sizes and combinations, not to mention occasional download bundles. Most people who think they know the label and the collective will probably have a convenient musical category to put everything in. But they should think again. Fence may have dwelled primarily on acoustic songwriters since its birth, but it now encompasses far more, serving up a *smörgåsbord* of indie-rock, electronica, psychedelia, folk, noise and comedy at their live events and on record. It seems their spirit of eclecticism is deepening and widening.

Kenny Anderson sets it straight. 'We're seen as an alt-folk label, and that may backfire one day, but we don't just release that kind of music. Listen to Kid Canaveral, The Red Well, The Shivers and Deaf Mutes.' Johnny Lynch continues: 'The folk thing is interesting, because the thing we have in common with the folk tradition is sharing songs and people covering other people's songs. In that way, Fence is folk, just not in the acoustic, traditional sense. We just put out stuff we like. The Picket Fence series opened everything out for us – The Süpergun was rock, Clock was happy hardcore – so after that we thought we could do anything. If the Eigg band The Massacre Cave came to us with an incredible full-on metal record, maybe we would release that just to be perverse.'

But the truth is that Fence was stuck with the alt-folk, nu-folk, New Acoustic Movement tags from the moment the public and the media set eyes and ears upon them. Johnny is honest: 'There's a part of me that suspects Fence got a lucky break because we came at the right time. We were one of the few labels releasing that kind of music. Cottage-industry and CD labels were just starting, and we had some good music. It was also quite rural, not a city thing. But certain people think they know what Fence is. A Radio 2 DJ was saying recently that he knew all about Fence. I was like: "Really? How many Art Pedro CDs do you own? Have you heard Hardsparrow? Do you know any Pictish Trail or James Yorkston, even?"'

Whether you're a purist or not, whether you've been there since the start or you're a newbie, if you examine the label's release schedule and back catalogue you'll discover a world of diversity. Johnny says: 'I love electronic and dance music, and I've tried to incorporate it into the Fence events, though I know some people are put off by Kid Canaveral, Silver Columns and the more rock, indie and dance elements. You don't get to choose your audience.'

The proliferation of decent, affordable home recording equipment has helped create a boom in new music never seen before. Johnny says: 'It's grown out of the realisation that people can do music themselves. The whole MySpace thing, CD machines and more sophisticated computer software for home-recordings; you don't need a studio. But what's the best type of home-recording? It's the simple stuff – an acoustic guitar, a voice and maybe one other thing.' Perhaps that's why the alt-folk tag has stuck – it's what most people are capable of creating in their bedroom on a tiny budget. As with the 1960s beat explosion, punk, hip-hop and acid house, the available technology often dictates the terms of the music.

Although Kenny Anderson is hugely wary of the internet, there is no doubt in anyone's mind that Fence was nurtured by the growing presence of music fans online. With the rise of internet forums, online pseudonyms and chat rooms, music obsessives and those yearning to be part of something could venture into a new world and call it their own. On Fence there's an online community who spend most days on the 'Beef' board, swapping information, ideas and gossip. And once they buy into something, they want to collect it all. Fence fans have so far remained extremely loyal to the collective, helping the label champion new names. Fence fans seem to be a creative bunch too, with some even being signed to the label. Rozi Plain, whose brother Sam was a big Fence fan, was inspired by them to set up their own Cleaner Records label and collective in Bristol.

Is there a typical Fence fan? Do they all adhere to the indie cliché of beards, woolly hats and checked shirts? Johnny says: 'I think there probably are people who look a certain way and live their life in a certain way, to whom Fence and our events are appealing. It's what they like about music. But things changed a lot when Kenny got bigger, and KT Tunstall brought a lot of people into Fence. There are a lot of hardcore fans who came in via Kate and are really excited about the music. There are more young people at the shows now, and more folk dancing – there was never anyone dancing before.'

But if the label and the collective ideas are growing, there is still an attention to detail and a desire to stand apart that pushes them forward. Johnny admits: 'There's more and more choice nowadays, but we've made it harder and harder for folk to get into the shows. If you want to be part of the Fence thing, you have to make an effort. You have to own the vinyl and have the physical product – we're not on Spotify or iTunes or any of these things. We don't want to make it easy, because the experience is so much better when you're more involved. Buying the records is only one part of it now. We're releasing less stuff and putting on more events. To have the experience you have to see the show and see it on our turf.' It's true that the label is releasing fewer CDs and even full releases. Neither Kenny nor Johnny has as much time, with their own careers and touring schedules. Still, as Johnny says: 'Sometimes a record comes in that you *have* to put out.'

In these austere times, format ideas come thick and fast from Fence. To keep things fresh and an audience hooked, perhaps this is the only way. Kenny and Johnny evangelise about vinyl, and have introduced a series in which a download code may only become available when the vinyl has sold out. Increasingly they arrange launch gigs to promote new releases, and subscriptions to the Buff Tracks or Chart Ruse series, where an artist does three tracks and then there's a remix by another member of the collective. When releasing a full album, they make a quality, heavyweight-vinyl record with a CD included. This is more expensive and higher-priced, but all these schemes are a big part of the Fence experience and a way to demand attention and devotion. Johnny adds: 'Kenny and I have been having these weird ideas on how to release records that make it even more difficult and inspire even more fanaticism. For example, an album is only made available on one cassette in a library: you rent it out for, say, £5 and have it for a week or two weeks, and if you're a day late there's a £10 fine per day! You can then copy it, but you're not going to make a great copy of it, are you? But to be honest, that's maybe one of our more shit ideas!'

He elaborates: 'You have to have ideas. You can't just do the same thing as everyone else. That's why the record industry failed, because people tried to use the same methods as everyone else while undercutting each other. They tried to make everything cheaper and cheaper and cheaper, making everything less and less valuable. You should do the thing you want to do and do it really well, and people will pay. I don't want our records to be throwaway things. Incorporating events makes an experience out of it.'

These ideas have had a profound effect on others making music and starting labels or collectives. 'It's really flattering when you hear someone's inspired by you,' Johnny says. 'There are a few bands who have said that recently, such as Monoganon and Randolph's Leap. But it's more from other labels, like Song, by Toad, for example.'

Fence's cachet has undoubtedly grown, with author Ian Rankin, actors Christopher Eccleston and Warwick Davis, and BBC DJs Rob Da Bank, Lauren Laverne, Marc Riley and Dermot O'Leary as fans and supporters. Plenty of musicians doff their caps to King Creosote and co., including Chris Martin of Coldplay, Hot Chip and Kenny's teenage favourites The Bluebells, whose frontman Ken McCluskey was recently discovered to be Johnny Lynch's second cousin. But there is ambition and division within the Fence hierarchy itself. Johnny wants to secure overseas distribution and a more international profile. He'd like to see the label expand in the live arena and on record while keeping the personal touch and homespun philosophy. Kenny is perhaps more conservative, having been burned by the corporate machine. Running a new project called The Alter Ego Trading Company he leans towards a more localised and decentralised collective, based in his beloved Fife and of an easily manageable size. We can only hope they both get their way and can coexist.

The extensive back catalogue is there for further investigation, but what will the future be like for the label, and can the collective keep growing? Johnny says: 'I think it will, though some people will fall by the wayside. The thing is, it doesn't have to be a career. There are some folk who do it full-time and others who treat it as a hobby. Maybe Fence will go by the wayside itself and be seen in years to come as some trendy movement of the time. I don't think Fence will ever stop doing what it does, but we might not be the flavour of the month any more. I just hope that there's going to be an audience that will stick with it.'

Live events are the lifeblood of the Fence community, from Aikman's to the Sunday Socials via micro-gigs in Anstruther's Ship Tavern, through the UK's small-venue and festival circuit, finally to their signature Homegame and other key festivals including Eye o' the Dug, Haarfest, Hott Logs, The Bun Fight and Away Game. Booking shows nationwide has been vital for the label, but bringing audiences to its own home territory has been all Fence's own making. But why drag people all the way to Fife? Kenny Anderson says: 'It's an extension of the reason we stayed in Fife and did the label here. It's a beautiful part of the world and our live events here offer something different.' Johnny Lynch adds: 'I think Anstruther has developed a real character and identity off the back of the Homegame and Fence gigs. But we're not stupid; we know people don't just come for the music, they come because it's a nice place to be. You don't have to watch music, you can take a stroll around a relaxing place that isn't London, Manchester, Edinburgh or Glasgow.'

Kenny says: 'There's no festival that appeals to me enough to have me camping for three days in a row. Maybe at the age of seventeen or twenty-five, but not now. Not with toilets and queues and so on. I'm not into music *that* much.' Laurence Bell of Domino is more romantic about the idea. 'Hearing that music in that setting, in those villages, is magical. I imagine it's like hearing the Ramones in CBGB's or Fats Domino in New Orleans – it's genuine modern folk music in its natural setting.' Even lapsed Fifer and BBC presenter Edith Bowman, who grew up in Anstruther, has taken notice. In a radio documentary I made a few years ago for the BBC, she said: 'I think there is definitely something special about the East Neuk as an area. I never saw it when I lived there. It's only when I moved to London that I really appreciated the beauty and spirit of the place. As a teenager there, I was bored all the time and went looking for things to keep me occupied – that's why I joined bands and tried to persuade my mum to drive me to gigs. What's really nice is seeing a vibrant surge of creativeness in the area that's really accessible to people. That was never there when I was growing up.'

The Homegame kicked things off and is still the flagship event. Those lucky enough to have attended one or more will attest to the relaxed atmosphere, the diverse line-ups and the welcoming audience. 'There's something very exciting about it,' Kenny says, smiling. 'It's a chance to do our Fence thing on home turf.' Yet the first Homegame, in March 2004, was supposed to take place in a hostel in Inverness-shire. 'We didn't think we had the pulling power to get people along,' Kenny admits. Calling it Homegame because their recently released *Fence Reunited* album had a football theme, they tied it in with that, although Kenny stresses they're not big footie-heads.

For the very first event the Erskine Hall was a venue that could be used, but only with a maximum audience of a hundred and fifteen people. They hired a PA, a local barman said he'd do the bar, and they made a poster and announced it on the Fence website. With friends from labels 679, Twisted Nerve, and Analogue Catalogue on the bill, James Yorkston headlined the Friday evening gig and there was a full day of music on the Saturday, all taking place in one hall. As requested, they made only a hundred and fifteen tickets available, and sold out on the Friday at £15 a ticket.

Johnny says: 'We suddenly realised that Anstruther is a great place to visit! We thought it would be like a Sunday Social on a slightly bigger scale, but when it happened it was completely different from the Aikman's gigs. There were people up from London! We were thinking: "Who the hell are these people? How have they heard about this?" That amount of people at a local show, plus all the bands, was a big deal for us at the time.' With an out-of-town audience staying in the vicinity and renting cottages, out of peak season, they noticed the fishing village coming to life.

In 2005 they did it all again with more bands and extended time, but still in one hall. It had doubled in size, however, as key Fence artists had been touring the nation spreading the word. Kenny explains: 'After the first one, every night we played around the UK we'd mention the

Homegame on stage.' James Yorkston is effusive: 'Those first two Homegames were just extraordinary. Hardly anyone knew about it then, but the people who did know absolutely loved it. They had so much love for the music. You'd play a show and it would be silent, and then rapturous applause. We'd bring up bands we'd seen on the road, so you knew they'd be really good. You could go into any of the rooms and it would be good – Elaine Palmer, David Thomas Broughton, Viking Moses, Adrian Crowley, Catherine Williams, Seamus Fogarty and so on. They were unknown, but we were all unknown!'

For the third Homegame, in 2006, the festival doubled in size again, so they started using other halls and venues around Anstruther and Cellardyke. As the crowds expanded, so did the complaints about noise from humourless neighbours and local naysayers. Because of community pressure the council decreed that they couldn't use the hall, so a petition was launched, gaining a lot of publicity and even making the BBC's *Reporting Scotland*. Fence had made the news, if for the wrong reasons. 'People really wanted the event to happen,' Kenny now says. What didn't harm their cause was that his personal stock as King Creosote was rising. His music was infiltrating playlists, newspapers and magazines, and the public was becoming more and more aware of him and by extension Fence. It was up to Johnny Lynch, however, to take charge of the booking and organisation, due to Kenny's increasingly busy timetable.

By the fourth Homegame, in 2007, they had two main halls at their disposal and a staggering seven hundred people in attendance, their biggest audience so far. As a result they decided to strip back the fifth Homegame, in 2008, to a more manageable size, capped at five hundred people. Tickets sold out in five minutes, and Kenny now says: 'When you've got a small thing that everyone wants to be at, the people who aren't there are talking about it, and the people who are there will tell their friends it's the best thing ever.' Although the bill is dominated by the Fence roster, Johnny Lynch has gradually opened up the booking policy but kept the quality control high and the musical links personal. He explains: 'We only book people we like, people we're friends with and people we know and trust. It's mostly done via the artists, not through their agents. That's why we can't get too big, because with some artists it would just be another booking for them. We want people to have an emotional attachment to it. KT Tunstall didn't do it because of her agent, she did it because she's pals with Kenny.'

Demand was increasing year on year; it was the perfect example of a boutique festival. There were no corporate sponsors, no overpriced beer vendors, no mud-splattered campsites and no knife-wielding neds to ruin your fun. With minimal security, friendly faces on the doors and at merchandise stalls, home-baking and homespun fun, these were gatherings for music fans of epicurean tastes and rustic, down-to-earth values. The venues were little more than typical Scottish village pubs and church halls, with the occasional museum thrown in. Seeing Johnny Lynch stumble onstage as compere between outstanding and chaotic acts only made the days more enjoyable. On top of that the sea views, the cobbled streets and the supreme fish and chips and ice-cream all added to the experience. If your ears were hurting after too much music, you could duck out and enjoy a coastal stroll. As Kenny says, not everyone wants to watch twelve bands a day for two days.

If Homegame's maximum capacity had been reached, Fence would simply have to do what they did best: think outside the box. To supply increasing demand, more events were planned and organised. Their Hallowe'en nights were a little more low-key, like fancy-dress parties with added entertainment, but also a good chance for musicians and fans to get together towards the end of the season. Another autumn spectacular, Hott Loggs, saw them sell four hundred and fifty tickets without any external publicity, winning five-star reviews in the *Scotsman*, the *Herald* and the *List*. It was seen as a miniature Homegame. Such was their status that these smaller shows could be used as a launchpad for new Fence releases.

Haarfest became a summer fixture, with a line-up announced only a month beforehand. Knowing it was more difficult to organise something in summer, with competition from larger festivals and family holidays, week-long as well as day tickets were sold. Kenny wanted to reclaim some ownership of the events, having become more distanced from Homegame. 'Unless you're online on a certain day at a certain time, you won't get a Homegame ticket. We get a lot of grief from locals and friends. It was modelled on what we'd done at the Pittenweem Arts Festival over three or four nights. It was in the same hall, but I wanted it to be about more than the music.'

Art-pop ensemble FOUND did a technology workshop, Ben Milne did a bread-making one, Kenny did a songwriting clinic, James Yorkston's cousin and photographer Sean Dooley explained how to use a pin-hole camera, and so on. There were walks, films, art exhibitions and a sports day, all for roughly a hundred people. Kenny says: 'Nobody gets to see the whole of Homegame, so Haarfest allows everyone to see the same thing. It's also a chance for us to show off our home area and not run around like dafties all the time. Some people said it was the best thing we'd ever done.'

By 2010 they had decided to take a gamble and curate an event with all the Fence trademarks, but even further away from city life. Called the Away Game, it was to happen on Eigg, in the Inner Hebrides, in September. Its roots are again embedded in a personal relationship. Johnny's girlfriend Sarah Boden, former editor of the *Observer Music Monthly*, had booked King Creosote to play her thirtieth-birthday party on Eigg, and her father Alec had said: 'We never get Homegame tickets. It's the wrong time of year for us, we're so busy in the spring. Why don't you do an event over here?'

Announcing the scheme online a month before the tickets went on sale, saying only where and when it was going to be, Johnny finally explained on the website what the event was going be about just two weeks before it happened. When the three hundred tickets went on sale, they sold out in six minutes. Being the most expensive thing they'd ever done, at £90 a ticket (including ferry and camping), the label only just broke even, but it was worth it for the excitement of bands and fans and for the press coverage. It was great to see money going to the Eigg community too. With perfect weather and atmosphere, a shambolic PA system that didn't manage to quash anyone's enjoyment, and an eclectic bill that featured Brighton's indie oddballs British Sea Power, it was the quintessential Fence festival . . . and it had taken place hundreds of miles from Fife.

The word was definitely out, and Fence's contrary flag was flying higher than ever. Soon the label was approached by Fife Council to do a 2,000-capacity event but declined, preferring to do things on their own terms. As the eighth Homegame drew to a close in 2011, Fence announced it would take a year off, as their beloved AIA Hall was closed for building works and threatening not to open again. Kenny was also tiring of Homegame and needed a break. 'It was getting almost too big and becoming a job,' he says. This got Johnny thinking, though. His ambition to organise Fence's biggest event so far had yet to be achieved. With access to his old haunt of St Andrews student union, thanks to some kindred spirits at the university, and the possibility of using the renowned Younger Hall, he hatched a plan that would materialise as 2012's Eye o' the Dug extravaganza, named after a song on Steve Mason's debut 'King Biscuit Time' EP. (If you look at the East Neuk of Fife, it vaguely resembles a Scottie dog's head, and St Andrews is where the eye would be.)

Dividing opinion among Fence aficionados, Eye o' the Dug was much like a typical Fence festival but with extra added production. There was now a lighting rig, state-of-the-art PA and, most importantly, over a thousand paying punters, but it still felt like a special event. Using the student union on the Friday night, Fence curated its most glitzy and electrified bill yet, with Django Django, Dutch Uncles, Errors, François and the Atlas Mountains, Conquering Animal Sound and Hot Chip DJs. Johnny's dream of making St Andrews rock had come true, with real security, bouncers, bar staff and even a corporate sponsor in Dewar's Whisky. It was extraordinary how far they'd come.

At Saturday's Younger Hall show, the grassroots Fence sound of acoustic songwriters, art mavericks and indie-pop was back to soothe hangovers in the wood-panelled surroundings. As King Creosote and Jon Hopkins closed the show, playing *Diamond Mine* in its entirety, the audience marvelled at what these local chancers had achieved. What made it even more exceptional for Kenny Anderson though, was the fact that his mother and father were in the audience. It was the first time they'd witnessed their son doing what he'd done for over twenty years.

The second Away Game, in the summer of 2012, was yet another success, considering the wind and rain came out to play, and it looks like that event may be here to stay. Festivals and weekenders are as intrinsic to Fence now as their recordings. For the foreseeable future, their principal following will keep turning up for these communal gatherings in Fife or elsewhere. Does Johnny have a favourite live happening so far? With no curfew, no noise limitations and music until 8 a.m., he plumps for the first Away Game in 2010. 'I didn't think we could top that at a Fence event. Others since then have been great, but that was the best yet.'

As Johnny looks to the future, he says: 'We want to put on more live events. We won't flood the calendar, but if we put on a few three-hundred or four-hundred-capacity events and make them amazing, that's what I want to do. Our new Fence Records Ltd company will hopefully allow us to do that. I'm thinking of doing some daybreak events with our new signings Eagleowl, some weird little artier events that have really special moments. Something a bit different, not the normal gig thing.'

There is little fear that 'normal' will ever be a word associated with Fence live events, and I have utter faith in Johnny to push the boundaries wherever possible in the pursuit of fun. The Homegame may or may not return, and the more intimate one-off shows like Kenny's Alter Egos Night will of course fly under the radar to keep the hardcore Beefboarders and Fence obsessives happy.

17

Diamond Mine

The Future for Our Fifers

KENNY ANDERSON

Now in his mid-forties and showing no sign of slowing down with his prolific output, Kenny Anderson doesn't always like the twists and turns of modern life, as his occasional and famous fevered rants confirm. But he has resigned himself to the fact that he is Fife for life. 'I've not found anywhere better,' he admits. 'It's a sense of belonging. I belong here. I feel like I'm at home here. I'm not daunted by any of it. I love the sea. I love the people. My family are here. I couldn't live somewhere else.' He also credits his success to the region's capital, saying: 'Look at St Andrews. It's a very different town to anywhere else in Fife or Scotland. It has the university, and it's historically a place for thinking and change. There's a sense that you can do something in this town. It's isolated, and there's very little competition in anything. People are willing to get behind you, even though it's a hard place to show off in.'

Living happily in his beloved Fife and continuing to look after and encourage his daughter Beth, who will soon be a teenager, he technically still runs Fence with Johnny. For his own albums Kenny is established on Domino Records, thanks to the undying support of Johnny Bradshaw. Laurence Bell says: 'Johnny was right into it from the off. He, Bart and Claire from the office would go up to the Fence bashes and were always as excited about it as I was. Johnny has developed close working relationships with Kenny and co. He's been pivotal in bringing Kenny back to Domino.'

Through this return Kenny and the label have had one of the biggest successes of their careers so far. At the time of writing this book, *Diamond Mine*, the album by King Creosote and Jon Hopkins, has sold around 50,000 copies. Laurence Bell talks about hearing it for the first time: 'The project had been quietly evolving with Jon Hopkins, and I'd been hearing whispers of it for some time. We knew what an exceptional producer he was. When Jon premiered it to us in the office, I was spellbound. I put it on the big speakers and was enveloped by this huge sound as he took these songs and reframed them in his own sonic architecture. It was a modern ambient folk record and it just transported you.'

It was one of the most hi-fi recordings to bear the Fence hallmark and was a beautiful collection of songs, or re-appropriated segments from the King Creosote back catalogue, but no one expected it would get the reception it did. Laurence continues: 'We put it out, with no one expecting too much from this odd little collaboration. But we kept chipping away, it started to grow and it caught a little fire of its own. We got the Mercury Music Prize nomination and they did a fantastic performance on the night. It was a genuine word-of-mouth success. It was one of those records where everyone who bought it told five of their friends, who then went out and bought it.'

After countless self-released CDs, official records on Domino, and two major-label releases through Warners, many might have thought that King Creosote had had his chance and his time was up. No one guessed that this renaissance would come so late in his career, with his biggest sales and highest profile yet. James Yorkston says: 'I thought it was quite funny that Warners threw all that money at Kenny, with all the hype and videos, and then he put out *Diamond Mine* with Jon Hopkins on Domino, which was made for next to nothing, and it became a success through word of mouth and because people loved the music. It was his songwriting, his skill and his sense of humour that got him the Mercury nomination. I thought that was perfect.'

The album was an unquestionable success and arguably should have won the Mercury. With a win under their belt, Kenny and Jon could have made even more of an impact with the record. There are, of course, plans for a follow-up, but as the first record took seven years to make, don't hold your breath. Jon deadpans: 'Yes, we've pretty much got the tunes in place. Hopefully this time we'll manage to create something that will alienate his fans, my fans, and our joint fans.'

Kenny isn't waiting around, however. Since *Diamond Mine* he's released three 12-inch vinyl EPs – 'I Learned From The Gaels', 'To Deal

With Things' and 'It Turned Out For The Best' – through Domino. They are lovely artefacts, sporting Kenny's own artwork, and showcase full-band recordings of the songs from his low-key solo album *That Might Be It Darling*. The 'Three EPs' were bundled together as an album for those who didn't buy the initial vinyl for Record Store Day in April 2013.

Kenny has recently completed yet another album, *Greetings From Hamilton, Canada!*, which he plans to put out soon. It may have to be on Fence Records, however, as Laurence says: 'He's very prolific, and there's only so much you can put in the front line of the marketplace.' Kenny has also been working with Kate Tunstall and Johnny Lynch on some new material that may or may not be forthcoming on Fence. Kenny says of his old pal Kate: 'She's keen to be more involved. She is such an amazing backing-singer and keeps me in line. I wanted her doing the *Diamond Mine* live shows.'

Fence itself has a game plan of sorts, involving releasing more vinyl and putting on more live events. This year sees The Pictish Trail unleash *Secret Sounds Vol. 2*, as well as albums from new signings Randolph's Leap, Eagleowl and Monoganon. Kenny concedes: 'I've created something here that is as good as anywhere else. There's something about building something and then continuing to build on it . . .' But does he want Fence to grow massively? He replies frankly: 'No! Not in the number of acts. But, yes, in the number of events we put on and the number of releases we sell.' He may have a minor fight on his hands with his label co-boss, however, as Johnny Lynch has different ambitions for the label and the collective. There may be two separate labels under the Fence banner one day. Who knows?

Mentioning a 1960s rock 'n' roll band called The Rebels, who never left St Andrews and consequently never made it, Kenny says: 'They were probably just as good as any band cutting around the east end of London at the time.' But times have changed, and via convoluted routes, word of mouth and the power of the internet, music and ideas can spread far and wide. Yet every area needs a catalyst, and The Skuobhie Dubh Orchestra was perhaps that vehicle for change in this generation of Fife musicians. They were certainly important at the time and went on to influence Kate Tunstall, John Maclean, James Yorkston and others. Kenny ponders their influence and attributes it to a simple attitude: 'If they can do it, then we can do it!'

The Anderson brothers have all inspired each other too. Gordon has encouraged Kenny to do his own lo-fi recordings; Kenny then cherry-picked Gordon's recordings to make the albums he's released; and Een has been influenced by both, yet shown how great a musician he is. As James Yorkston says, there's an incredible amount of talent for one family.

Of all the musicians I have ever met, Kenny Anderson is the most productive. He simply has to make music. It pours out of him and will continue to do so until the blood pours out of him. In Fife or across the world, on major labels or on Fence, in front of 10,000 people in a stadium or ten in a pub, Kenny Anderson is a natural, a true original, and one of the finest songwriters around. Without him, as I said in my opening lines, this book and these stories would probably not exist.

GORDON ANDERSON

Even though he is continually working on sculptures, paintings and computer art, what's tragic is that the Lone Pigeon has stopped making music for the time being. There's a lot to be going on with, if you want to investigate – *Concubine Rice*, *Schoozzzmii* and the *Time Capsule* seven-CD box set – but he insists: 'I don't record anything any more. Nothing. For what reason? So it can end up on a record? So some guy can review it in a magazine? "Here's the nutcase who helped start The Beta Band with his psychedelic, folk, riff-raff, mumbo-jumbo songs . . . I'll give it three stars!"'

It seems he's lost his mojo for the moment. 'Musically I am happy not to do anything again *ever*. Certainly not gig-wise, as I find that all a bit embarrassing. But I do get the urge to finish so many songs that I'm working on. I'd love to record them some time.' But there is light at the end of the tunnel when it comes to art and creativity. 'I find it hard *not* to create,' says Gordon. 'I spent two months just creating pictures on my iPhone, making pictures I'd never seen on walls before. The amount of poetry I've written recently! I'm into UFOs just now, and film. I watch a lot of films. Some days I'm into making art, and sometimes I want to learn proper classical piano. I'm just into what I'm into just now.'

One should always take comments like these with a pinch of salt. Gordon is flighty and forever changing. His mercurial character can see him embrace a new idea in a split-second. He's impulsive and moody, and often says things for effect. Thankfully, he is still good friends and in touch with John, Robin and Steve Mason, whom he lives near and sees now and again, and confirms: 'Of course I would do another project with those guys, but not a band thing.' He says he's in the process of putting together another Aliens album with all the left-over material; there's a ton of it, apparently.

His fans continue to sing his praises. Laurence Bell says: 'I tried for years to get Lone Pigeon to work with us, but he went on a great journey, disappearing for months and walking to the Middle East etc. Then The Aliens happened, and after that it finally came around. Those marvellous records that had been out on Fence hadn't been distributed to the wider world, so there came a time when he was interested in us compiling the seven-CD box set. It was for the hard-core, but I would have loved to put them out at the time. I think we could have turned people on to it. The songs are just extraordinary.' James Yorkston adds: 'There's a rawness and an honesty. I like the close harmonies and the close-miking. You have the feeling you're right there with him. 28 Secret Tracks is extraordinary. Despite listening to John Peel all my life, it sounds like nothing I'd ever heard.' Gordon says, in a debatable judgement: 'I listen back to old tapes at the start before The Beta Band, and I knew what I was doing back then. I've never been able to match that.'

Ever the dreamer and utopian (or unsatisfied perfectionist?), he wishes for a simpler and purer way of making music. 'There was a time when people would watch the moonlight on a lake for an entire night, then come back and virtually transpose it into musical notes, somehow painting what they saw.' It's almost as though he's yearning for an old-fashioned, more basic life, as if he's out of step with the modern world – something that most of us can probably identify with. Like his brothers, he still loves Fife and life outside the cities. 'I realised I am a country boy. I can't even live in St Andrews nowadays. Quietness is something to adore. The countryside, the backwardness, the lack of phone signal, the endless country roads, the little villages cobbled together, the farms, the beaches, the rocks, the views, the cathedral, the history and the ancestry; it's all very inspiring.'

Sadly, at times he's estranged from his brother Kenny and what he's trying to achieve with the Fence Collective, remarking: 'I don't feel welcome playing at Fence events any more. I once felt part of a community in Fife doing music with my brothers, but not any more. I'm moving further and further away from music all the time. I feel like I'm in a stagnant pond and I'm not sure who or what or where or why. At the moment I don't think music is the way to help me sort it out, either.' Hopefully all this will change in due course. A man this talented, with a close family so absorbed in music . . . it can only be a matter of time until whatever hatchet needs to be buried is laid to rest and harmony can prevail once more. Kenny wants this to happen, as do the rest of the Fence Collective. Gordon is always welcome, and when rumours abound that Lone Pigeon is showing up to play, the hall is always full. Come back, Pigeon!

As you can tell, Gordon is a sensitive soul. There is chaos and confusion in his mind, and he needs support from those around him. There are many who continue to hold a candle to his music and his vast talent. In many ways he just needs reassurance and the ability to focus without all the unnecessary aspects of the cruel, commercial music industry. If only it were that easy! Gordon is direct: 'I don't think too much about tomorrow. It's too daunting. I'd love to make a few great albums, but would like to disconnect from all the other stuff, like interviews. If I could make those albums and no one knew it was me, that would be perfect.' When asked about Gordon's future and his health, John Maclean says: 'Will he be all right? How old is he now, forty? I think that's all right enough for him. He's reached forty, and he had his finger on the self-destruct button when we were thirteen. Nothing's changed. He's my best friend and I speak to him all the time.'

A little bewildered and occasionally disgruntled, Gordon seems fairly happy when I see or speak to him. He certainly appreciates the kingdom he lives in. 'Fife's the best place. It's beautiful! On certain days it's like being in Holland in the sixteenth century, if you get the right light. Anyone from this end of Fife will say they're blessed to come from here. You're always gobsmacked about how much you miss it and how lovely it is. It's like living in the past or something, especially after a couple of weeks in London or Los Angeles. It's all tractors and crows and seed!' He adds: 'St Andrews is the northern Jerusalem. At one point it had the largest cathedral in Europe, and it was the most religious place after

Jerusalem, with the bones of the first apostle of Christ. I see a resurgence of faith and I see St Andrews becoming a holy capital for a second time.'

Does he have any answers as to why Fife has produced so much great music lately? He says: 'It's probably because of the lack of a train line . . . it's this little untouched, forgotten Neuk with white houses from St Andrews down to Elie. It may also stem from my dad. If he hadn't done music, then neither would Kenny, Een and I, probably. It's also down to Kenny getting people interested more recently, and starting his own thing.'

EEN ANDERSON

Having met his girlfriend Lisa in 2001, Een Anderson is settled in Anstruther with two lovely daughters, Rosemary and Olivia. They're a charming, friendly family, and you can see how much they love each other and enjoy spending time together. Telling me he has moved house thirty-eight times since leaving his parents' home in the late 1980s, he seems more relaxed and comfortable in his skin than ever. He reflects on his previous life as a gigging musician, trailing across the land trying to establish himself as Pip Dylan. 'It's the only job where you're required to get drunk every night. After a big tour you have to drink for a few nights afterwards when you get home, just to deal with it. Now I'm through with that abuse and self-destruction. I've done it so, so many times, nearly every night of my life.'

Leaving that lifestyle behind and enjoying family life, he has also quit his instrument-making, going on to design and build wooden furniture with a difference. These wonky, angular chests of drawers and wardrobes are eccentric and beautiful, but also fully functional. Almost Gaudi-like in their proportions and design, they draw on Een's study of sacred geometry and the golden section. Still in the prototype stage, they are used by his children to see if they'll stand wear and tear. Unique, like his music and his instruments, they will probably only ever sell if he learns how to market himself or finds a manager.

As far as music is concerned he has two projects on the go. To earn money he plays Scottish country dance music with his dad, and has done since 2006. He admits: 'I hated it and would never listen to it.

But it's different now I'm playing it, because I've introduced an element of swing. It's given it a new life. My dad likes it too. He'll turn around and say: "That's magic, that!"' Een also admits that it has helped his musicianship. 'My dad doesn't do rehearsals. He says: "We're doing this tune, and it's in this key." Once you know the songs, you realise the order of how they all go. Doing that stuff has been invaluable for me technically, playing guitar. I didn't know anything about music before, but now I've learned all about modes and scales by reading books and trawling the net. That's what I've been doing for the last couple of years. Now I can play in any mode, in any key, on the entire neck of the guitar.'

Een now quite enjoys it. It pays a living wage and the gigs tend to be local. He turns up, plays for four hours, gets his cheque and is home in bed that night. Incorporating the typical ceilidh set of 'Dashing White Sergeant', 'Gay Gordons', 'Strip The Willow' and so on, his father's repertoire is huge. 'Dad probably knows an accordion piece or a tune from every country in the world.' With a stripped-back line-up of accordion, guitar and drums, they can also turn their hand to Beatles tunes, Fairport Convention, country songs, jazz, quicksteps and more. Een stresses: 'You play it so often that you get better and better, then change and adapt things to make them more fun.'

Aside from paying the bills by playing at weddings, parties and other celebrations, Een still harbours ambitions to show the world his musical virtuosity. He says: 'Since January 2012 I've been getting heavily back into flamenco guitar. I'm getting eleven pieces together that will last fifty minutes to an hour. That's all I want to play for the next year or so. Get them all recorded and then go out and start playing them in proper theatres, with quiet, sit-down audiences. That's what I'd like to do. It has nothing to do with Fence whatsoever. I want to do music that I genuinely like and am good at. I'm going to do it seriously again, and call myself *Hermano* – Spanish for "brother".'

As he distances himself from Pip Dylan and the whole indie music scene, he adds: 'If you're doing the style of music you did when you were young and continuing to do something similar, you turn up to a place and your audience is eighteen. That's why I'm into jazz and flamenco, because you can play to any age. Also, with flamenco guitar I can do it on my own. I don't need to rely on finding other players.' When he rattles through a few set-pieces, I am as astonished as ever. I am also pleased to find he still rehearses constantly, sometime up to eight hours a day.

With his loving family, furniture design, ceilidh band and flamenco ventures on the go, you might assume he's fairly content with his lot. But unlike his two brothers, he's not entirely enamoured of life in Fife, saying: 'If I had the opportunity to move elsewhere – probably another country – I would do it in a shot. If I came into lots of money, I wouldn't be sitting in Fife spending it. South of France here I come, or Spain here I come! It's the culture, the food, the climate. The only reason I'm still here is because nothing's ever come my way to provide the finances to move somewhere else.' This may only be indicative of his current mood, but it's sad to think Een should be discontented living in this beautiful part of the world. It is also sad to see his continual frustration at how he hasn't received his just rewards for his years of service to music. In answer to how all of these gifted musicians have come from the East Neuk, he responds: 'Inspiration-wise, a lot of my songs are about what I see around me here, but I'd do that wherever I was. A lot of artists come here because of the surroundings, the light, the sea and the shore. But there are just as many musicians in Fife who haven't made it.'

Talking about his negativity towards Fence, The Skuobhie Dubh Orchestra and his sibling rival Kenny in this book, he admits: 'I think I must have been depressed for the past fifteen years. It must have been fun, or I would have stopped. Somehow a lot of the memories have gone.' Asked whether he'll ever make music with his brothers again, he answers: 'You can never tell. Maybe there will be an opportunity or a window to do it again one day. Initially it was good until the egos crept in. Nowadays you can't get all three of us in the room before one of us falls out with the others. That's just the way it is and has always been.' He adds finally, in a typically self-deprecating way: 'Kenny got the brains, I got the looks and Gordon got the talent. I think that about sums us up. Of course, that's all changed now . . . the looks have gone.'

Despite varying degrees of dissatisfaction and disappointment, Een will surely make world-class music that one day may receive the recognition it deserves. The man is just too damn talented.

JOHN MACLEAN

John Maclean has had a chequered and colourful life since leaving home, that's for sure. With The Beta Band and The Aliens behind him, he is now engrossed in making his debut feature film. He says: 'I'm making a black-and-white film. It's a Western about a Scottish guy and an Irish guy out in the west. Michael Fassbender will be the Irish character, and I'm still looking for the Scottish actor.' Will it be art-house or blockbuster? 'I like the people in between. If you look at American cinema of the past ten years, you've got the Coen brothers, Tarantino, Paul Thomas Anderson, who are making these films that are arty and eccentric but are still entertaining.'

He believes art, film and music all come from the same place. 'It's all collage and montage and sampling. You hope that you're creating something new out of it all. Even when I was painting, I knew it wasn't my forte. Drawing I loved. If you want to be a great painter in this day and age, you have to have something very personal to say. I'm more of a people person, and I like to work with people who have something to say. Film is more collaborative and allows you to do that. A band is more like that too. Painting is a lonely, difficult thing to do. Gordon is more of a painter than I am, because he has that heartfelt passion to express himself. With film, you can be more of a producer.'

John hasn't just stepped out from behind the keyboards and sampler to pick up a camera. He was active in visuals, videos, spoof TV and film ideas in The Beta Band. The point when he knew he could do it properly and things could get serious was when he met and started working with Fassbender. He admits: 'That was the step between making stupid stuff and putting it online with mates, to being able to manage and get the most out of an actor, which is the other half of directing.' He created his first official short film, *Man on a Motorcycle*, entirely on a mobile phone. It was entered in the London Film Festival and appeared on the Bafta long-list, getting down to the last fifteen. His second short, *Pitch Black Heist*, filmed in November 2010, made it to the Bafta 2012 short-list, so he dug out his tuxedo and went to the ceremony. It won. 'It was crazy! Martin Scorsese, Brad Pitt and all these guys were in the front row. Michael was well chuffed! We worked on it together, so it was *our* film. I didn't expect to win, but when I watched the other shorts I thought I had a chance because mine was pretty different. I wasn't really bothered by what it meant. For some it's the be-all and end-all, but for me it's never why I'd make a film. But it was good that we won it. It was a fun night.' What gives him more pride however, is Fassbender's reaction to his work behind the camera. 'At the end of *Pitch Black Heist*, Michael said: "You've made me appreciate acting again," so I think he thinks I have the right ingredients to be a good director, which is getting the best out of people without being an egotistical twat.'

Working with a small team of people he trusts, his agent and producer take care of the business and networking side while John deals with the artistic and creative decisions. It's a sweet arrangement, but he does stress: 'As long as I have Michael! He's the key to getting the projects green-lit. If he dropped out it would be more difficult to get funding.' Is his leading man a fan of John's musical endeavours? John says: 'He's a big rock fan and likes Metallica and so on. He likes the full-on stuff. I imagine The Beta Band and The Aliens were a bit too whimsical for him. He plays guitar and I think he used to be in bands. Since working with me, I think he talks to his Hollywood chums and tells them about our stuff. I know Charlize Theron is a fan.' Reflecting on his career, it seems that everything has gone according to plan. With music, his band made a demo and were signed to EMI/Parlophone. In films, he laughs, 'I got lucky again!'

Would he ever consider a Beta Band reunion? 'I'd never say never, but not just now. Even if the money was amazing, I wouldn't reform the band until after this film. I've been working on this film for over two years, but I've been working on my film career for over ten years.' He adds that The Aliens never officially split and may join forces again, should it feel right. He says: 'I guess if we were going to do something again, I'd have to say something like "Let's make an album with Gordon and an acoustic guitar, using only two microphones and four tracks." That kind of rule!' However, the music of his second group lives on in recorded form and in TV and film, when a track is used in a scene or advertisement. Part of his management team still works away at this, as it's a money-spinner. 'Michelle has worked really hard to get us sync deals with film and TV. "Setting Sun" was on a trailer for an HBO show, a couple of ads used "Setting Sun" and "The Happy Song", and "I Am the Unknown" was in the soundtrack of the Hollywood film 21.'

Luck may have something to do with John's success, but so have inspiration and perspiration. When you meet him, he's very unpretentious and unaffected. Although determined to make it as a film director, he's also rooted in pragmatism and reality. Thankfully there is still a lot of humour that runs through what he does, stretching from The Beta Band through to *Pitch Black Heist* and beyond. He explains: 'It's probably quite a Fife thing. There's a sense of self-deprecation and a piss-taking humour in there.' He is based in London now, but always finds time to return home and join in the fun. 'I DJ at the end of Homegame now and have done for four years or something. It's like my little part of their thing. The Fence Collective is better for it and I'm better for it.' Put on the spot about why this little area of Scotland has been so productive over the past twenty years, his answer is straightforward. 'It's because of the Andersons, really. If the Andersons didn't exist you probably wouldn't have any of this. It usually comes from two or three people. The whole Manchester scene started like that. I can't imagine any of it happening without the Andersons.'

STEVE MASON

Still the outsider and something of a lone wolf, Steve Mason is undergoing a much anticipated renaissance as a singer and songwriter. After shooting blanks with his King Biscuit Time and Black Affair projects, his solo footing is a lot more secure as he continues under his own name and his own steam. 'All I ever wanted to do was make music,' he says. 'I think Gordon and me, and then The Beta Band, were a catalyst. We didn't see it as playing; we were on a fucking mission to change humanity through music, and that's a serious endeavour. You make that decision to devote your entire life to trying to get to where you want to go, to learn the craft of writing songs, making music and devoting your headspace to those things.' There can be little doubt that, through The Beta Band and as a solo artist, Steve has accomplished that. From the Fence Collective to The Stone Roses to Hollywood film-stars and the public at large, his fan base is respectful and cosmopolitan.

Confirming John Maclean's views, Steve says there are no plans to reform his old group but doesn't completely rule it out. He says he might take part in 'a project with Gordon'. And maybe The Beta Band? 'It might feel right at some point. I'm not against or pro-anything. But we've all got loads on our plates just now. I'm happy with myself just now.' It whets the appetite, though, and here's hoping that, after John's feature film and Steve's next album campaign, they might let bygones be bygones and tour that crazy psychedelic show one more time.

Considering his own status and impact on others, he says: 'People tell me about things they've seen that they think have come from The Beta Band. I'm aware of little things. I saw a band the other day and they had plants all over the stage, and I was like: "Oh yeah!" But I don't know how I feel about it, because I don't spend any time thinking about The Beta Band. I'm always looking forward. What's new, what's better, how can I improve it and make it more exciting, touching and beautiful? That's how it should be.'

Steve has been keeping himself busy since his comeback with *Boys Outside*. At the time of writing this book, his new album under his own name, *Monkey Minds In The Devil's Time*, was released on Domino, produced by dub reggae-loving Dan Carey, who has worked with many successful artists including Franz Ferdinand. The album is saturated in personal politics, its title referring to the Buddhist term for an easily distracted brain, and is shaped by the current global political climate. Boasting of 'Real tape hiss – none of that cheap imitation stuff!', it gathers another concise, intimate and personal set of songs segued with instrumental pieces. The trademark Mason falsetto, whispered vocals and a quasi-spiritual sense of euphoria are all there, with a new feeling of militancy. With a touring schedule to promote the new set, he's likely to gig with a backing band across the UK, Europe and possibly America, where The Beta Band were always popular.

Working between his home in Fife and his beloved London, he has branched out further into production, setting up his own Kronk Studios and acting as engineer and producer on his own digital and analogue set-up. As well as producing a few local-artist demos, releases by Scroobius Pip and even the song 'Coast On By' for King Creosote's album *Flick the V's*, he has remixed Miles Kane and Django Django, and recently scored the soundtrack of the *La La Land* comedy series for the

BBC. Composing thirty to forty pieces of music for the show, he says: 'I loved it! It was the biggest challenge ever.' His website also offers drum and ProTools tuition, showing his new will to diversify and earn extra cash. Steve seems to have his confidence back as well as his work ethic. As ever, his path is unpredictable but will doubtless be interesting and provocative.

He now contemplates his past and his life in Fife and its capital, saying: 'St Andrews can afford you a certain amount of space to think. It's an odd thing to be able to walk around and know every crack in the pavement. There's something that draws you back to a place that you know so well. What draws you back is the idea of checking whether those things are still there, because when those things go, a part of you is gone forever. It's how you deal with that, and how you feel about that, that's character-building. You can let it upset you or you can find the memories comforting and move on.' He continues: 'People who come here for The Beta Band or the Fence thing will be discovering an amazing part of the UK. I think we're living in a time when it's important to discover how amazing your own country is, because this country has a lot to offer. I think what Fence has done for tourism in the East Neuk cannot be overstated, and Fife Council should be applauding them and sponsoring them wherever possible.'

He knows his peers have done well for themselves, but is reluctant to be grouped with anyone local. He is not part of the Fence Collective or any other scene, and makes that very clear. He says: 'The Andersons are a musical family. I think Kenny and Een injected a more youthful take on traditional Scottish music. Gordon is incredibly talented and has a drive to be successful, but he needs the right people around him to help him make that happen.' He's also honest about James Yorkston. 'I've known him since school and he's a mate. He's absolutely immersed in folk and traditional music, but Scottish and English traditional music does absolutely nothing for me.'

Trying to explain this inspired bunch from the East Neuk, he puts his hands up and says: 'I don't know what it is. It's not like Dublin, where you walk into every pub and somebody's playing. The people who have made it from around here haven't had any help from the local venues and what have you. The Vic Café was the hub of all music from St Andrews, but those days are gone. Maybe it's because I'm reluctant to find something that binds all these people together, because I hate being part of any group, clique or gang. The thing that Kenny, Kate and I have in common is that we were determined to succeed.'

JAMES YORKSTON

James Yorkston is something of a national treasure these days, albeit a slightly grouchy, obstinate, vegan one. It suits him. With a collection of respected albums and a book of tour diaries behind him, he has made his own way through the music industry and kept his integrity and individuality intact. He is always honest, candid and grateful for his lot. 'There are songs I've released which I don't think are my best songs. Some people have said this or that is your best song, I love that song etc. But I can't play them live because I don't think they're strong enough. Another person saying something is really good doesn't change my opinion of it. It's amazing getting all the plaudits, and if everyone said what I did was two out of ten, I'd probably stop. Thankfully it's been mostly good.'

Never one to stray far from his beginnings, he still praises Fence and what it stands for. 'I thought it was a brilliant place to be grounded. I was touring, doing interviews and getting a certain amount of pretty and colourful people saying pretty and colourful things to me. The first period when Fence was really good for me was when I left Huckleberry and I was trying to find my own voice and my own way. I was going back to Fife, meeting Kenny, getting some confidence in what I was doing and enjoying music again. The second was when I came back from that first album and all the promotion. I was pretty shattered, and they were just there, really warm and really welcoming.'

However, if it hadn't been for his initial success, the collective might not have got the break it deserved. 'Everywhere I went I punted their stuff. I'd hand over a King Creosote CD or a Fence compilation. It was very easy and truthful for me to recommend those guys. Although I was doing well, I never considered myself better than them. I still consider Kenny an absolutely outstanding songwriter and producer of music and art. I almost thought: "How am I here and these guys aren't?" These guys are incredible. I remember one of the Domino guys saying: "I just don't get Kenny," and I thought: "How can you *not* get Kenny?"'

Discussing his most recent album, *I Was A Cat From A Book*, he explains: 'It was going to be with the Archie Bronson Outfit as my backing band, to make it loud and blaring punk rock. It was meant to be a fast, hard, punk-pop album. They didn't want to do it, so I did it with a jazz trio instead – Jon Thorne, who plays with Lamb, Luke Flowers, who plays with Cinematic Orchestra and various others, and John Ellis, who's played with John Squire, Lily Allen and Cinematic Orchestra. They play as a trio and Jon recommended them to me. I wanted people who would just fuckin' go for it! Not over-playing, but people who had energy and would follow me. It had me and David Wrench producing.'

This new set of instrumentalists worked out well for James, as Laurence Bell points out. 'It's gone down brilliantly and is as good as anything he's ever done. It's got this extra emotional resonance.' Earning yet more four-star and five star reviews everywhere, it seemed like the critics felt the same way. Sonically it didn't stray too far from his previous records, but perhaps returned to the immediacy of his debut album, notwithstanding the added emotion that personal domestic troubles had brought upon him. The song 'The Fire And The Flames' is an astonishingly truthful and heart-rending piece of work.

Now a family man in his early forties, and based back in Fife, he isn't quite sure what the future holds for him. 'I don't know what's going to happen, but I hope musicians like me can make a living off sales, so I don't have to be away from my family the whole time. I just caught the end of it with my first album, before the internet and downloading took hold. You just have to adapt. I'm lucky if I get two hundred people coming to see me in Stockholm or Paris. My next London show is nine hundred people, which is amazing for me even after all these years. But I don't get those numbers everywhere I go. It's hard work simply making a living. I'd love to get to the point when you were financially rewarded when people got your album.'

He is still positive about what's around the corner. 'There are loads of good things that have come out of the internet – less reliance on one or two magazines, word of mouth, music being released instantly, lots of positive things. I think scenes that produce their own music and are remotely like the Fence model are going to work, as long as they have the love of the music and the integrity to keep it going.'

The harsh realities of life as a working musician without celebrity status or great wealth do hit home, but he is gracious and pragmatic about his fate, saying: 'It's a little strange that you want to be a musician all your life, but just as you become one someone takes away the main income stream. Even if record sales were as they were twenty years ago, I still wouldn't be rich. Getting older and having a family to support, you realise you're missing half your revenue. That's a shame . . . but you're doing music for a living! You're playing for a living! It's fun. The good still outweighs the bad by forty country miles. If I were doing music for the money, I'd be an idiot. I'd be better off doing almost anything else than music to make money.'

Does he ever feel envious of Kate Tunstall's or Kenny Anderson's achievements? Immediately he retorts: 'No. Kenny's got fifty albums or whatever. He's a worker and he deserves it. I've got a great family, I make a living out of music and I've got great friends. They do well and they deserve to do well. I hear Kate in the Co-op the whole time and her songs always sound good.'

James is full of ideas for new work and says: 'Family allowing, I've got so many potential projects. A book of short stories, hopefully. I'd love to do an album with Suhail Yusuf Khan. There's always talk of a Three Craws album with Kenny, Johnny Lynch and me. There's talk of other collaborations too.' Elaborating on the Three Craws, he says: 'It came about as naturally as anything has ever come about. We were standing drunk on a pool table in the Ship Tavern in Anstruther and we took it in turn to sing each other's songs, HMS Ginafore songs and traditional songs. We carried it on for a while because it was a real laugh. We did stop it though, because Kenny and I thought it was the wrong thing to be doing at the time. I hope we do it again, though, but everyone has to be ready to do it and in the right frame of mind. It's a tricky thing, because there are three egos in there, whether you like it or not – three frontmen. Maybe we'll do it when we're a bit older. But for me there is nothing sweeter than sitting onstage with three voices harmonising and three guitars, just enjoying it, making up lyrics and joking about with no pressure.'

James still happily resides on Domino Records alongside Kenny, Steve, Gordon and Tom 'UNPOC' Beauchop as he moves into his second decade as a solo artist. Laurence Bell says: 'They're all still under this roof. As long as everyone is happy and we can make it all add up, we'll carry on. We've been working for a long time now; if it ain't broke, we won't need to fix it.' Crucially Laurence continues to be a staunch fan of James. 'I think he was working in a bookshop when I first met him. He's always had amazing taste, and would recommend to me books and music that I didn't know. It's hard making it all add up sometimes, but he's as entrenched as anyone on the label, and we'll make records with him as long as we can.'

Striving to find some explanation for this eruption of creativity in the East Neuk since the early 1990s, James is typically realistic. 'I don't think there is anything special about the East Neuk of Fife. There are dozens of places like it all around the UK and Ireland. We used to go to Skibbereen and Baltimore in Ireland and I'd think: "Why do I love it down here?", but it's because it's almost identical to Fife! I only worked that out recently.' He continues: 'I think a lot of it is coincidence, but there are two things. First, when Kenny started doing his own stuff and promoting it by himself, and when I left Huckleberry and started my own music by myself, we were doing it under the impression that no one would ever hear it outside St Andrews and possibly Edinburgh. It would be small gigs to local people. There was no pressure. Second, mainly because of Kenny building up the Fence name, it started to attract other people. There is magnetism there because of what's happened.'

With his young daughter's health improving and a loyal, loving family and fan base behind him, James is as centred and content as I've ever known him, and that's almost forty years. He has worked hard and put his considerable talent and uncompromising worldview to good use. His future as a musician, writer and performer is guaranteed for as long as he cares to continue. Nice one, Jamesy!

KT TUNSTALL

Kate Tunstall's life is slowly changing, and she seems to be enjoying it. After years of struggle followed by global success, she is in a contented position financially and artistically, and reaching for something meaningful in her life. She explains: 'I pretty much toured for eight years. I came back and made a record. I came back and got married. I went travelling for four months. But other than that we just toured constantly.

I haven't put as much time as I'd have liked into recording because I haven't enjoyed it. I always preferred playing live. But that's massively swung recently. I've got a much higher standard now. I can't just get up and play. I've got to be pushing myself. I've got to be playing these songs and be lost in them. When I started it was enough to get up and do "jazz hands" and say: "Hey, everybody, this is my album!" I'm just not as excited by that any more. I want to get up and express something.'

As always she is extremely busy, working on her forthcoming solo album, touring acoustically with the likes of Billy Bragg, and collaborating with Kenny and Johnny at Fence. She says: 'Johnny's been a massive inspiration to me. He's such a positive force.' Having done the 'Scarlet Tulip' EP at his encouragement, she says: 'I needed to get that out and sell it exclusively at gigs. There's no promotion, marketing or barcode on it. It's virtually a hand-made product and it's real.'

Since then they've been getting closer as friends and songwriters, as Johnny Lynch attests. 'Kenny and I have done a writing session with Kate, and then I did one with her on my own. We went into her studio and recorded together. It probably wouldn't be all that "Fence", either – it sounds big and epic and pop and it's her kind of thing. She is an amazing musician and she is very versatile, far more versatile than people give her credit for. She's a total perfectionist and has done things on her own terms.'

Kate seems to be finding solace and a sense of achievement in this partnership too. 'I've got a song, which will be on the next record, that I wrote with Johnny called "Out Of Touch", which is about being away from all the judgement. I find it intimidating. Now with all the social media, all you have to do is show your face on TV and you can be ripped to shreds. You have to not read it, and it's quite difficult not to. Sometimes I'll face up to it and take someone to task for it. Other times, it really makes me lose faith in the human spirit. It's not harmless all the time, it's hurtful.' As someone who lives her life in the public eye to a certain degree, she is learning to deal with the downside of celebrity.

People are frank but complimentary about her roots in Fife and her later success. Johnny says: 'I'd seen her play in St Andrews in the late 1990s in Elia Drew, with Uncle Beesly and Een Anderson, and it wasn't really my cup of tea. Then, years later, I saw her on *Later . . . with Jools Holland*, and I was really impressed by how she held the crowd with just her and the loop pedal. It sounded new, and she still does something new with that loop pedal. It wasn't necessarily the kind of music I would buy; it was quite commercial. Then Kenny pointed out that she had sung backing vocals in The Skuobhie Dubh Orchestra, which I hadn't known. We were about to release a Skuobhie Dubh Orchestra album with a Fencezine called *A New Cat*, and she was singing on it. She's an amazing singer and does pretty much everything in one take. She's one of the most instinctive singers I've ever met. She knew her music would never appeal to the Fence crowd, so she moved to London and did it that way. She made all the right decisions for her music the entire way.'

James Yorkston adds: 'I used to see Kate Tunstall and Een Anderson playing in St Andrews. I didn't really like her music, but I admired her enthusiasm and the fact she was doing it and booking her own gigs etc. At the time I was into Swans and Dead Kennedys, and her stuff was pure pop music, so it wasn't for me. When she sprang up with a big push behind her, she was brilliant. She was a great performer, simply because she'd done all those gigs in the Vic Café, the West Port Bar and Aikman's. I was delighted for her and thought she deserved it. She's a lovely girl, she's a hard worker and she's generous.'

Despite her fame and fortune, Kate has enjoyed returning to Fife on many occasions and thrown herself into performing in the collective spirit at Homegame and Eye o' the Dug. Kenny Anderson says: 'Kate Tunstall is a huge ambassador for Fence and she's a real sport. She once played a set in front of thirty people, accompanied by Michael Johnson on piano and John Maclean battering away on a guitar case with a pair of sandals. She was totally up for it. I want people like that involved.'

Johnny adds: 'I don't think she'd be comfortable releasing a pop record on Fence – she knows that's not her audience. But she does have a fascination with it, and she was definitely intimidated by it, as any musician is by music snobs of any description. But she's so open to playing and excited about playing, and that's quite a Fence attitude. She came on stage to sing with Kenny at the Shepherd's Bush Empire, probably his biggest headline gig to date, and she did backing vocals. She didn't cause any fuss or try to stand out. She just wanted to be a player.'

Aside from her own material and her allegiances to Fence, she has embarked on an electronic side project with highly praised producer Jim Abbiss, called *Ghost Pot*. Inspired by Johnny and his Silver Columns project, she says: 'Jim and I hit it off so well in terms of getting tracks going. We were creating these absolutely banging tracks that were just too hard for what I was doing. Basically we said we *have* to do something. We have to get together and make a dance record. We're both playing everything from electronics and sequencers to mandolin, bass and kazoos. There are guest vocals throughout and I'm hardly even singing on it. It's a concept album where every song is a chronological part of the story, and it's hopefully going to come out along with an animated film and computer game.'

It sounds intriguing and a whole lot of fun. There is no doubt that she has afforded herself the time and money to do what the hell she wants. She is taking that opportunity and having a blast. Could a family be on the cards at some point? She laughs: 'I'm so desperate for it! I'm ready for it . . . bring it on!' Luke, her husband, retorts: 'That's news to me!'

As she continues her career with getting into vinyl, again due to Kenny and Johnny, she says: 'I don't want people to get free downloads for something I've worked really hard for. I don't want much for it, but I wouldn't walk into an art gallery and expect to just take a painting or walk into a bookshop and take a book. You pay for it. I don't like that culture that is growing where music doesn't cost anything, because it certainly costs money to make. How are musicians supposed to make any money? You can't work a nine-to-five job and make albums . . . well, I can't, anyway.'

Mulling over her status as a singer-songwriter and role model, she states categorically: 'The important thing, in terms of a legacy and leaving something behind me as I go, is for young girls. I have a special relationship with teenage girls who come to gigs, who want to play and are really sick of the over-sexualised side of females in music just now. It's basically just tits and arse ruling the music scene. I find my relationship with bikini-clad women in music difficult. I think if you have a majority audience of very young girls, radically sexualising yourself is not that cool.

'Chrissie Hynde has the best quote on it: "Rock 'n' roll is all about fuck you, not fuck me." It's very difficult to talk about it without sounding like a total square, but I see this total dearth of girls in bands. I'm very glad I'm a guitar-toting female artist, because there aren't that many. Being self-sufficient in the music business is incredibly important – that's empowering to me. It's busking, isn't it? It's making your money by playing a song. I respect that. People pay good money, so I want to be good.'

Currently in the south of England, with her blooming career and a myriad of options at her fingertips, she ponders the Fife question and considers why the region has been so productive in her generation. 'The three things are isolation, boredom and weather. I see a similarity in Fife with Iceland. There's so much music coming from this tiny little island. It's concentrated, it's home-grown and there's a community feel to it, plus there's shit weather and not a lot to do.'

THE PICTISH TRAIL

Johnny Lynch is the ultimate polymath, wearing way too many hats at once but thriving on every minute of it. He makes music as The Pictish Trail and in Silver Columns, he runs and co-owns Fence Records, and he plots, strategises and books the vast and growing assortment of Fence live events. Sometimes he even sleeps.

All this would be tricky for anyone anywhere, but he manages to do it while living in the back of beyond. He explains: 'I'm living in two places just now. I have a caravan on Eigg which I get for almost free, and I share a flat with Hardsparrow in Anstruther. It's working really well. It's a lot of travelling between the two, but it's good. But Fife is always where Fence will be – definitely!' It's obvious he likes the challenge and the relative lack of anxiety. 'It's what attracted me to St Andrews and what attracted me to stay in the East Neuk. You can put something on and people will come to it. If not, then it's just a small town, doing something and not having to make it the biggest thing in the world. Being on Eigg is a similar thing. There's an element of removing yourself from the London thing. I like being in London and doing Silver Columns etc; that's fun and will still happen, but I like getting away and hunkering down to my own thing.'

But his own thing has taken on many new avenues as his career has deepened and been championed by new fans and supporters. His second album, *Secret Sounds Vol. 2*, has been released to flattering reviews, following up the first album perfectly. The *Skinny* magazine said on its release: 'Many artists develop signature sounds; rarer is the musician who accrues several. Johnny Lynch is one of the few to do so successfully, with a palette as diverse as roof-raising dance duo Silver Columns and *In Rooms'* playful genre experiments. For The Pictish Trail's second volume of *Secret Sounds,* the spectrum re-restricts to a core of folk-influenced balladry and warm electronics, but the variation on offer remains striking and enriching.' The *List* magazine expressed it succinctly: 'It's a rare album that manages to sound utterly immediate yet layered with hidden sounds and sensations, but as the name implies, this manages it. Deserved wider recognition surely awaits.'

It was recorded in January 2012 on Eigg with Sweet Baboo, also known as Stephen Black, a Welsh producer, member of Cate Le Bon's band and occasional multi-instrumentalist with Slow Club. Johnny says: 'I loved what he did on the last Euros Childs record and I wanted something a bit different.' As a part of Wales's close-knit independent music scene, which includes Super Furry Animals and other iconoclasts, Black mucked in, staying in a caravan, to help give the album its dreamy, hazy and vaguely psychedelic air. As a companion piece to Johnny's first official album, it bears all the trademarks that made its predecessor such an appealing listen. There are traces of US indie, sublime folk and skewed electronica as lo-fi instrumentals, digital washes of sound and ethereal, acoustic atmospheres place his songs in their own space. To play choice cuts from the two volumes on tour, Johnny has put a band together with a semi-solidified line-up, including members of Edinburgh indie-folk slow-core ensemble and new Fence signings Eagleowl. He stresses that they're not on the new album, but says: 'I want to do more with those guys. I want the live thing to be totally different from the record.'

Silver Columns are still on the go as well, although on the back-burner, considering how busy the duo are. Johnny is inundated with work, as we know, and Adem has recently started a family. They have been writing and recording, but find it a little difficult due to Johnny living on Eigg and Adem being in London. When they have had the chance to put down some ideas, Johnny is delighted that they have been immediate. 'The first record was electro-pop,' Johnny says, 'but the new stuff is much darker. It's definitely a progression. The next record is way more dance – there's less hi-hat and snare and more kick-drum and basslines.' We wait with bated breath.

As Kate Tunstall has pointed out, there have also been writing sessions with Kenny and Johnny that look like they will bear fruit. These may appear on Kate's new album, or perhaps an entirely new project will present itself. Again, an air of tangible promise hangs heavy in the air. And let's not forget the potential of a Three Craws album with Kenny and James Yorkston.

Johnny is busy, but he seems to cope. Perhaps this multi-faceted life is what keeps him interested. He ponders the whole collective idea and his second home in Fife, maintaining: 'Everyone records on their own. People are isolationist. There are wee pockets of individuals. The collaborative ethos comes to life more in the live setting. It's about removing yourself from a competitive crowd. You go to London and people take ages to make your voice heard, because you're too scared to compare it to what someone else has done.

'If Fence was in Edinburgh, everything we do would be compared to something else in Edinburgh. In Fife there's nothing else to compare it to, so everyone champions each other's stuff. The platforms you have for performing and being heard are the ones you yourself are making. It's small-town halls and club nights you're performing in with your friends. That's quite conducive to making great art and music. It takes the pressure off. People aren't so judgemental because they want stuff to happen and want to be part of it.'

Are other people moving to Fife? Johnny replies: 'They already have. Three or four people have bought houses in Cellardyke or Anstruther in the past year, and there are more people looking. James Yorkston's here, Steve Mason's here, Gordon's here – it's cheaper to live there than Edinburgh, Glasgow or London. You can live a very happy life and easy life if you've got something to keep you going. It's a great place to be creative because there are so few distractions.'

From that it's clear to see his love of the area and the collective ideal hasn't diminished one iota. With Domino Records signing many Fife-based artists over the past few years, Laurence Bell is also still passionate about their strength as a unit. 'I've been trying to get a Fence Collective record with everyone singing each other's songs in harmony,' Laurence says. 'You'd have moments with the Anderson brothers and James Yorkston. I want to make a document of that sound and those songs. Record it really well with songs from everyone's collections, like a classic folk ensemble. I think we could do something really special there.' I agree, and Johnny might be the man to pull it all together – if he has the time.

Johnny may or may not feel pressure as he helms the Fence ship and his own musical career and steers them through choppy waters ahead. But as a solo act, a band member, a record label boss or a festival booker, he does everything with will, spirit and enthusiasm. He forever seems to have a smile on his face and words of positivity for anyone who cares to listen. He's on a mission, and as his confidence and ambition grow, so do his chances of success and his developing qualities as an artist. With Kenny Anderson at his side and the collective all around, surely Fife, Fence and those lucky enough to embrace his music, humour, determination and talent are all the better for it.

Afterword
July 2013

So there you have it – the story so far. Almost! This book took well over a year to research and write, and largely contains material sourced from the musicians themselves, via one-to-one interviews and conversations. I only hope I've done everyone justice and been even-handed with the information on offer.

I wanted to document these stories before they splinter, scatter and dissolve into the mists of time. Rather than write about a dead musician whose story has a beginning and end, this is a book about a group of living, breathing individuals who are continually evolving and pushing forward with their music. There is no full-stop and no tangible end to these tales yet. Maybe there will be a part two of this book or a hugely extended second edition? We'll see . . . As it stands, 35,000 words were edited out to fit the format of what is ostensibly eight biographies in one. Since submitting the original text to my long-suffering editor, various complications and developments have arisen that could establish this book as something of a 'line in the sand'. Here are a few updates.

It seems as if the Fence Records of the last decade is now being disassembled and formed into separate pieces before our very eyes. Kenny Anderson, who set it up to release his own music and that of his brothers and friends, doesn't want to run a conventional label with an ambitious agenda to schedule releases and compete in a generic marketplace. He yearns for something simpler and less official, something more homespun, based in Fife, and easier to manage and control.

His right-hand man of the last ten years Johnny Lynch *does*, however, want to take Fence beyond these confines, and who can blame him? He wants to retain the DIY ethos but let it grow in size and stature as a force to be reckoned with in UK music. Therein lays the dilemma. The two men have been a great double-act over the last decade, and Kenny may never find someone quite so energetic and full of ideas to stand by his side. Hopefully they will be reconciled and come to some understanding . . . One thing is certain though, there's never a dull moment, and some incredible music is sure to head our way soon.

Unfortunately, Kate Tunstall recently announced some very sad changes in her personal life. Her father passed away at the end of 2012 and her marriage to Luke came to an end. To reflect these events, she has written, recorded and released a new album, *Invisible Empire/Crescent Moon*, which is a return to her more country-folk roots. It was recorded with Howe Gelb of Giant Sand in Tucson, Arizona, during two separate sessions and has garnered some of her best reviews since her break-through debut album. As you'd expect, the album deals with the themes of mortality and separation. Out of the ashes rises a phoenix . . .

Although James Yorkston's *I'm A Cat From A Book* album has been hugely acclaimed and seen as the most direct, immediate album he's released since his debut, the past few months have been tinged with sadness. His long-standing bass-player and friend Doogie Paul sadly lost his battle with cancer and died in November 2012. After an emotional funeral at which his old bandmates sang and played, James organised a charity concert in his honour with various Fence Collective members playing alongside headliners Mogwai.

In more positive news, Steve Mason's renaissance as an artist and songwriter continues with outstanding reviews for his new *Monkey Minds In The Devil's Time* album. With an almost unanimously positive reaction from fans and critics, the record is considered by many to be his best material since The Beta Band. Many of his previously disillusioned fans are returning to the fold, and Mason himself is out playing live shows to great acclaim. He seems more calm, confident and reassured than he has been for years, and it looks like he's enjoying himself.

And what of the others? Well, it is my pleasure to announce that Pip Dylan is playing again. After a triumphant return to the stage at the 2013 Fence Gnomegame (a smaller Homegame if you like!), it seems Een has let bygones be bygones and decided to dust off the back catalogue and his finger-picking guitar skills. With his flamenco work on offer and the return of Pip, compete with reissued back catalogue, the world is a better place for sure. Even the Lone Pigeon is rumoured to be thinking about playing again, albeit under a different pseudonym. I do know that Gordon is building an observatory in East Fife for a super-powered telescope he's acquired. His next-door neighbour, songwriter and former member of Arab Strap, Malcolm Middleton, has seen him working away at this new project. If you are in need of a Pigeon fix now, there are seven albums available in the *Time Capsule 001–010* box-set. And finally, the ever affable, friendly and helpful John MacLean is edging ever closer to shooting his debut feature film with Michael Fassbender in a starring role. I'll be first in line to see it on release.

I hope you've enjoyed Songs in the *Key of Fife* – now search out all the recordings and see these guys perform live when you can.

Acknowledgements

First, I'd like to say a massive thank you to all those who gave up their time and talked to me for this book – without you it wouldn't have been possible. Een, Gordon and Kenny Anderson, Robin Jones, Johnny Lynch, John MacLean, Steve Mason, Kate Tunstall and James Yorkston – this is a tribute to you and your music. I hope I did you all proud – and you won't now hunt me down.

For returning my emails and answering questions, thank you Tom Beauchop, Laurence Bell, Gavin Brown, Ziggy Campbell, Jon Hopkins, Kate Lazda, David MacGregor, Dave MacLean, Pete Macleod, Francois Marry, Tommy Perman, Rozi Plain, Andy Robinson, Alan Stewart and Dan Wilson.

Thanks also to Simon Banks, Charlotte Butler, Michael Curry, Stephanie Gibson, Carina Jirsch, Toby Malcolm, Bart McDonagh, Charlotte Neil, Domino Records and Fence Records for facts, figures, photographs and artwork.

Special thanks to Alison Rae for believing in me, ploughing through the mammoth edit and putting up with my missed deadlines, to Kevin Pocklington at Jenny Brown Associates for taking me on, encouraging me and ultimately making this happen, and to Polygon for releasing this mighty tome into the world.

One love to my BBC crew: Barbara, Chris, Gavin, Helen, Kirsten, Lee-Ann, Jo, Mandi, Muslim, Niall, Nick, Simone and anyone else who has produced, recorded, filmed or photographed me over the years. At least no one died . . .

Cheers to Suzy Clark and Stephen Marshall at Dewar's.

A big shout out to Mr Reuben 'The Cuban' Taylor – let me give you a hand with your organ!

Extra special thanks to Mum, Dad and Alan for tolerating my noise for over forty years – I love you all dearly! Specific thanks to Mum for cooking all the meals, listening to my rants and letting me write the majority of this book in her house for large chunks of time in 2012.

Respect to Miraclehead, Khartoum Heroes, Huckleberry, Hail Caesar! and Deaf Mutes.

Dougie Paul RIP.

Finally, thank you for buying, begging, borrowing or stealing this book – just as long as you read and enjoy it!

A Note on the Author

Vic Galloway is a broadcaster and journalist who has presented weekly music shows for over fourteen years on BBC Radio Scotland and BBC Radio 1. He has also worked for BBC 6 Music and made countless documentary, entertainment and educational series for different radio networks. His TV work includes many years of BBC1 and BBC2's T in the Park coverage, a series of *The Music Show*, an *Artworks* documentary on the South by South West Music Festival in Austin, Texas, as well as other music-presenting roles on BBC Scotland, BBC ALBA and Channel 4.

As a freelance journalist Vic has written for newspapers, magazines and websites, and currently contributes to the *Sunday Herald*. In the past, he has written for *The Times*, *The List*, *The Skinny* and *News of the World*.

Vic is often invited to host and chair events, and he now lectures to students with an interest in radio, TV, media and journalism. As a DJ, he has played at student unions, festivals and clubs across the UK and Europe. He is also a freelance podcaster and voiceover artist.

On top of that, he foolishly continues to write, perform and produce music of his own . . .

This is his first book.

You can contact him at www.twitter.com/vicgalloway